Legal Regime of Marine Environment in The Bay of Bengal

Legal Regime of Marine Environment in The Bay of Bengal

M. Habibur Rahman

ATLANTIC

PUBLISHERS & DISTRIBUTORS (P) LTD

Published by

ATLANTIC

PUBLISHERS & DISTRIBUTORS (P) LTD

B-2, Vishal Enclave, Opp. Rajouri Garden,
New Delhi-110027
Phones : 25413460, 25429987, 25466842

Sales Office
7/22, Ansari Road, Darya Ganj,
New Delhi-110002
Phones : 23273880, 23275880, 23280451
Fax : 91-11-23285873
web : www.atlanticbooks.com
e-mail : info@atlanticbooks.com

ISBN 81-269-0759-2

Printed in India
at Nice Printing Press, Delhi

Under the Sponsorship of
Max Planck Institute for
Comparative Public Law and International Law,
Heidelberg, Germany

CONTENTS

FOREWORD

The treatise on the legal regime of the marine environment in the Gulf of Bengal constitutes a comprehensive description and assessment of the legal regime governing this particular maritime area. It deals with fisheries as well as the protection of the environment against pollution and the discharge of waste from land. The study is embedded in the global perspective of the protection of the marine environment. It shall be of significant use to the practitioner as well as the scholar.

Rudiger Wolfrum
Director at the Max Planck Institute
for Comparative Public Law and
International Law, Heidelberg, Germany

ACKNOWLEDGEMENTS

It is my great privilege to put a few words as acknowledgement about my work: *Legal Regime of Marine Environment in the Bay of Bengal.* I am most grateful to Professor Dr. Rudiger Wolfrum, Director, Max Planck Institute for Comparative Public Law and International Law (MPIL), Heidelberg, Germany. Professor Wolfrum is a Judge of the International Tribunal for the Law of the Sea. His Excellency Judge Rudiger Wolfrum to whom I made contact expressing my wishes to carry out research on marine environment kindly helped me obtain a postdoctoral fellowship for six months. This work has been possible only because of Max Planck fellowship without which I could not be able to be in Germany. I express my gratitude to the Max Planck Institute authorities. My gratitude is also expressed to the Institute's Director Professor Dr. Armin von Bogdandy who was kind enough to endow me access to the library. I am deeply indebted to the Max Planck Institute library personnel for their wonderful cooperation for materials, which I needed in order to work. Without their cooperation, it would have been difficult for me to find the required working in the vast law library. The privileges and scope of research at the Max Planck Institute was beyond my imagination. In the field of International law to which I am somehow acquainted, a scholar can feel highly blessed if provided with an opportunity to pursue research at this Institute.

I cannot help mentioning a researcher of Heidelberg University's South Asia Institute, Mr. Matthew Paukert, who did a lot for me during my stay in Heidelberg. I am thankful to him. I extend my gratitude to Dr. Macalister Smith of MPIL for cooperation which I received in contemplating the work. The Royal Thai Embassy personnel in Germany deserve high esteem for clarification of some technical terms as applied in Thailand which I got from them. I thank MPIL Guest Professor Dr. Chang Jiwen of the Institute of Law, Chinese Academy of Social Sciences, Beijing with whom grew a cordial relationship while working on environment discipline.

It is, I feel an obligation, to extend my gratitude to the Max Planck Institute administrative personnel who met my queries very sincerely. I happened to go frequently to Professor Rudiger Wolfrum's secretariat. His secretary Frau Y. Klein was so cooperative to contact German Embassy in Dhaka enabling my family to accompany me to Germany. I extend my thanks to her. I am indebted to Professor Rahmatullah Khan of Jawaharlal Nehru University, New Delhi who was at Max Planck Institute while I was in contact with the Institute. He encouraged me to be in this Institute. I feel opportune to mention Professor Dr. M. Rezaul Karim of Biochemistry and Molecular Biology, and Professor Dr. M. Badaruddin, formerly Dean, Faculty of Law of Rajshahi University who contacted me and relieved me from feeling from homesick. I am indebted to the Rajshahi University authority and the Government of the People's Republic of Bangladesh for granting study leave for the pursuit of my research in the Max Planck Institute. My wife Syeda Morjina Khatun, a lawyer, with our youngest son Shahriar Rahman staying in Bangladesh, my son Niat Mahmud Rahman, an engineer, pursuing higher studies in the United States, and my daughter Dr. Humairath Hilmi Rahman, a physician pursuing higher studies in Britain and myself in

Germany were in frequent contact through mail although far from each other. This in fact kept me relieved from loneliness, worries and home sickness.

To end, I feel obliged to remember and express my indebtedness to some intellectuals and institutes with whom I was in contact directly or through correspondence that made me committed to study law of the sea the outcome of which has resulted in the research work at the Max Planck Institute. Among them are, late Professor D.H.N. Johnson and Professor L.F.E. Goldie (deceased), Professor Wolfgang Graf Vitzthum, Judge Shigeru Oda, Professor E.D. Brown, Professor R.P. Anand, Secretariat of the International Tribunal for the Law of the Sea, UN Law of the Sea Secretariat and the Secretariat of the International Seabed Authority.

M. HABIBUR RAHMAN

PREFACE

This study deals with the marine environment related to the Bay of Bengal. Environment is an all-embracing matter, as such there is a wide scope to work on it. Virtually, the law of the environment is in a somewhat different category. Not limited in location, the environment is pervasive, extending into the domain of territorial sovereignty as well as the common areas of the Earth (and, in some sense beyond, into outer space). International spaces are, however, more extensive than sovereign areas. They are particularly open to depoliation of the environment in the absence of unified legal regulation. Because state boundaries do not generally provide physical frontiers to environmental effects, activities in international spaces that affect the environment can readily carry over into the sovereign areas of states and vice versa.

Since the 1960s awareness of the serious consequences of environmental neglect has been growing steadily. The composition of the atmosphere is changing, the ozone shield is being depleted, marine life is threatened by pollution and over-exploitation, and rapid population growth in certain areas has created an alarming imbalance between population and resources.

The UN Conference on the Human Environment held in Stockholm in 1972 marked the beginning of the phase of development of international environmental law by "soft law" mechanism, such as UN resolutions and declarations at international conferences. Spurred by a number of ecological disasters and realisation that such damage was both prohibitively expensive and detrimental to human well-being, representatives from 113 states adopted, by acclamation, the Stockholm Declaration on the Human Environment, together with an "Action Plan for the Human Environment" comprising of 109 recommendations and a resolution for the creation of UNEP. The Declaration sets out a number of principles (26 Principles) relating to the safeguarding of the natural environment, use of renewable resources, protection of flora and fauna, restriction of the discharge of toxic substances, prevention of marine pollution, and the relationship of environmental protection to economic development. Importantly, it recognised not just oil and minerals, but also air, water, plants, animals and earth, as natural resources to be protected and preserved in the interest of future generations. These emerging principles, many of which are now considered to have attained the status of customary norms, found further expression in numerous UN and other international declarations and resolutions, culminating in the World Charter for Nature, 1982.

Also significant was the adoption of the UN Convention on the Law of the Sea, 1982 (LOS Convention). This imposes on state parties the obligation to protect all of the marine environment, including all the resources therein. This obligation extends both to areas outside and those within a state's jurisdiction. It also contains provisions relating to the protection of the marine environment from marine and land-based pollution.

In 1989, the General Assembly decided to hold a second UN Conference on Environment and Development in 1992 in order to encourage pursuit of the development of international environmental law, taking into account the Stockholm Declaration and the particular needs of developing countries. One outcome of the so-called "Earth Summit", which met in

Rio de Janeiro in June 1992, was the Rio Declaration on Environment and Development. The Rio Declaration, adopted by consensus by more than 175 states, is a statement of principles (27 Principles) or goals, some of which have already been incorporated into treaties and into domestic state practice and may, therefore, constitute customary norms. It also adopted the equally non-binding, but very influential, Agenda 21. In reality, Agenda 21 seems to be titled under Stockholm's Principle 21 whose contents are identically adopted in Rio's Principle 2. This Agenda 21 is a comprehensive 800-page action plan covering all aspects of the environment and development, which is intended as a guide for states in designing and pursuing their environmental and developmental policies and international relations into the twenty-first century. The Conference also produced the Biodiversity Convention and the Framework Convention on Climate Change (the Climate Change Convention). Agenda 21 consists of 40 chapters of which Chapter 17 relates to Seas and Ocean matters. Specifically, it deals with "Protection of Oceans, All Kinds of Seas, Including Enclosed and Semi-Enclosed Seas, and Coastal Areas and the Protection, Rational Use and Development of their Living Resources". Chapter 17 embodies 137 titles devoted to the promotion of marine environment.

The Bay of Bengal is much more than the eastern segment of the Indian Ocean; the maritime region encompassing the countries around the littoral of the Bay always maintained a thriving contact through movement of trade, people, religious, cultural and political missions, which gave the region an autonomous character. The littoral states Bangladesh, India, Myanmar, Sri Lanka, Thailand and Maldives have specific concerns with environmental issues of the Bay of Bengal. As environment is no one's exclusive matter, other states might have pleas in respect of the Bay of Bengal environment. It is a fact that the Indian Ocean is in the realm of tectonic activity. The very recent tsunami that occurred in the Indian Ocean envisages states to be in cooperation to overcome calamity—the mission to all intents and purposes is inevitable for the marine environment.

As a matter of fact, there are a number of regional and sub-regional agreements through which states have common objectives towards protection and preservation of marine environment. The South Asian Association for Regional Cooperation (SAARC) embodying Bangladesh, Bhutan, India, Maldives, Nepal, Pakistan, and Sri Lanka as launched in 1987 is not specific to marine environmental matters although it appears to be to some extent concerned. The recently emerged BIMST-EC (Bangladesh-India-Myanmar-Sri Lanka-Thailand including Bhutan and Nepal Economic Cooperation in 2001) coming now as "the Bay of Bengal Initiative for Multi-Sectoral Concern for the Technical and Economic Cooperation" seems somehow to deal with environment. But there seems no vigour in it towards promotion of the marine environment. The Bay of Bengal Community under the auspices of the Bay of Bengal Programme-Intergovernmental Organisation (BOBP-IGO) since 2001 is aiming to address regional programme for fish stocks assessment in the Bay. This statement gives rise to an assumption that as time passes, the Bay of Bengal bordering states are realising necessity of protecting and preserving the Bay of Bengal not only for its resources but also, for its environment as well. As a first study of its kind, *Legal Regime of Marine Environment in the Bay of Bengal* is commited to the promotion of its environment. In reality, obligation for protection and preservation of the Bay of Bengal Environment lies with the Bay of Bengal Community.

M. HABIBUR RAHMAN

ABBREVIATIONS

ADB	Asian Development Bank
AJIL	American Journal of International Law
ALGS	Asia Least Cost Greenhouse Gas Abatement Strategy
ASEAN	Association of South-East Asian Nations
BFDC	Bangladesh Fisheries Development Corporation
BIMST-EC	Bangladesh-India-Myanmar-Sri Lanka-Thailand including Bhutan and Nepal for the Bay of Bengal Initiative for Multi-Sectoral Technical and Economic Cooperation
BMR	Bangkok Metropolitan Region
BOBMEX	Bay of Bengal Monsoon Experiment
BOBP	Bay of Bengal Programme
BOBP-IGO	The Bay of Bengal Programme-Intergovernmental Organisation
BOD	Biochemical Oxygen Demand
BYIL	British Yearbook of International Law
CAPE	Convective Available Potential Energy
CEPM	Committee on Environmental Policy and Management
CEPOM	Committee on Environmental Policy and Management
CITES	Convention on International Trade

	on Endangered Species of Wild Fauna and Flora
CRZ	Coastal Regulation Zone
CSD	Commission for Sustainable Development
DOALOS	UN Division of Ocean Affairs and the Law of the Sea
DOD	Department of Ocean Development
DOF	Department of Fisheries
EEZ	Exclusive Economic Zone
EGDT	Electricity Generating Development Authority
EQS	Environment Quality Standards
ESBN	Estuaries Set Bag Net
ESCAP	Economic and Social Commission for Asia and the Pacific
FAD	Fish Aggregated Devices
FAO	Food and Agriculture Organisation
GDP	Gross Demography of Production
GHG	Green House Gas
GIS	Geographical Information Systems
GOOS	Global Ocean Observing System
GNP	Gross National Product
GPA	Global Programme Action
ICLQ	International and Comparative Law Quarterly
ICOM	Integrated Coastal and Ocean Management
ICSU	International Council of Scientific Union
IJIL	Indian Journal of International Law
IOFC	Indian Ocean Fisheries Commission

IOMAC	Indian Ocean Maritime Affairs Cooperation
IPCC	Inter-governmental Panel on Climate Change
ISO 1400	The Standard of Environmental Management issued by International Organization for Standardization
LOS Convention	United Nations Convention on the Law of the Sea, 1982
MARPOL	International Convention for the Prevention of Marine Pollution
MEF	Ministry of Environment and Forestry
MFAA	Marine Fishing and Agriculture Act
MLD	Million Litters Per Day
MOFA	Ministry of Fisheries and Agriculture
MOFL	Ministry of Fisheries and Livestock
MSY	Maximum Sustainable Yield
PAH	Polycyclic Aromatic Hydrocarbons
NCPC	National Cleaner Production Centre
NCS	National Conservation Strategy
NEA	National Environmental Act
NEMAP	National Environment Management Action Plan
NGO	Non-governmental Organization
NPA	National Plan of Action
NLD	National League for Democracy
NYIL	Netherlands Yearbook of International Law
OOIS	Ocean Observation and Information Service
Rio Declaration/ Earth Summit	United Nations Conference on Environment and Development, 1992
RSP	Regional Seas Programme

Stockholm Declaration	United Nation Conference on the Human Environment, 1972
UNCED	United Nations Conference on Environment and Development, 1992
UNCLOS III	Third United Nations Conference on the Law of the Sea
USCSP	United States Country Study Programme
UNEP	United Nations Environment Programme
UNFCCC	United Nations Framework Convention on Climate Change
UT	Union Territory of India
WMO	World Maritime Organization

TABLE OF CASES

1

INTRODUCTION

1.1 General Approach

The concept of integrated coastal and ocean management (ICOM) in international law first began to germinate in the 1970s in two areas: environmental and oceans governance. These two subjects are not discrete topics and have frequently been addressed in the same document. Although there were a number of regional initiatives in the 1970s that saw the convergence of the two domains, it is only in the 1990s that they have been formally combined as a new oceans governance regime at the global level. One of the first fusions of international environmental law with international oceans governance occurred during the historic 1972 United Nations Conference on the Human Environment. The Conference resulted in the signing of the 1972 Stockholm Declaration of the United Nations Conference on the Human Environment (Stockholm Declaration),[1] an aspirational declaration setting out 26 key environmental principles. In addition to providing the foundation for subsequent international law developments, the Stockholm Declaration takes important steps to link environmental law with oceans governance in a number of provisions. First, Principle 7 provides a general provision for ocean pollution prevention:

> States shall take all possible steps to prevent pollution of the seas by substances that are liable to create hazards to human health, to harm living resources and marine life, to damage amenities or to interfere with other legitimate uses of the sea.

The importance of public participation in environmental decision-making "...by citizens and communities and by enterprises and institutions at every level" is emphasised in paragraph 7 of the Preamble. Principle 14 sets out the need to use rational planning to reconcile development aspirations with environmental protection.

This fusion of environmental principles with basic integrated oceans governance represents a shift from international oceans governance conferences or documents that merely concerned themselves with the assertion of maritime jurisdiction.[2] However, the Stockholm Declaration is not without limitations. Firstly, it is a non-binding declaration that explicitly recognises state sovereignty in environmental decision-making in Principle 21. Second, Principle 18 places heavy reliance on the use of science and the technology to identify, avoid, and control environmental risks. This reliance suggests that action is to be taken only when there is scientific proof of environmental harm and not to prevent taking action against its occurrence. Despite these limitations, the Stockholm Declaration is helpful for setting out basic oceans governance and environmental law provisions.[3]

Another result of the 1972 Conference that advanced the development of ICOM was the creation of the United Nations Environment Programme (UNEP)[4] to promote UN-led environmental efforts. One of the most important ICOM initiatives of UNEP was the development of the Regional Seas Programme, which promotes the idea of "...special protective systems for regional seas."[5] The approach taken by UNEP in establishing Regional Seas Programmes is a "...cross-sectoral and problem-oriented management philosophy...in dealing with environment degradation is a problem of reconciliation between development and the environment in search of sustainable development."[6]

The next major initiative that combined oceans governance with environmental laws was the Third United Nations Conference on the Law of the Sea (UNCLOS III) which held its first session in 1973. During its third and last session in December 1982, the participating states produced the United

Nations Convention on the Law of the Sea (LOS Convention), a key document in oceans governance.[7]

The theme of the work will be firmly based on the international legal documents. Furthermore, attempts will be made in this work to present state practices, LOS Convention and related convention/declaration provisions. From a practical consideration, the study has a major base of the Earth Summit, 1992 (Rio Declaration) taking into account the Stockholm Declaration, 1972. Along with this, it deals with the UN Convention on the Law of the Sea, 1982 (particularly its Part XII: Protection and Preservation of Marine Environment, Part XIII: Marine Scientific Research, and Part XIV: Development and Transfer of Marine Technology). It is inevitable for the study to devote to chapter 17 of Agenda 21 which based on Principle 21 (Stockholm Declaration), came into being in the Earth Summit (Rio Declaration). That is to say, an analytical evaluation is needed to focus on marine environment under the specified chapter that deals with "Protection of Oceans, All kinds of Seas, Including Enclosed and Semi-Enclosed Seas, and Coastal Areas and the Protection, Rational Use and Development of their Living Resources."[8] There is until now no specific study on the Bay of Bengal Environment.[9] Truly, there are a lot of regional and sub-regional agreements in the world through which marine matters have developed in respect of their resources and environment as well. The Bay of Bengal littoral states, as time passes, are although late but feeling for protection and preservation of Bay's resources and as such its environment as well. The research work will be prepared through the use of traditional, analytical and empirical methods. Besides these, the modern methods of internet browsing will be exhaustively used for collection of most recent literatures on the subject.

From a traditional point of view, the seas provide economic sustenance that results from fisheries. There is therefore the need to make a reading on fisheries. Fisheries in the Bay of Bengal[10] are now regionally governed by the BOBP-IGO. Along with this, the study will address "Legal Regime of Marine Environment in the Bay of Bengal" laying emphasis on cooperative mechanism considering it as a path for the better, to begin with a full look at the worst.

1.2. Fisheries Management Programme in the Bay of Bengal

BOBP-IGO proposes to take up the following fisheries management programmes.

Regional Programme on Safety at Sea for Artisanal and Small-Scale Fishermen: Fishing at sea is probably the most dangerous occupation in the world and every year thousands of fishermen die worldwide on account of poor safety regimes. The problem is all the more acute in the Bay of Bengal region, where sea safety measures among artisanal and small scale fishermen are rudimentary or non-existent. The factors that endanger safety of fishermen at sea include excessive fishing efforts, increased competition, dissatisfactory vessel maintenance, equipment and manpower, fatigue, recklessness, fisheries management measures that do not pay attention to fishermen's safety and diversifying operations without training fishermen. The erstwhile BOBP during 8-12 October 2001 organised a Regional Workshop on Safety at Sea for Artisanal and small-scale Fishermen in Chennai, India, with support from the FAO. It suggested a Regional Programme on Sea Safety for Artisanal and Small Scale Fishermen, which could formulate a holistic long-term approach to improve safety at sea for small-scale fishermen (Chennai Declaration). Necessary measures would include analysis of accident data; education and training of trainers, extensionists, fishermen and inspectors; better fisheries management and enforcement; stronger collaboration between fishermen, fishermen's organisations and governments.

1.2.a. Regional Programme for Fish Stocks Assessment

Information on the fish stocks in the Bay of Bengal is sparse. A characteristic feature of fisheries in the Bay of Bengal region is open access that causes excessive fishing capacity and gives rise to resource conflicts. While inshore stocks are either optimally exploited or overexploited, little is known about offshore resources or their exploitation. Illegal fishing by fleets from other countries is said to be rampant and fish stocks in several parts of the Bay are threatened. The proposed Programme on Fish Stocks Assessment, would seek to provide a mechanism through which member countries could participate in a regional stocks assessment Programme and also develop their national capacities to carry out resources surveys and improve fishery statistics in support of fisheries management.

1.2.b. Setting Up of Regional Information Network

This Programme is aimed at providing appropriate information for development, planning, research and training through web-based networking. This will assist member countries in strengthening national capabilities in development and management of coastal fisheries.

1.3. Marine Environment Pollution : Indian Ocean Paradigm

Since 1960 arms race of the super powers gave rise to world states threats to the oceans to be grabbed by those powers. Steps to save the oceans ultimately came into being through the United Nations. In 1970, the General Assembly adopted a Declaration of Principles (General Assembly resolution 2749 (XXV), following upon negotiations which took place in the Sea-Bed Committee, which solemnly declared that "The sea-bed and ocean floor, and the subsoil thereof, beyond the limits of national jurisdiction...as well as the resources of the area, are the common heritage of mankind" and "shall not be subject to appropriation by any means by States or persons." In addition, it was declared that this area "shall be open to use exclusively for peaceful purposes by all states...without discrimination." Thus the common heritage formally spelled out. As a matter of fact, ocean affairs are at all levels for peaceful purposes. The Indian Ocean seems to have obtained similar approaches, being declared as the peace of zone. Where there is peace, there is environment to prevail and marine environment cannot be viewed other than for peaceful purposes. There is a need to spell out the pollution of marine environment to enable measures to be taken accordingly. Conventionally it is said:

> 'Pollution of marine environment' means the introduction by man, directly or indirectly, of substances or energy into the marine environment, including estuaries, which results

> or is likely to result in such deleterious effects as harm to living resources and marine life, hazards to human health, hindrance to marine activities, including fishing and other legitimate uses of the sea, impairment of quality for use of sea water and reduction of amenities.[11]

Pollution of marine environment was verily known to occur by oil and radioactive substances. But with the development of science and technology more and more pollutant materials have been known to activate marine pollution. In addition to oil and radioactive materials, a number of other substances must be considered as actual or potential "hazardous substances" in relation to marine pollution. There seem to be ten major categories of marine pollution in addition to oil and radioactive materials: domestic sewage, pesticides, inorganic wastes, including pulp and paper wastes, military wastes, heat, detergents, solid objects, and dredging spoil and inert wastes. These various materials reach the sea by a variety of routes: by discharge through pipelines from land; by agricultural run-off; by deliberate dumping; by exploration and exploitation of seabed resources; by transfer from the atmosphere; and by spillages from ships carrying such hazardous substances as cargo.[12]

The legal regime of marine environment in the Bay of Bengal is indivisible with the concerns of the Indian Ocean. As matters stand, the Indian Ocean has been a peace of zone. This was adopted by two resolutions of the UN General Assembly. The first resolution was adopted on 16 December 1971 and the second on 15 December 1972. Both were adopted by an overwhelming majority without any opposition though the two super powers and some other nations had abstained from voting. The groundwork for these resolutions had been laid down by the Lusaka Conference of Non-aligned Countries in 1970 and the Singapore Commonwealth Prime Ministers' Conference in 1971. The principle was reaffirmed at the Conference of the Foreign Ministers of the Non-aligned Countries held at Georgetown (Guyana) in August 1972 and the Commonwealth Parliamentary Conference at Blantyre in October 1972.

The first resolution was actuated by the need "to consider and respect the Indian Ocean as a zone of peace for which the great power rivalries and competition as well as bases conceived in the context of such rivalries and competition should be excluded and declaring that the area should also be free of nuclear weapons." It was thought desirable to ensure "the maintenance of such conditions in the area by means other than the military alliances". The General Assembly was concerned at "the extension of the arms race into the Indian Ocean area, thereby posing a serious threat to the maintenance of such conditions in the area." It, therefore, declared that "the Indian Ocean within the limits to be determined, together with the airspace above and the ocean floor subjacent thereto, is hereby designated for all times as a zone of peace."

The General Assembly called upon "the great powers, in conformity with this Declaration, to enter into immediate consultations with the littoral States of the Indian Ocean with a view to (a) Halting the further escalation and expansion of their military presence in the Indian Ocean; and (b) Eliminating from the Indian Ocean all bases, military installations, logistical supply facilities, the disposition of nuclear weapons and weapons of mass destruction and any manifestation of military presence in the Indian Ocean conceived in the context of great power rivalry." It also called upon "the littoral and hinterland States of the Indian Ocean, the permanent members of the Security Council and other major maritime users of the Indian Ocean, in pursuit of the objective of establishing a system of universal collective security through regional and other co-operation, to enter into consultations with a view to the implementation of this Declaration and such action as may be necessary to ensure that: warships and military aircraft may not use the Indian Ocean for any threat or use of force against the sovereignty, territorial integrity or independence of any littoral or hinterland States of the Indian Ocean in contravention of the purposes and principles of the Charter of the United Nations."

The second resolution after recalling the first resolution noted that the consultations envisaged therein did not take place and agreed that further steps should be taken towards the implementation of the first resolution. It, therefore, appointed an Ad Hoc Committee to study the implications of the resolution and to report on it. The Ad Hoc Committee held certain meetings between February and October 1973 and submitted its report. The deliberations of the Committee were mostly exploratory.[13]

Pollution of marine environment occurs from (a) land-based sources,[14] (b) sea-bed activities subject to national jurisdiction,[15] (c) activities in the Area,[16] (d) by dumping,[17] (e) from vessel,[18] and (f) from or through the atmosphere.[19] The study here is aimed to make an acquaintance with general approach rather than an in-depth approach about marine pollution.

1.4. The Bay of Bengal : BOBP-IGO Mission

The Bay of Bengal is a sea that forms the north-eastern part of the Indian Ocean, 1,300 miles (2,090 km) long and 1,000 miles (1,610 km) wide, bordered on the west by Sri Lanka and India, on the north by Bangladesh, and on the east by Myanmar and Thailand; the Andaman and Nicobar Islands separate it from the Andaman Sea, its eastern arm. It resembles a triangle in shape, and is bordered on the east by the Malay Peninsula, and on the west by the Indian subcontinent; on the northern tip of the "bay" lie the Indian state of West Bengal and the country of Bangladesh, thus the name. The southern extremes reach the island country of Sri Lanka, and the Indian Union Territory Andaman and Nicobar Islands.

Many major rivers of India flow west to east into the Bay of Bengal : in the north, the Ganges River (or Ganga), Meghna and Brahmaputra rivers, and in the south Mahanadi, Godavari, Krishna and Kaveri (sometimes written as Cauvery) rivers. The Sundarbans mangrove forest is formed at the delta of the Ganga, Brahmaputra and Meghna rivers on the Bay of Bengal. The Irrawaddy River of Burma also flows into the bay.

The bay receives many large rivers including the Ayeyarwady, Ganges-Brahmaputra, Mahanadi, Godavari, Krishna, and Kaveri, all forming fertile, heavily populated deltas. Sediment from the rivers has made the bay a shallow sea, and the waters have reduced the salinity of surface waters along the shore. Monsoon rains and destructive cyclone storms have caused great loss of life along the bay's northern coast. The main ports are Vishakhapatnam, Paradip, Madras, and Calcutta (India); Chittagong (Bangladesh); and Sittwe (Myanmar).

The Bay of Bengal Programme Inter-Governmental Organisation (BOBP-IGO) has evolved from the erstwhile Bay of Bengal Programme of the Food and Agriculture Organization of the United Nations. The establishment of the BOBP-IGO was conceived during the early stages of the Third Phase of the BOBP (1994-2000) and finally endorsed through a resolution at the 24th Meeting of the Advisory Committee of the erstwhile BOBP, held at Phuket, Thailand in October 1999 (Phuket Resolution). BOBP-IGO Agreement was formally signed by the Governments of Bangladesh, India and Sri Lanka at Chennai on 26 April 2003 and by the Government of Maldives at Chennai on 21 May 2003 (BOBP-IGO Agreement).

1.4.a. What is the Mission?

The mission is to promote, facilitate and secure the long-term development and utilisation of coastal fisheries resources of the Bay of Bengal based on responsible fishing practices and environmentally sound management programs. The goal is to connect member countries to knowledge, experience and resources to help their fisher folk build a better life.

1.4.b. What are the Objectives?

The core objectives are to : increase awareness and knowledge of the needs, benefits and practices of coastal fisheries management; enhance skills through training and education; transfer appropriate technologies and techniques for development of small-scale fisheries; establish a regional information networking; and promote women's participation in coastal fisheries development at all levels. Emphatically, the BOBP-IGO seems to be the forwarding body that can contribute towards promotion of the Bay of Bengal environment. The BOBP-IGO is a unique regional fisheries body, specifically mandated to assist the member countries in increasing the livelihood opportunities and improving the quality of life of the small scale artisanal fisher folk in the Bay of Bengal region. The forerunner, the BOBP, with a relentless focus on quality and objectivity, has already set international benchmarks in execution of programs and activities in the field of small scale fisheries that has translated into measurable benefits for the member countries. Emphatically, the BOBP-IGO seems to be the forwarding body that can contribute towards promotion of the Bay of Bengal environment.

1.4.c. The Members

Currently, member governments of BOBP-IGO are Bangladesh, India, Maldives and Sri Lanka.

1.4.c.i. Bangladesh[20]

Location : Between latitude 20°34' and 26°39' north and longitude 80°00' and 92°41' east

Length of Coastline: 710 km

Population : 123 million

Number of fishermen : 1.2 million full-time, 11 million part time

Contribution of fisheries : 6.15 per cent of the GDP, 6.28 per cent of foreign exchange earnings through export

Average annual growth rate of fish production : 8 per cent

Total fish production : 1,544,170 mt (1999), 846,144 mt (1990).

No. of artisanal boats : 45,500 (including 10,500 mechanised boats)

Export : 28,477 mt (1998-99), mainly frozen shrimp and fish.

Bangladesh lies between the Himalayan mountains and the Bay of Bengal in the delta of the River Ganges and Brahmaputra. It commands jurisdiction over 1,66,000 sq. km of water area, including the 200-mile EEZ. One-fifth of the population lives in coastal areas. Most of them depend on marine resources for their livelihood. Fisheries play a conspicuous role—through nutrition, employment generation and foreign exchange earnings.

Marine fishing is largely confined within a depth of 100 meters. Nearly 70 trawlers and 51,000 mechanized and non-mechanized boats are active in fishing. Pelagic and deep-sea resources are largely untapped.

Till the mid-1960s, fishing in the estuaries and coastal waters was carried out by traditional craft. Mechanization of boats started in 1975 and has been steadily increasing since. Mechanized boats generally fish with drift gill nets and long lines and vary in length from 5 m to 15 m. They operate with 22-60 hp engines and a crew of 14-18.

Small scale fishermen, who contribute about 95 per cent of the total marine production of the country, make their living from the sea using crafts such as dinghies, chandi and balam. The major fishing gear employed in the estuaries and coastal areas are gill net, set bag net, trammel net, long line and beach seine.

The traditional estuarine set bag net (ESBN) fishery is not merely the major employer of poor rural inhabitants, but is also responsible for much of the country's marine and brackish water capture fisheries production.

Some half a million people are engaged in marine artisanal fisheries. Most coastal fishermen operate in the coastal zone. Most of them own neither land nor assets. With the rapid increase in fisher folk population, fishing in coastal areas is characterized by low catches and fishing rights conflicts. Fishermen are now opting to fish away from the coast.

It is assumed that substantial harvestable resources exist for pelagic stocks like mackerel, tuna, shark, anchovy, sardine, cephalopod, etc. No detailed surveys have been conducted for pelagic fishery resource for a long time. Thus, there is a need for fresh surveys to assess the present stock position.

Frozen shrimp and fish together accounted for more than 26,000 mt., out of the total of 28,477 mt. of fish exported during 1998-99. About 95 per cent of fish products are exported to European countries, USA and Japan.

The Ministry of Fisheries and Livestock (MOFL) is the nodal Ministry for fisheries and aquaculture development in Bangladesh. The Department of Fisheries (DOF) heads institutional support to fisheries in the country and is headed by a Director General. The DOF operates three fish inspection and quality control stations, a Marine Fisheries Station, Fisheries Training Centres and farms and hatcheries.

The Bangladesh Fisheries Research Institute (BFRI), an autonomous organisation under the MOFL, was established in 1984 and has six stations located at Mymen Singh, Chandpur, Rangamati, Cox's Bazar, Paikgacha (Khulna) and Santahar (Naogaon). The Bangladesh Fisheries Development Corporation (BFDC), established in 1964, helps to harvest fisheries resources and develop marketing facilities. BFDC has established fish harbour, landing and distribution centres, ice plants and processing plants. National fisheries policy has been adopted to increase fish production through optimum utilization of resources. Other objectives are employment generation and poverty alleviation.

1.4.c.ii. India[21]

Coastline : 8,118 km

Total population : 1,000 million

Annual fish production : (1999-2000) 5.66 million metric tons (2.83 million-mt marine fish, 2.82 million mt inland fish)

Fisherfolk population : 6 million

Contribution of fisheries to GDP : Rs. 2,223 million (1999-2000) (1.8 per cent of GDP)

Harvestable resource potential : 3.934 million mt (1.9 million mt demersal, 1.7 million mt pelagic and 0.2 million mt oceanic)

Export of fish and fish product : Rs. 51,167 million (1999-2000)

Main fish species exported : Shrimp, squid, cuttlefish

Fishing craft : 2,80,491 (1,81,284 traditional craft, 44,578 motorized traditional, 53,684 mechanised)

Growth rate of fish production : 4.12 per cent during the 1990s (6.5 per cent inland fisheries, 2.19 per cent).

Fisheries play an important socio-economic role—it supplies cheap and nutritious food, generates employment and income, earns foreign exchange through export and stimulates subsidiary industries. More than six million fishermen and fish farmers in the country depend on fisheries and aquaculture for their livelihood. The harvestable potential of marine fishery resources in the Indian EEZ has been estimated at about 3.9234 million tonnes (mt). About 58 per cent of the resources are available at a depth of 0-50 metres, 35 per cent at 50-200 metre depth and 7 per cent in depths beyond 200 metres. The marine fishing fleet comprises nearly 3,35,000 craft, which includes about 2,81,000 traditional craft. India's inshore waters have been exploited almost to the sustainable level, but the contribution to production from the deep sea has been insignificant. Annual fish production in 1999-2000 was estimated at 5.66 mt – 2.834 mt from the marine sector (against a potential of 3,934 mt), and 2.823 mt from the inland sector against a potential of 4.5 mt. Of the total marine production, about 31.5 per cent comes from the east coast (Bay of Bengal) and 68.5 per cent from the west coast (Arabian Sea).

The major pelagic resources identified for exploitation are coastal tuna, carangid, ribbon fish, mackerel and pelagic shark, yellow fin tuna and skipjack tuna in the EEZ. Penaeid shrimps, which dominate the export front, are at their optimum exploitation levels. Tuna and cephalopods are the two least exploited fisheries because of the limited operational range of the majority of present fishing fleets and the lack of suitable technology. Presently, some 25 per cent of the marine fish production is caught by artisanal boats, and 74 per cent by small mechanised boats. Only about one per cent is from the deep-sea fishing vessels now in operation. India exported marine fish and fish products worth Rs. 51,167 million in 1999-2000 against Rs. 17,674.3 million during 1992-1993. The exports go to some 70 countries, with Japan being the single largest market. Imports, so far, are negligible. Development and management of marine fishery resources poses problems for a number of reasons. The Indian sub-continent covers a vast region with long coastlines and different ecosystems, both on land and in the sea. The fishery resources are diverse; artisanal and small scale fishermen operate from thousands of landing places dispersed along the coast and live within socially and culturally disparate communities. Responsibilities and programmes for fisheries management and development are split between the Union Government and State/Union Territory Governments, which differ in their policies, programmes and approaches.

The open-access nature of marine capture fisheries in India is one of the major reasons for depletion, economic waste and conflict among user groups. There are laws that restrict fishing seasons, fishing areas and the mesh sizes of gear, but there is no satisfactory monitoring and surveillance mechanism available to ensure implementation. To avoid over-capitalisation and to ensure sound growth, the country is adopting a rationalised approach to determining the number and size of fishing vessels, the type of fishing gear and operational equipment.

A growth rate of 2.5 per cent has been proposed for marine fisheries during the Tenth Five-Year Plan (2002—2007), and a growth rate of 8 per cent for inland open water fisheries and aquaculture development. This will enable a total fish production of 8.09 million tonnes (3.26 million tonnes from the marine sector and 4.83 million tonnes from the inland sector) at the end of the Tenth Plan, according to estimates.

1.4.c.iii Maldives[22]

Population : 3,00,000

No. of coral islands : 1,190 (of which 200 are inhabited)

No. of full-time fishermen : 19,108 (2000 census)

Contribution of fisheries : 10 per cent of GDP, 76 per cent of exports.

Main fisheries : Tuna, yellow fin, live bait fish, grouper, aquarium, sea cucumber

No of fishing vessels : 5,187 (including 2009 mechanized masdhonis)

Fish, reef production : 1,23,000 metric tons

Exports : 70,800 mt (1999) (frozen tuna, yellowfin tuna).

The Republic of Maldives consists of 1,190 coral islands spread over 90,000 sq kilometres in the Indian Ocean, some 400 miles southwest of Sri Lanka. Two hundred of the islands are inhabited and have a total population of about 3,00,000. In recent decades, tourism has become the highest foreign exchange earner, but fisheries and related industries have always been the main source of employment and nutrition. The fisheries sector employs nearly 20,000 people, accounts for about 10 per cent of the country's GDP and 76 per cent of the exports.

The fishing waters of the Maldives are divided into two zones—the Coastal Fishery Zone and the Exclusive Economic Zone (EEZ). The Coastal Fishery Zone, extending to 75 miles offshore, is meant for the exclusive use of Maldivian fishermen. The EEZ has an area of about 1.2 million sq. km, and prior consent is required for the entry of fishing vessels to this zone.

The main fisheries in the Maldives are the tuna, large yellow fin tuna, live bait, reef fish, grouper, aquarium and sea cucumber fisheries. The main tuna species caught are skipjack tuna (Katsuwonus pelamis), yellowfin tuna (Thunnus albacares), and to a lesser extent bigeye tuna (Thunnus obesus). These fish are caught in open waters, around fish aggregating devices (FADs), drifting flotsam and along the reef edge. Pole and line fishing for tuna takes place throughout the year.

Since the early 1980s, Maldives has seen the emergence of a new fisheries that targets reef species. This includes the export-oriented grouper fishery, the marine aquarium fish trade, the beche-de-mer fishery and the giant clam fishery. High export demand and a small resource base have together caused severe pressure on these fisheries. Maldives has therefore initiated a Reef Resources Management Programme.

The total fish landings in Maldives have increased in recent years from some 1,04,000 metric tons to 1,23,000 metric tons between 1995 and 2000 with an average increase of 4 per cent per annum. Exports, comprising mainly of frozen tuna, chilled or fresh yellow fin tuna, chilled or live grouper, canned tuna, traditionally processed fish and others, totalled 70,800 mt during 1999.

Traditionally-processed fish in the Maldives falls into four broad categories based on processing: smoked-dried skipjack, salted-dried skipjack, salted-dried reef fish and reef-associated fish. Smoked-dried skipjack, also known as "Maldive Fish" is highly sought after in Sri Lanka where it is sold at a premium.

During 2000, a total of 5,187 fishing vessels were enumerated in the Republic. Mechanised masdhonis formed the bulk (2,009) of the fleet. A dramatic change has taken place in the design and construction of fishing vessels in the Maldives during the past three years. The change has primarily been an increase in vessel size, now 20-30 metres in length, with bigger engines. The fishing range has also extended, to over 75 miles offshore. There are 82 such vessels in operation, with about 30 more under construction.

The Ministry of Fisheries, Agriculture and Marine Resources is the nodal ministry for fisheries development in the country. The Marine Research Centre under the Ministry is the nodal facility for R&D activities in marine fisheries in the country. To ensure sustainable resource development, Maldives plans to strengthen its institutional capacity to monitor and enforce fisheries management, improve knowledge and ensure better utilization of tuna and pelagic resources in the EEZ area; and organise long-term scientific research.

1.4.c.iv. Sri Lanka[23]

Area and population : 65,000 sq.km, 15 million.

Length of coastline : 800 km

Shelf area (up to 180 m depth) : 31,250 sq.km

Strength of fishing fleet : 28,000 craft (including 1,500 multi-day boats)

Traditional craft : Oru, vallam, theppam, kattumaram.

Fishing methods : Drift gillnetting, longlining, trawling, line fishing, trolling, beach seining

National fish production: 3,04,380 mt (2000) (marine 2,67,680 mt, inland 29,730 mt, aquaculture 6,970 mt)

Fisherfolk population : 150 Related occupations 50,000

Maximum sustainable yield : 2,50,000 mt (1,70,000 mt pelagic, 80,000 mt demersal)

Pelagic species: Sardine, scad, mackerel, anchovy, seer fish, tuna

Demersal species : Bream, snappers, groupers.

Exports : Rs. 10,328 million (2000)

Imports : Rs. 4,951 million (2000)

Fishing and fish production are vital to the Sri Lankan economy in terms of employment, food and nutrition, security and foreign exchange earnings. Over 7,00,000 people depend on fisheries for their livelihood. The per capita consumption of fish is around 16 kg. Sri Lanka's continental shelf area is estimated at 31,250 sq. km but its width varies. Most of the fish resources are found within the continental shelf. The 1,800 km. long coastline comprises a vast area of marine habitat sandy beaches, extensive lagoons, mangroves and coastal marshes. Over 50 per cent of the population resides in the coastal areas of the country. Of the island's 28,000 craft, some 46 per cent are motoris.

The main fishing method is drift gill netting, which accounts for about 60 per cent of the total catch. Long-lining, trawling, line fishing, trolling and beach seining are the other important methods of fishing. Some 1,500 multi-day boats operate in the offshore/oceanic area. Presently, over 75 per cent of the multi-day boats are equipped with SSB radio, and satellite navigators have been provided under various government development schemes. Fisheries in the island can be broadly divided into four categories: coastal or inshore fisheries, offshore or deep-sea fisheries, inland fisheries and coastal aquaculture. Fisheries on the shelf are supported by a wide range of coastal pelagic and demersal species, typical of tropical multi-species fisheries. The maximum sustainable yield (MSY) of the coastal marine resources in Sri Lanka was estimated in 1979-1980 at about 2,50,000 metric tonnes (mt), of which up to 1,70,000 mt were pelagic fish (small and medium-sized sardine, scad, mackerel, anchovy, seer fish and tuna) and up to 80,000 mt were demersal or semi-demersal (bream, snappers, groupers, etc.).

Fisheries in the offshore or deep-sea waters are supported by medium-sized and large pelagics, mainly tuna, and an exotic range of deep-water demersal species. There has been a marked increase in fish production from offshore or deep-sea areas owing to the introduction of better-equipped multi-day boats. The production from the offshore and deep-sea sector increased from 800 mt in 1972 to 84,400 mt in 2000. Coastal aquaculture in Sri Lanka is presently confined to shrimp farming in the north-western province and a National Aquaculture Development Authority has been set up in the country to regulate shrimp aquaculture. The ornamental fish trade in Sri Lanka has developed into a valuable foreign exchange earner. Sixty fresh water species and over 200 marine species are collected and exported to over 25 countries. However, management measures are urgent for the Exclusive sustainability of the aquarium industry. The export of fish and fish products is an important source of foreign exchange. However, Sri Lanka is a net importer of fish. With high per capita consumption, demand exceeds supply. Fish imports consisted mainly of dried and canned fish. They amounted to 77,338 mt, valued at Rs. 4,951 million.

A new Fisheries and Aquatic Resources Act was promulgated by Sri Lanka in 1996, following clear evidence that coastal fishing exceeded sustainable limits. This Act lays greater emphasis on management and sustainable development of fisheries through 10 sections that address (i) Licensing of all major fishing operations, (ii) Declaration of areas for fisheries management, and (iii) Conservation of fisheries and aquatic resources.

1.5. The Bay of Bengal : Fisheries Regime

The littoral states of the Bay of Bengal have their own Acts to govern fisheries particularly in their seas within national jurisdiction.[24] Fisheries in the Bay of Bengal are now regionally governed by the BOBP-IGO. BOBP-IGO proposes to take up regional programme on safety at sea for artisanal and small-scale fishermen.[25]

While inshore stocks are either optimally exploited or overexploited, little is known about offshore resources or their exploitation. Illegal fishing by fleets from other countries is said to be rampant and fish stocks in several parts of the Bay are threatened. The proposed programme on fish stocks assessment, would seek to provide a mechanism through which member countries could participate in a regional stocks assessment programme and also develop their national capacities to carry out resources surveys and improve fishery statistics in support of fisheries management. Along with this, it is imperative to consider environmental matters for protecting and promoting ecosystems which are practically related with fisheries and all other species. Until and unless there is no environmental regime, there will be no ecosystem to prevail.

1.5.a. Capacity Building and Information Services for Fisheries Development and Management

There is strong optimism that the Bay of Bengal region can produce significantly more fish than it does at present, through better management of the resources. What is needed, apart from appropriate technology inputs, are institutional capacity building, better all-round awareness of management and adoption of a community-based participatory approach.

The BOBP-IGO is aimed to address these issues, with funding support from member countries and other agencies. It is suggested to construe a code of conduct on responsible fisheries at grassroots level. To this end the erstwhile BOBP implemented several activities which aimed at popularisation of the code amongst government functionary stakeholders, including the fisher community. The activities included translation of the main Code and its concise version.

The BOBP-IGO will address these issues, with funding support from member countries and other agencies. Taking the code of conduct for responsible fisheries to the grassroots level the third phase of the erstwhile BOBP implemented many activities, which aimed at popularisation of the code amongst government functionaries and other stakeholders, including the fisher community. The activities included translation of the main code and its concise version. The Code of Conduct was propounded to be effective into national languages of the member countries (Bengali, Dhivehi, Sinhales, Thai, Oriya, Tamil, Telugu, Gujrati, Hindi and Marathi). The BOBP-IGO will continue the activities and translation of the main code and its technical guidelines into the remaining national languages so that the code and its technical guidelines are read and understood by the grassroots fisheries practitioners in the region. Popularisation and adaptation of the code will also be carried out through conduct of national workshops/seminars and organisation of fisher folk weeks in the member countries.

1.6. Biodiversity and Climate Impact

Biodiversity is a term which is often used in environmental literature and yet seldom properly understood.[26] Climate has an inevitable pulse in the Indian subcontinent. Monsoon is the governing parameter of the climate in this area.[27]

> *"Biodiversity is the totality of genes, species, and ecosystems in a region..."*

Biodiversity can be divided into three hierarchical categories—genes, species, and ecosystems—that describe quite different aspects of living systems and that scientists measure in different ways.

Genetic diversity refers to the variation of genes within species. This covers distinct populations of the same species (such as the thousands of traditional rice varieties in India) or genetic variation within a population (high among Indian rhinos, and very low among cheetahs)....

Species diversity refers to the variety of species within a region. Such diversity can be measured in many ways, and scientists have not settled on a single best method. The number of species in a region—its species "richness"—is an often-used measure, but a more precise measurement, "taxonomic diversity", also considers the relationship of species to each other. For example, an island with two species of birds and one species of lizard has a greater taxonomic diversity than an island with three species of birds but no lizards....

Ecosystem diversity is harder to measure than species or genetic diversity because the "boundaries" of communities—associations of species—and ecosystems are elusive. Nevertheless, as long as a consistent set of criteria is used to define communities and ecosystems, their numbers and distribution can be measured."[28]

There are three general kinds of biodiversity: habitat diversity, genetic diversity, and species diversity. The survival of each is linked to the health of the other two, and together they comprise the wealth of ecosystems.

Habitat diversity refers to the variety of places where life exists—coral reefs, old-growth forests in the Pacific Northwest, tall grass prairie, coastal wetlands, and many others. Each broad type of habitat is the home for numerous species, most of which are utterly dependent on that habitat. So when a type of habitat disappears, a vast number of species disappear as well. More often, an entire habitat does not completely disappear but instead is nibbled away, acre by acre, until only small patches remain. This has happened to old-growth forest and coastal wetlands in the United States and is now in full swing in tropical forests throughout the world. Elimination of small patches of habitat can lead to the extinction of those species that live only in small regions of the habitat. Elimination of all but small patches is especially damaging because it not only eliminates many localized species but also threatens those species that are dependent on vast acreages for their survival.

To understand genetic diversity, it helps to first clarify what biologists mean when they refer to as 'population.' Consider the song sparrows in the neighbourhood. They are a population—individuals of a species that live together, in the sense that mates are chosen from within the group. The sparrows in the population share more of their genes with each other than they do with other individuals from populations of the same species elsewhere, because individuals in one population rarely breed with those in another. Although each population within a species contains some genetic information unique to that population, individuals in all populations share in common the genetic information that defines their species.

In principle, individuals from one population could mate with individuals from another population of the same species. That is a definition of what a species is—a collection of individuals that could, in principle, interbreed. In practice, individuals from different populations within a species rarely interbreed because of geographic isolation.

The genetic diversity within a species is primarily the variety of populations that comprise it. Species reduced to a single population (like the California condor) generally contain less genetic diversity than those consisting of many populations. Song sparrows, found over much of North America, occur in numerous populations and thus maintain considerable genetic diversity within the species. Biologists care about the survival of populations, as well as species, because of the unique genetic information contained within populations.

The very survival of a species is dependent on the survival of its populations, for if only a few populations remain, there are few survival tactics that the species can deploy in the face of threats (such as global warming). Each population contains a distinct set of genetic instructions for how the species might adapt to threats. Nature, in other words, figured out long ago not to put all its eggs in one basket.

Finally, there is species diversity, which is what most people mean when they talk about what includes the genus, the family, the order, the class, the phylum, and the kingdom. Consider people, whose species name is *Homo sapiens*. *Homo* is the genus, and *sapiens* biodiversity. The designation "species" is one level of classification in a taxonomic hierarchy. We happen, now, to be the only living species in the genus *Homo*.

We are in the family Hominidae (apes and man), the order of Primates (femurs, monkeys, apes, and man), the class Mammalia, the phylum Chordata (or vertebrates), and the kingdom animal.

There are about one and a half million named species on earth, but we know that many unnamed species exist, and the total number is probably between 5 and 15 million. Most of the evidence for numerous unnamed species comes from studies of insects in tropical forests: when the canopy of a tropical tree is fumigated and all the dead insects are collected, large numbers of hitherto unknown insects are frequently collected.

One of the most important components of climate change is the variation of temperature at the Earth's surface. Because temperature changes at the surface affect the distribution of temperature in the subsurface, ground temperatures comprise an archive of signal of past climate. Thermal regime at shallow depths of the crust is controlled by the temperature condition at the surface and the heat flowing from deeper part of the Earth. In an idealized homogeneous crust, if the surface temperature is steady, the distribution of ground temperature is a linear function of depth. However, if the surface temperature changes with time, the ground temperature will depart from the linear distribution which is governed by heat flow and thermal conductivity.[29]

The threats of climate change[30] are potentially serious and demand the concerted attention of the world community. But in light of all the scientific and economic uncertainties, climate change might best be viewed as presenting a heroic problem in risk management. That conception reminds us that the aim is not to avoid all the perils that greenhousing may present, on a worst-case scenario, at any cost; the goal is to reduce the sum of the costs of avoiding, controlling and insuring the risks.

The proposition that the world faces serious global environmental problems hardly needs demonstration or rehearsal. It was the reason that led to the establishment of the United Nations Conference on Environment and Development to begin with. Ozone depletion,[31] climate change and biodiversity are the issues that have the most public prominence, but there are many others. They include the quality and supply of fresh water; protection of the oceans; deforestation. desertification and drought; the management of biotechnology; the management of wastes, including toxic chemicals and other hazardous wastes; urban slums; and poor human health conditions. In recent times, the issues have been coached in security terms. Security of adequate food supplies is an obvious one, but the issues of energy can be dealt with from the same angle. It is worthy to note if global environmental security is taken to mean security against those risks that threaten our common survival, the focus of collective legal action may indeed be sharpened considerably. A tentative priority list of genuine survival risks would thus, as a minimum, have to include the following essential concerns:

- climate security
- biological security
- chemical security[32]

A myriad of other issues concern the health of our planet and the capacity to sustain life upon it. The whole question was summed up by the World Commission on Environment and Development as one of sustainable development. To produce the conditions necessary for sustainable development, a great deal more in the way of regulation and prohibition will be required at the international level. At present, environmental responsibilities are divided among a number of the specialized agencies, including the Food and Agriculture Organization, the World Health Organization, the World Meteorological Organization, the International Maritime Organization, the UN Educational, Scientific and Cultural Organization and the UN Development Programme, with a coordinating and catalytic role assigned to the UN Environment Programme (UNEP).[33]

1.7. Need for a Legal Regime for the Bay of Bengal Environment

The Bay of Bengal is very much related with its littoral states. Bangladesh, India, Maldives, Myanmar, and Sri Lanka have so much dependence on the Bay of Bengal. The rivers of the littoral states carry colossal amount of silts to the bay and sediments are being deposited in the coastal regions of the bay. In the case of Bangladesh it is true in entirety.[34]

The legal regime of environment internationally paved the way since the Stockholm Declaration. The new environmental consciousness among nations started with the Stockholm Conference in 1972, not a moment too soon. The Stockholm Declaration of the United Nations Conference on the Human Environment attracted 103 affirmative votes, 12 abstentions and not a single negative vote.[35] In some respects the declaration was a masterpiece of international drafting. The document suggests that we have a right now to a life of dignity and equality in an environment of quality, but that we also have a "solemn responsibility to protect and improve the environment for present and future generations."[36]

In order to promote environment and development there arises an issue of financial resources and technological cooperation. The primary responsibility to deal with global threats like climate change rests with industrialized countries. Transfer of additional resources to developing nations must initially apply to poverty-related environmental problems that receive priority among the Third World nations themselves.[37]

The oceans cover 70 per cent of the surface of the globe and play a dominant and decisive role in the biogeochemical processes of the planet on local, regional, and global scales. The global energy budget, climate and weather, the hydrological and carbo cycles, and atmospheric and physical processes are critically influenced by the properties of the oceanic processes. Most of the earth's life, expressed as biomass, exists within the vast volume of the oceans. The fertility of the seas is determined by the abundance of the phytoplankton. The annual phytoplankton production is estimated at between 15 and 30 billion tons of carbon. The annual world fish production is estimated at almost 30 million tons of carbon. Yet these processes are less understood than those occurring in the terrestrial environment and atmosphere. Long-term management and sustainable development of the world's resources must be based on a sound understanding of the role of the ocean in shaping conditions on the globe and on a proper evaluation of the benefits of the marine resource base for development.

In relation to development, the oceans have traditionally provided a medium for the transportation of goods, fishing, and recreation, as well as repository for wastes. Uses of ocean and coastal space are multiple and serve many and diverse purposes. The traditional ones include the production of food, sources of energy, minerals and other raw materials, a base for tourism, recreation, settlement, transport, and the location of both aquatic and semi-aquatic farming. Over the years, offshore oil production has greatly increased and new technological developments have opened greater areas of the sea floor to drilling and production. World sea-borne trade in oil and cargo has also grown enormously in the past decades. This includes changes in the type of vessels requiring new port development and major channel dredging. In addition, the oceans have been used as a free dump service for sewage and wastes, without the proper inclusion of damage costs.

Turning to fisheries, the oceans are sources of living and non-living resources, which are currently treated as open access goods. The marine catch is close to the maximum production obtainable, nearly 80 million metric tonnes, of which 90 per cent is estimated to be from coastal areas. Mariculture yields approximately five million metric tonnes and by now it is almost double. Increases in marine catches in the last two decades are the result of different events such as the discovery of the new resources, the introduction of new fishing technologies, changes as a result of the law of the sea, and major environmental changes. Artisanal fisheries are socially important since they contribute significantly to fisheries employment, particularly in developing countries.

Aside from living resources, the high seas seem to be largely unaffected, but the physical and ecological degradation of coastal areas and the increase in pollution from land-based sources are greatly increasing. The interface between the land and the sea, the coastal zone, is a band of highly diverse and biologically productive ecosystems and habitats. The coastal zone supports much of the world's population. The root cause of coastal management problems lies in the distribution, absolute size, and the rate of growth of human populations. Rapid growth of coastal settlements, expansion of recreational areas and centres of marine transport, and concentration of industrial development along the coast, all result in accelerated coastal degradation. Sixty-five per cent of cities with populations above 2.5 million inhabitants are coastal, and at present 20 per cent of the world population lives in coastal urban centres and approximately 60 per cent increasing human impacts on one of the most productive of ecosystems, the shallow marine and brackish-water areas. The situation in many enclosed and semi-enclosed seas is of particular concern.

Although international conventions have been developed for pollution from shipping, for dumping and major oil spills, and for oil pollution, the coastal zone is highly degraded by other factors not yet covered by conventions. Coastal areas are the receiving end of upstream activities, including the discharge of pollutants to rivers and of changing water regimes due to damming rivers and deforestation. Considerable international cooperation exists in marine research and development, but much larger efforts are required to ensure global participation and benefits. A much stronger commitment is required on behalf of governments in order to obtain the benefits of opportunities for development inherent in the marine environment.

The capabilities of most countries to manage current problems are still insufficient and limit future choices for meeting the challenge of sustainable development. Management units for ocean and coastal affairs are generally weak and dispersed. They currently reflect agencies' sectoral responsibilities rather than the boundaries of coastal systems. There is now a widespread recognition that sectoral approaches to managing coastal zones fail to resolve conflict. The responsibilities of national agencies must integrate the environmental limits of the ecosystems under management with the sectoral economic interests.

Moreover, current patterns of management and exploitation in the marine environment reflect historical conditions of use which no longer apply. Numbers of people in the coastal areas were low and technologies less advanced, so the supply of ocean goods and services was little impacted by demand. Free use and open access when demand is low pose no problem. However, when demand nears or exceeds supply, policies of open access on the ocean environment create conflict among users and significant resources and environmental degradation. In general, there is not an efficient user-rights system in the exclusive economic zones at the national level and in open seas at the international level.

Historically, ocean legal regimes have been reactive. Few recent legal regimes have been designed to operate in a proactive manner and avoid conflict. Legal instruments need to be more closely correlated with anticipatory environmental planning and management approaches designed to incorporate new perceptions of ocean uses. The new approach to ocean management must recognize the need for proactive and anticipatory regimes that could avoid conflict and must prevent environmental damage and economic loss, as an alternative to the traditional view, which has been centred on reactions to conflicts in resource use, environmental degradation, and prescriptive actions.

Geopolitical and administrative boundaries have no meaning in environmental terms since marine living resources and ecosystems do not correspond to these man-made limit. The need to maintain the natural functioning of the oceans in the face of increasing uses may result in viewing ocean space in ecosystem terms. The scales of management and the economic and legal regimes must therefore be adjusted so as to reflect not only the political administrative boundaries but the real physical and biological units being managed, e.g., large marine ecosystems, marine catchment basins, and species ranges.

Public perception of ocean issues is in transition. Society is gradually appreciating that the impact of intensified human activities no longer permits a casual approach to oceans as an unlimited receptacle for wastes and an endless supply of free and open access resources. The increasing active support of significant non-governmental organizations is placing ocean management on centre stage as a significant public policy issue. Broader educational and public awareness programmes are essential to enhance participation in decision-making debates. In this connection, the value of ocean coastal areas for tourism and the role of coastal ecosystems in terms of erosion control and protection against storm and episodic damage are rarely included in economic or social evaluations.

Management refers to the attempt to provide order for a detected balance between and among the various uses of ocean space, as well as to protecting the ocean environmental viability. It encompasses several steps which include: collection, organisation and analysis of data; setting of priorities; making choices related to policy directives, laws, and regulations; implementation of policies; surveillance and enforcement of rules; and evaluation of results. Technical solutions for many of the problems are quite well known and action is needed. However, there are still critical uncertainties for management purposes. Significant among the challenges for future ocean management are the availability, incorporation, and utilization of scientific and technical information in the policy process, jurisdictional problems, the nature of ocean political constituencies, and the costs associated with management efforts.

The overall objective for future ocean management lies in utilizing the environmental and economic goods and services provided by marine and coastal ecosystems to meet development objectives while at the same time ensuring the long-term maintenance of marine environmental health, resource quality, and ecological integrity. The oceans and coastal areas need to be viewed as a positive asset presenting opportunities for sustainable development. This will only be possible under an holistic and integrated management approach to their utilization. The ocean requires a full evaluation of the marine coastal resource base and of opportunities and constraints provided within a given area or country. Where marine resources and ecosystems are shared with other states, cooperative approaches will be necessary.[38] This ensures the needs for a legal regime of marine environment for every area of the oceans. Hence the legal regime of marine environment in the Bay of Bengal is warranted.

References

1. Stockholm Declaration of the United Nations Conference on the Human Environment, 16 June 1972 (cited as Stockholm Declaration). UNDoc.A/CONF.48/14, reprinted in *International Legal Materials* (hereafter cited as ILM), 11(1972) 14-21.
2. The 27th Session of the UN General Assembly passed a series of resolutions which resulted in the creation of the UNEP: 2994(XXVII) – UN Conference on the Human Environment; 2995(XXVII) – Cooperation between States in the Field of the Environment; 2996 (XXVII) – International Responsibility of States in Regard to the Environment; 2997(XXVII) – Institutional and Financial Arrangements for International Environmental Cooperation; 3001 (XXVII) – Measures for Protecting and Enhancing the Environment; 3002 (XXVII) – Development and Environment.
3. The oceans governance is inevitable in the sense that the oceans, for example, while at one time seemed so vast that no amount of waste disposal could cause a pollution problem now represent a serious area of environmental overload. Each year it is estimated that 5,00,000 chemical compounds are put into the air and that most of them find their way into the oceans. Lead from petrol falls into the sea at the rate of 2,50,000 tons per year. Mercury used in agriculture, where it functions as a very effective fungicide, has entered the oceans at a rate of 4,000 to 5,000 tons per year. Current estimates of oil losses in the oceans due to leakage and spillage are calculated at 1 per cent of the total transported volume of 10,00,000 tons per year. The burning of fossil fuels releases great quantities of carbon dioxide into the atmosphere, which have deleterious effects on the ocean's photosynthesis process. See H.L. Dickstein, "International Law and the Environment: Evolving Concepts", 26(1972) *The Year Book of World Affairs* 1972, 246.
4. *Supra*, n 2.
5. D. Vander Zwaag and D.M. Johnston, "Toward the Management of the Gulf of Thailand: Charting the Course of Cooperation", in D.M. Johnston (ed) *SEAPOL Integrated Studies of the Gulf of Thailand* (Bangkok: SEAPOL, 1998) vol. 1, pp. 60-135 at 81.
6. The first UNEP-led Programme was in the Mediterranean, wherein the participating states signed an umbrella framework convention, the 1976 Barcelona Convention, about specific protocols to address particular environmental problems. The Mediterranean Programme is significant in the development of regional ICOM initiatives as it was the model for regional governance for the 12 other Seas Programmes led by UNEP. See the Convention for the Protection of the Mediterranean Sea against Pollution, 16 February 1976, reprinted in ILM 15(1976); 285-318

(Barcelona Convention): the Protocol for the Prevention of Pollution of the Mediterranean Sea by Dumping from Ships and Aircraft, 16 February 1976, reprinted in ILM 15(1976):300-306; and the Protocol Concerning Cooperation in Combating Pollution in the Mediterranean Sea by Oil and Other Harmful Substances in Cases of Emergency, 16 February 1976, reprinted in ILM 15(1976): 306-310. Also see D. Vander Zwaag and D.M. Johnston, "Toward the Management of the Gulf of Thailand: Charting the Course of Cooperation," in *SEAPOL Integrated Studies of the Gulf of Thailand,* vol. 1, D.M. Johnston (ed) (Bangkok: SEAPOL, 1998), pp. 69-135 at 81.

7. United Nations Convention on the Law of the Sea, 10 December 1982, UN. Doc.A/CONF. 62/122, reprinted in ILM 21(1982); 1261. LOS Convention was signed by 159 states by the close of signature on 9 December 1984 and entered into force upon the 60th ratification on 16 November 1994 (hereafter cited as LOS Convention).

8. Chapter XVII of Principle 21 specifies the seas, oceans and the parts thereof in "common noun" form to be its concerns. That means, the Bay of Bengal subsumes in the provisions of this chapter. The coasts of the Bay of Bengal do not belong to a single State, as such Article 10 of the LOS Convention relating to "Bays" is not applicable. The map of the Bay has been appended in Annex E.

9. In order to intensify marine environment concerns, clarification is almost re-added to the relevant infrastructure of the Bay of Bengal. The Bay of Bengal is a northern extended arm of the Indian ocean, located between latitudes 5°N and 22°N and longitudes 80°E and 100°E. It is bounded in the west by the east coasts of Sri Lanka and India, on the north by the deltaic region of the Ganges-Brahmaputra-Meghna river system, and on the east by the Myanmar peninsula extended up to the Andaman-Nicobar ridges. The southern boundary of the Bay is approximately along the line drawn from Dondra Head in the south of Sri Lanka to the north tip of Sumatra. The Bay occupies an area of about 2.2 million sq km and the average depth is 2,600m with a maximum depth of 5,258m. Bangladesh is situated at the head of the Bay of Bengal, characterised by a broad U-shaped basin with its south opening to the Indian Ocean. A thick uniform abyssal plain occupies almost the entire Bay of Bengal gently sloping southward at an angle of 8°-10°. In many places underwater valleys dissect this plain mass.

   Surface hydrology of the Bay of Bengal is basically determined by the monsoon winds and to some extent by the hydrological characteristics of the open part of the Indian Ocean. Fresh water from the rivers largely influences the coastal northern part of the Bay. The rivers of Bangladesh discharge a vast amount of 1,222 million cubic metres of fresh water (excluding evaporation, deep percolation losses and evapotranspiration) into the Bay. The temperature, salinity and density of the water of the southern part of the Bay of Bengal is, almost the same as in the open part of the ocean. In the coastal region of the Bay and in the north-eastern part of the Andaman Sea where a significant influence of river water is present, the temperature and salinity are seen to be different from the open part of the Bay. The waves and ripples entering from the southern part of the Bay provide energy for mixing the water and consequently bring uniformity in its chemical and physical properties. Tidal action is also very great in the shallow coastal zone. Marine environment of the Bay of Bengal is directly or indirectly becoming polluted due to addition of so many polluting agents.

10. The Bay of Bengal is much more than the eastern segment of the Indian Ocean; the maritime region encompassing the countries around the littoral of the Bay always maintained a thriving contact through movement of trade, people, religious, cultural and political missions, which gave the region an autonomous character. The Bay of Bengal was a linking factor between the countries bordering on it and the cultural and trade links forged by the Bay stretched from China to the east, to West Asia and Africa to the west. This was the picture which clearly emerged once again from the papers presented to the seminar on the trade and cultural links in the Bay of Bengal, held in Delhi, 16-20 December 1994, organized jointly by the ICHR, Delhi and the MSH, Paris. Visit http://iias.leidenuniv.nl/iiasn5/soutasia/bengal.html Pursuant to the version of South Asia Analysis Group there is to point out that as time passes, the Bay of Bengal is becoming an important concern for its community (the Bay of Bengal Community). There are many factors politically and strategically varying not only to the interests of its littoral states but also to some concerns of certain big powers as well. Visit http// www.saag.org/papers3/papers215 htm
11. LOS Convention, Art 1(4).
12. E.D. Brown, *The Legal Regime of Hydrospace,* (Steven & Sons, London, 1971) 103.
13. V.S. Deshpande, "Indian Ocean as a Peace of Zone – Evolving the Legal Process", 14(1974) IJIL 160-161.

    See Resolution 3259 (XXIX). Implementation of the Declaration of the Indian Ocean as a Zone of Peace (9 December 1974) Votes: A-103-0-26 (recorded) B-adopted without vote. Reported in this volume at 490-492.
14. LOS Convention, Art 207.
15. *Ibid.,* Art 208.
16. *Ibid.,* Art 209.
17. *Ibid.,* Art 210.
18. *Ibid.,* Art 211.
19. *Ibid.,* Art 212.
20. http:/www.cia.gov/cia/publication/factbook/geos/bg.html
21. http://www.cia.gov/cia/publication/factbook/geosin.html
22. http://www.cia.gov/cia/publication/factbook/geos/mv.html
23. http://www.cia.gov/cia/publication/factbook/geos/ce.html
24. According to the LOS Convention the seas within national jurisdiction are considered to be internal waters (Art 18), territorial sea (Art 2), contiguous

zone (Art 33), exclusive economic zone (Art 55), and the continental shelf (Art 76).

25. See 1.2.

26. There has developed a lot on the concept of biodiversity. Visit : http://www.defenders.org/bio-bioohtml

27. Visit : http://eprints.iisc.ernet.in/archive/00001891 and alternative location. The first observational experiment under the Indian Climate Research Programme, called the Bay of Bengal Monsoon Experiment (BOBMEX), was carried out during July-August 1999. BOBMEX was aimed at measurements of important variables of the atmosphere, ocean, and their interface to gain deeper insight into some of the processes that govern the variability of organized convection over the bay. Simultaneous time series observations were carried out in the northern and southern Bay of Bengal from ships and moored buoys. About 80 scientists from 15 different institutions in India collaborated during BOBMEX to make observations in most-hostile conditions of the raging monsoon. In this paper, the objectives and the design of BOBMEX are described and some initial results presented. During the BOBMEX field phase there were several active spells of convection over the bay, separated by weak spells. Observation with high-resolution radiosondes, launched for the first time over the northern bay, showed that the magnitudes of the convective available potential energy (CAPE) and the convective inhibition energy were comparable to those for the atmosphere over the west Pacific warm pool. CAPE decreased by 2-3 kJ kg(-1) following convection, and recovered in a time period of 1-2 days. The surface wind speed was generally higher than 8 m. s(-1). The thermohaline structure as well as its time evolution during the BOBMEX field phase were found to be different in the northern bay than in the southern bay. Over both the regions, the SST decreased during rain events and increased in cloud-free conditions. Over the season as a whole, the upper-layer salinity decreased for the north bay and increased for the south bay. The variation in SST during 1999 was found to be of smaller amplitude than in 1998. Further analysis of the surface fluxes and currents is expected to give insight into the nature of coupling. E Print Type: Journal (Paginated) Subjects: Division of Mechanical Sciences Centre for Atmospheric & Oceanic Sciences ID Code: 1859 Deposited By:

    Ravi V. Nandhan, Deposited On: 16 September 2004 Additional Information: Copyright of this article belongs to American Meteorological Soiety. Alternative Locations: http://caos.iisc.ernet.in/faculty/dsen/bobmex.pdf

28. http://www.ceres.ca.gov/biodiv/Biodiversity/biodiv_def2.htmal. This gives a scope to come through Edward Grumbine, «Ghost Bears: Exploring the Biodiversity Crisis,» 1993.

29. For a brief introduction to the geothermal approach of climate reconstruction go to: http://www.geo.isa.umich.edu/climate/approach.htmal.

30. Most important to the more concerned wing of the scientific community, the global temperature represents an average across the world, one that

would not be spread evenly across regions. Some areas generally supposed to be those closer to the equator, would experience relatively little of the increase, while areas in high latitudes it occurs differently.

31 In a study Dr. Harold Johnston of the University of California at Berkeley, estimated that if commercial supersonic airliners come into regularly scheduled service they will rapidly deplete the ozone layer in the atmosphere and thereby jeopardise continued life on this planet (*The New York Times,* May 30, 1971, s. 3, p. 2, Dr. Johnston is also credited with being the first, in 1951, to measure the rate at which nitric oxide breaks down ozone). Supersonic transports area threat to life because the nitric oxide in their exhaust would convert ozone into oxygen gas, which is not a complete shield against ultraviolet rays. Without an atmospheric ozone layer, ultra-violet rays would, according to Dr. Johnston, blind humans and animals, burn land plants and probably make higher forms of life on this planet impossible. Even more frightening is the prospect that the introduction of a large quantity of nitric oxide into the stratosphere would set in motion an irreversible chemical reaction, which would go on destroying ozone even if mankind then halted supersonic transports flights. See H. L. Dickstein, "International Law and the Environment: Evolving Concepts", 26(1972) *The Year Book of World Affairs* 1972, 245.

32. Geoffrey Palme, "New Ways to make International Environmental Law", 86(1992) *AJIL* 260.

33. *Ibid.*, 260.

34. Vast reserves of natural gas—both onshore and offshore in the Bay of Bengal – have been discovered in Bangladesh since the mid-1990s. Total proven reserves amount to 301 trillion cu m, but actual reserve may be much greater. Natural gas is the principal energy resource in Bangladesh and an important ingredient in the manufacture of nitrogenous fertilizers which are part and parcel of its agriculture. Its irrigation is endowed by such fertilizers. Visit : http://www.encarta.msn.com/enclopedia_761553817/Bangladesh.htmlttp3

35. Stockholm Declaration, Section 1 of Report of the United Nations Conference on the Human Environment, UN Doc.A/CONF.48/14 and Corr.1(1972), reprinted in 11 ILM 1416 (1972) (adopted with no roll-call vote recorded)[hereinafter Stockholm Declaration]. See also BASIC DOCUMENTS IN INTERNATIONAL LAW AND WORLD ORDER 691, 943 (B. Weston, R. Falk & A. D'Amato 2nd ed. 1990).

36. Principle 1 of Stockholm Declaration.

37. Svante Bodin's speech quoted in Alastair Couper & Egar Gold (ed), *The Marine Environment and Sustainable Development: Law. Policy, and Science* (1993), The Law of the Sea Institute, Twenty-fifth Annual Conference, August 1991, Malmo, Sweden, p. 8.

38. Alicia Barcena, "Some Reflections on a New Approach to Ocean and Coastal Management", *The Marine Environment and Sustainable Development: Law, Policy, and Science* (1993), The Law of the Sea Institute Twenty-fifth Annual Conference, 23-27.

2

ENVIRONMENTAL REGIME FOR THE BAY OF BENGAL

2.1. The Bay of Bengal Approach

The environmental regime for the Bay of Bengal is concerned with its surrounding littoral states. The Bay of Bengal, a northern extended arm of the Indian Ocean, is located between latitudes 5°N and 22°N and longitudes 80°E and 100°E. It is bounded in the west by the east coasts of Sri Lanka and India, on the north by the deltaic region of the Ganges-Brahmaputra-Meghna river system, and on the east by the Myanmar peninsula extending up to the Andaman-Nicobar ridges. The southern boundary of the Bay is approximately along the line drawn from Dondra Head in the south of Sri Lanka to the north tip of Sumatra. The Bay occupies an area of about 2.2 million sq km and the average depth is 2,600m with a maximum depth of 5,258m[1].

2.1.a. Bottom Topography

The Bay of Bengal is characterised by a broad U-shaped basin with its south opening to the Indian Ocean. A thick uniform abyssal plain occupies almost the entire Bay gently sloping southward at an angle of 8°-10°. In many places underwater valleys dissect this plain mass.

The bottom topography is influenced by sediment deposits carried by the rivers of the surrounding states. Moreover, ocean surges together with tectonic activities, influence the topography of the Bay. The width of the continental shelf off the coast of

Bangladesh varies considerably. It is less than 100 km off the south coast between Hiron Point and the Swatch of no Ground and more than 250 km off the coast of Cox's Bazar. Sediments are fine seaward and westward with the thickest accumulation of mud near the submarine canyon, the Swatch of no Ground. The shallow part (less than 20m) of the continental shelf off the coast of Chittagong and Teknaf is covered by sand and the intertidal areas show well-developed sandy beaches. The shallower part of southern continental shelf off the coast of the Sundarbans, Patuakhali and Noakhali is covered by silt and clay; and extensive muddy tidal flats are developed along the shoreline. Some of the shoals and sand ridges present on this part of the continental shelf show an elongation pattern pointed towards the Swatch of no Ground. The entire topographical situation is related to the surrounding littoral states.[2]

2.1.b. Swatch of no Ground/Ganga Trough

Swatch of no Ground has a comparatively flat floor 5 to 7 km wide and walls of about 12° inclination. At the edge of the shelf, depths in the trough are about 1,200m. The Swatch of no Ground has a seaward continuation for almost 2,000 km down the Bay of Bengal in the form of fan valleys with levees. The sandbars and ridges near the mouth of the Ganges-Brahmaputra delta pointing toward the Swatch of no Ground showing sediments are tunnelled through this trough into the deeper part of the Bay of Bengal. The Swatch of no Ground feeds the Bengal Deep Sea Fan by turbidity currents.

2.1.c. Sunda Trench/Java Trench

Running parallel along the west side of the arc of the Nicobar and Andaman islands it is extended northward up to 10°N into the Bay and joins the eastern limit of the Himalayan range. It originated tectonically at the junction of the Indian and Myanmar plates.

Ninety East Ridge, a major feature of the Indian Ocean runs in a north-south direction approximately along the longitude 90°E. It lies at the immediate outboard of the Sunda Trench between the Bengal Fan and the Nicobar Fan. The

Ninety East Ridge has existed since early in the formation of the Bay of Bengal. The ridge represents the trace of a hot spot formed during the northward flight of India and its associated oceanic lithosphere of the Bay of Bengal.

Eighty-five Ridge, is a ridge along 85°E longitude. More than 5 km thick sediments have been deposited on either sides of the ridge. The main turbidity current channel of the sub-aerial drainage pattern lies immediately east of the buried ridge.

Bengal Deep Sea Fan the world's largest submarine fan is also known as Bengal Fan. Together with its eastern lobe, the Nicobar fan, it covers an area of 3106 sq. km. It is 2,800 to 3,000 km. long, 830 to 1,430 km wide and more than 16 km. thick beneath the northern Bay of Bengal. Sediments are tunnelled to the fan via a delta-front trough, the Swatch of no Ground. It can be divided into three parts: upper fan, middle fan and lower fan. Rapid terrigenous sedimentation on an incipient Bengal fan began in the Eocene age (58 to 37 million years ago) as a response to the first intra-plate collision and continued to the present, building the world's largest submarine fan.

2.1.d. Geo-hydrographical Characteristics

Hydrological conditions, e.g., surface hydrology of the Bay of Bengal is basically determined by the monsoon winds and to some extent by the hydrological characteristics of the open part of the Indian Ocean. Fresh water from the rivers largely influences the coastal northern part of the Bay. The rivers of Bangladesh discharge the vast amount of 1,222 million cubic metres of fresh water (excluding evaporation, deep percolation losses and evapotranspiration) into the Bay. The temperature, salinity and density of the water of the southern part of the Bay of Bengal is, almost the same as in the open part of the ocean. In the coastal region of the Bay and in the north-eastern part of the Andaman Sea where a significant influence of river water is present, the temperature and salinity are seen to be different from the open part of the Bay. The waves and ripples entering from the southern part of the Bay provide energy for mixing the water and consequently bring uniformity in its chemical and physical properties. Tidal action is also very great in the shallow coastal zones.[3]

Temperature—the mean annual temperature of the surface water is about 28°C. The maximum temperature is observed in May (30°C) and the minimum (25°C) in January-February. But the annual variation in temperature is not great, about 2°C in the south and 5°C in the north.

Salinity—the surface salinity in the open part of the Bay oscillates from 32% to 34.5% (parts per thousand, i.e., grams per kilogram of sea water) and in the coastal region varies from 10% to 25%. But at the river mouths, the surface salinity decreases to 5% or even less. The coastal water is significantly diluted throughout the year, although the river water is greatly reduced during winter. Along the coast of the Ganges-Brahmaputra Delta, salinity decreases to 1% during summer and increases up to 15% to 20% in winter. Salinity gradually increases from the coast towards the open part of the Bay. The surface salinity at the mouths of some large rivers like the Ganges, Brahmaputra, Irrawaddy and some Indian rivers like the Krishna, Godavari, Cauvery and Mahanadi varies widely from one day to another, especially in summer. Salinity of water also changes vertically. The influence of the fresh water is experienced up to depths of 200-300m. From the surface, the salinity gradually increases downward, at about 200-300m it reaches 35% and at about 500m the salinity is more than 35.10%. But at 1,000m it decreases slightly and attains 34.95%. With further increase of depth salinity decreases and at 4,500m it is close to 34.7%.

Tides—semi-diurnal type of tides, i.e., two high and two low tides during the period of 24 hours and 52 minutes. The highest tide is seen where the influence of bottom relief and the configuration of the coast are prominent, i.e., in shallow water and in the Bay and estuary. The average height of tidal waves at the coast of Sri Lanka is 0.7m and in the deltaic coast of the Ganges it is 4.71m. In the Bay of Bengal tidal currents specially develop in the mouths of the rivers, like the Hoogly and the Meghna.

Colour and water transparency—the colour of the water in the open part of the Bay is dark blue which gradually changes to light blue to greenish towards the coast. Transparency is great, 40-50m in some places. In the central part of the Bay of Bengal, the anticyclone circulation is generated and in the centre of this lies the zone of convergence. This region is characterised as a rule by high transparency of water. Regions of low transparency and turbid water exist in the limited area of the pre-deltaic part of the rivers Ganges and Brahmaputra.

Sea Level—due to the influence of water density and wind the seasonal changes of the sea level in the Bay are remarkable and one of the highest in the world. The range at Khidirpur is 166 cm, at Kolkata 130 cm and at Chittagong 118 cm. But towards the south-western coast at Madras and Vishakhapatnam the range is small compared to the northern and north-eastern coasts of the Bay. The lowest variation of sea level at the south-eastern coast of India is due to its geographical location at the edge of a comparatively deep sea.

Ocean Current—surface circulation is found to be generally clockwise from January to July and counter-clockwise from August to December, in accordance with the reversible monsoon wind systems. The flow is not constant and depends on the strength and duration of the winds. The effects of a strong wind blowing for a few consecutive days are reflected in the rate of flow. Currents to the north-east generally persist longer and flow at greater speed because of the stronger south-west monsoons. An important vertical circulation in the Bay of Bengal is up-welling. In this process, sub-surface water is brought toward the surface, and conversely a downward displacement is called down-welling or sinking.

Up-welling and down-welling are seasonal, being created by monsoon winds that blow from the south-west during the summer, then reverse direction and come from the north-east during the winter. The persistence of the monsoon, especially from the south-west and the orientation of the coasts cause up-welling to occur along most of the east coast of India. That is why in the east coast of India the up-welling takes place in summer and down welling in winter, and in the eastern part of the Bay of Bengal and in the Myanmar coast, up-welling occurs in winter and the down-welling in summer. However, the duration and intensity of vertical movement of water on both sides of the Bay of Bengal is not as great as on the Somali or North and South American coasts. But it does have a profound effect on the food economy of the sea through its influence on chemical properties and biological populations.

2.1.e. Biological Characteristics

The occurrence of marine species—both plants and animals—has largely been controlled by the physico-chemical properties of ocean water. Water discharges from the surrounding river catchments carry huge influx of sediments full of nutrients to the Bay, particularly along the near shore region. This has turned the Bay into a fertile marine fishing ground of the region. The near-shore up-welling zone not only has a high yield of nutrients, but also is a high primary production area for the phytoplankton and related zooplankton zones.

Fishing—the hydrological conditions of the Bay of Bengal are favourable for a variety of shrimps and fishes. Although fishes remain scattered in the Bay in some places they get concentrated and constitute important fishing grounds. Four fishing grounds have been identified so far. They are south patches, south of south patches, middle ground and Swatch of no Ground.

South patches located at 91.30°E to 92.10°E and 20.55°S to 21.52°S, having a total area of 3,662 sq km. Depth ranges from 10m to 100m, but 90% of the total area is less than 40m deep. Bottom sediment is sandy or slightly muddy sand. Nearest distance of the ground from Chittagong and Cox's Bazar is 40 km and 10 km respectively. Salinity in surface water ranges from 26% to 32% and 30% to 35% in bottom water. Water temperature varies between 20 and 28°C.

South of south patches located at 91.30°E to 92.20°E and 20.15°S 20.50°S, having an area of 2,538 sq km. The nearest boundary of this area is 5 km from Teknaf. Depth ranges from 10m to 100m. Within this ground 75% of the area is more than 40m deep. Bottom is sandy or muddy sand. Surface salinity ranges from 18% to 34% and bottom water salinity from 28% to 38%. Water temperature ranges between 22°C and 30°C.

Middle ground located at 90.20°E to 91.30°E and 20.25°S to 21.20°S, having a total area of about 4,600 sq km. The nearest distance from Cox's Bazar is about 65 km. The depth of 70% of the total area is more than 40m. Bottom sediment is soft mud or muddy sand. Surface salinity ranges from 22% to 34% and bottom salinity 28% to 35%. Water temperature is between 26°C and 28°C.

Swatch of no Ground located at 89.35°E to 90.10°E and 20.55°S to 21.55°S, about 30 km away from Dublarchar and 40 km from Sunarchar. Total area is about 3,800 sq km, of which 70% is more than 40m deep. Overall depth of the area ranges from 10m to 100m. Bottom sediment consists of muddy sand. Surface salinity is 28% to 34%, while the bottom salinity is 30% to 35%. Water temperature falls within 24°C to 30°C.

All these fishing grounds are potential reserves for fish and shrimp. Most of the known commercial species of shrimps and fish are harvested from these areas by trawlers or mechanized fishing boats. Commercially important shrimp and fish species include tiger shrimp, karuma shrimp, cat fish, Bombay duck, snapper, flounder, Indian salmon, crocker, seabream, jawfish, mullet, pomfret, ribbon fish, anchovy, hilsa, oil sardine, tuna, mackerel and skipjack.

Pollution—marine environment of Bangladesh is directly or indirectly becoming polluted due to addition of many polluting agents. To protect water from pollution and control of mine drainage, large scale drilling and production of natural gas from the Sangu offshore gasfield, discovery of Kutubdia offshore gasfield and exploration of beach sand placer deposits from the offshore islands of Chittagong and Cox's Bazar districts must follow standard regulations both from mine safety and environmental protection point of view. Sangu gasfield is located about 50 km south-west of Chittagong City and stands at a depth of 10m water in the Bay of Bengal. Kutubdia gasfield is about 92 km south-west of Chittagong.

The coastal environment of Bangladesh is contaminated by oil tanker traffic, harbour operations and effluents discharged from petroleum processing. Sewage deposit by the Karnafuli and Pasur rivers into the Bay of Bengal contains higher concentration of Biochemical Oxygen Demand (BOD) and faecal coliform. Moreover, the coastal environment of Bangladesh has also been affected by industrial effluents, agricultural residues, some other human activities like deforestation and irrational expansion of coastal shrimp farming, etc. resulting in ecological degradation. Identical activities of the littoral states are causing injuries to the coastal environment and as such, the environment in the Bay of Bengal almost in entirety.[4] Overfishing and dumping of discarded fish in these areas are becoming a threat to the resourcefulness of the fishing grounds. Only proper management of the existing grounds and finding new fishing grounds can ensure the continuous harvest of fisheries resources.[5]

2.2. The Bay of Bengal Littoral States

The study here about marine environment in relation to the Bay of Bengal deals mainly with the littoral states like Bangladesh, India, Maldives, Myanmar, and Sri Lanka. States like Thailand, Malaysia and Indonesia too may be taken to some extent to enrich the study about marine environment in the Bay of Bengal. Geographical, geological, geomorphologic and oceanographic features of the littoral states have been considered here.

2.2.a. Bangladesh

2.2.a.i. Background

Bangladesh is one of the world's most densely populated countries, with its people crammed into a delta of rivers that empties into the Bay of Bengal. Poverty is deep and widespread, although Bangladesh has made progress in reducing population growth and improving health and education. The country is vulnerable to flooding and cyclones. The major employer is agriculture, but it is unable to meet the demand for jobs. So many Bangladeshis—in common with citizens from other countries in the region—seek work abroad. The country is trying to diversify its economy, with industrial development a priority. Bangladesh came into existence in 1971 when Bengali East Pakistan seceded from its union with West Pakistan. Bangladesh is situated at the head of the Bay of Bengal. About a third of this extremely poor country gets annual floods during the monsoons, hampering economic development.

Geographical Location: Between 20°34' and 26°38' north latitude and between 88°01' and 92°41' east longitude.

Area	: 1,47,570 sq.km. or 57,295 sq.miles.
Boundary	: India
West	: India
East	: India and Myanmar
South	: Bay of Bengal
Land boundaries	: Total: 4,246 km, border countries: Myanmar: 193 km, India 4,053 km
Maritime claims	: Territorial sea: 12 nm, contiguous zone 18 nm, exclusive economic zone: 200 nm, continental shelf: up to the outer limits of the continental margin
Climate	: Tropical: mild winter (October to March); hot, humid summer (March to June); humid, warm rainy monsoon (June to October).
Terrain	: Mostly flat alluvial plain; hilly in south-east.
Elevation	: Lowest point: Indian Ocean 0 m, highest point: 1,230 m.
Population	: 129.2 million (Growth rate 1.45%, 2001)
Sea Ports	: Chittagong and Mongla.[6]

The Bay of Bengal has provided Bangladesh with the world's largest beach as well as a rich coastal area filled with unique and diverse biodiversity. The coastal zone of Bangladesh is 710 km long, which is unique and complex. It has a great natural ecosystem value not only for its multiple renewable resources of direct economic benefit to the nation but also for its outstanding aesthetic value and scientific interest. Burdened with a large population lacking adequate natural resources on land, Bangladesh will have to depend more and more on her sea territories. But increased pollution, destruction of biodiversity and mis-management of seaport has become a major concern for the country.

Bangladesh Government enacted the Territorial Water and Maritime Zones Act, 1974 (Act No XXVI of 1974), which contains some provisions to prevent marine pollution.[7] According to section 6 of this Act the Government may, by Gazette notification, establish conservation zones in the sea for maintenance of the living resources.[8] Section 8 of the Act empowers government to take such measures, as it deems appropriate for preventing and controlling marine pollution and preserving the quality and ecological balance in the marine environment in high seas adjacent to the territorial waters.[9]

According to section 26 of the Marine Fisheries Ordinance, 1983 use or attempts to use of any explosive, poison or other noxious substances in water is an offence. Section 28 empowers government to declare any portion of Bangladesh fisheries water as marine reserve for special protection of aquatic flora and fauna therein.

Again according to section 41A of The Chittagong Port Authority Ordinance, 1976 (Ordinance No. LII of 1976) causing pollution of the water or environment in the port area shall be punishable with fine, which may extend to one lakh taka.

All these provisions have a great significance in preserving the sea resources including fish stocks and preventing pollution in marine environment. But all these provisions are not utilised and enforced adequately and effectively.

2.2.a.ii. Major International Conventions/ Protocols Signed and Ratified by Bangladesh are as follows:

(1) International Convention for the Prevention of Pollution of the Sea by Oil, 1981.

(2) Basel Convention on the Control of Transboundary Movements of Hazardous Wastes and their Disposal, 1989.

(3) Plant Protection Agreement for the South East Asia and Pacific Region, 1974.

(4) Treaty Banning Nuclear Weapon Tests in the Atmosphere, in Outer Space and Under Water, 1985.

(5) Convention on International Trade in Endangered Species of Wild Fauna and Flora (CITES), 1973.

(6) Vienna Convention for the Protection of the Ozone Layer, 1985.

(7) Montreal Protocol on Substances that Deplete the Ozone Layer, 1987.

(8) The London Amendment to the Montreal Protocol, 1990.

(9) Convention on Wetlands of International Improtance Specially Waterfowl Habitats (the Ramsar Convention).

(10) International Framework Convention on Climate Change, 1992.

(11) Convention on Biological Diversity, 1992.

(12) Convention to Combat Desertification.

2.2.a.iii. Major Constraints in the Implementation of Agenda 21

(1) Lack of domestic financial resources and appropriate technology.

(2) Poor inflow of financial and technical assistance against commitments made under different conventions.

(3) Legal and institutional weakness and lack of trained human resources.

(4) Lack of high-quality data.

(5) Coordination among so many different actors.

2.2.a.iv. Overview

(a) Bangladesh recognizes the vital importance of participating in global attempts to halt the process of environmental deterioration. Bangladesh was actively involved in the proceedings of the UNCED, signed the Rio Declaration and endorsed Agenda 21. This reflects the strong commitment of Bangladesh towards promoting environmental management and sustainable development.

(b) The priority areas of concern in Bangladesh are (1) Disaster Management; (2) Deforestation, including mangroves; (3) Biodiveristy losses; (4) Water Pollution; (5) Land Degradation; and (6) Air Pollution.

(c) A National Conservation Strategy (NCS) has been prepared in line with the World Conservation Strategy. The NCS has identified problems in eighteen different sectors and made recommendations for addressing these problems. In December 1996, the NCS is in its final draft stage and expected to go ahead.

(d) A National Environment Management Action Plan (NEMAP) has been prepared identifying the key environmental issues and actions required to halt or reduce the rate of environmental degradation, to improve the natural and man-made environment, to conserve habitats and biodiversity, to promote sustainable development, and to improve qualitative indicators of human life. The NEMAP can be considered to be the first initiative towards the preparation of a National Agenda 21. The NEMAP has outlined an action plan to address the environmental issues of Bangladesh.

(e) A National Environment Committee with the Head of the Government as its Chairperson has been set up to ensure an effective top-level management of the environment and to integrate development and environment at the national level.

(f) Bangladesh has developed Draft Environmental Quality Standards (EQS) for (1) water pollution; (2) air pollution; (3) noise pollution; (4) sewage pollution; and (5) industrial pollution. By approving the EQS, the Government will ensure compliance through monitoring. The development of indicators is also needed in this respect.

(g) A country study on climate change has just been completed under the United States Country Study Programme (USCSP). Another project on Asia Least Cost Greenhouse Gas Abatement Strategy (ALGAS) is in progress with the support of the ADB. Under these studies, an inventory of GHG emissions and an analysis of vulnerability impacts have been completed and both are in their refinement and updating stages.

(h) Bangladesh has prepared a National Phase Out Plan of Ozone Depleting Substances, which is currently being implemented with assistance from the Montreal Multilateral Fund.

(i) Bangladesh has adopted an Environment Protection Act in 1995 for the preservation of the environment.

(j) Bangladesh has carried out inventories of its forest resources and biological diversity in both dryland and wetlands. Reliable and high-quality data is expected to become available after the completion of these inventories. After this, Bangladesh will be able to develop indicators for sustainable management of these resources. In order to be able to develop and test indicators for sustainable development, Bangladesh needs financial and technical support for other inventories, and data and information collection.

2.2.b. Sri Lanka[10]

Sri Lanka takes interests in promoting marine environment. The country acknowledges that degradation of marine environment from land based activities is a current global concern. In reaffirming the Rio declaration, the global community adopted implementation of a Global Programme of Action (GPA) for the protection of the marine environment from land based activities in 1995. The United Nations Environment Programme (UNEP) was designated as the Secretariat of the GPA, and since then UNEP played a vital role in assisting countries in the South Asian region, including Sri Lanka to develop a National Programme of Action (NPA), in accordance with country specific policies, priorities and resources and to implement the same. Sri Lanka was provided funding for this activity in 2003, and this assistance has been instrumental in the development of a National Program of Action for the protection of the marine environment in Sri Lanka, taking an integrated river basin management approach.

2.2.b.i. Background

Sri Lanka is an island in the Indian Ocean located between 5°34' and 9°52' Northern latitudes and between 79°39' and 81°53' Eastern longitudes. Sri Lanka has a land area of 65,610 sq km. The Exclusive Economic Zone of the country covers an area of 4,37,000 sq km and the Maritime waters of the country extend up to 4,89,000 sq km in accordance with the UN Convention of the Law of the Seas.

Scattered around the coast line of Sri Lanka there are a number of features that are imperative for the well-being of the oceans and its resources. Some of them are:

Coastal structures in Sri Lanka and their Extent

Feature	Extent
Sandy beaches, and sand pits	5,620 ha
Dunes	15,930 ha
Lagoons	36,300 ha
Estuaries	90,960 ha
Mangroves	4,640 ha
Marshy wetlands	880 ha

The central mountain region of the country, which rises to an elevation of 2,524 m. is the birthplace of the country's major rivers. There are 103 river basins in the country and most of these rivers radiate from the hill country to flow down to the sea forming estuaries/lagoons. These rivers transport a large amount of sand, silt and clay for the formation of beaches.[11]

2.2.b.ii. Economic Structure

Sri Lanka's population is around 19 million and the per capita income in year 2003 was US$ 897. Annual growth rate in 2003 was 4%. When sectoral composition of the GDP is considered, 26% of the GDP is made up from the Industry sector and 20% comes from the Agriculture/fisheries allied activities.

Coastal GDP contributed to 35% of the national GDP in 1983, while it increased to 40% by the year 1989. The coastal region is the hub of industrial production and contains around 62% of all industrial units. This region also contributes to the tourism industry, which is a major income earner. Hence, as could be expected, more than 70% of hotels are located within the coastal region. The Country's economy is also enhanced by commercial ports, fishery harbours and anchorages.

2.2.b.iii. Pollution and Degradation of the Environment

Pollution of the marine environment from land based activities in Sri Lanka is on the increase. Streams and rivers, estuaries and lagoons continuously bring in heavy loads of pollutants to the sea. Pollutants derived from developmental activities and from human settlements without adequate sewage facilities pose the risk of degrading the waters from hilltops to oceans. Degraded water quality in turn adversely affects not only economic activities such as industries and tourism, but also the health of the people.

Main source of pollution include partly treated or raw sewage released to water bodies; chemicals released from industries; agrochemical and nutrient run off from agricultural activities; and solid waste dumped in or around waterways. Accidental spills of oil as well as intentional release of oil from fishing boats and commercial boats, harbours and even service stations pose a threat to the waters. Most of the land based activities are unplanned and haphazard and, therefore, such activities cause rapid deterioration and degradation of the marine environment and its biodiversity, thereby affecting the socio-economic benefits and public health of communities.

2.2.b.iv. Institutional and Legal Framework

The long felt need for the protection of the environment is signified in the Constitution of the Democratic Socialist Republic of Sri Lanka. In line with the Constitution, the National Environment Act (NEA) has provisions which serve directly or indirectly in protecting the marine environment and river basins from developmental activities.

The National Environmental Action Plan (Caring for Environment), the main policy document of Sri Lanka, covers 6 main areas and accordingly to look after these areas, 6 committees have been established. These Committees on Environmental Policy and Management (CEPOM) are chaired by the Secretary of the Environment ministry and co-chaired by the Secretary of the ministry in-charge of the subject of environment. Each CEPOM focuses its attention on actions within its area of authority that affect the whole or any part of the environment.

Other than the NEA, several legislative enactments could be used for implementing the NPA including the Forestry Ordinance, Fauna and Flora Protection Ordinance, Urban Development Ordinance, and the Marine Pollution Prevention Act. These legislations are conducive to conserving the environment from upper reaches of the river basin down to the ocean.

The major Act that is instrumental in protection of the coastal areas from erosion, encroachment and in mitigation is the Coast Conservation Act. The Department of Coast Conservation has taken steps to implement a Coastal Zone Management Plan in Sri Lanka. The NPA planning process has identified that this plan concentrates mainly on the coastal zone, and hence the Core Group decided that the NPA should take an integrated river basin to sea management approach.

2.2.b.v. Developing the National Programme of Action

Sri Lanka embarked on the formulation of the National Program of Action (NPA), by adopting the framework offered by the Global Program of Action for the Protection of the Marine Environment from Land based activities. Accordingly, an integrated approach was taken, incorporating river basins and the ocean into the action plan, which demanded broad-based stakeholder participation throughout the planning process.

Priority issues that should be addressed were identified through literature review, field surveys and stakeholder workshops, in collaboration with all the relevant stakeholder participation. Issues identified were reviewed by the Core Group, comprising of senior members from relevant ministries, agencies and organizations.

Development of the NPA involved the identification of pilot projects which could be used to showcase successful activities implemented for the protection of the marine environment.

2.2.b.vi. The National Programme of Action

The NPA, Sri Lanka identifies four priority areas which need to be addressed as urgent requirements of the country. These areas were prioritized based on the severity of the problem; their effect on food security and poverty alleviation; impacts on public health; effect on ecosystem health; and effects on cultural values. The prioritized areas are Coastal and Marine Pollution, Coastal Erosion, Degradation of Marine habitats and their Biodiversity, and the Deterioration of Environmental quality in sites of Special Significance.

For these priority areas Management Objectives were developed, and in line with these policies were adopted. Strategies were suggested to achieve the objective of each policy. Activities have been proposed, specifying performance indicators.

The NPA has identified all the elements required for sustaining the marine and coastal ecosystems—technology, community involvement, capacity building, private sector, institutional arrangements, partnerships and financing.

The challenge that Sri Lanka will be facing is to be committed to the NPA, which specify short-term, time bound targets and long-term goals. It has been attempted to define a conducive environment for implementing the plan, with an effective monitoring and evaluation system with indicators.

2.2.b.vii. Implementation Process

Policies and strategies spelt out in the NPA, Sri Lanka requires the implementation of a series of actions that are logical and well-organized. This calls for an innovative approach in the implementation procedure where a greater emphasis is placed on the active participation of all stakeholders of the relevant priority areas, including the civil society. Activities of the NPA are based on introducing appropriate market based instruments to ensure sustainability through securing partnerships with local authorities, private sector and communities. Creating awareness and strengthening existing enforcement have been given priority.

All the activities of the NPA require the involvement of a multiplicity of agencies and institutions with their own legal framework. It is envisaged that the establishment of an effective monitoring and evaluation mechanisms and strengthening institutional coordination will be facilitated through the NPA. With this in view, an effective inter-agency coordination mechanism has been proposed. This coordinating body will also be involved in monitoring and evaluation of the implementation process.

It is expected that policies developed would be implemented more efficiently and effectively when tasks are assigned to relevant line ministries and agencies, rather than being handled by the ministry that overseas coordination.

Such institutional fragmentation might result in competing roles among governmental ministries and agencies to a certain extent. This situation is aggravated when two agencies handling related fields are assigned two different roles—one agency implementing and the other overseeing. Therefore, it is necessary to overcome such adverse competition.

However, such dispersion will facilitate appropriate division of labour, pooled resources and shared responsibility among ministries. Furthermore, if frequent communication lines are not opened, coordination problems may arise that will hinder effective implementation of the NPA. In order to overcome these, it is necessary to reform and create new or revised legal frameworks, information management systems, networking and partnerships which will do away with distrust.

2.2.b.viii. Monitoring and Evaluation of the Implementation

Sri Lanka will not consider the formulation of the NPA as end of the process. The implementation process would be instrumental in formulation of future policies, better suited for the protection of the marine environment from land based activities.

Once activities are being implemented by relevant agencies, they will keep the CEPOM (Committee for Environmental Policy and Management) informed about their progress and any issues that need to be resolved. Since the Secretary of the Ministry of Environment co-chairs the committees, the ministry will be able to monitor the overall progress of the NPA. Depending on the successes and failures encountered in the implementation process, the Ministry will review the NPA and periodic revisions will be undertaken through the CEPOM itself. Periodically, the Cabinet of Ministers will be informed of the progress of the implementation of the NPA and approval will be sought for new policies and activities.

Further to the CEPOM mechanism, is the Committee of Secretaries, and conflicting issues will be taken up at this committee.

2.2.b.ix. Important Initiatives

Presently Sri Lanka has taken several initiatives to facilitate participation of stakeholders for the protection of the environment. Ministry has identified that pollution signifies inefficiency of the system, and hence wastage of resources. This has led to the formulation of a National Cleaner Production Policy, Strategy. It is expected to implement CP action plans in sectors such as tourism, health and agriculture, with a view to preventing pollution. In minimizing pollution in the industrial sector, the National Cleaner Production Center (NCPC), works in close collaboration with the industries.

The Ministry of Environment is implementing a Clean River program in collaboration with all relevant stakeholders, where decisions are taken jointly, and implemented at local level, specially by the relevant local authorities. This Program launched the first ever transparent mechanism in Sri Lanka, where Water Quality Information Boards have been established along side the Kelani River, informing the general public about the quality of water. Through these Boards, it is expected that polluting industries, relevant institutions and local authorities will make an attempt to improve the water quality.

2.2.b.x. Pilot Projects

Formulation and implementation of pilot projects have been undertaken with a view to develop the conceptual basis for future programs. These 6 projects have been developed by stakeholder agencies, in accordance to the priority areas identified by the broad based stakeholder group. These pilot projects are:

- Integrated solid waste management Pilot Program for the Wattala Local Authority area, Western Province.
- Selection and design of an appropriate sewage system for new and improved settlements under the Lunawa Environment Improvement and Community Development Program, Western Province.
- Study of economic significance of the coastal region in the context of social, political and environmental changes that occurred during the last decade.[12]
- Pilot scale zoning plan for aquaculture development, in order to overcome adverse affects of upcoming unplanned aquaculture development, in the Southern Province.

- Pilot project to control river-sand mining in Deduru Oya River Basin to mitigate marine and coastal environmental degradation in North-Western Province.
- Study on assessment of squatter settlements and their contribution to coastal pollution along a prioritized, selected area of the coastline.

It is envisaged that once implemented successfully, the selected pilot projects will demonstrate its benefits, so that it could be replicated in other areas of the country. Pollution and degradation of ecosystems defies boundaries. Therefore, the need for integrated cooperative solutions is particularly urgent in the management of river basins thereby creating awareness for protecting and preserving marine environment in Sri Lanka.[13]

2.2.c. Myanmar (Burma)[14]

2.2.c.i. Background

Britain conquered and ruled Burma over a period of 62 years (1824-1886) and incorporated it into its Indian Empire. Burma was administered as a province of India until 1937 when it became a separate, self-governing colony; independence outside of the Commonwealth was attained in 1948. Gen. Ne Win dominated the government from 1962 to 1988, first as military ruler, then as president, and later as political kingmaker. Despite multiparty elections in 1990 that resulted in the main opposition party—the National League for Democracy (NLD)—winning a landslide victory, the ruling junta refused to hand over power. NLD leader and Nobel Peace Prize recipient Aung San Suu Kyi, who was under house arrest from 1989 to 1995 and 2000 to 2002, was arrested in May 2003 and is currently under house arrest.

Location	:	South-eastern Asia, bordering the Andaman Sea and the Bay of Bengal, between Bangladesh and Thailand
Geographic coordinates	:	22,00 N, 98,00 E
Area	:	Total: 6,78,500 sq.km., land: 6,57,740 sq.km., water: 20,760 sq.km.

Land boundaries	: Total: 5,876 km., border countries: Bangladesh: 193 km., China: 2,185 km., India: 1,463 km., Laos: 235 km., Thailand: 1,800 km., Coastline: 1,930 km.
Maritime claims	: Territorial sea: 12 nm, contiguous zone: 24 nm, exclusive economic zone: 200 nm, continental shelf: 200 nm or to the edge of the continental margin.
Population	: 42,510 million (2002 est), GDP per capita: purchasing power Power parity $1,700 (2002 est).
Natural hazards	: Destructive earthquakes and cyclones; flooding and landslides common during rainy season (June to September); periodic droughts.

Environment-current issues: deforestation; industrial pollution of air, soil, and water; inadequate sanitation and water treatment contribute to disease.

2.2.c.ii. National Commission for Environmental Affairs

The National Commission for Environmental Affairs (NCEA) drafted the National Environment Policy, which was adopted on 5 December 1994. The Policy calls for harmony and balance between environmental development through the integration of environmental considerations into the development process. National environment policy forms the basis for developing environmental strategies, programmes and plans. With a view to implementing the National Environmental Policy of Myanmar, the National Commission for Environment Affairs initiated the drafting of the Myanmar Agenda 21 in 1995 based on the Agenda 21 laid down by the United Nations Environment and Development Conference in 1992 for achieving sustainable development. The drafting of Myanmar Agenda 21 was carried out with the participation of all government departments concerned. Workshops were held to seek suggestions and proposals from various departments. The first workshop took place in February 1995 and the second in October 1995. The Myanmar Agenda 21 was published in June 1997 and distributed to the United Nations and UN agencies and the government departments at home and abroad.

2.2.c.iii. National Environmental Policy

To establish sound environment policies in the utilization of water, land, forests, mineral, marine resources and other natural resources in order to conserve the environment and prevent its degradation, the Government of the Union of Myanmar hereby adopts the following policy:

> The wealth of a nation is its people, its cultural heritage, its environment and its natural resources. The objective of Myanmar's environment policy is aimed at achieving harmony and balance between these through the integration of environmental considerations into the development process to enhance the quality of the life of all its citizens. Every nation has the sovereign right to utilize its natural resources in accordance with its environmental policies; but great care must be taken not to exceed its jurisdiction or infringe upon the interests of other nations. It is the responsibility of the State and every citizen to preserve its natural resources in the interest of present and future generations. Environmental protection should always be the primary objective in seeking development.

The said policy was proclaimed through the Gazette in accordance with Notification No. 26/94 dated 5 December 1994 of the Government of the Union of Myanmar.

2.2.c.iv. Major Environmental Legislation

As to the concerns of environment—the marine environment in consequence, Myanmar has legislations like:

> Forestry Law, Protection of Wildlife and Wild Plants and Conservation of Natural Areas Law, Public Health Law, Factory Act, Territorial Sea and Maritime Zone Law, Marine Fisheries Law, Fishing Rights of Foreign Vessels Law, National Environment Policy, Year (1951, 1972, 1977, 1989, 1990, 1992, 1994).

Purpose

To implement the forest policy and the environmental conservation policy, to promote the sector of public cooperation in implementing these policies, to develop the economy of the State, to prevent the dangers of destruction of forest and biodiversity, to carry out simultaneously, conservation of natural forests and establishment of forest plantations and to contribute towards the fuel requirement of the country.

To protect wildlife, wild plants and conserve natural areas, to contribute towards works of natural scientific research, and to establish zoological gardens and botanical gardens.

To promote and safeguard public health and to take necessary measures in respect of environmental health.

To make effective arrangement in every factory for disposal of waste and effluents, and spreading awareness on health, cleanliness and precaution against danger.

To define and determine maritime zone, contiguous zone, exclusive economic zone and continental shelf and the right of the Union of Myanmar to exercise general and exclusive jurisdiction over these zones and continental shelf with respect to preservation and protection of marine environment, its resources and prevention of marine pollution.

To conserve fisheries water and to enable systematic operation in fisheries with participation of foreign investors.

To establish sound environment policies in the utilization of water, land, forest, mineral resources and other natural resources in order to conserve the environment and prevent its degradation.

Environmental Institutions

National Commission for Environment Affairs (NCEA), Ministry of Foreign Affairs

Environmental Impact Assessment

The drafting of EIA Law is in process.

Key environment Issues

Deforestation
Inland Water Pollution
Urban Pollution, Waste Management
Soil Erosion

UNEP on-going project/activities

Institutional Capacity Building in Myanmar Project (SoE Reporting) – UNEP-RRC.AP

NGOs Active in Environmental Activities

Forest Resource and Environment Development Association (FREDA).

2.2.c.v. Myanmar Agenda 21

The formulation of Myanmar Agenda 21 is part of the country's effort to fulfil its commitments to the historic Earth Summit in 1992. This document is an expression of the political commitment of the Government to sustainable development.

Myanmar Agenda 21 seeks to achieve four main objectives:

(a) To provide a forum and context for the debate on sustainable development and the articulation of collective vision for the future;

(b) To provide a framework for negotiation, mediation, and consensus-building in the country to achieve development with due regard to the environment, to focus the entire country on a common set of priority issues;

(c) To provide strategy and implementation plans for the changing and strengthening of values, knowledge, technologies and institutions with respect to environmental protection and development; and

(d) To provide the impetus and the framework for the development of organizational capacities and institutions required for sustainable development.

Myanmar Agenda 21 is organized into four main parts.

Part – I

This section addresses the social dimensions of sustainable development and as such deals with population dynamics, consumption patterns, poverty alleviation and border area development, human health issues and the development of human settlements.

Part – II

This section addresses economic and infrastructural support for sustainable development, first in broad overview in relation to the development of economic policies and instruments for sustainable development. Subsequently each sector that contributes to economic development in Myanmar is addressed separately: agriculture, livestock and fisheries, energy production and consumption, industrial development and transport and communications, tourism, and finally environmental management and enhancement. The forestry sector which also contributes to economic development is addressed in part III.

Part – III

This section highlights environmental and natural resource conservation through an analysis of the impacts of socio-economic development and examination of conservation and management approaches. This is addressed sectorally in the areas of integrated management of land resources, fresh water resources, management, coastal and marine ecosystems management, forest resources management, biodiversity conservation, development of mineral resources, and preservation of cultural heritage. The section stresses the need to conserve these resources to ensure the sustainability of the ecosystem and maintains cultural diversity.

Part – IV

This final section addresses the development of policy changes and support systems for sustainable development. It emphasizes the need for the enhancement of policy support systems for sustainable development and stresses the importance of appropriate legislation and the strengthening of institutions to enable them to implement Myanmar Agenda 21. Also addressed are the incorporation of environment and sustainable development concerns in processes of policy formulation and national development and sectoral planning. Public participation in sustainable development is addressed through formal and non-formal education programmes, promotion of general awareness and information dissemination, all with a view to encouraging participation and involvement of all stakeholders. Each chapter of Myanmar Agenda 21 begins with an introduction outlining the role of the sector in the context of sustainable economic development, and then identifies key programme areas. Each programme area is elaborated upon in a sub-section on basis of action which presents a more detailed description of the programme area and outlines the objectives of that programme area. Then, specific activities to be achieved are laid out.

2.2.c.vi. Coastal Marine Diversity

Myanmar is a maritime country in Southeast Asia having a coastline some 2800 km. in length which faces the Andaman Sea and the Bay of Bengal. The coastal region is rich in marine resources and is a source of foreign exchange and employment opportunities for the local populace.

The project site, the Myeik Archipelago, is unique in that it has more than 800 coastal islands lying on a broad continental shelf. The shallow waterways among the islands are a fertile source of resources for commercial fishing enterprises. All coastal bio-systems including mangroves, sea-grass, coral reefs, mud flats and sandy beaches commonly occur on and near the coasts of both the mainland and on the islands of the archipelago. This habitat is home to a rich and varied population of sea life.

Although Myanmar's richest fishing grounds lie in the Myeik Archipelago Region, there has been little research on its biodiversity. Waters of the region receive little pressure from human activities at present but there is a potential for pollution and severe depletion of fishery resources in the coming years.

2.2.c.vii. Environment—International Agreements

Party to: Biodiversity, Climate Change, Climate Change-Kyoto Protocol, Desertification, Endangered Species, Law of the Sea, Ozone Layer Protection, Ship Pollution, Tropical Timber 83, Tropical Timber 94 signed, but not ratified: none of the selected agreements.

2.2.c.viii. International Organization Participation

ARF, ADB, ASEAN, CP, FAO, G-77, IAEA, IBRD, ICAO, ICRM, IDA, IFAD, IFC, IFRCS, IHO, ILO, IMF, IMO, Interpol, IOC, ITU, NAM, OPCW (signatory), UN, UNCTAD, UNESCO, UNIDO, UPU, WCO, WHO, WIPO, WMO, WTO

2.2.c.ix. Economy—Overview

Burma is a resource-rich country that suffers from government controls and abject rural poverty. The military regime took steps in the early 1990s to liberalize the economy after decades of failure under the "Burmese Way to Socialism", but those efforts have since stalled.

Burma has been unable to achieve monetary or fiscal stability, resulting in an economy that suffers from serious macro-economic imbalances—including a steep inflation rate and an official exchange rate that overvalues the Burmese kyat by more than 100 times the market rate. In addition, most overseas development assistance ceased after the junta suppressed the democracy movement in 1988 and subsequently ignored the results of the 1990 election. A crisis in the private banking sector in early 2003 followed by economic moves against Burma by the United States, the European Union, and Japan—including a US ban on imports from Burma and a Japanese freeze on new bilateral economic aid—further weakened the Burmese economy. Burma is data poor, and official statistics are often dated and inaccurate. Published estimates of Burma's foreign trade are greatly understated because of the size of the black market and border trade—often estimated to be one to two times the official economy. Better relations with foreign countries and relaxed controls at home are needed to promote foreign investment, exports, and tourism. In February 2003, a major banking crisis hit the country's 20 private banks, shutting them down and disrupting the economy. In July and August 2003, the United States imposed a ban on all Burmese imports and a ban on provision of financial services, hampering Burma's ability to obtain foreign exchange. As of January 2004, the largest private banks remained moribund, leaving the private sector with little formal access to credit outside of government contracts.

2.2.d. Maldives

The Maldives were long a sultanate, first under Dutch and then under British protection. They became a republic in 1968, three years after independence. Tourism and fishing are developed on the archipelago.[15]

Location	:	Southern Asia, group of atolls in the Indian Ocean, south-southwest of India, within 3°15', 73°00' E.
Area	:	300 sq.km.
Coastline	:	644 km.
Maritime claims	:	measured from claimed archipelagic straight baselines, territorial sea: 12 nm, contiguous zone: 24 nm, exclusive economic zone: 200 nm. The only natural resources being explored are fish.[16]

2.2.d.i. Environmental Measures

The Ministry of Planning, Human Resources and Environment is responsible for developing all aspects of environmental policy and enforcement of Environmental Protection and Preservation Act. The Ministry also acts as the secretariat for the National Commission for the Protection of the Environment.

The Planning Section is responsible for overall development planning and monitoring which includes coordinating the preparation of the National Development Plan, the Perspective Plans, Regional Development Plans and project monitoring and evaluation. The Environment Section within this Ministry deals with all issues of the environment including global environmental issues.

The National Commission for the Protection of the Environment (NCPE), which was appointed by the President in 1989, advises the Minister of Planning, Human Resources and Environment on issues related to the responsibilities stated above.

A National Agenda 21 is not in place but a number of sustainable development plans have been prepared since the Earth Summit. The fourth National Development Plan formalizes the planning process by reviewing the current economic situation, medium-term prospects and constraints on development; describing recent sectoral development, establishing development objectives, priorities and strategies; identifying and prioritizing development projects and identifying financing sources for the projects.

Detailed sector analysis forms the basis for identifying projects which are included in the plan. The Plan provides the basis for discussions with foreign donors relating to the financing of priority projects.

In order to evaluate the longer term development prospects, the Government of the Maldives has prepared a Perspective Plan for the next ten years with the assistance of the Asian Development Bank, setting out a vision of life in the Maldives in the year 2005 and what is required to achieve the vision. It is intended to serve as a guide to the nation's long-term social and economic development; establish a clear and consistent policy framework for the formulation of development priorities; and the integration of sector strategies. Regional development is a priority objective of the Perspective Plan.

To address sustainable development of tourism in the Maldives, the government has formulated the Tourism Master Plan covering the period 1996-2005.

To date, the first National Environment Action Plan (NEAP), developed in 1989 to address the environmental planning and management needs of the country has been followed as the overall strategy of the Government in the environment sector.

It is expected that in 1997 a National Agenda 21 will be developed. As a first step, the first National Environment Action Plan will be reviewed and a second National Environment Action Plan formulated for the future.

The Maldives was among the first countries to ratify the Convention on Biological Diversity. With GEF assistance, the Maldives will be formulating its National Biodiversity Conservation Strategy in 1997. The lack of a biodiversity inventory is a major constraint in formulating appropriate policies for the sustainable utilization of marine resources. Coral reefs of the Maldives are renowned for their aesthetic beauty and species diversity and the reefs support stocks of endangered species such as green and hawksbill turtles, giant clams and black coral. Fifteen sites and a number of species have been declared protected.

The Maldives has ratified the UN Framework Convention on Climate Change but participants noted with serious concern the slow progress in the global implementation of the convention.

Environmental Law: the Environmental Protection and Preservation Act established a framework upon which regulations and policies can be developed to protect and preserve the natural environment and resources for the benefit of future generations. Environmental Impact Assessments have been made mandatory for large scale projects.

Recommendations

(i) The Maldives urgently needs a national sustainable development strategy to harmonize the various policies and plans that are being developed to address issues like population growth, solid waste, freshwater, sanitation, transport, energy, industrial development and conservation;

(ii) Test in the Maldives, the set of sustainable development indicators developed by UNDPCSD and use them as yardstick in measuring progress towards sustainable development;

(iii) Pay special attention to human resource development at the island and national levels so that better informed decisions can be made towards sustainable development; and

(iv) Continue the nationwide campaign on increasing environmental awareness among the people.

2.2.d.ii. Protected Marine Areas in the Maldives

Protected Marine Sites

The concentration of an increased population on some atolls and new developments, including tourism, has created a threat to marine environment. Activities such as sand and coral mining, waste disposal and fishing are degrading the fragile and vulnerable marine life.

The survey carried out by the Marine Research section of the Ministry of Fisheries and Agriculture in 1992 estimated that (US$) 2 million per annum was spent by divers to watch sharks. It also states that reef sharks are worth 100 times more alive as generators of diving revenue, than they are caught or dead in fishing boats. Therefore, they recommended protecting reef sharks within the tourism zone as it clearly sounded a positive economic case. It estimated that up to 80% of world marine protected areas are protected in name only and are not actively managed.

The Marine Research Section of MOFA selected 30 different sites with the help of diving schools across the tourism zone and made a proposal, which was discussed with other concerned government agencies, to finalise, protected areas. From the proposed sites, 15 sites were declared as protected marine areas in June 1995 under the Environment Act (4/93) and were registered under the name of the Ministry of Tourism in the Ministry of Planning, Human Resources and Environment.

As the importance of protected marine parks shows a common interest, the government declared more sites as protected marine areas in October 1999. Within these protected marine areas, the following activities are prohibited.

Anchoring (except in an emergency)

Coral and sand mining

Rubbish dumping

Removal of any natural object or living creatures

Fishing of any kind (e.g., for sharks reef fish or aquarium fish) with exception of traditional live bait fishing

Any other activity which may cause damage to the area or its associated marine life

Managing and Monitoring the Sites.

Only less than one per cent of the world's oceans is protected from exploitation, and most of the area protected is not adequately managed. This is one of the core problems faced by the Maldives. Maldives has very little resources to dispense in monitoring the life in these protected areas. Since 1998, Marine Research Section of the Maldives has been conducting a monitoring scheme of some of the reefs. In September 2003, Marine Research Section surveyed the reefs of Finey, Hirimaradhoo, and Hondaa islands of Haa Dhaalu atoll under the Marine Research Center's reef-surveying project. In these surveys information about the reef's condition and coral bleaching in general is collected according to the Centre.

2.2.d.iii. Overview

Fishing is the largest industry, employing 25% of the work force and accounting for over 60% of exports. Over 90% of government tax revenue comes from import duties and tourism-related taxes. During the 1980s, tourism became one of the most important and highest growth sectors of the economy. In 1993, tourism accounted for 17% of GDP and more than 60% of the Maldives' foreign exchange receipts. The Maldivian government initiated an economic reform program in 1989 initially by lifting import quotas and opening some exports to the private sector. Subsequently, it has liberalized regulations to allow more foreign investment. Agriculture and manufacturing continue to play a minor role in the economy, constrained by the limited availability of cultivable land and the shortage of domestic labor. Most staple foods must be imported. In 1993, industry which consisted mainly of garment production, boat building, and handicrafts accounted for about 6% of GDP.[17]

2.2.e. India[18]

2.2.e.i. Background

The Indus Valley civilization, one of the oldest in the world, dates back at least 5,000 years. Aryan tribes from the north-west invaded in about 1500 B.C.; their merger with the earlier inhabitants created the classical Indian culture. Arab incursions starting in the 8th century and Turkish in the 12th were followed by European traders, beginning in the late 15th century. By the 19th century, Britain had assumed political control of virtually all Indian lands when Gandhi and Jawaharlal Nehru led India to independence in 1947. The subcontinent was divided into the secular state of India and the smaller Muslim state of Pakistan. A third war between the two countries in 1971 resulted in East Pakistan becoming the separate nation of Bangladesh. Fundamental concerns in India include the ongoing dispute with Pakistan over Kashmir, massive overpopulation, environmental degradation, extensive poverty, and ethnic and religious strife, all this, despite impressive gains in economic investment and output.

2.2.e.ii. Geography

Location	: Southern Asia, bordering the Arabian Sea and the Bay of Bengal, Burma and Pakistan
Geographic coordinates	: 20°00' N, 77°00' E
Area	: Total: 32,87,590 sq. km.
Land	: 29,73,190 sq. km.
Water	: 3,14,400 sq. km.
Land boundaries	: Total: 14,103 km.
Border countries	: Bangladesh 4,053 km, Bhutan 605 km, Burma 1,463 km, China 3,380 km, Nepal 1,690 km, Pakistan 2,912 km
Coastline	: 7,000 km

Maritime claims	:	Territorial sea: 12 nm
Contiguous zone	:	24 nm
Exclusive economic zone	:	200 nm
Continental shelf	:	200 nm or to the edge of the continental margin.
Climate	:	varies from tropical monsoon in south to temperate in north.
Terrain	:	upland plain (Deccan Plateau) in south, flat to rolling plain along the Ganges, deserts in west, Himalayas in north
Elevation extremes	:	lowest point Indian Ocean 0 m. highest point: Kanchenjunga 8,598 m.
Natural hazards	:	droughts; flash floods, as well as widespread and destructive flooding from monsoonal rains; severe thunderstorms; earthquakes.

India has a coastline of 7,516 km. It has an Exclusive Economic Zone of 2.02 million km^2. Out of its 1 billion population, nearly 20% live in the coastal areas. Many highly populated and industrialised cities like Bombay, Madras, Calcutta, Cochin, Visakhapatnam are located along/near the coastal areas. There are 11 major ports and a number of minor ports handling shipping to various degrees of intensity. The coastline of the mainland belongs to nine States and two Union Territories. The coastline of the islands of Andaman, Nicobar and Lakshadweep (Laccadives) group of islands constitute nearly 2,000 km.[19]

The details on various coastal ecosystems, environmental problems due to prevalence of various activities and management needed are given below:

2.2.e.iii. Coastal Eco-Systems

Along the Indian coastline, the brackishwater areas including marshes, backwaters, mangroves, inter- and sub-tidal measure about 14,16,300 hectares. These areas act as feeding and nursery grounds for a variety of commercially important fish, prawn and crabs, media for inland transportation, fishing etc.

2.2.e.iii.(a) Mangroves

Along the Indian coast mangroves are found along the islands, major deltas, estuaries and backwaters of the east coast of India. They also exist along the oceanic island groups of the Andaman and Nicobar. The total mangrove area is estimated to be 6,81,976 hectares. While the mangroves along the west coast of India are dense, they are scattered and comparatively small in area along the West coast. Gangetic Sunderbans (4,18,888 ha), Andaman-Nicobar Islands (1,15,000 ha), Krishna, Kaveri and Godavari deltas and Mahanadi delta are some of the best mangrove formations of India.

There are about 45 mangrove species along the Indian coast. The dominant genera are *Rhizophora, Avicennia, Bruguiera, Sonneratia, Canocarpus, Heretiera, Xylocarpus, Ceriops,* and *Exoecaria.*

Mangrove forests mainly function as spawning, breeding and nursery grounds for nearshore estuarine organisms like fishes, crabs, prawns, molluscs, etc. Some of the common and economically important species are *Mugil cephalus*, *Hilsa ilisha*, *Lates calcarifer*, *Scylla serata*, *Meretrix casta, Crassostrea grephoides,* and *Penaeus* spp.

Apart from the captive and culture fisheries, mangroves are also important as "coastal stabilizers" and "shelter belt areas". These formations protect the coasts and the landward areas from erosion and cyclonic destructions to some extent. Apart from these the mangrove forests of India have importance from a wildlife, recreation and education point of view. "Project Tiger" of Sunderbans and "Crocodile Sanctuary" in the Mahanadi delta are examples of such activities.

2.2.e.iii.(b) Coral reefs

Around India, coral reef formations are found in the Palk Bay, Gulf of Mannar, Gulf of Kutch, Central West coast of India, Lakshadweep atolls, and Andaman-Nicobar Islands. Both the coral atoll and the fringing coral reefs are of utmost significance in Indian waters. A few species of corals have recently been reported from the Malvan (Maharashtra) coast. Some 32 genera from Minicoy Islands, 34 genera from Palk Bay and Gulf of Mannar, 25 genera from Andaman Islands, 9 genera from Lakshadweep and 3 genera from Nicobar Islands have also been reported. A total of 342 species belonging to 76 genera from the seas around India have been described.

Primary productivity studies of coral reefs in Indian waters indicated comparable rates with other reefs and marine ecosystems. Often the large benthic algal communities and extensive seagrass beds are equally important as the energy released from them is transferred to higher trophic levels by way of the detrital food chain.

2.2.e.iii.(c) Marine Parks and Marine Sanctuaries

On account of their high bio-diversity, the Gulf of Mannar and Wandoor (Andaman) have been declared as Marine National Parks and Malvan coast (Maharashtra), Gulf of Kutch, Jamnagar as Marine Sanctuaries. There are a number of other specialised ecosystems which exhibit a large variety of marine life and they include Chilka and Pulicat Lakes, Point Calimere, etc.

2.2.e.iv. Activities in Marine Areas and Environmental Problems

India's nation building activitities are wide. As time passes, the country is advancing. Its technological capabilities are competitive with the world's. The country is already aware of the dire consequences of pollution of environment and has planned activities accordingly.

2.2.e.iv.(a) Land-based activities causing Pollution

Demographic pressure in the urban cities and towns has resulted in the production of enormous amounts of domestic waste materials. These materials reach the marine environment either directly or indirectly through rivers, creeks, bays, etc. The domestic sewage contributes to the largest amount of waste and it has been estimated that approximately 18,240 million liters per day (MLD) (as of 1994) reach the coastal environment of the country. These wastes predominantly contain degradable organic matter which utilises enormous amount of oxygen from seawater for its oxidation. The low oxygenated seawater leads to decrease of population of flora and fauna.

Domestic wastes are discharged mostly in untreated condition due to the lack of treatment facilities in most of the cities and towns. It has been reported that only primary treatment facilities are available in cities and towns where the population is more than 1,00,000 and the capacity of the plants is not adequate for the treatment of the total waste generated in the city. For example, in Bombay, the treatment facilities are available only for 390 MLD as against 1,200 MLD of domestic sewage which is generated. Due to such partial treatment, the chemical characteristics of the wastewater retain almost their original features and cause damage to the environmental water quality.

2.2.e.iv.(b) Discharge of Industrial Waste

India is one of the largest industrialised nations in the world. Major industrial cities and towns of the country such as Surat, Bombay, Cochin, Madras, Visakhapatnam and Calcutta are situated on or near the coastline. The total quantity of wastes discharged by these industries is estimated to be 0.67×10^9 m^3 (as of 1994). While the major industries discharge treated effluents into the sea, numerous small and medium scale industries discharge the untreated effluents into the adjoining wastewater canals, municipal drains, creeks, etc.

2.2.e.iv.(c) Non-point Sources of Pollution

India being an agricultural country, uses large quantities of fertilizers and pesticides to sustain its agricultural production. This is essential in order to meet the food requirements of its population. The run-off from the agricultural fields reaches the rivers. Since the riverine flow is very much less during the dry period, the chemical elements present in the run-off undergo biogeochemical changes in the riverine environment itself with minimum input into the sea.

2.2.e.v. Status of Marine Pollution

A nation-wide marine pollution monitoring programme operating for the last 10 years has identified areas of clean sea, low levels of pollution and areas of concern. It has been found that the sea beyond 2 km all along the coast except in Bombay is clean. In case of Bombay, the sea beyond 5 km is clean. The inland port/creek waters of Veraval (Gujarat) and Bombay were identified as areas of concern.

2.2.e.vi. Other activities causing Environmental problems

The coastal engineering studies have revealed that the construction of breakwaters alter the sediment transport mechanism in the coastal areas, thereby causing erosion and accretion, depending on the direction of the littoral drift. Such impacts have already been noticed due to construction of port of Madras (Chennai), Paradip, etc. It has been found that due to the establishment of Madras port, an accretion of 75 acres occurred in the last 60 years south of the port as well as severe erosion in the north resulting in the loss of 83 acres of land.

Serious coastal erosion problems are also experienced in the western part of India due to intense monsoonal activity. In the State of Karnataka, nearly 0.2 metric ton of sand material is lost per year due to monsoons and resultant sand drift. The cyclonic weather which is common along the East coast (175 cyclones in the last 100 years along the east coast; only 31 in the west coast during the same period) also causes severe erosion problems reported in north of between Point Calimere and Visakhapatnam. The navigational channel from Bay of Bengal to the Hooghly estuary (Calcutta and Haldia are two inland Major ports in India) is causing severe erosion problems in Saugar and Niachara islands.

The State of Kerala has been experiencing a coastal erosion problem in a severe manner. Besides the causes mentioned above for coastal erosion, the additional factors that are also responsible for causing coastal erosion in this State are:

(a) Mud-bank formation along the coasts influencing the shore processes and disturbing the equilibrium conditions of the coast adjoining them, thereby causing erosion problems on the down drift side.

(b) The bank shore level is low in many places causing severe tidal overflow during monsoon seasons.

(c) Lack of supply of littoral materials due to influence of mud banks, littoral barriers like water channels and non-replenishment of sediments from land to the shore as these sediments are trapped in the extensive network of backwaters.

(d) Inappropriately designed and constructed coastal protection structures.

Due to the above factors, out of 590 km length of coastline, nearly 90% is facing the problem of erosion.

2.2.e.vi.(a) Accretion

The littoral drift along the coastal area, caused by reversing monsoonal surface circulation, leads to erosion and accretional problems. The beach sand eroded in the area is deposited either offshore or north or south of that area depending on the direction of the drift. Deposition of sand and sediment by perennial rivers also cause sandpits and small islets. For example, deposition of silt load of 9.4 m^3 by the Mahanadi river over the years has led to the formation of Hukitola island. Similarly, the Chilka lake, the largest brackishwater lake in Asia, is facing a heavy siltation problem due to sand deposition at its mouth. Formation of sandbars due to nourishment also leads to poor exchange of tidal water with the adjoining brackishwater ecosystem which is being slowly converted to freshwater ecosystem of adverse dimension. This has been affecting the marine life and also the nesting of migratory birds which rely on the marine ecosystem for its food.

2.2.e.vi.(b) Ship-breaking Industries

At present, the activities related to the breaking of ships have been reported from the coasts of Gujarat, Maharashtra and, to a certain extent, off Tamil Nadu. During the ship-breaking activities, the major components like engine, etc. are removed and offloaded to the shore. The hull and other steel parts are cut into different sizes and transported as scrap. During the operation, the iron particles and the paint containing lead, get into the marine environment while the soluble matter contaminates the surrounding environment. The iron particles settle in the sediment. Increased concentrations of lead in sea water is lethal to organisms and the iron debris settling in the sediment causes damage to the benthic organisms particularly the filter feeders like clams, mussels, etc.

2.2.e.vi.(c) Sea-based activities causing Environmental Disturbances and Pollution

Oil pollution is one of the major sources of pollution due to the sea-based activities. India imports nearly 30 metric tons of petroleum products every year through its major ports located at Kandla, Bombay, Cochin, Madras and Calcutta. India also produces oil through its inshore and offshore oil fields. The details of tanker terminals, oil depots, refineries as well as offshore oil fields in India are given below:

Port/Area	Function
Gulf of Kutch	Ship to ship transfer
Port Kandla	Single point Mooring Buoy
Vadinar	Single point Mooring Buoy
Bombay High	Offshore oil field
Bombay (Offshore)	Ship to ship transfer
Bassein	Offshore oil field
Ratna/Heera	Offshore oil field
Butcher Island	Marine Terminal
Bombay	Refinery/Depot
Goa	Marine Terminal
Mangalore	Marine Terminal
Cochin	Marine Terminal
Tuticorin	Marine Terminal
Cauveri	Offshore oil field
Madras (Offshore)	Ship to ship transfer
Madras	Marine Terminal
Vishakhapatnam	Marine Terminal
Vishakhapatnam	Offshore oil berth VIZAG
Krishna	Offshore oil field
Godavari	Offshore oil field
Mahanadi	Offshore oil field
Haldia	Marine Terminal, Refinery/Depot
Calcutta	Marine Terminal

2.2.e.vi.(d) Oil Production in Offshore Platforms and handling in Ports

The total quantity of oil produced from the offshore wells along the Western coast of India is approximately 30 million tons per day. This oil is transported mainly through pipelines and oil tankers. Additionally, approximately 30 million tons of crude oil imported from foreign countries is handled at major ports. The total quantity of petroleum products handled in major ports is about 50 million tons per year at present and is likely to increase in future. This crude oil is carried by tankers and ships which number more than 1,600 per year. The Shipping Corporation of India (SCI) also operates more than 24 crude carriers which carry imported oil to the major ports of the country.

The western part of the Indian Exclusive Economic Zone, i.e., Arabian Sea adjoining peninsular India, forms the main international tanker route for oil tankers originating from the Persian Gulf. It has been estimated that some 330 million tons of crude oil is transported annually along this route, involving approximately 2,500 laden tankers. The preferred route is through the 9° channel between the Maldives and Lakshadweep Islands, during the Southwest monsoon (May to September), and north of Lakshadweep following the 200-m depth curve west of Mangalore, at other times. Considering the large volume of oil transported and high rate of tanker movement the probability of tanker accident is high—once every few years. The last major accident in the area occurred in January 1993 when two tons of oil spilled in the Nicobar Sea.

2.2.e.vii. Radioactive and Thermal Wastes

Although power generation is mostly thermal in India, nuclear power is also being generated. So far no serious harm has been reported from these sources, but fly ash from thermal power plants invariably creates environmental problems.

Radioactive wastes from nuclear power plants are normally disposed of according to strict international conventions. However, their heat generation poses several problems. Nuclear power plants normally release 50% of their generated heat to the coastal marine environment. Localised damage to ambient flora and fauna appears to be unavoidable.

2.2.e.viii. Coastal Laws

The national laws governing coastal zone related issues are as follows:

(i) Merchant Shipping Act, 1954
- Deals with prevention and control of pollution arising from ships and offshore oil platform.

(ii) Wildlife (Protection) Act, 1972
- Deals with protection and conservation of marine life and establishment of marine parks, sanctuaries etc.

(iii) Water Act, 1974
- Deals with control of marine pollution and land based sources.

(iv) Maritime Zone Act, 1974
- Defines various maritime zones like territorial waters, exclusive economic zone and the continental shelf.

(v) Environment Protection Act, 1986
- An umbrella Act containing provisions for all environment related issues.

2.2.e.ix. Activities Relating to Integrated Coastal Area Management

The Government of India, in 1991, issued a major notification under the Environment Protection Act, 1986, framing rules for regulation of various coastal zone activities. These rules are called the Coastal Regulation Zone (CRZ) Rules. Under these Rules, the entire coastal stretch from the lowest low tide to highest high tide line and the coastal land within 500 m from the high tide line on the landward side is termed as Coastal Regulation Zone (CRZ). The latter is classified into four categories, namely:

Category-I (CRZ-I)

Areas that are ecologically sensitive and important, such as national parks/marine parks, sanctuaries, reserve forests, wildlife habitats, mangroves, corals/coral reefs, areas close to breeding and spawning grounds of fish and other marine life, areas of outstanding natural beauty/historically/heritage areas, areas rich in genetic diversity, areas likely to be inundated due to rise in sea level as a consequence of global warming and such other areas as may be declared by the Central Government or the concerned authorities at the State/Union Territory level from time to time.

Category-II (CRZ-II)

The areas that have already been developed up to or close to the shoreline. For this purpose, "developed area" is referred to as that area within the municipal limits or in other legally designated urban areas which is already substantially built up and which has been provided with drainage and approach roads and other infrastructural facilities, such as water supply and sewage mains.

Category-III (CRZ-III)

Areas that are relatively undisturbed and those which do not belong to either Category-I or II. These will include coastal zone in the rural areas (developed and undeveloped) and also areas within Municipal limits or in other legally designated urban areas which are not substantially built up.

Category-IV (CRZ-IV)

Coastal stretches in the Andaman and Nicobar, Lakshadweep and small islands, except those designated as CRZ-I, CRZ-II or CRZ-III.

Prohibited and regulated activities have been listed for each zone. The 9 coastal states and 5 Union Territories (including the Andaman and Nicobar and Lakshadweep group of islands) have prepared Coastal Zone Management Plans which delineates the areas included under the above categories.

2.2.e.ix.(a) Capacity Building in the ICM areas

The Government of India in the Department of Ocean Development (DOD) is undertaking capacity building and infrastructural development activities. These aim at the development of expertise in ICM oriented activities, and dissemination of knowledge gained to the users like coastal states through organised training programmes. Towards accomplishing these objectives, the following priority activities are being undertaken:

(i) Determination of designated use of coastal waters.

(ii) Development of GIS based information system for critical habitats like mangroves, coral reefs, turtle breeding grounds, etc. containing all information necessary to prepare management plans.

(iii) Determination of waste load allocation based on waste assimilation characteristics of Tapi estuary (Gujarat), Ennore creek (Chennai), and Cochin/ Hooghly/Vizag harbour.

(iv) Development of EIA guidelines for major coastal developmental and other activities like development of ports, harbours, waste disposal from domestic and industrial sources, tourist beaches, etc.

(v) Development of model ICM plans for Chennai, Goa and Gulf of Kutch.

Out of the five priority activities proposed above, assistance from the World Bank in the form of International Development Association (IDA) credit has been obtained for projects 2 to 5, under the project like Coastal and Marine Area Management through an umbrella project on Environment Management Capacity Building which is coordinated by the Ministry of Environment and Forests (MEF). The DOD has established a unit namely Integrated Coastal and Marine Area Management (ICMAM) Project Directorate in Chennai (Madras) to implement the above activities. The Institute for Ocean Management, Anna University and the National Institution of Ocean Technology, Chennai will work as partners with the Project Directorate in implementing the proposed activities. In addition to the Coastal State Governments, a number of National and State Institutions and Consultants are also involved in the implementation of the activities.

2.2.e.ix.(b) Expected Benefits from ICM

The implementation of ICM is expected to yield the following benefits:

(i) Knowledge and expertise in the country for the development of ICMAM plans and infrastructural facilities for training in this area for all future requirements. This will help India to develop and implement the plans with local efforts. Once the plans are implemented, it is expected that there will be a systematic management of the coastal and marine environment leading to preservation, conservation and sustainable development of its resources on which the coastal population depends for their livelihood.

(ii) Minimize conflicts arising from the incompatible uses of coastal land areas and adjoining sea area through an established coordination mechanism as defined in the plans.

(iii) Protection of critical habitats leading to conservation of marine bio-diversity and protection of endangered species which facilitate maintenance of ecological balance to ensure a healthy coastal environment.

(iv) Systematic management of marine environment from pollution by using waste load limits. This will facilitate sustainable development of estuaries and coastal waters and minimize their degradation.

(v) The proposed environmental guidelines for developmental activities would ensure minimized adverse impact of activities on the ecology of the marine environment.

The above information was provided by the Government of India to the fifth and seventh sessions of the United Nations Commission on Sustainable Development.[20]

2.2.e.x. Integrated Coastal and Marine Area Management (ICMAM)

The Coastal Ocean Monitoring and Prediction Systems (COMAPS) is a programme being carried by the Department of Ocean Development since 1990-91 with the objective of constantly assessing the health of Indian seas on a long-term basis. The status of marine pollution in the coastal waters has been assessed and current level of pollution into the waters has also been determined.

Further, it is planned to include physical oceanographic studies and incorporate the techniques for determination of waste assimilation capacity of water bodies to have predictive capabilities on pollution levels, which will enable establishing site specific regulatory measures to maintain the desired quality of the coastal waters.

In 1998, the Department took up an infrastructure development and capacity building programme to facilitate adoption of the concept of Integrated Coastal and Marine Area Management (ICMAM) by coastal areas in the coming years. The programme focuses on development of expertise in ICMAM oriented activities and dissemination of knowledge gained to the coastal areas through organized training programmes.

2.2.e.x.(a) National Facility for ICMAM

Since the ICMAM related activities are long-term in nature, DOD is establishing a National facility on ICMAM in the new National Institute of Ocean Technology campus to undertake the above activities on a long-term basis. Besides regular long-term training programmes on preparation of ICMAM plans and an information system needed for the management of critical habitats, it will also undertake all other ICMAM related activities like determination of use classification of coastal waters, and water quality criteria for different uses of sea, determination of impact zone for developmental activities in critical habitats, etc. DOD also envisions ICMAM to become a regional training centre for South Asian countries and implement international coastal zone programmes.

The above information was provided by the Government of India to the fifth and seventh sessions of the United Nations Commission on Sustainable Development (Last update: February 1999).[21]

2.2.e.x.(b) Integrated Decision-Making

In India, the UN Convention on the Law of the Sea was signed in 1995 and ratified in June 1996. India has also ratified the international Convention for the Prevention of Pollution from Ships (MARPOL Convention 73/78) and adopted the provisions in the Merchant Shipping Act. Fisheries are regulated under the Marine Fishing Regulation Act (MFRA).

The Ministry of Environment and Forests, New Delhi and Department of Ocean Development are responsible for decision-making in the area of oceans and seas. A national and 13 State/U.T. level coastal management Authorities have been set up to identify and prepare an Integrated Coastal Zone Management Plan for ecologically important stretches.

The Notification on Coastal Regulation Zone 1991 (as amended from time to time) lists certain prohibited and regulated activities related to integrated coastal zone management and sustainable development. Its provisions also prohibit and regulate developmental activities in the Coastal Regulation Zone. The effluents/discharges from various resources have to meet the standards listed in the Environment Protection Act, 1986 before being discharged in the marine waters.

The management of resources in high seas is the responsibility of Department of Ocean Development, while management of resources in the Coastal Water lies with Ministry of Environment and Forests.

2.2.e.xi. Assessment of Marine Living Resources

Over the years the Fisheries Survey of India has assessed the fishing resources up to 50-70 m. depth and published the fishery atlas. It is also noted that the fishery resources in India's coastal waters up to 50-70 m. depth is almost fully exploited. Some of the species are over-exploited and are endangered. In addition, marine pollution has led to degradation of the marine resource potential and marine biodiversity. Indian R&D institutes have carried out studies on fish biology and technologies for culture fisheries, controlled harvesting, etc. to aid sustainable resource utilisation. The Department of Ocean Development has initiated a multi-disciplinary and multi-institutional programme aimed at making an assessment of the marine living resources beyond 70 m. depth within the Indian EEZ and correlating the marine living resources potential with the oceanographic parameters in 1997-98. The major objectives of this programme are to have realistic and reliable information on the potential of marine living resources in the Indian EEZ for sustainable development and management and to enhance the marine living resource potential of Indian seas.

In addition, it is planned to develop technologies and implement pilot projects to increase the productivity of India's coastal waters selectively by sea ranching and mariculture and thereby augmenting the sea food production and improving the life of our coastal community.

To address the preservation and sustainable use of fragile ecosystems, State/Union Territory level Waste Zone Management Authorities have been set up, and these will prepare an Integrated Coastal Zone Management Plan for ecologically important zones.

To address integrated coastal zone management and sustainable development, the following legislations have been adopted:

- Environment Protection Act (EPA), 1986, under which Coastal Regulation Zone 1991 has been notified.
- Forest Conservation Act, 1980.
- Standards for discharging effluents are listed in the Environmental Protection Act, 1986.

In the area of fisheries development, the following are the legislation/rules/Acts in force in the country:

> The Maritime Zones of India (Regulation of fishing by Foreign Vessels) Act, 1981 provides fishing regulations for foreign fishing vessels for operation in Indian waters. The Coast Guard and the State/UT Police has been authorised under the Act to apprehend and prosecute unauthorized foreign fishing vessels/crew for fishing/poaching in Indian waters.

The Marine Fishing Regulation Acts enforced by the coastal States of India provide for regulating fishing and conservation measures in the territorial waters. These include: regulation of mesh size to avoid catching of juvenile fish, regulation of gear to avoid over-exploitation of certain species, reservation of zones for various fishing sectors to provide exclusive rights to traditional fishermen to fish unhindered in near shore areas and also for declaration of closed seasons during fish breeding period to avoid catching of young juvenile fish.

A committee was constituted by the Government of India in March, 1995 to review the Deep Sea Fishing Policy. On the basis of the recommendations of this Committee, the Deep Sea Fishing Policy of 1991 was rescinded and no new permits, extensions or renewal of the permits under the above policies has been given. The Government has also constituted a National Level Review Committee in 1996 to assess the area-wise requirements of different categories of fishing vessels below 20 m and conservation of fishery resources, etc. A number of measures have also been taken by the government to conserve marine fishery resources and over-exploitation as per the provisions made in the Central/State Acts/Rules. Measures have also been taken to introduce resource-specific fishing vessels for oceanic fisheries.

In addition, the following Guidelines have been adopted:

- Guidelines under Environment Impact Assessment (EIA) notification for setting and operating various projects.
- Guidelines on Sustainable Aquaculture Development for regulating coastal aquaculture.

Major Groups are involved through public hearings that have been made mandatory before any project listed in EIA notification is cleared.

2.2.e.xii. Status

Fisheries: Fisheries play an important role in the Indian economy and supports about 6.0 million full time or occasional fishermen. It continues to be a thrust area of India's development programmes due to its vital contributions to employment generation, food security and foreign exchange earnings.

Fish production in India reached a level of about 5.40 million tons in 1998 and the country is now sixth largest producer of fish in the world. Out of this, 2.90 million tons is from the marine sector. The earnings from export of fish and fishery products crossed US$1.30 billion in 1998. While fish production from 0-50 m. zone has been harvested to maximum sustainable yield levels, the zone beyond 50-200 m. and 200-500 m. has been harvested up to about 50% levels. The oceanic resources are harvested up to 10% of the potential.

In the Indian Ocean context, the over-exploitation and destruction of eco-system and habitat is not so alarming as in some other parts of the world. The recent review of the state of world fishery resources by FAO has revealed that while the Atlantic Ocean and in different parts of the Pacific Ocean the fishery resources are largely over-exploited, in the Indian Ocean fish production is on the increase with relative stability and healthy state of fish stocks. Various measures are being undertaken to optimise and rationalise the fishing fleet as well as the fishing effort by area-wise deployment of different categories of fishing vessels, regulation of fishing, gear and mesh size, uniform closed fishing season, development of deep sea fishing including diversified fishing, replenishment of fish stocks by undertaking projects on sea ranching, setting up of artificial reef, etc. Anyway, care must be taken to maintain ecosystems in each and every region of the global ocean.

2.2.e.xii.(a) Enhancement of Marine Living Resources

The seas around India, including Island Groups, are endowed with a variety of finfish and shellfish resources. The over-exploitation of these commercially important resources has resulted in significant depletion of their population. The objectives of the work contemplated in the present technology development programme are steps towards conservation of these resources through breeding and sea ranching.

2.2.e.xii.(b) Oil Spills and Shipping

The western part of the Indian Exclusive Economic Zone, i.e., the Arabian Sea adjoining the peninsular India, forms the main international route for oil tankers originating from the Gulf. It has been estimated that some 450 mt. of crude oil is transported annually along this route, involving approximately 2,500 laden tankers. Considering the large volume of oil transported and increased ocean traffic, the probability of tanker accidents is high. The last major accident in the area occurred in January 1993 when a few thousand tonnes of oil spilled into the Andaman Sea. Any accidental spillage of oil along the tanker route will cause severe and in some cases irreparable damage to the marine ecosystem.

In addition to offshore oil exploration and production activities, transfer operations of oil at single buoy mooring stations, as well as lightening and bunkering operations in major ports, cause spillage of oil.

2.2.e.xii.(c) Disposal of Domestic and Industrial Waste

It has been estimated that a large quantum of domestic sewage reaches the coastal environment each day. These wastes contain degradable organic matter, which utilizes enormous amounts of oxygen from seawater for its oxidation. The resultant fall in oxygen in seawater leads to a decrease in the population of marine flora and fauna. Domestic wastes in certain coastal areas are discharged without treatment due to lack of such facilities in most cities and towns.

2.2.e.xiii. Information

Oceanographic data are essential for understanding the oceanic processes and undertaking developments relating to ocean sector. The UNCED (1992) emphasizes the need for Global Ocean Observing System (GOOS) to collect long-term systematic scientific oceanographic data at a national, regional and global level. The world climate research programme needs effective contributions for oceanographic observations. Thus the need of the hour is reliable oceanographic data and data products of quality which are application oriented and user driven. The application areas are weather/climate prediction, fisheries, port and harbour development, navigation and shipping, environment pollution monitoring, coastal area development and R & D in oceanography.

With a view to synergise and generate reliable coastal and ocean data and data products, the various related projects of the Department of Ocean Development were restructured and reoriented in 1997-98 as Ocean Observation and Information Services (OOIS). This programme has four major elements viz., Ocean Observing System using Conventional and Satellite Remote Sensing Observations, Ocean Information Services, networking different ocean observations and marine data centres to serve the user demands, Satellite and Coastal Oceanographic Research utilising the advances in Satellite Remote Sensing Technology, and Ocean Dynamics & Modelling to establish predictive capacity of ocean parameters.

Geographic Information System has been introduced as a means of Decision Supporting System in the management of critical habitats like mangroves, coral reefs, areas rich in biodiversity, etc., under the Integrated Coastal and Marine Area Management programme.

For acquiring surface meteorological and upper oceanographic parameters on real-time basis, 12 moored data buoys have been deployed along the Indian coastline at selected locations. These buoys are equipped with sensors for accurate measurement of a number of oceanographic parameters. The data are disseminated to the India Meteorological Department for forecast of cyclones, and to other scientific and research institutes, port authorities, National Hydrographic Office, etc., for wider utility and application. The transmission of the data between the buoys and a store station is effected through a two-way communication system of INMARSAT-C satellite. The oceanographic data are also collected through drifting buoys and are transmitted via ARGOS satellite to various user agencies. A website has been set up for dissemination of information pertaining to the policies and programmes of the Government in the field of ocean science and technology.

Under the Integrated Coastal and Marine Area Management Programme of the Department, waste assimilation capacity and preparation of model Integrated Coastal and Marine Area Management plans, etc., have been envisaged. With a view to control marine pollution from land based activities information relating to assimilation capacity of coastal waters, particularly with reference to the thermal waste discharges including fly ash, aquaculture waste and sewage and other industrial wastes. Studies have been initiated on discharge and assimilation of fly ash and other pollutants from industries located along Ennore Creek, north off Chennai. Application of modern tools like computer based modelling for prediction of the impact of the various integrated activities occurring in the coastal areas is also incorporated in the Integrated Coastal and Marine Area Management Programme.

Constant monitoring of the health of the seas and taking up remedial measures for preventing and controlling pollution from land based activities is another activity, for ensuring sustainable development of the seas around India. The various measures taken up by the Government for regulating the activities along the coastal zone, fishing and fisheries, etc., have a definite role to play in sustainable development and utilisation of the ocean and its resources.

The programme and activities of the Department of Ocean Development are fully funded by the Government of India, from the National Budget. External assistance is also available for specific programmes such as National Data Buoy Programme and the Capacity Building Component of Integrated Coastal and Marine Area Management from NORAD and World Bank, respectively.

2.2.e.xiv. Environment—Current Issues

Deforestation, soil erosion, overgrazing, desertification, air pollution from industrial effluents and vehicle emissions, water pollution from raw sewage and runoff of agricultural pesticides, huge and growing population—all these are overstraining natural resources in India.

2.2.e.xv. Environment – International Agreements

India as party to: Antarctic-Environmental Protocol, Antarctic-Marine Living Resources, Antarctic Treaty, Biodiversity, Climate Change, Climate Change-Kyoto Protocol, Desertification, Endangered Species, Environmental Modification, Hazardous Wastes, Law of the Sea, Ozone Layer Protection, Ship Pollution, Tropical Timber 83, Tropical Timber 94, Wetlands, Whaling signed, but not ratified none of the selected agreements

2.2.e.xvi. International Organization Participation

AfDB, ARF, AsDB, ASEAN (dialogue partner), BIS, C, CP, FAO, G-6, G-15, G-19, G-24, G-77, IAEA, IBRD, ICAO, ICC, ICFTU, ICRM, IDA, IFAD, IFC, IFRCS, IHO, ILO, IMF, IMO, Interpol, IOC, IOM (observer), ISO, ITU, MICAH, MONUC, NAM, OAS (observer), OPCW, PCA, SAARC, UN, UNCTAD, UNESCO, UNHCR, UNIDO, UNIFIL, UNMEE, UNMIK, UNMOVIC, UPU, WCL, WCO, WFTU, WHO, WIPO, WMO, WTO.

2.2.e.xvii. Disputes—International

Kashmir remains the world's most highly militarized territorial dispute with portions under the de facto administration of China (Aksai Chin), India (Jammu and Kashmir), and Pakistan (Azad Kashmir and Northern Areas), but recent discussions and confidence-building measures among parties are beginning to defuse tensions; India does not recognize Pakistan's ceding lands to China in the 1965 boundary agreement; disputes with Pakistan over Indus River water sharing and the terminus of the Sir Creek Estuary at the mouth of the Rann of Kutch, which prevents maritime boundary delimitation; Pakistani maps continue to show Junagadh claim in Indian Gujarat State; most of the rugged, militarized boundary with China is in dispute, but sides have committed to begin resolution with discussions on the least disputed Middle Sector; Joint Border Committee with Nepal continues to work on resolution of minor disputed boundary sections; discussions with Bangladesh remain stalled to delimit a small section of river boundary, to exchange certain enclaves in both countries, to allocate divided villages, and to stop illegal cross-border trade, migration, and violence; Bangladesh protests India's attempts to fence off high-traffic sections of the porous boundary; dispute with Bangladesh over volcanic New Moore/ South Talpatty/Purbasha Island in the Bay of Bengal deters maritime boundary delimitation; India seeks cooperation from Bhutan and Burma to keep out Indian Nagaland insurgents; joint border commission continues to work on small disputed sections of boundary with Nepal; India has instituted a stricter border regime to restrict transit of Maoist insurgents and illegal cross-border activities from Nepal. Recent river linking projects are causing differences between India and Bangladesh.[22]

2.2.e.xviii. Agenda 21

Humanity stands at a defining moment in history. Confrontations are not unusual with perpetuation of disparities between and within nations, a worsening of poverty, hunger, ill-health and illiteracy, and the continuing deterioration of the ecosystems on which human beings depend for their well-being. However, integration of environment and development concerns and greater attention to them will lead to the fulfilment of basic needs, improved living standards for all, better protected and managed ecosystems and a safer, more prosperous future. No nation can achieve this on its own; but together we can—in a global partnership for sustainable development.

This global partnership must build on the premises of General Assembly resolution 44/228 of 22 December 1989, which was adopted when the nations of the world called for the United Nations Conference on Environment and Development, and on the acceptance of the need to take a balanced and integrated approach to environment and development questions.

Agenda 21 addresses the pressing problems of today and also aims at preparing the world for the challenges of the next century. It reflects a global consensus and political commitment at the highest level on development and environment cooperation. Its successful implementation is first and foremost the responsibility of Governments. National strategies, plans, policies and processes are crucial in achieving this. International cooperation should support and supplement such national efforts. In this context, the United Nations system has a key role to play. Other international, regional and sub-regional organizations are also called upon to contribute to this effort. The broadest public participation and the active involvement of the non-governmental organizations and other groups should also be encouraged.

The developmental and environmental objectives of Agenda 21 will require a substantial flow of new and additional financial resources to developing countries, in order to cover the incremental costs for the actions they have to undertake to deal with global environmental problems and to accelerate sustainable development. Financial resources are also required for strengthening the capacity of international institutions for the implementation of Agenda 21. An indicative order-of-magnitude assessment of costs is included in each of the programme areas. This assessment will need to be examined and refined by the relevant implementing agencies and organizations.

In the implementation of the relevant programme areas identified in Agenda 21, special attention should be given to the particular circumstances facing the economies in transition. It must also be recognized that these countries are facing unprecedented challenges in transforming their economies, in some cases in the midst of considerable social and political tension.

The programme areas that constitute Agenda 21 are described in terms of the basis for action, objectives, activities and means of implementation. Agenda 21 is a dynamic programme. It will be carried out by the various actors according to the different situations, capacities and priorities of countries and regions with respect to the principles contained in the Rio Declaration on Environment and Development. It could evolve over time in the light of changing needs and circumstances. This process marks the beginning of a new global partnership for sustainable development. In matters of marine environment India seems to be playing a great role, and is committed to promote the Bay of Bengal environment in partnership modality with the littoral states.

2.2.e.xix. Economy—Overview

India's economy encompasses traditional village farming, modern agriculture, handicrafts, a wide range of modern industries, and a multitude of support services. Government controls have been reduced on foreign trade and investment, and privatization of domestic output has proceeded slowly. The economy has posted an excellent average growth rate of 6% since 1990, reducing poverty by about 10 percentage points. India is capitalizing on its large numbers of well-educated people skilled in the English language to become a major exporter of software services and software workers. Despite strong growth, the World Bank and others worry about the continuing public-sector budget deficit, running at approximately 60% of GDP.[23]

2.2.f. Thailand[24]

2.2.f.i. Background

A unified Thai kingdom was established in the mid-14th century. Known as Siam until 1939, Thailand is the only South-east Asian country never to have been taken over by a European power. A bloodless revolution in 1932 led to a constitutional monarchy. In alliance with Japan during World War II, Thailand became a US ally following the conflict. Thailand is currently facing armed violence in its five Muslim-majority southern provinces.

Location	:	South-eastern Asia, bordering the Andaman Sea and the Gulf of Thailand, south-east of Burma
Geographic coordinates	:	15°00' N, 100°00' E
Area	:	Total: 5,14,000 sq. km., land: 5,11,770 sq. km., water: 2,230 sq. km.
Land boundaries	:	Total: 4,863 km., border countries: Burma 1,800 km., Cambodia

		803 km., Laos 1,754 km., Malaysia 506 km.
Coastline	:	3,219 km.
Maritime claims	:	Territorial sea: 12 nm, exclusive economic zone: 200 nm, continental shelf: 200-m depth or to the depth of exploitation
Climate	:	Tropical; rainy, warm, cloudy south-west monsoon (mid-May to September); dry, cool north-east monsoon (November to mid-March); southern isthmus always hot and humid
Terrain	:	Central plain; Khorat Plateau in the east; mountains elsewhere
Elevation extremes	:	Lowest point: Gulf of Thailand 0 m, highest point: Doi Inthanon 2,576 m.

2.2.f.ii. Environmental Issues

In addition to abruptly halting Thailand's decade-long economic boom, the 1997 financial crisis that swept across Asia focused attention on the negative environmental effects of Thailand's rapid industrialization. While Thailand, as one of the "East Asian tigers", was lauded for its strong economic growth during the expansion years, the country also suffered from increased levels of industrial wastewater, a dramatic rise in domestic sewage and hazardous wastes, and severe degradation of its water and coastal resources. Increased levels of air and water pollution and the loss of natural habitats—primarily due to deforestation—were some of the most visible negative environmental consequences of Thailand's unrestrained growth.

As Thailand's economy continues to recover from the effects of the 1997 financial crisis, more attention is being focused on the country's environmental problems. The country's return to economic growth has brought with it renewed threats to Thailand's environment, but there is increased awareness that Thailand's economic development must take into greater account the environment in order to be sustainable in the longer-term. The Thai government hopes that a stronger commitment to environmental protection will help the country deal with the environmental challenges that it now faces.

2.2.f.iii. Oceans and Coastal Areas

As to the sea location Thailand is bordered on the Andaman Sea and the Gulf of Thailand adjoining the Bay of Bengal of the Indian Ocean.

2.2.f.iii.(a) Decision-Making: Coordinating Bodies

In Thailand, different agencies are responsible for coastal zones under their own mandates. Integrated coastal zone management is generally coordinated by the Office of Environmental Policy and Planning. The National Environmental Board is the main body to determine the national coastal resource and environment policy. Other agencies playing major roles in coastal resource management include: the Pollution Control Department, the Harbor Department, the Department of Fisheries, the Royal Forestry Department, the Department of Local Administration, the City Planning Department, the Department of Industrial Work, and the Department of Environmental Quality Promotion.

The Pollution Control Department is also the main responsible agency for marine environmental protection. Other agencies include: the Department of Local Administration, the Department of Fisheries, the Royal Forestry Department, the Harbor Department, the Department of Industrial Work, the Royal Navy, and the Office of Environmental Policy and Planning.

In the area of sustainable use and conservation of marine living resources, the Fisheries Department, the Royal Forestry and the Harbor Department are responsible. Coordination takes place through the committees in which concerned agencies are members. At the policy level, there is the National Environmental Board. At the planning and operational level, coordination is facilitated primarily through the Office of

Environmental Policy and Planning and the Pollution Control Department.

2.2.f.iii.(b) Decision-Making: Legislation and Regulations

Thailand's legislation affecting integrated coastal zone management and sustainable development includes the following:

- Fisheries Act, 1994
- National Marine Park Act, 1961
- Environmental Quality Standards established by the Pollution Control Department
- Environmental Impact Assessment required for large and environmentally-sensitive establishments
- Environmental Conservation Zone
- Factory Act, 1992

Thailand has continuously revised the laws and legislation to meet international standards, although many still need revision.

Legislation in the area of marine environmental protection includes:

- Navigation in Thai Water Act, 1961
- Fisheries Act, 1994
- Enhancement and Conservation of National Environmental Quality Act, 1992
- Factory Act, 1992
- Pollutant Control Zone
- Building Effluent Standards
- Industrial Effluent Standards
- Coastal Water Quality Standards

Legislation affecting the sustainable use and conservation of marine living resources includes:

- Fisheries Act, 1994
- Prohibition of certain types of fishing gear within three kilometers from the coastal line

- Three-month prohibition of fishing during spawning period of economically-important fish species in the Gulf of Thailand
- National Forest Act

In general, the established guidelines and standards are made mandatory to compel the involved activities.

2.2.f.iii.(c) Decision-Making: Strategies, Policies and Plans

There is no specific national policy on oceans and seas. Thailand has established a National Committee on Sustainable Development of the Sea. In general, representatives of stakeholders have been nominated as committee members. The local communities are encouraged to participate in the public hearing of any major development that potentially generates environmental impacts. The new constitution has promoted information and management transparency. Access to development information must be open to the public.

There are also policies that cover the major issues, such as:

- The Policy and Perspective Plan for Enhancement and Conservation of National Environmental Quality (1997-2016), and
- The Five-Year National Economic and Social Development Plan (the eighth such plan, 1997-2001).

Policies for integrated coastal zone management and sustainable development are directed toward:

Fully protecting the remaining mangrove areas;

- Minimizing the environmental impacts on coastal areas, especially from urban and industrial centres;
- Promoting eco-tourism to protect the coastal environment; and
- Developing the seawater irrigation system for coastal aquaculture.

Marine environmental protection policies address the following:

- Polluters must be responsible for the cleaning of the environment;

- Participation of the private sector in coastal environmental management is promoted;
- Water quality in the major rivers is improved.

Policies for sustainable use and conservation of marine living resources aim at the following:

- Government control of the mesh size and limits to the period of catch to minimize by-catch of the target and non-target species;
- Periodical closure of the Gulf of Thailand;
- Promotion of the community collective management system to protect the coastal resources; and
- Protection and rehabilitation of the coral reefs.

Other related measures include:

- A Cabinet Resolution to prohibit the use of conserved mangrove forests;
- Urgent Measures for Mangrove and Coral Reef Management;
- The Master Plan for Coral Reef Management;
- Policies, Measures and Action Plans for Coastal Resource and Environmental Management;
- National Oil Spill Contingency Plan;
- The Five-Year Natural Resource Management Action Plan;
- The Provincial Environmental Management Plan;
- A Cabinet Resolution to demarcate conserved coastal forests;
- Prohibition on fishing in protected areas that are critical, such as coral reefs, sea grass, and mangroves, which are important nursing and spawning grounds.

2.2.f.iii.(d) Programmes and Projects

Among the programmes that have been developed to address the issues enumerated above are included:

- Program to install artificial reefs along the twenty-three coastal provinces of Thailand;

- Programs to install the gloating anchor for boats in environmentally critical areas;
- Development of an *Action Plan and Pollution Sources Control* to Improve the Coastal Water Quality in the Gulf of Thailand and Andaman Coast; and
- Development of a Mathematical Model for Predictions of the Movement of Oil Spills.

2.2.f.iii.(e) Status

The major current uses of the coastal areas in Thailand are fishing, aquaculture and tourism. The percentage of the economy contributed by fishing is about two per cent of GDP.

Methods in place to encourage sustainable use and conservation of marine living resources include:

- Control of the number and type of fishing gear and vessels;
- Prohibition of new trawlers;
- Improvement of laws and regulation, such as licensing system;
- Periodical ban of fishing in the Gulf of Thailand
- Prevention of specific fishing gear within three kilometres from the coast line; and
- Promotion of tripartite institution-setting (government, private sector and the public) in formulating plans and monitoring coastal resources.

Shipping impacts sustainable development mainly through improper waste management, especially in relation to the ship cleaning. Oil spills from ships also generate a major impact. In addition, there is conflict over land use in port development.

Impacts from other coastal- and marine-based industries are several. Over-fishing deteriorates the fishery resources. Conversion of mangrove forest to shrimp farms affects the coastal resources. There is over-capacity utilization of tourism resources, especially in the coral reef areas, and improper management of pollution in the areas. Oil and gas operations and transportation increase the risk to the coastal and marine environment. Operational discharges from offshore oil and gas exploration and exploitation generate pollutants, including oil produced in water, oil contaminated drill cuttings, like oil-based mud, production of chemicals, like residual drilling additives and well treatment agents, and other discharges and emissions, like sewage, garbage, deck drainage, heavy metal, aromatics and naturally occurring radioactive materials.

The primary sources of land-based pollution are domestic sources, industrial development areas and tourism areas, especially beach resorts and agriculture and aquaculture activities. There is also pollution from non-point sources, such as agriculture and urban runoff and coastal erosion.

The primary sources of sea-based pollution are offshore oil and gas operations, wastes from maritime transportation, shipping, oil spills, dredging and the red tide and harmful algal bloom.

The command and control approach has been strengthened through decentralization of resource and environmental management. Local communities are encouraged to play increasing roles in sustainable use of resources. There are *National Action Plans* for mangrove, coral reefs and seagrass management. A seawater irrigation system has been implemented to reduce the pollution of shrimp farms. Central domestic wastewater treatment plants have been developed in the major cities, especially in the coastal areas.

2.2.f.iii.(f) Challenges

One of the main constraints recently faced by Thailand is the economic crisis that accelerates resource exploitation, reduces budgets available for ocean and coastal resource management. The unilateral action in using environmental issues as trade barriers of developed countries also seriously affects the livelihoods of the small fishing households.

Other constraints include:

- Some duplication of efforts undertaken by various government agencies involved;

- The limited human and financial resources to oversee the coastal areas of the length of 2,600 kms, and
- The lack of knowledge and skills of the multi-ecosystem of tropical zones.

2.2.f.iv. Capacity-building, Education, Training and Awareness-raising

Programmes to educate policy-makers include seminars and study tours for new approaches in sustainable coastal management, such as the use of economic instruments, integrated coastal resource management, integrated watershed management. Regional meetings and cooperation, such as ASEAN, APEC, and ESCAP, also provide opportunity to exchange experiences at the policy-making level.

Capacity-building training programmes for the local administration organizations are being implemented for preparing resource and environmental management plans. Support to the factories to adopt ISO 14000 has been provided with training, auditing, etc. Local communities are also trained by NGOs to enhance their capability in managing coastal resources in their areas.

The Environmental Promotion Department regularly conducts campaigns for raising public awareness in protecting ocean and coastal resources. Similarly, the Fisheries Department also actively promotes the rehabilitation of fishery resources.

2.2.f.v. Information

National fishery statistics include the number of catch, types of vessels, fishing gear, number of fishing households, and registered vessels, research works on sustainable fishing, fishing efforts, etc.

Information on water quality is available in the coastal urban centres, coastal sea water quality, ocean pollution warning systems, etc. There are also statistics on oil spills in Thai waters.

Thailand has national mineral statistics, mineral deposit mapping, and a master plan for national mineral resource management.

With respect to critical uncertainties, Thailand maintains the following information: national GHG inventory for 1990 and mitigation policies to cope with climate change vulnerability and adaptation; and assessment of these uncertainties by the Meteorological Department. There is GIS on coastal areas, and it has been utilized in marine and coastal resource management and planning, such as Songkla Basin and Phanga Bay. The Department of Fisheries has recently begun to set up GIS to assist decision-makers and planners.

Information is mainly used by the public agencies and academic institutes. Simple indicators have been recommended for use at the provincial level in the preparation of provincial environmental action plans. At the national level, the sustainable yield of fishery resources is estimated, while the Green Account of Gross National Product is being developed. Water quality standards of the seawater are also regularly monitored.

2.2.f.vi. Research and Technologies

Basically, the lack of appropriate technology transfer is the major issue impeding the development of innovative approaches to sustainable coastal resource utilization. The proposed technology should be effective and suitable to the areas. It should be cost-effective and harmonized with the local government. In general, all activities are financed by the national budget. Some external assistance has been provided through research works under bilateral or multi-lateral programmes.

2.2.f.vii. Cooperation

Thailand is party to several Conventions relevant to oceans and seas, including:

Framework Convention on Climate Change

- MARPOL;
- SEAPOL;
- CITES;
- CBD (to be signed);
- RAMSAR; and
- The Convention Concerning the Protection of the World Cultural and Natural Heritage.

Thailand is in the process of ratifying the Basel Convention on the Control of Transboundary Movement of Hazardous Wastes and their Disposal, and it is in the process of becoming party to the following Conventions: the International Convention for Prevention of Pollution from Ships; the International Convention on Oil Pollution Preparedness Response and Cooperation; and the International Convention on Civil Liability.

Thailand is also a member of or party to the following:

- The ASEAN Working Group on ASEAN Seas and Marine Environment and the Sub-Committee on Marine Science;
- The Regional Programme on Prevention and Management of Marine Pollution in the East Asian Sea;
- The ASEAN Agreement on The Conservation of Nature and Natural Resources;
- Agreement on the Network of Aquaculture Centres in Asia and the Pacific; and
- The Southeast Asian Fisheries Development Centre.

Other bilateral, multilateral and international cooperation in this area includes:

- APEC Marine Resource Conservation Working Group;
- APEC Fisheries Working Group;
- The Danish Cooperation for Environment and Development;
- The PECC Task Force on Fisheries Development and Cooperation; and
- ASEAN-Dialogue Partners Cooperation Programme (ASEAN-Australia Project; ASEAN-EU Project; ASEAN-Canada Project; ASEAN-Korea Project; ASEAN-Japan Project).[25]

2.2.f.viii. Air and Marine Pollution

Air and water pollution are two of the biggest environmental problems in Thailand. As such, the Thai government is taking steps to clean up the damage that has already been done and attempting to implement policies geared to prevent further pollution from taking place.

(i) *Air Pollution*

Thailand's most significant environmental threat is that of urban air pollution, and the capital city of Bangkok stands out as the worst among urban areas in Thailand in the country. In 1992, the United Nations Environment Program (UNEP) reported that the Thai capital was one of the most air-polluted cities in the world due to the city's notorious traffic problems. Approximately one million Bangkok residents are thought to suffer from allergies and respiratory problems due to air pollution. In 2001, airborne particulate matter was estimated to have caused 3,300 premature deaths and to have led to almost 17,000 hospital admissions, at a total health care cost of up to $6.3 billion.

Approximately 350 miles north of Bangkok, the area surrounding the 2.6-GW capacity Mae Moh thermal power plant complex has recorded a large number of deaths from heart failure and a high occurrence of chronic respiratory problems. The excessive levels of sulphur dioxide (SO_2) being emitted in the Mae Moh valley can be attributed to 13 coal-fired power plants at the complex. There have been several notable environmental incidents involving the complex, including one instance in 1992 when excessive SO_2 emissions from the power plants sent more than 1,200 villagers to the hospital. The Electricity Generating Authority (Goa) has responded with the installation of sulphur scrubbers and has promised to take further remedial actions at its other sites.

(ii) *Marine Pollution*

Marine pollution is considered a severe threat to the health of Thailand's people as well as its economy. Agricultural run-off, coastal aquaculture, industrial effluents and domestic sewage are responsible for the pollution of coastal, surface and groundwater in Thailand. Water pollution is most severe in the BMR due to the high concentration of industrial activity;

however, areas all over the country have been affected by current water use trends.

As a result of rapid coastal development, it has been estimated that more than half of all mangrove forest areas in Thailand have been depleted. Although agriculture is considered to be the primary factor behind this, expansion of marine-based activities such as offshore oil and gas exploration in the Gulf of Thailand is expected to increase the risk of marine pollution in Thailand. Indeed, a planned 140-mile offshore gas pipeline, designed to carry gas to southern Thailand from the Malaysia-Thailand Joint Development Area along the two countries' maritime border, has been the focus of vehement environmental opposition. Construction of the pipeline, along with a two-unit gas separation plant at a point along the pipeline in the Songkhla province, has been delayed by strong opposition from Thai environmental groups worried about the risks of further marine pollution.

2.2.f.ix. International Organization Participation

APEC, ARF, AsDB, ASEAN, BIS, CP, FAO, G-77, IAEA, IBRD, ICAO, ICC, ICCt (signatory), ICFTU, ICRM, IDA, IFAD, IFC, IFRCS, IHO, ILO, IMF, IMO, Interpol, IOC, IOM, ISO, ITU, NAM, OAS (observer), OIC (observer), OPCW, OSCE (partner), PCA, UN, UNAMSIL, UNCTAD, UNESCO, UNHCR, UNIDO, UNMISET, UPU, WCL, WCO, WFTU, WHO, WIPO, WMO, WTO.

(i) *Economy—Overview*

Thailand has a free-enterprise economy and welcomes foreign investment. Exports feature textiles and footwear, fishery products, rice, rubber, jewelry, automobiles, computers and electrical appliances. Thailand has recovered from the 1997-98 Asian Financial Crisis and was one of East Asia's best performers in 2002. Increased consumption and investment spending and strong export growth pushed GDP growth up to 6.3% in 2003 despite a sluggish global economy. The highly popular government has pushed an expansionist policy, including major support of village economic development.

2.2.f.x. Reality

Of late, it is now in master plan for each and every state to address environment and development. In environment matters multi-nature factors are involved, in consequence, it is not possible to single out any environment matter from others. Marine environment is not an exception to this stance. Environment regime at present cannot be said as a virgin discipline. Helsinki 21 Principle enabled to evolve a 'package' Agenda 21 which is now the realm of environment and development. Every state of the world is serious to its environment vulnerability.[26]

The Earth Summit (Rio Declaration) is multi-faceted and represents a monument to international co-operation in the treaty-making process; the need to elaborate a new and comprehensive regime for environment and development was perceived, and the international community expressed its collective will to cooperate in this effort on a scale the magnitude of which was unprecedented in the history of treaties. The elaboration of the Summit represents an attempt to establish a true and universal effort to achieve a "just and equitable international economic order" governing environment and development.

The touchstone of the package of the Summit is the notion that the enjoyment of rights and benefits involves the concomitant undertaking of duties and obligations, so that an overall equitable order may be created. The paramount duty of all states parties is to respect the rights of others; however, some duties may entail more executory acts. The duty to give due notice of hazards would be an example of the latter kind of duty.

Among the package deal of environment and development, the Summit lays stress on ecological and environmental issues. The general principles and policies governing prevention, reduction and control of pollution throughout the marine environment are established, as are the specific rights and duties of states concerned for the realization of their environmental and ecological goals. The allocation of the rights and the burden of the duties would vary depending upon the location and/or the type of pollution involved, and specific safeguard and enforcement provisions are reiterated.

As a matter of fact, the commitment to sustainable development is concerned, Agenda 21 is indeed a worthy document. It was the product of an exhaustive process of consultation and in itself a remarkable tribute to the almost indefatigable energies of the exiguous UNCED secretariat and its Secretary-General, Maurice Strong. But Agenda 21 may suffer from its own sheer bulkiness as well as from the fact that it does not lay down any mandatory rules, nor on the whole does it require truly bankable commitments to be made by any of the parties involved. Agenda 21 is in reality the softest of "soft law", exhortatory in nature, a cafeteria where self-service is the order of the day.

Much hope is placed in the 'follow-up process", i.e., how the implementation of Agenda 21 at national and international level will be monitored, but this is an area where much confusion still has to be dissipated.

UNCED agreed on new institutional arrangements, particularly an inter-governmental Commission on Sustainable Development reporting to the General Assembly through ECOSOC, whose primary responsibility would be to investigate the extent to which states were fulfilling their duties under Agenda 21.[27] By this time Agenda 21 has drawn attention of each and every state. States have provided their reports. But the matter to remember is that countries, particularly the developing countries are seen to miss certain information. This is owing to their lacking expertise. It is almost common to see the lack of financial supports to enable the financially unsound developing countries, especially in the case of the Bay of Bengal littoral States.

The chapter on oceans is the longest and one of the most complex chapters of Agenda 21.[28]

Chapter 17 contains the areas such as: Integrated coastal zone management; marine environmental protection (including land- and sea-based sources of marine pollution); sustainable use and conservation of high seas living resources; sustainable use of living marine resources under national jurisdiction; addressing critical uncertainties for the management of marine environment and climate change; strengthening international, including regional, cooperation and coordination; and sustainable development of islands. Summarily, the main focus of chapter 17 is on protection of the oceans, all kinds of seas, including enclosed and semi-enclosed seas, and coastal areas and the protection, rational use and development of their living resources.

The marine environment – including the oceans and all seas and adjacent coastal areas – forms an integrated whole that is an essential component of the global life-support system and a positive asset that presents opportunities for sustainable development. International law, as reflected in the provisions of the United Nations Convention on the Law of the Sea sets forth rights and obligations of states and provides the international basis upon which to pursue the protection and sustainable development of the marine and coastal environment and its resources. This requires new approaches to marine and coastal area management and development, at the national, sub-regional, regional and global levels, approaches that are integrated in content and are precautionary and anticipatory in ambit, as reflected in the areas relating to:

(a) Integrated management and sustainable development of coastal areas, including exclusive economic zones;

(b) Marine environment protection;

(c) Sustainable use and conserving of marine living resources of the high seas;

(d) Sustainable use and conservation of marine living resources under national jurisdiction;

(e) Addressing critical uncertainties for the management of the marine environment and climate change;

(f) Strengthening international, including regional, cooperation and coordination; and

(g) Sustainable development of small islands.

The implementation by developing countries of the activities shall be commensurate with their individual technological and financial capacities and priorities in allocating resources for development needs and ultimately depends on the technology transfer and financial resources required and made available to them.

2.3. Integrated Management and Sustainable Development of Coastal and Marine Areas, including Exclusive Economic Zones

The coastal area contains diverse and productive habitats important for human settlements, development and local subsistence. More than half the world's population lives within 60 km. of the shoreline, and this could rise to three quarters by the year 2020. Many of the world's poor are crowded in coastal areas. Coastal resources are vital for many local communities and indigenous people. The exclusive economic zone (EEZ) is also an important marine area where the states manage the development and conservation of natural resources for the benefit of their people. For small island states or countries, these are the areas most available for development activities.

Despite national, subregional, regional and global efforts, current approaches to the management of marine and coastal resources have not always proved capable of achieving sustainable development, and coastal resources and the coastal environment are being rapidly degraded and eroded in many parts of the world.

There is a need for the coastal states to promote integrated management and sustainable development of coastal areas. That is to say, coastal states commit themselves to integrated management and sustainable development of coastal areas and the marine environment under their national jurisdiction. To this end, it is necessary to, *inter alia*

(h) provide for an integrated policy and decision-making process, including all involved sectors, to promote compatibility and a balance of uses;

(i) identify existing and projected uses of coastal areas and their interactions;

(j) concentrate on well-defined issues concerning coastal management;

(k) apply preventive and precautionary approaches in project planning and implementation, including prior assessment and systematic observation of the impacts of major projects;

(l) promote the development and application of methods, such as national resource and environmental accounting, that reflect changes in value resulting from uses of coastal and marine areas, including pollution, marine erosion, loss of resources and habitat destruction;

(m) provided access, as far as possible, for concerned individuals, groups and organizations to relevant information and opportunities for construction and participation in planning and decision-making at appropriate levels.[29]

There is a need for coastal states to be particular to take measures for protection of marine environment. To this end, it is necessary, to address the causes of pollution of marine environment.

2.4. Marine Environment Pollution

(i) Degradation of the marine environment can result from a wide range of sources. Land-based sources contribute 70 per cent of marine pollution, while maritime transport and dumping at sea activities contribute 10 per cent each. The contaminants that pose the greatest threat to the marine environment are, in variable order of importance and depending on deferring national or regional situations: sewage, nutrients, synthetic organic compounds, sediments, litter and plastics, metals, radionuclides, oil/hydrocarbons and polycyclic aromatic hydrocarbons (PAHs). Many of the polluting substances originating from land-based sources are of particular concern to the marine environment since they exhibit at the same time toxicity, persistence and bioaccumulation in the food chain.

(ii) Degradation of the marine environment can also result from a wide range of activities on land. Human settlements, land use, construction of coastal infrastructure, agriculture, forestry, urban development, tourism and industry can affect the marine environment. Coastal erosion and siltation are of particular concern.

(iii) Marine pollution is also caused by shipping and sea-based activities. Approximately 6,00,000 tons of oil enter the oceans each year as a result of normal shipping operations, accidents and illegal discharges. With respect to offshore oil and gas activities, currently machinery space discharges are regulated internationally and six regional conventions to control platform discharges have been under consideration. The nature and extent of environmental impacts from offshore oil exploration and production activities generally account for a very small proportion of marine pollution.

(iv) A precautionary and anticipatory rather than a reactive approach is necessary to prevent the degradation of the marine environment. This requires, *inter alia*,the adoption of precautionary measures, environmental impact assessments, clean production techniques, recycling, waste audits and minimization, construction and /or improvement of sewage treatment facilities, quality management criteria for the proper handling of hazardous substances, and a comprehensive approach to damaging impacts from air, land and water. Any management framework must include the improvements of coastal human settlements and the integrated management and development of coastal area.[30]

With the passage of time, states are approaching towards commitments to Agenda 21, nationally, regionally to enrich global impacts on environment and development. As for instance, since the Rio Declaration Johannesburg Summit, 2002 gave incentives to states parties to acquiescence in environment and development and the point to this end is to applaud regional feeling of African states to stress for them to be treated as to their situations.[31]

2.5. The Bay of Bengal Resources Impact

The Bay of Bengal and its littoral states are integrated as a whole in respect of their interactions with the environment. The littoral states have dependence on the Bay in the sense that their climate, marine life as well as economy, to an extent, are governed by it. As a part of the Indian Ocean, the Bay of Bengal provides natural resources like oil and gas fields, fish, shrimp, sand and gravel, aggregates, placer deposit, polymetallic nodules too. Both living and mineral resources of the Bay have a great role in the economy of the littoral states. The matter can be clarified by way of the following table.[32]

Region	Natural Resources
Bangladesh	Natural gas, arable land, timber, coal
India	Coal (fourth largest reserve in the world), iron ore, manganese, mica, bauxite, titanium ore, chromites, natural gas, diamonds, petroleum, limestone, arable land
Maldives	Fish
Myanmar (Burma)	Petroleum, timber, tin, antimony, zinc, copper, tungsten, lead, coal, some marble, limestone, precious stone, natural gas, hydropower
Sri Lanka	Limestone, graphite, mineral sands, gems, phosphates, chug, hydropower
Thailand	Tin, rubber, natural gas, tungsten, tantalum, timber, lead, fish, gypsum, lignite, fluorite, arable land
Malaysia	Tin, petroleum, timber, copper, iron ore, natural gas, bauxite
Indonesia	Petroleum, tin, natural gas, nickel, timber, bauxite, copper, fertile soils, coal, gold, silver

Each of the states has some source of the resources in the Bay, as a result, their dependence on it is indispensable. More clarification can be made through the following table:[33]

Region Export	Commodities	Import Commodities
Bangladesh	Garments, jute & jute goods, leather, frozen fish, and seafood	Machinery and equipment, chemicals, iron and steel, textiles, foodstuffs, petroleum products, cement
India	Textile goods, gems and jewellery, engineering goods, chemicals, leather manufactures	Crude oil, machinery, gems, fertilizer, chemicals
Maldives	Fish, clothing	Consumer goods, intermediate and capital goods, petroleum products
Myanmar (Burma)	Apparel, foodstuffs, wood products, precious stones	Fabric, petroleum products, plastics, machinery, transport equipment, construction materials, crude oil, food products
Sri Lanka	Textile and apparel, tea, diamond, coconut products, petroleum products	Textiles, mineral products, petroleum, food stuffs, machinery, and equipment
Thailand	Computers, office machine parts, transistors, rubber, vehicles (cars & trucks), plastics, seafood	Capital goods, industrial trial goods and raw materials, consumer goods, fuels

It is clear that Bangladesh has an export earning from frozen fish and seafood and Maldives from fish. Sri Lanka can have export earning from coconut which is very much dependent on sea waters, Thailand can boost export earning from seafood. India is a vast country whose number of islands/group of islands are linked with the Bay of Bengal. In the case of islands/fringe of islands Myanmar steps in sea interests for preserving environment and accelerating development. As sediment deposits in the river beds and estuaries, and erosion and tidal bores have been a continuous casualty, the entire Gangetic deltaic Bangladesh sees no alternative to the promotion of environment and its development. Malaysia and Indonesia seem to some extent concerned, but their issues are not vital exclusively regarding the Bay of Bengal. Their concerns are substantive while marine environment is considered as a matter of broader perspective for South Asian/South-East Asian concerns.

The Bay of Bengal is rich in living and non-living resources. Their preservation in the interests of the littoral states is inevitable. This can be reiterated through integrated spirit. If so, it can result in ensuring and promoting environment and development in the Bay. In other words, such a move can succeed in evolving a legal regime of the environment in the Bay of Bengal.

References

1. http://www.hurricanealley.net/bob.htm; http://banglapedia.search.com.bd/HT/B_0361.HTM
2. See *infra*.at 2.2.b.iii, 2.2.e.(iv)(a, b. c), 2.2.e.vi.(a, b, c, d), 2.2.e.vii.
3. http://www.banglapedia.search.com.bd/HT/B_0361.HTM
4. See *infra* 2.2.b.iii., 2.2.c.i., 2.2.e.v., 2.2.e.vi.(a, b, c, d), 2.2.e.vii.
5. See http://www.banglapedia.search.com.bd/HT/B_0361.HTM
6. See http://www.bgmea.com/ban.htm
7. See National Legislation – DOALOS/OLA – United Nations.
8. E.g. The Government may, with a view to the maintenance of the productivity of the living resources of the sea, by notification in official Gazette, establish conservation zones in such areas of the sea adjacent to the territorial waters as may be specified in the notification and may take such conservation measures in any zone so established as it may deem appropriate for the purpose including measures to protect the living resources of the sea from indiscriminate exploration, depletion or destruction.
9. E.g. The Government may, with a view to preventing and controlling marine pollution and preserving the quality and econological balance in the marine environment in the high seas adjacent to the territorial waters, take such measures as it may deem appropriate for the purpose. It is also stated in section 9(2)(e) the measures to be taken by the Government to "prevent and control marine pollution of the high seas."
10. http://www.cia.gov/cia/publications/factbook/geos/ce.html
11. For administrative purposes, Sri Lanka is divided into 9 Provinces and under these there are 309 local authorities. Provinces are vested with authority under the 13th Amendment to the Constitution. Local authorities are of 3 types – Urban Councils, Municipal Councils, and Pradeshiya Sabha. Local authorities are empowered by their own acts for activities related to the protection of environment.

    Sri Lanka is divided into 25 Administrative Districts under the Central Government, and out of these 14 Districts have maritime boundaries. Around 10.79 million people live in these coastal districts, which is around

58% of the total population. Out of this, only 16.5% have access to pipe borne water. It should be noted that 65% of the coastal districts are categorized as urbanized areas of the country.

12. Oceans and Coastal Areas

The Department of Fisheries and Coast Conservation, under the Ministry of Fisheries, is responsible for policy-making and implementation. The major policy decisions are approved by the Cabinet.

Decision-Making Legislation and Regulations: The Government of Sri Lanka has various laws, rules, and regulations for dealing with activities in the coastal zone. Regulations have been developed to prevent over-fishing, and the coastal management plan provides for zones to conserve marine species threatened by indiscriminate fishing and the use of inappropriate fishing techniques. A Coastal Zone Management Plan has been prepared by the Ministry of Fisheries in order to adopt an integrated approach the management of coastal resources and to involve local communities in the planning and implementation of programmes for the conservation and sustainable use of marine resources and the conservation of the coastline. The Department of Fisheries and Coast Conservation, under the Ministry of Fisheries, is responsible for policy-making and implementation. The major policy decisions are approved by the Cabinet. The policy on coastal fishing has been oriented towards mitigating the adverse effects on the environment and maximizing the protection of fish in a sustainable manner. A national contingency plan to deal with oil spills is also under consideration.

13. Membership of international organizations: ARF, ADB, ASEAN, CP, ESCAP, FAO, G-77, IAEA, IBRD.

14. http://www.free-living.com/Country Profiles/burma/profile.htm

15. See http://www.cia.gov/cia/publications/factbook/geos/mv.html

16. There is a fear that as sea levels rise, island countries such as the Maldives and the Marshall Islands will simply be swamped and disappear. For the moment the country is portrayed by travel companies as a tropical paradise with sandy beaches and coral reefs. The economy is highly-dependent on revenues from its tourism industry. Seventy-four islands have been developed for the top end of the tourist market and they are favoured by scuba divers because of their abundant marine life. Aside from the island capital Male, outsiders are only permitted onto inhabited islands for brief visits, thereby limiting their impact on traditional Muslim communities. The Maldives has made progress in developing its infrastructure and industries, including the fisheries sector, and in improving health, education and literacy. See http://www.news.bbc.co.uk/1hi/world/south_asia/country_profiles/1166...

17. See http://www.theodora.com/wfb/maldives_economy.html

18. http://www.cia.gov/cia/publications/factbook/geos/in.html

19. CIA World Factbook, 1999. See http://www.globaloceans.org/country/india/india.html

20. See http://www.un.org/esa/agen
da21/natlinfo/countr/india/index.htm

21. See http://www.un.org/esa/agenda21/natlinfo/countr/india/index.htm

22. India is set to complete at least 30 of its river linking projects in the current year although it has been saying the project plan is still on the drawing board, said leaders of the Bangladesh Poribesh Andolon (BAPA). Bangladesh Poribesh Andolon (BAPA) will forge an alliance with local, regional and international organisations in favour of "ecological approach to rivers" and wage a movement across the subcontinent against the proposed Indian river-linking project. httt://www.bangladesh-web.com/news/view.php?hidDate=2005-0...

http://www.financialexpress-bd.com/index3.asp?cnd=2/25/2005&s...

23. See http://www.globaloceans.org/country/india/india.html

24. http://www.cia.gov/cia/publications/factbook/geos.th.html

25. This information was provided by the Government of Thailand to the fifth and seventh sessions of the United Nations Commission on Sustainable Development, Last Update: February 1999. See http://www.un.org/esa/agenda 21/natinfo/countr/thai/natur.htm#oceans

26. See Stanley P. Johnson, *The* Earth *Summit: The United Nations Conference on Environment and Development (UNCED),* Martinus Nijhoff (1993) 5.

27. *Ibid.*, 6.

28. After intensive negotiations throughout both PrepComs III and IV, all of the difficult issues were resolved with the exception of the issue of straddling and migratory fish stocks. Rather than allowing lengthy and acrimonious discussions in the Main Committee, Koh requested that the US hold informal consultations to achieve a compromise between Canada and the EC. Twenty-four hours later a compromise was in hand. The resulting text was similar to text proposed at the end of PrepCom IV. The new text for paragraph 17.52 reads: "States should convene an inter-governmental conference under UN auspices with a view to promoting effective implementation of the provisions of the Law of the Sea on straddling and highly migratory fish stocks." The EC was able to accept this language once text was added to say that the conference would draw on scientific and technical studies by the FAO and be fully consistent with the provisions of the Law of the Sea, in particular the right and obligations of coastal states and states fishing on the high seas. *Ibid.*, 307.

29. *Ibid.*, 308-09.

30. *Ibid.*, 311.

31. The Summit (Johannesburg 26 August - 4 September 2002) reaffirmed sustainable development as a central element of the international agenda and gave new impetus to global action to fight poverty and protect the environment. The understanding of sustainable development was broadened and strengthened as a result of the Summit, particularly the important linkages between poverty, the environment and the use of natural

resources. Governments agreed to and reaffirmed a wide range of concrete commitments and targets for action to achieve more effective implementation of sustainable development objectives. Energy and sanitation issues were critical elements of the negotiations and outcomes to a greater degree than in previous international meetings on sustainable development. Support for the establishment of a world solidarity fund for the eradication of poverty was a positive step forward. Africa was identified for special attention and support by the international community to better focus efforts to address the development needs of Africa. The views of civil society were given prominence at the Summit in recognition of the key role of civil society in implementing the outcomes and in promoting partnership initiatives. Over 8,000 civil society participants attended the Summit, reinforced by parallel events which included major groups, such as, NGOs, women, indigenous people, youth, farmers, trade unions, business leaders, the scientific and technological community and local authorities as well as Chief Justices from various countries. The concept of partnerships between governments, business and civil society was given a large boost by the Summit and the Plan of Implementation. Over 220 partnerships (with $235 million in resources) were identified in advance of the Summit and around 60 partnerships were announced during the Summit by a variety of countries.

32. See http://www.faqs.org/docs/factbook/fields/2111.html

33. See http://www.cia:govt/cia/publications/factbook/fields/2058.html

3

INTERNATIONAL DOCUMENTS TOWARDS MARINE ENVIRONMENT

The study of marine environment has been an all-discipline topic. As such, it is one of the most rapidly expanding fields in the modern social, behavioural and engineering sciences. In 1972, the United Nations convened the first international summit conference on Earth's environment: the UN Conference on the Human Environment. Since then, both internationally and domestically nations have enacted statutes, entered into international agreements, and established new environmental protections agencies, all designed to observe the fundamental obligations of states to "ensure that activities within their jurisdiction or control do not cause damage to the environment of other states or of areas beyond the limits of national jurisdiction."[1] In the years since 1972, the new field of environmental law has come into existence, and its reach extends from the village ordinance to national legislation, to the treaties that would integrate and harmonise the human laws that govern society's relations with nature and the "laws of nature."[2] States have, in accordance with the Charter of the United Nations and the principles of international law, the sovereign right to exploit their own resources pursuant to their own environmental policies, and the responsibility to ensure that activities within their jurisdiction or control do not cause damage to the environment of their States or of area beyond the limits of national jurisdiction.[3] Subject to the rights of other states, and except as otherwise expressly provided in this Convention, provisions of this Convention apply, in relation to each contracting Party:

(a) In the case of components of biological diversity, in areas within the limits of national jurisdiction; and

(b) In the case of processes and activities regardless of where their effects occur carries out under its jurisdiction or control, within the area of national jurisdiction or beyond the limits of national jurisdiction.[4]

The provisions of this Convention shall not affect the rights and obligations of any contracting Party deriving from any existing international agreements except those rights and obligations that would cause a serious damage to biological diversity.

Contracting Parties shall implement this condition with respect to the marine environment consistently with rights and obligations of states under the law of the sea.[5]

3.1. Globalism and Regionalism in Marine Environment

No study of the international law relating to protection of the marine environment can fail to note the interplay of global, regional, sub-regional and national rules and institutions, or the variety of interrelated and sometimes overlapping treaties which deal with the marine environment at these various levels.[6] Whether regional regimes are part of or separate from a global framework of regulations but unquestioned is the aspect of the relationship between global, regional and sub-regional approaches to protection of the marine environment. More important for policy-makers is to have an understanding of the comparative advantages and disadvantages of global or regional approaches when deciding whether to regulate and how to do so. Both the Arctic and the Antarctic illustrate well sometimes difficult choices which may have to be made between these different levels of international protection. Decision-makers must deal not only with the question whether to initiate action at a regional or sub-regional level, rather than a global level; they must also consider what constitutes a 'region' or a 'sub-region'. The variety of answers to this question reflects both the diversity of state practice, and the complexity of international legal and political responses to the problems of protecting and preserving the marine environment.[7]

3.1.a. Regionalism in the pre-UNCLOS III: Law of the Sea Context

The law of the sea is inherently global. The International Law Commission assumed as much in its codification of the subject in the 1950s; and the words 'region' and 'regional' appear only twice in the four Geneva Conventions of 1958.[8] Nor has there been any suggestion in the case law of the International Court of Justice as it is applying local or regional customary law when adjudicating law of the sea disputes. While the Court's decisions to take account of special circumstances, such as geography, or dependence on fisheries,[9] naturally pay particular attention to the practice/practices in dispute, the Court has always been careful to articulate its conclusions in terms of a general law of the sea applicable to all states. The Court's general approach suggests that, while there may be, for example, a Latin American perspective on the law of the sea, or Latin American practice contributing to the development of the law of the sea,[10] there can be no Latin American law of the sea distinct from what prevails elsewhere. That means, the pre-UNCLOS III period gives no emphasis on regional concept in the context of the law of the sea.

3.1.b. Regionalism in the LOS Convention

The U.N Convention on the Law of the Sea, 1982 presents a more complex picture, however. On the one hand its explicit purpose is to articulate a comprehensive, uniform and global legal order for the world's oceans, and it seeks to sustain that legal order in several ways. Article 309 forbids reservations and thus compels states to make an 'all or nothing' choice when deciding whether to become a party to the Convention. Article 311 gives the Convention pre-eminence over other agreements; it specially limits the freedom of parties to create new agreements which are incompatible with the effective execution of the object and purposes of the Convention or which affect either the application of "the basic principles embodied herein" or the rights and obligations of other parties. This article thus provides a significant constraint on the making of regional agreements by parties to the LOS Convention. At the same time, Article 237 specifically preserves the freedom of states to make further agreements relating to the protection and preservation of the marine environment, provided these are "concluded in furtherance of the general principles and objectives of this Convention." The same article also preserves obligations under existing agreements on the marine environment, but requires them to be "carried out in a manner consistent with the general principles and objectives" of the LOS convention.

Moreover, Part XV of the Convention subjects disputes concerning the interpretation or application of the Convention to compulsory, binding dispute settlement. Although there are certain exceptions to this principle, disputes concerning the Convention's articles on protection of the marine environment will generally be subject to the requirement of compulsory settlement.[11] Regional agreements which derogate from the Convention in violation of Article 311 would therefore be open to unilateral challenge by other states parties in one or other of the various fora on which the Convention confers jurisdiction.

The Convention is thus equipped with strong and sophisticated mechanisms intended to preserve its integrity and universality. On the other hand, while recognising that the problems of ocean space are 'closely interrelated' and 'need to be considered as a whole,[12] the Convention is replete with reference to regional rules, regional programmes, regional cooperation and so on. It makes specific provision for regional cooperation in the case of enclosed and semi-enclosed seas.[13] Moreover, in the case of fisheries management, regional coopertion and regulation are required if the provisions of the Convention[14] and the Implementation Agreement on Straddling and Highly Migratory Stocks, 1995[15] are to be implemented effectively. Part XII of the Convention dealing with protection of the marine environment, also makes significant reference to regional rules and standards in various contexts.

It is clear, therefore, that a global law of the sea can accommodate regional approaches to certain problems, including protection of the marine environment. There will be no necessary incompatibility with the LOS Convention, provided any regional arrangements are consistent with object and purpose of the Convention as set out in Article 237 and 311, and provided they comply with the framework for regulation of the marine environment established by Part XII.

3.1.c. Regionalism in Part XII of the LOS Convention

The interplay between globalism and regionalism in the law of the sea is too complex in Part XII of the LOS Convention. There is no doubt that the fundamental elements of the law of the marine environment—both conventional and customary—are found in these articles of the Convention. They not only build on pre-existing law, including prior regional agreements, but have provided the basis for subsequent developments, whether at global, regional or national level. There are important linkages between this part of the Convention and other, sectoral, treaties dealing with the marine environment, including the Convention on the Prevention of Marine Pollution by Dumping of Wastes and Other Matter (London [Dumping] Convention) and its successor Protocol of 1996,[16] as well as the International Convention for the Prevention of Pollution from Ships, 1973 as modified by the Protocol of 1978 (MARPOL 73/78[17] and other IMO conventions. Part XII also provided the framework for Chapter 17 of Agenda 21 of the Report of the Rio Conference on Environment and Development, 1992 and is specifically referred to in that report as representing the international law on the subject.[18] If that view is correct, then it is merely regional arrangements between parties to the Convention which must comply with the constraints of Part XII: so must regional arrangements between non-parties, who will be bound as a matter of customary law.[19]

While setting out a global framework of rules and principles governing marine pollution and protection of marine ecosystems, Part XII also reflects a pragmatic acceptance that, in certain instances, regional approaches will be necessary or more appropriate even within a broadly uniform and comprehensive global legal order. It does, however, treat different sources of pollution differently in this respect. Within the global framework, two contrasting models of regionalism can be noted—one restrictive, the other more liberal.[20]

3.1.d. The Restrictive Model of Regionalism

This model is exemplified by the provisions of the LOS Convention on dumping at sea and pollution from ships.[21] Here the function of regional rules or treaties is relatively limited: it is to reinforce enforcement and application of the global rules found in the LOS convention itself and in the London Convention, 1972 and MARPOL 73/78. These latter conventions are also global; neither permits regional derogation or the separate adoption of lower regional standards. Their purpose is to provide international *minimum* standards, especially for flag states, and the LOS Convention articles serve to reinforce this objective.

At the same time, some elements of regionalism are permissible even here. Although dumping at sea is now globally almost entirely prohibited,[22] regional treaties had for some time been more stringent than was required by the London Convention, 1972 in its original form.[23] Neither the LOS convention nor the London Convention in any way limits the freedom exercised by states to impose additional controls on dumping in response to the environmental circumstances of certain regional seas, including those, such as the Baltic, that are shallow and semi-enclosed.

The scope for regionalism with regard to pollution from ships is somehow more limited. In the interests of freedom of navigation, MARPOL 73/78 is not merely a minimum standard for flag states, it is also a maximum standard for exclusive economic zone regulation by coastal states.[24] There is some room for additional regional action, however, MARPOL 73/78 itself provides for stricter discharge rules in designated special areas,[25] while the LOS Convention does not prevent coastal states from exercising some control over navigation in environmentally sensitive areas,[26] or the exercise of port state control over compliance with international rules and standards.[27] Article 234 of the LOS Convention also permits additional measures to be taken nationally, or regionally to control pollution from ships in ice-covered areas, while Article 211(6) allows for other special areas to be designated by IMO. Under this article IMO has a special responsibility for ensuring that regional or national action affecting navigation falls within the narrow boundaries of acceptability under the LOS Convention and its own conventions. It is really only under Article 234 that there is a significant autonomous discretion conferred on coastal states.[28]

3.1.e. Liberal Model of Regionalism

The more liberal approach is found in the LOS Convention's articles on land-based (including airborne) sources of pollution, and in the practice of states on these. Here, although the negotiation of global rules and standards is encouraged by its Articles 207 and 212, no attempt is made in the LOS Convention either to impose a uniform global standard comparable to that for ships, or even a minimum standard comparable to that for dumping at sea. Indeed, no such global standards exist for land-based or airborne pollution, nor are they likely to be agreed, given the great diversity of sources and the widely differing socio-economic priorities of states hence asked to control pollution originating in industrial and agricultural activities. Instead, states are free to set their own standards of regulation, provided only that these meet the more general requirements of Article 194 of the LOS Convention. Briefly, this article requires states to take 'all measures consistent with this Convention that are necessary to prevent, reduce and control pollution of the marine environment from any source, using for this purpose the best practicable means at their disposal'. These measures must minimise to the fullest extent the release of toxic, harmful or noxious substances. States are free to take such measures nationally or jointly, including regionally, as they deem appropriate.

In practice, international action to tackle these sources of pollution remains almost entirely regional. Prior to the 1992 Rio Conference, no agreement could be reached on a stronger global approach to land-based marine pollution. Since Rio, there has been the adoption in 1995 of the non-binding Washington Declaration and the Global Plan of Action for the Protection of the Marine Environment from Land-Based Activities,[29] but this neither sets global standards of pollution control nor does it limit or preclude regional action.[30] Precisely because it does so little, it does not alter the liberal attitude of the LOS Convention towards regionalism in the control of these sources of pollution.

3.1.f. Conceptual Aspect of 'Region'

The terms 'region' or 'regional', both of which appear in the LOS Convention are not defined by that convention nor by any other relevant instrument, including Agenda 21. This omission has not hindered reliance on the concept of regionalism, it gives it an amorphous and open-textured character which makes any attempt at definition essentially descriptive rather than prescriptive.

Literature on the subject distinguishes two or possibly three senses in which the term 'region' has been used in a maritime context: the formal, the functional and the political.[31] A formal definition of a marine region would focus on its physical and geographical character, such as the fact that it is an enclosed or semi-enclosed sea. A functional definition would concentrate on patterns of use—resource exploitation, navigation, fisheries, defence and so on. A political region is essentially defined by little more than the decision of a group of states to cooperate, although some element of geographical propinquity may be implicit even here,[32] for example, an agreement among members of the British Commonwealth should probably not be described as 'regional' in any sense.

These descriptions are probably of more use in understanding how a particular region comes to be composed than in telling us what a region is. Not surprising, after considering the use of the term 'region' in the LOS Convention, it is not out of place to conclude that 'any kind of cooperation developed by states in a given part of the ocean is regional'.[33]

3.2. Regional Sea Agreements Relevant to Pollution

Two regional agreements focusing on regional sea management may serve as avenues for controlling land-based pollution: Paris Convention for the Protection of the Marine Environment of the North-East Atlantic, 1992 and the Convention on the Protection of the Marine Environment of the Baltic Sea Area, 1992 (the latter often referred to as the Helsinki Convention, 1992).

3.2.a. The Paris Convention, 1992

Applying to parties of the northeast Atlantic and Arctic Ocean, this Convention includes several provisions supportive of the precautionary and pollution prevention approaches. Parties are required by Article 2(2)(a) to apply the precautionary principle. Article 2(2)(a) requires parties to "take all possible steps to prevent and eliminate pollution" and "take the necessary measures to protect the maritime area against the adverse effects of human activities". Annex 1, detailing commitments on the prevention and elimination of land-based sources, calls for consideration of using clean technologies.[34]

3.2.b. The Helsinki Convention, 1992

The Baltic Sea, surrounded by nine countries (Denmark, Estonia, Finland, Germany, Latvia, Lithuania, Poland, Russia and Sweden) has a population of approximately 66 million living around its drainage basin area.[35] Thus, there is considerable potential for long-range transboundary atmospheric pollution from the region as well as the potential sources linked to the Arctic.

The Helsinki Convention, 1992 promotes precautionary and pollution prevention approaches in various ways. The parties are required to apply the precautionary principle where introduced substances or energy may create environmental hazards. The parties are further required to take all appropriate legislative and administrative measures to prevent and eliminate pollution, so as to promote ecological restoration and to preserve the ecological balance of the Baltic sea area. Annex 1, dealing with harmful substances, prohibits the use of certain substances, such as DDT and its derivatives and PCBs (except in closed system equipment). The Annex also bans (or at least requires reduction of) various pesticides, among them many types of POPs (persistent organic pollutants).

The Baltic Marine Environment Protection Commission (Helsinki Commission) has adopted numerous recommendations on land-based pollution measures. For example, at its meeting in March 1996, the Commission recommended reduction of atmospheric emissions from pulp and paper mills, waste water discharge standards of chemical industries, emission limits from incineration of household wastes and discharge reductions from textile plants.[36]

3.3. Implementation and Monitoring Bodies

In order to implement and monitor the international conventions the United Nations activate through some specific bodies. With regard to environment there are certain bodies which work to achieve the goal.

3.3.a. Framework Convention on Climate Change (UNFCC)

The Environmental Bodies as construed by the United Nations work in matters of environment. Each such body has a secretariat in the name Secretariat of the UN Framework. The Framework Convention on Climate Change (UNFCC) was opened for signature at the Earth Summit, 1992 (United Nations Conference on Environment and Development) in June 1992, and entered into force in March 1994. The Convention has received 188 instruments of ratification as of 17 February 2003.

> The Convention provides for a Conference of the Parties, as the supreme body (i.e., the highest decision-making authority), a subsidiary body for implementation, a subsidiary body on scientific and technological advice, and a secretariat. The 'ultimate objective' of the Convention is to stabilise greenhouse gas concentrations in the atmosphere at a level that would prevent dangerous anthropogenic interference with the climate system. Such a level is expected to be achieved within a time-frame sufficient to allow ecosystems to adapt naturally to climate change, to ensure

that food production is not threatened, and to enable economic development to proceed in a sustainable manner.

3.3.b. Intergovernmental Panel on Climate Change (IPCC)

The Intergovernmental Panel of Climate Change (IPCC) was established in 1988 jointly by the United Nations Environment Programme and World Meteorological Organization to:

Assess available factual information on the science, impacts and economics of climate change, and on the response options available to address it.

Assess, and develop as needed, methodologies such as the IPCC Guidelines for National Greenhouse Gas Inventories.

Provide, on request, scientific/technical/socio-economic advice to the Conference of the Parties to the UN Framework Convention on Climate Change (UNFCC) and its bodies.

All Member States of the UN and Members of the WMO are members of the IPCC. The Panel has three working groups: Group I (science), Group II (impacts, adaptation with associated costs) and Group III (mitigation with associated costs and cross-cutting issues).

The Panel makes decisions at its plenary sessions and is assisted by a Bureau comprising 30 members. It also has a Task Force on National Greenhouse Gas Inventories.

3.3.c. Ozone Secretariat, Secretariat for the Vienna Convention for the Protection of the Ozone Layer and the Montreal Protocol on Substances that Deplete the Ozone Layer

The Ozone Secretariat services the Vienna Convention for the Protection of the Ozone Layer and its Montreal Protocol on Substances that Deplete the Ozone Layer. The Ozone Secretariat was established and its duties defined by Article 7 of the Vienna Convention and Articles 12 and 14 of the Montreal Protocol.

The Vienna Convention for the Protection of the Ozone Layer was adopted in 1985 as a result of negotiations facilitated by UNP in cooperation with WMO. The Vienna Convention laid down a general commitment to protect the ozone layer and focuses on scientific cooperation. As of February 2003, 185 Parties had ratified the Convention. It is governed by a Conference of the Parties which meet every three years. The last meeting was held in Rome, Italy, in November 2002.

The Montreal Protocol sets targets for phasing out production and consumption of ozone-depleting substances, and included other measures for the protection of the ozone layer, including controls on trade in ozone-depleting substances and a multilateral fund for meeting the incremental costs of developing countries in implementing the control measures. As of February 2003, 184 Parties had ratified the Protocol.

3.3.d. Secretariat of the Convention on Biological Diversity (CBD)

The Convention on Biological Diversity was negotiated under UNEP auspices, and was signed by 157 countries at the 1992 Earth Summit (United Nations Conference on Environment and Development) in June 1992. It entered into force in December 1993, and has now been ratified by 186 countries and the European Community.

The Convention has three objectives: conservation of biological diversity; the sustainable use of its components; and the fair and equitable sharing of the benefits arising out of the utilisation of genetic resources, including by appropriate access to genetic resources and by appropriate transfer of relevant technologies, taking into account all rights over those resources and technologies, and by appropriate funding.

The Convention provides for a Conference of the Parties (COP), a Subsidiary Body on Scientific, Technical and Technological Advice (SBTTA) and a Secretariat. The Secretariat services the Conference of the Parties and its subsidiary bodies, performs functions assigned to it by any protocol, and coordinates with other international bodies and processes.

The Conference of the Parties has met six times and adopted work programmes on various thematic areas (forests, inland waters, marine and coastal, dry and sub-humid lands and agriculture biodiversity) and cross-cutting issues (traditional knowledge, innovations and practices, intellectual property rights, indicators, taxonomy, incentive measures, etc). Secretariat of the Convention on International Trade in Endangered Species of Wild Fauna and Flora (CITES) services the Convention on International Trade in Endangered Species of Wild Fauna and Flora. This Convention was adopted in March 1973 and entered into force in July 1975. It has been ratified by 161 countries as of 19 March 2003. The objective of the Convention is to ensure that no species of wild fauna or flora becomes or remains subject to unsustainable exploitation because of international trade. To this end it provides an international as well as national regulatory framework.

The Conference is governed by the Conference of the Parties, and serviced by a Standing Committee and by the Secretariat. The Animals and Plants Committees are Committees of the experts established to fill gaps in biological and other specialised knowledge regarding species of animals and plants that (or might become) subject to CITES trade controls, and their role is to provide technical support to decision-making about these specifies.[37]

As a matter of fact, marine issues are too multidimensional in the sense that there are many issues to be taken into consideration. It should be noted that marine matters that should be dealt with are (i) seabed, and ocean floor; (ii) subsoil of seabed and ocean floor; (iii) water area; and (iv) air space. Thus, the law of the sea seems to be concerned with four dimensional matters whereas the law of the land deals with (i) land surface, (ii) subsoil of the land, and (iii) air space. Whatever regime is designed regarding the marine environment, inevitable are the measures for implementation and monitoring. That is to say, if implementation and monitoring measures are practically taken, marine environment regime will be substantial.

As the marine matters are not a single party's concern, should be taken global, regional, sub-region and national measures to promote a legal regime to this end.

3.4. Legal Framework for Marine Pollution

The law regulating marine pollution draws from the same sources and follows the same law-making processes as international law generally. Thus, the legal framework governing marine pollution in the Bay of Bengal is undergirded by the sources of international law, including primarily international treaties, international customary law and general principles of law. However, the international legal framework for regulating marine pollution also draws considerably from so-called 'soft law' instruments that are formally non-binding and are often adopted through the decisions of international organisations. Not surprisingly, though international law governing marine pollution has developed since the early 1950s mainly through a process of multilateral actions, complemented by national actions.[38] The pillars of international marine pollution law today stand mainly as certain normative principles accepted as customary law and as various international conventions intended to regulate pollution activities in the oceans. First, to undergird contemporary international environmental law, a customary norm has arisen embodying the general obligation to protect the marine environment from pollution. This general norm has evolved from the entire body of legal instruments adopted relating to marine pollution, and is clearly and explicitly codified in Article 192 of the LOS Convention, 1982: 'States have the obligation to protect and preserve the marine environment'.[39]

As a second principle, states are obliged not to transfer pollution from one area to another or to transform one type of pollution to another. As stipulated by Article 195 of the LOS Convention:

> In taking measures to prevent, reduce and control pollution of the marine environment, States shall act so as not to transfer, directly or indirectly, damage or hazardous from one area to another or transform one type of pollution into another.

Finally, environmental monitoring and assessment also emerge as autonomous and effective obligations for protection of the marine environment. International norms on marine pollution thus tend to have certain basic contents. They include mainline fundamental rules (rules that prohibit activities or establish standards) and enforcement rules, normally coupled with safeguards. Marine pollution norms usually provide for rules on global and regional cooperation, including environmental monitoring and assessment, technical assistance and varying kinds of responsibility for pollution, liability and settlement of environmental disputes. This general framework is set out in the Environmental Protocol, 1991 for specific application.[40] There is then an opening to apply these norms in the protection and preservation of marine environment in any area of the sea and hence, in the Bay of Bengal.

3.5. Towards the Bay of Bengal Marine Environment

The Bay of Bengal as part of the Indian Ocean is not unknown but there is no comprehensive work exclusively concerned with its environment. The piecemeal works of UNEP Regional Seas Programme (RSP), the East and South Asian Seas are—along with the Southwest Atlantic and the Black Sea—those regions where comprehensive-sectoral frameworks are under preparation.[41] Although the two regions have their distinct characteristics, they directly border each other and form an important parts of the wider Indian Ocean region, with the East Asian Seas also bordering the West Pacific.

Within the RSP context, all surrounding regions—the Persian Gulf, Red Sea and Gulf of Aden, Eastern Africa, and Southwest Pacific—are already covered by complex Action Plans and regional Conventions with respective Protocols. The East and South Asian Seas' frameworks form, thus, an important missing link in adequate coverage of the wider Indian Ocean region and its transposition into the Pacific.

The two missing frameworks are at present nearing completion. In particular, the two UNEP Meetings of Legal and Technical Experts to review the Proposed Legal Frameworks of the Action Plans for the South Asian Seas (SAS) and East Asian Seas (EAS) regions, held in Bangkok on 5-8 and 12-15

February 1990 respectively, have revised the draft conventions together with two draft protocols on dumping and on pollution emergencies to be adopted in these regions.[42] The EAS region is somewhat more advanced, as its Manila Action Plan for the Protection and Development of the Marine and Coastal Areas was already adopted in 1981.[43] In the SAS region—which was included into RSP—an Action Plan is only under preparation.[44]

By and large, the progress in both the EAS and SAS regions has been perceived as rather slow, giving rise to growing criticism. The momentum of the initial phase of the Action Plan for the region has been steadily decreasing since its adoption. The low level of the East Asian Seas Trust Fund, the exclusion of international and intergovernmental organizations from the Plan's implementation, and the failure of most of the implementation projects to have any real impact on the management of the region's environmental problems have all contributed to the lack of real progress.[45]

Although partly justified, addressing of above criticism only to the EAS region seems somewhat exaggerated, as similar pessimism could also be raised in relation to SAS and other developing state RSP regions.[46] The study of Peter Sand—the Principal Legal Officer of the United Nations Conference on Environment and development seems to be viable. He rightly submits that our generation bears a heavier responsibility for the future of Earth than any generation before it has, because first "we know better" and second "we can do better."[47] In the context of the marine environment, this approach is based on Sand's recognition of "the integenerational social contract or 'planetary trust' between ourselves and those yet unborn members of the human specifies whose survival will depend on our ability to preserve the Blue Planet's marine sphere".[48]

One could add to it that since industrialized states both know and can do better than the developing countries, the former states bear a special responsibility for preserving the environment of our planet Earth. This, as Edith Brown Weiss would put it, is an aspect of "intergenerational" equity which requires attention for the purpose of the fulfilment of "intergenerational" obligations for the environment.[49]

Keeping this aspect in mind, several factors require to be addressed that may be of relevance in assessing specific prospects for the East and South Asian Seas regions.[50]

The role played by UNEP in RSP in general and in EAS and SAS in particular is one of important factors in assessment of prospects for the two regions. As a matter of policy, UNEP plays a catalytic and generally coordinating role by providing financial and institutional support in the initial stage of regional programs covered by the RSP, upon understanding that the states concerned will take over responsibility for the implementation of respective Action Plans.

The problem is that since cooperation in developing state regions will require outside financial and other support for at least a generation, the presently limited UNEP's catalytic role could be considered sufficient only if sound mechanisms of development cooperation (aid) with industrialized states and the competent international organizations existed otherwise this, however, is clearly not yet the case in the present inter-state relations, in which the impressive commitments of the developed states,[51] are in practice countered by their clearly self-protective and ruthlessly paternalistic measures. From amongst a wide range of complex factors involved, one could mention a strong preference by the donor developed states to fund bilateral development cooperation with a view to reinforce their foreign policy objectives, rather than to support multilateral program which are indispensable for promotion of the protection of the environment in general and of marine environment in particular.[52]

Problems for promoting any development work for developing countries are not only due to lacking of funds but also a lack of cordial cooperation. Economic constraints and political instability have been so far obstacles to their development. In spite of that organizational efforts are indispensable to ameliorate their position in particular in marine environment. National and organizational efforts should aim to do as such. That is to say, more effective arrangements must be provided to ensure the effective and comprehensive coordination and direction of environmental activities in the

United Nations system to enable it to meet the new and expanding requirements placed upon by the ever-increasing urgency and complexity of international and related environmental challenges facing the international community. Due to the innumerable drawbacks and problems of developing countries, it is not easy to overcome their problems, but it would appear that industrialized states, with their incomparable advantages in terms of knowledge and means to act, bear a primary responsibility for this process.

Amongst the problems requiring an adequate perspective is a global strategic sensitivity to the East and South Asian Seas regions, which coupled with the particular—as compared to other RSP areas—complexity of inter-state relations in both these regions, makes any undertakings of regional states especially difficult.[53]

States bordering the South China Sea—which have a long history of interplay with non-regional powers and which so far merely partly participate in the UNEP EAS program—only since 1990s to consider advantages of developing "a sense of community" amongst themselves, and of transforming the South China Sea from a potential for conflict into a potential for cooperation.[54] As Douglas Johnston and Mark Valencia emphasize, it is only now that for the first time it seems realistic to review a range of diplomatic options available to the parties to some of the most serious disputes, and in some cases to evaluate the merits of fairly ambitious experiments in cooperative development and management of marine resources.[55]

A notable step towards such cooperative development is reflected by the initiation of negotiations between both the "blue South" (non-communist) members of the Association of South-East Asian Nations (ASEAN) and the "red North" (China, Vietnam and Kampuchea) Southeast Asian states on cooperation in the South China Sea, especially the disputed Spratly Islands.[56] Meaningfully, these negotiations—notwithstanding their essential importance for regional states concerned—are carried out on the basis of non-regional (in particular Canadian) funding as supported by Indonesia. A complex and politically sensitive situation in the region clearly explains the reasons for what is perceived as slow progress in the UNEP EAS program.

The five Indian Ocean states participating in the UNEP SAS program, i.e., India, Pakistan, Maldives, Bangladesh, Sri Lanka, are not divided by such strong ideological differences as are the EAS states. All these five states, along with the land-locked Bhutan and Nepal, are the members of a major political organization, the South Asian Association for Regional Cooperation (SAARC), and also participate (except for two land-locked states) in the UN Ad Hoc Committee on the Indian Ocean.

However, apart from its geostrategic sensitivity and its level of economic development considerably lower than that of the EAS region, the SAS region would appear to be disadvantaged in terms of any cooperative efforts due to divergent security perceptions of its bordering states, and especially India's increasing military (including nuclear) power and domination in South Asia. India's hegemonism, accompanied by its almost obsessed reluctancy to accept foreign funding, e.g., for the development of SAARC and for cooperation of SAARC with pro-Western oriented ASEAN or even with such an innocuous organization as the Canadian International Development Research Centre (CIDRC), while strengthening India's authority, impedes at the same time the development of a meaningful cooperation in the region.[57]

For instance, India not only did not join a remarkable regional effort aimed to develop ocean affairs through the Indian Ocean Marine Affairs Cooperation (IOMAC), but also actively discourages bilateral and multilateral donors from extending their support to this new organization.[58] This example also illustrates the complexity of factors which render development cooperation an extremely difficult and sometimes ineffective process. In particular, through exerting just political influence to effectively prevent a major UN regional commission, the Economic and Social Commission for Asia and the Pacific (ESCAP), from funding IOMAC's activities, India importantly diminished IOMAC's chances, as the bilateral donors would, by means of procedural routine, direct funding of regional programmes such as IOMAC to ESCAP, which in this case remains inoperative. This is particularly regrettable in view of IOMAC's potential for activating integrated ocean management with a view to meet the formidable demands of regional states for resources located in the Indian Ocean.

The political and socio-economic situation in the EAS and SAS regions, apart from affecting to varying degrees the actual operation of marine affairs cooperation in these regions, is also of important influence on the geographical scope of the respective sea areas covered. In 1988, Peter San suggested that:

> It would indeed be futile to rationalize in respect of the geographical selection and delimitation of these [UNEP] regions, which was to a very large extent dictated by *pragmatic considerations of political feasibility* (emphasis added).[59]

A detailed discussion on EAS regions, ASEAN, UNEP and RSP matters gives rise to inter-regional cooperation to be promoted.[60] That means, EAS coverage extended to at least the whole of Southeast Asia could also provide a basis for adequate inter-regional cooperation between the EAS and SAS. Such inter-regional collaboration, which generally appears to be rather underestimated within the UNEP-RSP, would be of major importance for subregions which are bordered by states of both these regions. This relates especially to the Andaman Sea, bordered by Myanmar, Thailand, Malaysia, Indonesia, and India, and to the Bay of Bengal, bordered by Bangladesh, Myanmar, India, Indonesia, Malaysia, Maldives, Sri Lanka, and Thailand. Myanmar is the most isolated amongst these states and presently participates in neither of the two programmes.[61] Some basis for cooperative interaction between these states is already provided by the IOMAC as well as programmes such as the FAO-IPFC and the Committee for the Development and Management of Fisheries in the Bay of Bengal (BOBC) of the FAO Indian Fishery Commission (IOFC).[62]

It is viewed that integrated ocean management in both the EAS and SAS regions would, moreover, importantly benefit from the adoption of the Protected Areas Protocol.[63] Finally, it seems worth mentioning that both EAS and SAS states are directly concerned with the problems pertaining to ecological and socio-economic impacts of global warming,[64] as evidenced by the International Conference on Global Warming and Climate Change from Developing Countries Perspective, which was organized by the Tata Energy Research Institute (New Delhi) in association with Woods Hole Oceanographic Institution (USA) and with the co-sponsorship of UNEP in New Delhi in February 1989. The Conference expressed serious concern with the issue of sea level rise and recommended the setting up by regional organizations such as SAARC or ASEAN of Regional Climate Monitoring and Management Boards. Another conference held on this issue in Maldives in November 1989 adopted the Male Declaration on Global Warming and Sea Level Rise, which provided for development of a programme of action for cooperation and exchange of information on strategies in relation to climate change, global warming, and sea level rise. The importance of these issues has specifically been recognized by the July 1990 ASEAN Ministerial Meeting on the Environment, which recommended establishment of a working group to assess the implications of the proposed Framework Convention on Climate Change to the ASEAN region.

The ongoing approaches of the EAS and SAS region states enable to reiterate that prospects for political accommodation of divergent national positions, which would further pave the way to effective regional cooperation, may be more apparent in the case of EAS and SAS. But these prospects could be enhanced in both regions if UNCED succeeded in stimulating adequate adjustments of the coordinating mechanisms within UNEP and respective funding agencies. The Bay of Bengal littoral states should take views for protecting and preserving marine environment not only for national interests but also for regional interests. This will result as a part in promoting global objectives for mankind as a whole.

3.6. Towards International Regime

In governing the relation of states, traditional international law focused on recognizing and preserving each state's sovereignty. Its underlying assumption was the freedom of control over activities within a state's national jurisdiction. The 1933 Montevideo Convention on the Rights and Duties of State sets out the fundamental character of this freedom. It provides that "no state has the right to intervene in the internal or external affairs of another."[65] Early in its history, the United States Supreme Court affirmed the principle of the "full and absolute territorial jurisdiction...of every sovereign."[66]

International law clearly emerged and developed unaware of and seemingly unaffected by global environmental interdependence. The scope of activities taking place within national jurisdictions, but which affect the environmental interests of the international community, is larger than previously imagined. The basic linkages between actions and effects in different parts of the world are being recognized in the depletion of the ozone layer, the threat of global climate change, and the loss of the world's genetic diversity. From an environmental perspective, political boundaries have little meaning.[67]

State responsibility with regard to international environmental law is unclear at best. However, such responsibility is developing through both customary international law and international case law. The principle of state responsibility for international environmental damage showed its face in 1935 during a dispute between the United States and Canada. The United States complained to the Canadian government that sulphur fumes discharged from the smelter of Consolidated Mining and Smelting located in Trail, British Columbia, caused damage in the State of Washington.[68] The smelter located on the Columbia River about eleven miles from the Washington border emitted sulphur dioxide as a result of its lead and zinc ore smelting operations. The dioxide drifted down the Columbia River Valley and harmed crops, woodlands and fisheries in the State of Washington. The United States and Canada established which was authorized to "apply the principles of both in international law and of the jurisprudence developed by the United States courts in disputes between states of the Union."[69]

The tribunal concluded that "No State has the right to use or permit the use of its territory in such a manner as to cause injury by fumes in or to the territory of another State or the properties or persons therein, when the case is of serious consequence and the injury is established by clear and convincing evidence."[70] The court also held that "A State owes at all times a duty to protect other States against injurious acts by individuals within its jurisdiction."[71]

Conventional international law recognized the potential problems of unfettered action within state boundaries. The earliest limitations on activities within national boundaries consisted of narrow formulations based on the general international law obligation that no State should permit its territory to be used to harm its neighbours. In the *Corfu Channel* case, the International Court of Justice decided that every State is under an obligation "not to allow knowingly its territory to be used for acts contrary to the rights of other States."[72] This case involved a dispute between the United Kingdom and Albania. The United Kingdom complained to the Albanian government that a minefield in its (Albanian) territorial waters cause the deaths and/or injuries of 44 British officers and men in the international seaway of the Corfu Strait. In addition, the U.K. complained that the Albanian government did not notify as to the existence of the mines in accord with both international law and the Hague Convention.[73]

The issue presented to the International Court of Justice was whether "Albania was responsible under international law for the explosions which occurred on the 22nd October 1946 in Albanian waters and for the damage and loss of human life which resulted from them and is there any duty to pay compensation."[74] The International Court concluded that Albania was indeed responsible for the explosions and the resultant damage and loss of life.[75] The court concluded that it had jurisdiction to determine the amount of compensation but held that further proceedings were necessary before reaching any specific amount.[76] Yet, in the context of extensive transboundary effects caused by global environmental problems, such a narrowly formulated limitation on national sovereignty is not sufficient.

The international law principle that a state must refrain causing damage in other states has been applied for many years in domestic property law under the term *sic utero tuo ut alienum non laedas*, which prohibits the use of one's property in any manner that injures another's property.[77] Another case often cited is the *Lake Lanoux Arbitral Decision* of 1957 which reiterated the *sic utero* principle in the international environment.[78] In this decision, the International Arbitration Awards panel concluded that France did not violate Spain's rights by replacing water flow from France into Spain from another source.[79]

The Restatement (Third) of the Foreign Relations Law of the United States addresses the issue of State responsibility in the international community. In Section 601(1)(b), the Restatement makes clear that a State is obliged to "Ensure that activities within its jurisdiction are conducted so as not to cause significant injury to the environment of another State or of areas beyond the limits of national jurisdiction." In addition, sub-section (3) makes clear that a state is responsible for any such serious injury to person or property.[80] What does that responsibility include? A state may be held responsible for its activities as well as the activities of individuals and private corporations under its jurisdiction.[81] Consequently, a State which is injured by acts of another State is entitled to money damages under a proximate cause theory.[82] In January 1990, the International Law Commission produced a draft on the topic of "International Liability for the Injurious Consequences of Acts Not Prohibited by International Law." The commission relied on environmental protection precedents such as the *Trail Smelter Arbitration* and the *Corfu Channel Case*.[83]

There have been several attempts to go beyond the more restrictive traditional interpretations of sovereignty. The last thirty-two years since the 1972 Stockholm Conference on the Human Environment has evidenced the increasing international and national concern for environmental protection. There has been a growing realization that the ecosystem is complex and interrelated and the approach to combat environmental harm must also be interrelated and integrated among States.

International law has been based on the relationship between independent States that exercise exclusive national sovereignty over their territories. Global change is altering this vision by causing States to realize that they are locked together in sharing the use of a common global environment. While human activities have always contributed to environmental change, it is only within the last half of this century that their effects have become global and serious, and in many cases irreversible. This has led to a growing awareness that the interests of humankind must not constrain the interests of individual States. Moreover, actors other than States have become essential to managing global environmental change. These developments are leading to a fundamental shift in the paradigm of international law that is evolving in the international environmental field.

3.7. International Conferences Impasse

Concern primarily shown by industrialized countries about the serious risk of environmental harm to countries around the world motivated to convene the 1972 Conference on the Human Environment.

At the time of Stockholm Conference countries were deeply divided over the issue of whether environmental protection and economic development were compatible. The conceptual breakthrough that provided the paradigm for joining these two important goals emerged from a meeting of experts held in Founex, Switzerland, just prior to the Stockholm Conference. Today countries recognize that sound economic development must be environmentally sustainable and are concerned about how to do this. They realize that we need to substantially increase the living standards of the poor in a manner that is environmentally sustainable. This issue in 1992 that divides countries is an equity one: how to finance environmentally sustainable economic development for present and future generations.

Twenty years after the Stockholm Conference, countries are concerned with global environmental problems that were then, either not yet identified or barely addressed. These include acid precipitation, ozone depletion, climate change, hazardous wastes disposal, loss of biological diversity, and forest degradation and loss and land-based sources of pollution.[84]

In the past, pollution and environmental degradation have operated largely on the local level and hence their effects have been isolated in impact. Given the increasingly global scale of environmental degradation and the ever-increasing volume of pollutants entering the environment, however, their effects are now being felt on regional and global levels. In addition, the scope and irreversible nature of some global changes reach through time to affect the well-being of future generations.

Marine pollution has caused great concern for several decades. Under the auspices of the International Maritime Organization (IMO), formerly called the International Maritime Consultative Organization (IMCO), the United Nations Environmental Programme (UNEP) and regional oganizations, many conventions have been adopted dealing with *inter alia,* design and construction of ships, oil pollution damage, a compensation fund, the dumping of wastes at sea.[85]

There are a number of regional agreements dealing with the maritime environment.[86] But the efficacy of the conventions has been frustrated to a great extent by lack of ratification and lack of consequent necessary domestic implementation. Enforcement mechanisms are at present seen to some extent existing but practically not effective. At the 1992 United Nations Conference on Environment and Development in Rio de Janeiro emphasis was laid on the crucial need for such full participation.

The most ambitious attempt to protect the marine environment is to be found in the provisions of the 1982 Convention on the Law of the Sea. At the onset of negotiations, Canada, among other states, in a working paper presented to the Seabed Committee called for treaty provisions which would provide a comprehensive framework for the conclusion of a complete network of treaties dealing with all aspects of marine pollution.[87] This approach is reflected in the 1982 Convention, Part XII which [now that it is in force since November 1994] will have the effect of committing all states parties to taking measures, nationally and internally, to prevent pollution from the principal sources of marine pollution: land, sea, continental shelf and atmosphere. States parties will be under an obligation to conclude international conventions dealing with the different manifestations of pollution of the marine environment or to take measures at least as effective as "generally accepted international standards." Failure to leave up to such minimum international standards will constitute a violation of the Law of the Sea Convention and in appropriate circumstances will give rise to state responsibility.

The Convention contains general provisions committing states to protect the marine environment from pollution from all sources and prohibiting the transfer of pollution from one area to another.[88] The text also provides for global and regional cooperation, notification of other states in the event of imminent or actual damage, the preparation of data, and technical assistance. The subsequent articles will have the effect of committing states to develop national and international rules on pollution from land-based sources, seabed activities, and ocean dumping. Complementary articles deal with enforcement of these rules. Articles 211 and 217 to 236 deal with pollution caused by ships. Traditional flag state obligations are somewhat strengthened. Most noteworthy are the new rules allowing limited jurisdiction to 'coastal' and 'port' states to enforce international rules and standards against foreign ships in strictly defined circumstances. Of great interest to Canada is article 234 allowing coastal states broad jurisdiction to adopt and enforce their own rules for the prevention, reduction and control of marine pollution from ships in "ice-covered areas" within the limits of the exclusive economic zone. This authority shall have due regard to navigation.

Perhaps the most significant development of the Convention is the duty set out in Article 194(2) not to "cause damage by pollution to other states and their environment" which, coupled with Article 235 on liability and responsibility, will make states liable for damages attributable to ensure prompt adequate recourse against persons under their jurisdiction who cause pollution affecting other states or their nationals. Failure to respect this obligation or other international treaty obligations will make the state responsible and liable to compensate the injured party. States parties are obliged to cooperate also in the development of criteria and procedures for payment of adequate compensation, such as compulsory insurance or compensation funds.[89]

The 1982 Convention on the Law of the Sea and related treaties have significantly developed the rules of international law applicable to the preservation of the marine environment and illustrate the evolution of state responsibility. In point of fact, states are under the obligation to ensure that activities under their jurisdiction or control "are so conducted as not to cause damage by pollution to other states and their environment" and that any pollution arising from such activities "does not spread beyond the areas where they exercise sovereign rights." The activities included in this obligation are those undertaken both by the state and by entities of a private nature under state jurisdiction and control. It is also quite apparent that this provision covers not only transboundary effects of pollution but also harm to areas beyond national jurisdiction. In other words, the global scale of environmental effects is incorporated into this particular regime.

This regime encompasses all sources of pollution, a further indication of the broadening concern and scope of international law. In addition, a broad definition of pollution of the marine environment is included in this and other treaty regimes as an expression of the very same concern. Important IMO and related conventions have developed a well-structured normative regime dealing with specific questions of marine pollution particularly in terms of oil pollution, discharge and dumping of waste, and safety at sea. To all intents and purposes, the conferences, global and regional gave impasses to environmental regime internationally to activate interests of all states in check and balance process through an intergenerational equity regime.

As a practical consideration, the largest contributors to ocean pollution, as well as to air pollution, are the industrial nations. Their ranks will be swollen when the developing nations acquire their factories and plants. The problem will not go away; it will increase in intensity. The problem cannot be solved by one nation alone. Its solution will require cooperative action of all nations.[90] The legal regime of marine environment in any area of the ocean seeks concerned states cooperation for its protection and preservation. Climatically, the Bay of Bengal littoral states seem identical, but practically their interests are so diverse. Whatever factors are seen to be involved, in marine environment matters they need to come close to promote a sound and effective legal regime of environment in the Bay of Bengal.

3.8. Essence of Marine Environment

There have been several attempts to go beyond the more restrictive traditional interpretations of sovereignty. The 1872 United Nations Conference on the Human environment held in Stockholm represented the first international forum to consider the protection of the environment on a comprehensive basis.[91] The Stockholm Conference issued a Declaration on the Human Environment and adopted twenty-six Principles meant to inspire and set down the basic tenets for world cooperation to preserve and enhance the human environment. A key provision at the Stockholm Conference involved Principle 21, This principle recognized the consequences of the global environment of a definition of national sovereignty limited only by a narrow interpretation of transboundary effects. The following adopted text attempts to define the relationship between a nation's freedom of action over its natural resources and its responsibility to prevent extraterritorial damage:

> States have, in accordance with the Charter of the United Nations and the principles of international law, the sovereign right to exploit their own resources pursuant to their own environmental policies and the responsibility to

ensure that activities within their jurisdiction or control do not cause damage to the environment of other States or areas beyond the limits of national jurisdiction.[92]

Although unanimously adopted in solemn form by the Conference, the Declaration and Principles are not technically binding. The Principle protecting state sovereignty limits legal obligations to those instances in which a state consents to be bound. While consent does not have to be explicit, consensus on a Declaration or a Principle is not commitment to any legal obligation.[93]

Guidelines, declarations, and principles are essentially an effective, non-threatening way to encourage cooperation among states with different views on the appropriate response to a particular problem. The negotiation and adoption of the Principles in their domestic laws in this important global forum does, however, imbue them with normative impact. As a result, states may well implement certain Principles, thereby facilitating their subsequent development into customary international law.[94]

Support for the Stockholm Principles, and particularly Principles 21 and 22, was confirmed by the General Assembly of the United Nations in Resolution 2996(XXVII).[95] General Assembly Resolution 2996 states that Principles 21 and 22 effectively set out the basic rules governing international environmental law and provides further that no resolution adopted at the 27th session should negatively impact those Principles.[96] As a matter of international law, however, the effect of resolutions issued by the United Nations General Assembly is virtually identical to that of the Stockholm Declaration and Principles themselves. That is, the General Assembly of the United Nations is empowered to "initiate studies and make recommendations for the purpose of... encouraging the progressive development of international law and its codification."[97] Thus, although these resolutions adopting declarations, recommendations, or principles are evidence of customary international law, they are not themselves a form of international legislation. Indeed, the General Assembly has recommended its resolutions be taken into consideration by the International Court of Justice as one way in which "the development of international law may be reflected."[98]

Beyond its recognition of the Stockholm Principles, the General Assembly of the United Nations has taken other similar stances. Despite reaffirming the principle of the permanent sovereignty of states over natural resources on a number of occasions,[99] the General Assembly solemnly invited Member States in Resolution 35/7 "to conduct their activities in recognition of the supreme importance of protecting natural systems, maintaining the balance and quality of nature and conserving natural resources, in the interests of present and future generations."[100]

Both Principle 21 and General Assembly Resolution 35/7 are important because to some extent they go beyond the more restrictive traditional interpretation of sovereignty. Principle 21 holds the state responsible for all activities within its territory. It also proclaims a state's duty to protect "areas beyond the limits of national jurisdiction." Meanwhile, Resolution 35/7 refers specifically to the interests of future generations, thereby implying that there may be an obligation to prevent damage to those interests.

The Principle and Resolution, however, are limited in their effect. In particular, Principle 21 does not detail the actions that states are expected to take to prevent environmental damage nor is it explicit about the nature of a state's liability should extraterritorial damage occur. Similarly, Resolution 35/7 goes no further than simply inviting Member States to consider its content. The lack of detail and more forceful language indicates adopting a general rule of state environmental responsibility. Thus, both the Principle and the Resolution can be seen as manifestations of the evolution of thought in the 1970s and early 1980s on the relationship of sovereignty to state responsibility for environmental protection.[101]

In international forum since the United Nations Conference on Trade and Development (UNCTAD), 1964 seems to be dialogue of differentiation on a matter of interest between the developing nations and the developed states. States have not been able to reconcile the concept of national sovereignty with the need for a global approach to environmental problems. Indeed, the tension between nationalism and internationalism appears to cause the North-South gap replaced the East-West struggle in international relations.

At the Ministerial Conference on Environment and Development held in Beijing from June 18-19, 1991 forty-one developing countries declared:

> International cooperation in the field of environmental protection should be based on the principle of equality among sovereign states. The developing countries have the sovereign right to use their own natural resources in keeping with their developmental and environmental objectives and principles. Furthermore, environmental considerations should not be used as an excuse for interference in the international affairs of the developing countries, nor should these be used to introduce any forms of conditionality in aid or development financing or to impose trade barriers affecting the export and development efforts of the developing countries.[102]

The Group of 77, composed of most of the governments of developing countries from Asia, Africa, Latin America, and the Caribbean, reiterated the sentiment when at the summit of the Preparatory Committee and Development held in Geneva in August and September 1991, it stated: "We haven't come here to negotiate away our permanent sovereignty over natural resources." Thus, it seems clear that developing countries continue to view a global approach to the environmental dilemma as an effort to challenge traditional notions of national sovereignty.

The essence of environmental matters stands in two avenues—avenues of the developing nations and the avenues of the developed countries. As to genetic and technological resources it is quite interesting to see pro-sovereignty claim of the developing states and pro-global free access approach of the developed countries.

3.9. Pro-Sovereignty Claim v. Pro-Free Global Access Approach

The issues of sovereignty and responsibility are most graphically displayed in the discussions surrounding the question of access to genetic resources and technology. The provisions on access impinge on the national economic interests of both developed and developing countries. Developing countries emphasize that access to genetic resources shall not be free and must also be linked with access to technology.[103] Developing countries assert that they will not tolerate any obligation which they perceive as an infringement of their sovereign rights. By contrast, industrialized countries argue for a system of 'open' access[104] to genetic resources. They speak in terms of global responsibility for a resource they would prefer to regard as part of the common heritage of humankind. In response, developing countries are wary of the industrialized world's enthusiasm for habitat set-asides and for concepts that regard genetic resources as the common heritage of humankind.[105] They fear the possible impact of the North's supported concepts and implied obligations on their fragile economies.

In asserting their sovereign rights over genetic resources and resisting obligations, developing countries effectively emphasize the first half of Stockholm Principle 21 on national sovereignty. In contrast, industrialized countries are paying due regard to the second half of the Principle as they promote some formulation of a common heritage regime and qualifying national sovereignty over genetic resources. In effect, industrialized countries maintain that conservation responsibilities are attached to a common heritage resource. Under this interpretation, the prevention of extraterritorial harm would be broadened to include responsibility for actions which unsustainably deplete the common heritage resource.[106]

The declining state of the global environment demonstrate that the traditional legal order must evolve or be superseded. Protection of the environment must be translated into a legal duty and not simply a political preference. Traditional customary international law actually gave license to damaging behaviour by its principle of national sovereignty. The limitation that territory not be knowingly used to harm the territory of another state was an attempt to moderate the harsh effect of a unconstrained principle of national sovereignty. Principle 21 of the Stockholm Declaration recognized that the real issue is one of state responsibility. The Principle moved the development of international law forward through its effort to express the basic rule of state responsibility for environmental protection.

It is now time to clarify the notion of state responsibility for environmental protection. It is no longer sufficient to talk of state responsibility for environmental damage. The context must change to reflect state responsibility for the preservation of global environmental well-being. Global environmental interrelatedness requires a corresponding rule that states the international environmental responsibility of individual states.

The loss of biological diversity, like the depletion of the ozone layer and climate change, is caused by a variety of factors, the effects of which may neither be immediately felt nor readily identified. Nevertheless, it is precisely this kind of environmental harm for which states must collectively take responsibility despite the implications for national sovereignty.

National boundaries have become so porous that traditional distinctions between local, national, and international issues have become blurred. Policies formerly considered to be exclusively matters of "national concern" now have an impact on the ecological bases of other nations' development and survival. Conversely, the growing reach of some nations' policies—economic, trade, monetary, and most sectoral policies—into the "sovereign" territory of other nations limits the affected nation' options in devising national solutions to their 'own' problems. This fast-changing context for national action has introduced new imperatives and new opportunities for international cooperation.

The international legal framework must also be significantly strengthened in support of sustainable development. Although international law related to environment has evolved rapidly since the 1972 Stockholm Conference, major gaps and deficiencies must still be overcome as part of the transition to sustainable development.[107]

The origins of sustainable development results in follow-up to two previous studies on the future of the world after the year 2000—one by former German Prime Minister Willie Brandt and the other by Scandinavian leader, Olfe Palme—and United Nations General Assembly resolution, No. 38/161, the World Commission on Environment and Development was set up. The UN asked Mrs. Gro Harlem Brundtland, Prime Minister of Norway, to chair the Commission in December, 1983. Their purpose would be to formulate a "global agenda for change" which would among other goals, (1) "propose long-term environmental strategies for achieving sustainable development by the year 2000 and beyond" and (2) "recommend ways in which concern for the environment may be translated into greater co-operation among developing countries..." The Commission was comprised of 22 members in addition to Mrs. Brundtland. With the exception perhaps of William Ruckelschaus from the United States, the commissioners were from socialist (including social democrat), fascist or communist countries. Two of the more interesting members of the Commission are Maurice Strong who called for the first UN environmental conference in 1972, who served as Secretary-General of United Nations Environment Programme and who was the Secretary-General of the "Rio Earth Summit" in 1992 and Sir Shridath Ramphal who was co-Chairman of The Commission for Global Governance, the group which succeeded the World Commission. Their study, *Our Global Neighbourhood*, appears to carry the globalist agenda to a final conclusion environmentally, legally, socially and economically.[108]

Our Common Future is considered one of the main reference books of the UN environmental agenda as it contains the official UN definition of sustainable development which is "development that meets the needs of the present without compromising the ability of future generations to meet their own needs." It goes on to define "needs" to mean the world's poor "to which overriding priority should be given and the idea of limitations imposed by the state of technology and social organization on the environment's ability to meet present and future needs." The reports of the Commission's three Advisory Panels were published under the titles *Energy 2000, Industry 2000,* and *Food 2000* and are constantly referred to by the UN today.

Where does the concept of sustainable development come from? First, it is part of the Declaration of the UN Conference on the Human Environment, chaired in 1972 by Maurice Strong. In their Declaration, Principle 1 states, "Man has the fundamental right to freedom, equality and adequate conditions of life, in an environment of a quality that permits a life of dignity and well-being, and he bears a solemn responsibility to protect and improve the environment for present and future generations." Another principle (Principle 2) states, "The natural resources of the earth, including the air, water, land, flora and fauna and especially representative samples of natural ecosystems, must be safeguarded for the benefit of present and future generations through careful planning or management, as appropriate."

Since this concept is not found in the US Constitution, the writer started to look at socialism and communism and found it in the 1977 Constitution of the USSR, Chapter 2, Article 18 e.g.

In the interests of the present and future generations, the necessary steps are taken in the USSR to protect and make scientific, rational use of the land and its mineral and water resources, and the plant and animal kingdoms, to preserve the purity of air and water, ensure reproduction of natural wealth, and improve the human environment.

To understand how accepted sustainable development is at the global level, the Prince of Wales delivered a keynote address to the World Commission on Environment and Development on April 11, 1992 in which he said,

> There is little doubt that your commission's report, in 1987, was the single most important document of the decade on this subject, bringing the phrase 'sustainable development into all our vocabularies.... Your commission also pointed out the importance of democracy and

> individual participation in achieving a more sustainable world....' the future of our planet is in the balance...we should not, I believe, just be 'managing the Earth's resources more efficiently' (relying on a traditional utilitarian ethic), but seeking to live in balance with the rest of creation, even if we cannot discern any direct and immediate material benefit to ourselves...this of course, points to the need for a fundamental shift in attitudes...a new triad should be recognized: environment plus development plus democracy...A first requirement will be a strong commitment by one and all to create a balance, within nations, between nations and between generations.

The Rio Declaration of Environment and Development, 1992 has promoted basically the essence of Stockholm Declaration. Principle 21 (Stockholm Declaration) is embodied in Principle 2 (Rio Declaration), in addition, the Rio has taken into account more economic parameters to be concerned with environment and development. It has innovated "sustainable development"[109] and given stress on equitable economic regime to prevail. Principle 8 of the Rio Declaration addresses:

> To achieve sustainable development and a higher quality of life for all people, States should reduce and eliminate unsustainable patterns of production and consumption and promote appropriate demographic policies.

According to the official UN definition, sustainable development is "development that meets the needs of the present without compromising the ability of future generations to meet their own needs." It goes on to define "needs" to mean the world's poor "to which overriding priority should be given and the idea of limitations imposed by the state of technology and social organization on the environment's ability to meet present and future needs."[110] The evolution of the concept of sustainable development appears to be highly concerned with Environment and Development. The Rio Declaration clarifies as well as further defines the current concept of sustainable development. It includes elements regarding state responsibility for the well-being of its citizens and for causes by them to the environment. In striking the balance it recognizes the primacy of development.

The Stockholm Declaration, while bringing the environment into the international political agenda, did not say anything about how its aims were to be achieved. The Rio Declaration introduces procedural requirements for implementing the concept of sustainable development and goes beyond looking at technological solutions to environmental problems.

The Rio Declaration of Environment and Development, unlike the Stockholm Declaration on the Human Environment attaches greater importance to the social rather than physical environment. Principle 21 of the Stockholm Declaration, a principle recognized as soft international environmental law, has been amended by stipulating that states have a right to exploit their own resources pursuant to their own environmental and developmental policies. The addition reflects the recognition that development must not be constrained by the generalized rules of international law for the environment. This principle, along with the addition, has been incorporated in the Framework Convention on Climate Change, giving it legal validity and wider acceptance.[111]

The Rio Declaration achieves a balance between the substantive requirements of development and the procedural requirements for implementing environmental protection. In relations between states, the Declaration recognizes that:

- human beings are at the centre of concerns;[112]
- a right to development exists;[113]
- environmental protection is an integral part of the development process;[114]
- eradicating poverty is an indispensable requirement for sustainable development.[115]

The Declaration also requires states to adopt certain procedures to ensure that environmental considerations are integrated into the decision-making process, including:

1. effective environmental legislation;[116]

2. public participation in environmental decision-making;[117]
3. application of the precautionary approach;[118]
4. promotion of the polluter pays principle;[119]
5. adoption of environmental impact assessment;[120]
6. notification in the case of emergencies and activities with significant transboundary effect.[121]

For the first time in international environmental negotiations focusing on economic issues, elements of international cooperation for sustainable development are also laid out to:

1. decrease disparities in the standard of living;[122]
2. strengthen endogenous capacity building by improving scientific understanding and transfer of technologies;[123]
3. promote a supportive and open international economic system;[124]
4. prevent the transfer of harmful activities and substances;[125] and
5. develop a legal liability regime as a transboundary regulatory instrument.[126]

The Declaration envisions a "global partnership" to not only conserve and protect but also to restore the "integrity and health of the earth's ecosystem" through steps like:

- reducing and eliminating unsustainable patterns of production and consumption;[127]
- promoting appropriate demographic policies;[128]
- exchanging scientific and technological knowledge;[129]
- enhancing the development, adaptation, diffusion, and transfer of new and innovative technologies;[130] and
- promoting a supportive and open international economic system.[131]

Principle of the Declaration relating to the priority to be given to the eradication of poverty and to adopting precautionary measures for environmental protection have been incorporated into the Framework Convention on Climate

Change[132] and the Convention on Biological Diversity,[133] making them a part of international law. Policies fleshing out these legal concepts will follow two parallel tracks. First, the Rio Declaration achieves a balance between the obligations accepted by the developing countries to prevent further deterioration of the environment and the responsibilities of the developed countries for causing the damage. Thus, the principle of common but differentiated responsibility for global environmental degradation has been accepted, with the developed countries acknowledging their responsibility "in view of the pressures their societies place on the global environment and of the technologies and financial resources they command."[134] The case has been made for transfer of resources and technology based on the economic advantages that have accrued to developed countries—and not on purely altruistic considerations.

Next, while the Stockholm Declaration was concerned with the conflict between the sustainable use of natural resources and transboundary pollution, twenty years later the understanding of both the content and the context of human interference with the ecosystem has changed. The policy focus is no longer the apprehension that environmental considerations will restrict the right of states to exploit their natural resources but the impact on sovereignty of restrictions over activities affecting the natural environment. With the widening scope of accepted restrictions, sovereignty is acquiring a new meaning. The restrictions affect a range of economic activities from those likely to cause irreversible environmental damage to those maintaining an open and fair trading system.

The significance of the Rio Declaration lies in its requirement that for the fulfilment of its principles, further development of international law in the field of sustainable development, not only in the field of environment, is needed.[135] The policy focus now is on the content and pattern of economic growth itself. The future debate on implementing sustainable development will encompass several areas, including: the economic instruments for determining the relative importance of production or consumption activities to the measures for reducing degradation; the approach to long-term risk management; equity considerations relating to social change; instrumental barriers to incorporating environmental costs in the pricing of commodities; and the transfer and adoption of environmentally sound technologies.[136]

The twentieth century has witnessed a growing awareness of environmental concerns. "Where nations and states once viewed regulation of pollution and natural resources as a local or national issue, economic, political, and institutional forces have now pushed them to see many environmental problems as global in scope."[137] This internationalization of environmental regulation" is the result of an increase in scientific understanding, public awareness, environmental groups, and media coverage. The people of the world have come to understand that preservation and protection of our environment, a shared world environment, can only be accomplished by way of international cooperation. Environmentalists have told us for many decades that in nature all ecosystems are inextricably intertwined. Chloroflouro carbons (CFCs) emitted in China affect the populations of South America. The nuclear accident at Chernobyl affects all of Europe. In short, each individual, national and international action affects the world environment.[138]

The emphasis in framing issues on sustainable development has shifted from legal notion of "common heritage" to political "common concerns." The driving force has so far been the determination of technical standards based on the physical and natural sciences and environmental law. These standards and their origin will continue to be important for interpretation and dispute settlement. The future evolution of sustainable development issues, however, will be driven by the choice of policy instruments based on environmental concerns that impart on interrelated flows of trade, investment, technology. and institutional arrangements. The Maastricht Treaty, as an example, recognized that environment takes precedence over commercial policy.[139]

The concept of sustainable development has evolved and will continue to evolve in a fragmented, but not incoherent, manner. Stockholm, in 1972, was concerned with specifying the causality and significance of the problem. Rio, in 1992, dealt with assessing options for action. The next conference, in 2012, will make and implement decisions within the structure of a truly global partnership based on mutual benefits and interests.[140]

As a matter of fact, political friction between nations involves the conflicting interests of states in maintaining ecological order of the oceans. Coastal states place priority on preserving their fisheries, conserving off-shore resources for their own use, as well as protecting their beaches and waters from contamination. They favour extended municipal jurisdiction in these areas. Non-coastal states insist on an equitable distribution of the ocean wealth. Consequently, they do not favour extending municipal jurisdiction. Maritime nations desire as much freedom of the high seas as possible for their warships and passenger, merchant and fishing vessels, and competitive access to the rich mineral resources of the seabed.[141]

3.10. Goal to Forward

The 1972 Conference on the Environment (held in Stockholm) was the first of the United Nations "mega-conferences", in which governments from around the world were brought together to discuss the United Nations' work in economic and social cooperation. The mega-conference represented a new form of diplomacy. It was not a conference to discuss common problems and suggest ideas on how they could be solved; it was not creating a treaty as such and so was not as ambitious as the usual diplomatic conference. But it was also, in a sense, more ambitious in that, freed from the requirements to remain focused on a particular issue, it could roam freely over a range of issues and encourage governments to think about these problems. To use the jargon of that era, it was a consciousness-raising conference designed to encourage governments to think more creatively about international cooperation. The main focus of the 1972 conference was cleaning up the environment and preventing pollution.[142]

Fifteen years later, the UN General Assembly set up the World Commission on Environment and Development (WCED), the so-called Brundtland Commission. By then the emphasis had shifted to combining environmental integrity with the processes of development. The report of the WCED made popular the concept of sustainable development, which was stated to be "development that meets the needs of the present without comprising the ability of future generations to meet their own needs."[143] This concept of sustainable development has achieved a large degree of international consensus and was unanimously endorsed by the world leaders gathered in Rio in 1992.

In reality, one of the most significant principles of international environmental law to emerge is the concept of "sustainable development", which recognises that the twin goals of environmental protection and economic development are mutually supportive and interdependent, rather than contradictory. Wide scale recognition of sustainable development lowered what was once a substantial barrier to international environmental cooperation between the developed and developing nations.[144]

Prior to the 1980s, a widely held belief was that socio-economic development and environmental protection were contrary goals and that to attain one the other had to be sacrificed. Thus, the developed and developing nations were divided over the importance of environmental regulation. Now, most countries realize that socio-economic development and environmental quality are convergent goals and that failure to control pollution will have both global socio-economic and global environmental repercussions. As a result, industrialized and developing nations now understand that economic and technological aid must be combined with environmental regulation to sustain development. Professors Schoenbaum and Rosenber explain that there are several reasons for increased international awareness of environmental issues. It is now realized that the earth is a fragile, interdependent biosphere, which has already been affected to some extent by mankind's technological activities. For instance, it is now quite evident that the use of chlorfluorocarbons (CFCs) as refrigerants and aerosol propellants has caused some destruction of the stratospheric ozone layer, a thin layer of gases that protect the planet from ultraviolet radiation.[145]

The Brundtland definition of sustainability has, however, been criticized by Starik and Rands as not being adequate in decision-making situations. According to them, the concept is (a) anthropocentric, (b) indefinite on what the needs are and whose needs have priority, (c) silent on changes in technology, resource distribution, and quality, and (d) unclear regarding the benefits. Costs, and strategies of intergenerational sacrifice and transfer and in a more comprehensive definition of sustainability, concepts like irreplaceability, biodiversity carrying capacity, socio-economic and ecological system resilience, and futurity need to be included.[146]

However, though it may be extremely difficult to apply the concept of sustainable development unambiguously in specific decision-making situations, it is a very powerful, though simple, idea. As with many powerful and simple ideas, it has become a buzzword and is used by many different groups to express a diversity of value judgments disguised in seemingly value-neutral language.

Another difficulty is that, in the broadest sense, sustainable development applies to many different policy areas that are usually thought of separately and appeal to different constituencies. It involves technical, economic, social, environmental, and cultural factors that interact with each other in complex and often unpredictable ways. Thus, it is a highly multidisciplinary concept that is very hard for one expert analyst or policy-maker to encompass.

Also, though intergenerational equity is central to the implementation of the concept of sustainability, it does not follow that achieving it is a zero sum game between ourselves and our descendants. The reason is that sustainability combines quantities that are finite (resources and environmental assimilative capacity) with others that are enhanced rather than depleted (knowledge and human capacities) when they are used for human benefit. Knowledge widely added to resources can thus be the source of new wealth and human capacity, both individual and collective, thereby opening up new options and possibilities for making economic and social growth compatible with sustainability.[147]

In matters of marine environment relating to the sea it is required to be generally conversant among others, with the coastal sea. The coastal zone—where land meets sea and where fresh and salt waters mix—contains many of the earth's most complex, diverse, and productive ecological systems. It functions as a protective buffer and filter between the land and the sea and is increasingly valued for recreational and aesthetic purposes. Coastal regions contain a high proportion of the world's most productive and biologically diverse ecosystems. The produce the bulk of the world's fish catch, support a major portion of the world's agriculture, industry, and tourism, and absorb most of the wastes. The pace of change—environmental, social, and institutional—is accelerating and therefore becoming more complex and challenging.

The Rio Conference of 1992 laid great stress on the management of coastal zones. The coastal system's problems can be addressed by systems analysis, and a large number of such analyses have been made.[148] Weide has schematized the coast as consisting of the natural subsystem, which can be further broken down into its biotic and abiotic components and the socio-economic system., including the users of the coastal resources and the required physical and social infrastructure. Weide's system can represent a specific coastal area or may be extended to include the entire global system. In all cases, appropriate input scenarios are required to account for the interaction of the socio-economic system and the physical and social environment.[149]

As time passes, environment consciousness is increasing at all levels. In spite of that, it is inherently difficult to deal with multi-issued environment discipline for an unambiguous consensus even on a burning topic like "sustainable development." Be that as it may, human efforts will go ahead for evolving and promoting a congenial environment at all spheres of the earth. In achieving a consensual view of the desirable future state, it is sometimes suggested that traditional cultural and religious/spiritual views could provide the necessary context. Most religions have very positive views on the environment. The United Nations Environmental Programme has shown how major religions like Buddhism, Christianity, Islam and Judaism have views that are very much in tune with the concept of sustainable development.[150]

As matters go, the international legal community was not alone in formulating international approach to oceans management. In the early 1980s, biologists, oceanographers, and ecologists commenced a series of international symposia to research the possibility of management of large marine ecosystems (LMEs).[151] Besides on an ecosystem approach, the management of LMEs incorporates two trends in oceans management: the search for meaningful parameters in oceans management rather than strict jurisdictions and the gradual progression towards marine regional cooperation at the international level. As laudable as the LME notion is, the establishment and enforcement of LME management has obvious political limitations. As Belsky observes:

> The management of large marine ecosystems...depends almost entirely on the voluntary agreement of individual countries. They must believe such management is in the best interests of their own nation. Hence, while there are few legal impediments to the comprehensive management of ecosystems, neither are there many legal incentives.[152]

While most authors acknowledge the political and legal difficulties associated with managing LMEs, the multilateral management thereof is a notion that is increasingly gaining acceptance in the international academic community. Despite the fact that the notion of LMEs has not been formally adopted by any international legal document, its development in international fora is part of a growing acknowledgement of the need to manage sea activities on a spatial rather than legal basis.

So far, the notion "sustainable" has approached a "... minimum, sustainable development must not endanger the natural systems that support life on Earth: the atmosphere, the waters, the soils, and the living beings."[153] Despite defining sustainability in the negative, the Brundtland Report acknowledges the importance of sustaining the natural world in which humans live with other life forms. Furthermore, "development" is defined as including economic as well as non-economic dimensions as it is "...a progressive transformation of economy and society."[154] Accordingly, the sustainable development of sea resources demands that the ecological aspects of a sea area be considered at the same time as the other dimensions, such as economic, social, and political ones. Thus, the articulation of the notion of sustainable development may be considered a shift in oceans resource management, as it calls for a continuous decision-making process, allowing changes to be made when new factors or uses emerge.[155]

Parallel to these ICOM (Integrated Coastal and Ocean Management)-related articulations in the 1980s was the strengthening and establishment of regional cooperation efforts around the world. This consisted continued efforts on the part of UNEP's Regional Seas Programme,[156] and the formation of regional cooperation bodies, such as the Gulf of Maine Council on the Marine Environment between two Canadian provinces and three American states.[157]

As a matter of fact, the 1992 United Nations Conference on Environment and Development (UNCED) was instrumental in popularizing and entrenching the principles of ICOM in international law.[158] The documents produced at UNCED went beyond a simple acknowledgement of the interrelationships between the land, sea and air. Not only did they encourage the use of integrated decision making in sea use governance, but more importantly, they emphasized the importance of using the precautionary approach in such a process. The precautionary approach to oceans' governance is revolutionary as it necessitates action or cessation of activity to prevent harm to the environment before such an occurrence becomes imminent.

Although the precautionary approach was originally a notion found in German federal law,[159] and although it has been introduced in a number of international law documents prior to 1992,[160] it was UNCED that popularized the precautionary approach in international environmental law and oceans' governance.

A key UNCED document is the Rio Declaration on Environment and Development, a set of 27 aspirational principles, articulating the environmental notions key to ICOM. Its opening principle reinforces the recommendations of the Brundtland Report as it makes individuals responsible for ensuring the sustainable development of natural resources. The Declaration requires states to ensure sustainable development of the resources in the following manners: by taking a precautionary approach to prevent environmental degradation;[161] by following an integrated ecosystem approach to oceans' governance;[162] by preventing pollution;[163] by undertaking environmental assessments;[164] and by seeking the input of the public and local and aboriginal populations.[165] These principles are key to ICOM as they compel states to manage their resources by using an integrated decision-making model and to act before scientific evidence is present to prove environmental degradation.

An important and striking UNCED document is Agenda 21: Programme of Action for Sustainable Development,[166] a 40-chapter action programme that attempts to operationalize the decision-making principles found in the Rio Declaration. Chapter 17 of Agenda 21, "Protection of the Oceans, All Kinds of Seas, Including Enclosed and Semi-enclosed Seas, and Coastal Areas and the Protection, Rational Use and Developments of Their Living Resources", the longest chapter of the document, promotes the sustainable use of the marine and coastal areas and resources. Chapter 17 requires that a precautionary and anticipatory rather than a reactive approach be taken by states to prevent the degradation of the marine environment[167] and that states commit to integrated management and sustainable development in the use of resources by the use of environmental impact assessments.[168]

Finally, the Convention on Biological Diversity (CBD),[169] is another UNCED document that incorporates ICOM principles. Although the CBD does not specifically address the oceans' environment, it emphasizes the importance of promoting and preserving biological diversity in general. This emphasis shifts the concept of sustainable development from one defined in terms of its utility to human tone that recognizes the intrinsic value on the preservation of the natural environment and other species. Therefore, the CBD expands upon the somewhat anthropocentric definition of sustainable development found in the Brundtland Report by including biological diversity as an implicit and necessary part of sustainable development. In the Preamble, it compels states to preserve biological diversity according to the principles of the precautionary approach.[170] Besides articulating the need to promote biodiversity and the use of the precautionary approach, the CBD was important in the development of ICOM as it spawned the Jakarta Mandate.[171] The Jakarta Mandate specifically addresses coastal and oceans' management and recommends that states manage their marine resources by using precautionary ecosystem management approaches and by establishing marine protected areas where necessary.[172]

In the past international law had largely focused on interstate relations and taken almost a hands off approach to interfering with national sovereignty including states' rights to exploit natural resources...UNCED articulated numerous soft principles that should guide not only international but also national ocean law and policy reforms. Those principles include integration, precaution, pollution prevention, international equity, polluter pays, public participation, community-based management, indigenous rights and women in development.[173]

Unlike the Stockholm Declaration and the LOS Convention, these documents articulate the goal of oceans' governance as being the sustainable use of the resources as opposed to the mere prevention of pollution. They go beyond merely recognizing the importance of interrelationships as they explicitly identify the public, local and indigenous populations as parties whose views must be considered by the various levels of government. Also, by requiring that states be guided by the precautionary approach, these documents compel states to manage their ocean resources before environmental harm ensues.

Although not a 'space', nor falling within the description 'between' states, the environment has attracted increasing attention as evidence of the potential for damage to it from human activity. This potential is not only within the Earth's biosphere itself, but already extends to pollution of outer space. International law here provides examples of development through custom, general principle and treaty. The major part of international environmental law is in emerging treaty form. As such, the content is a political product. The challenge for the lawyer is to identify what is clear law for application to particular activities, what are legal policies, trends or principles for contribution to development of law, and the powers, responsibilities and procedures of international organizations in taking forward the law globally.[174] In environment matters, it is taken into fact that the basic duty of states is to act so as not to harm the interests of other states.[175] The principle seems to have been accepted in documents globally, regionally and nationally as effective. As time passes, submission to environmental regime is increasing and as such, its recognition is not questioned. The International Court of Justice has accepted its viability that can be known in its advisory opinion. That is to say:

> The Court...recognizes that the environment is not an abstraction but represents the living space, the quality of life and the very health of beings, including generations unborn. The existence of the general obligation of States to ensure that activities within their jurisdiction and control respect the environment of other States or of areas beyond national control is now part of the corpus of international law relating to the environment.[176]

At present environment matter cannot be said to be inadequate as to materials and documents that give rise to promotion of a legal regime. It is now possible to promote a legal regime of environment through available materials and documents enabling its protection and preservation. Thus, it results in increasing concern to the international community—the responsibility that states owe for environment damage caused by economic activity, and the loss of species and habits to human development.[177] As to a goal, the marine environment is required to be endowed with measures for the states to be taken in such accord.

3.11. Goal for the Bay of Bengal

The Bay of Bengal is bordered by a number of coastal states principally by five coastal states like Bangladesh, India, Maldives, Myanmar (Burma), and Sri Lanka. Although Indonesia, Malaysia, and Thailand are considered here, their position in relation to the Bay is not like the five states. Environment concerns relating to the Bay of Bengal are not at all at an advanced stage like other areas of the oceans. There is no major work dealing with the environment regime of the Bay. As a matter of fact, the Bay is a domain of tidal bores and bestows monsoon that governs climate of the littoral states. It is inevitable for the littoral states to take steps to monitor the Bay. The Bay is rich both in living and natural resources, in consequence, the Bay is drawing attention at national, regional and global level. The Bay of Bengal Programme-Non-governmental Organization (BOBP-NGO) has taken initiatives towards fisheries management. The littoral states are taking interest in matters of environment regime the Bay. As a matter of fact, environment is now a common matter at all levels to be maintained and promoted. All concerned states should be attentive towards obligations for protection and preservation of environment in compliance with the global regime. Special situations that are inevitable should not be ignored in the interests of the state but not at the cost of others.

It is true that the nations of the world are confronted with major disagreements, mutual fears, distracting domestic political problems. But almost for the first time, it is being to be realised that no nation, not even the richest nor the strongest, can solve the problems of trade, money, pollution etc. without common action to deal with common world problems.

For too long, these problems have been left to the technicians, brought up in their own limited techno-structures and unable to comprehend the imperatives of a global setting. Efforts are being made to weave, out of seemingly chaotic strands, a pattern for individual and joint action to further the cause of prosperity.

The world situation today provides the International Law Association with "an impetus for a new period of endeavour" in aid of the statesmen of different nations, and in pursuit of work designed to evolve further the International Law on Development and Cooperation, to infuse it with a dynamic capacity to keep pace with international life, and to secure for it a catalytic role in furthering progress in directions and towards goals accepted by the international community. It is now required for all concerned to bestow their best thought in the promotion of environment regime taking into account the problems posed by the inequality of economic power in the states, to induce the states enjoying the panoply of power to be conscious of their responsibilities, to provide possible expertise for the use of their capabilities to the benefit of international cooperation. Truly, such step enshrines to evolve concepts and to introduce normative criteria in tune with the vision embodied in the U.N. Charter and thus to foster conditions in which international machinery is effectively employed for the fulfilment of commitments made by the international community to the people of the world.[178]

The world has been changing recently. The neat divisions and categories observed in earlier times no longer apply to current crises. Bridges and connections have been constructed between today's issues in a manner inconceivable only a few years ago. These issues include humanitarian assistance and international security; humanitarian protection and human rights; human rights and regional stability; peace, democracy, human rights, and the requirements of development; development and security; and the environment and development. The fabric of international society has grown ever more intricate and complex. The potential for effective international action and a broad role for the United Nations, albeit a very demanding one, has grown correspondingly.[179]

It is a well-recognized observation that environmental control, and in particular the protection against pollution, is to a very large extent a matter of international concern. Similar concern for marine environment cannot be ruled out. Satisfactory solutions can only be reached through international cooperation and the development of adequate rules of international law.[180] As a practical consideration, it is now possible to deal with environment matters that seem almost blessed with materials and documents and in the case of marine environment it is as well. Truly, the concerned Bay of Bengal regional concept is the first of its kind, where both enforcement and implementation are placed under one authority. Now is the time to coordinate the efforts of governments in the Bay of Bengal to afford a broad approach to its environment.[181] In regard to regional impact, there is now a regional organization in the name of South Asian Association for Regional Cooperation (SAARC).[182] It has as its members Bhutan, Nepal and Pakistan which, though coastal, is not bordered on the Bay of Bengal. Moreover, the littoral states like Myanmar and the rest those are not in SAARC tie. There is then a problem to construe a marine environment regime under its themes. But it is essential for countries in the region to cooperate in the development of uniform environmental standards and to prevent the danger of downward harmonization. It is possible that a country with the lowest environmental standards and no enforcement could be most successful in attracting international organizations or NGOs whose financial involvement may be needed.

As matters appear, with the advancement of science and technology there is a growing concern over the radical effects of technology on all phases of human life and, more specifically, over the prospects of shaping international law and institutions capable of dealing with these changes. The detailed principles of international environmental law have evolved from Principle 21. The principle is considered primarily an obligation to prevent pollution, and is generally accepted as customary international law. As a matter of fact, two Declarations (Stockholm and Rio Declarations), the products of conferences on environmental issues, provided a good illustration of the development of international environmental law. Important for mankind as part of the effort to achieve respect for the environment, for the international lawyer major issues are the legal effect of these instruments and how they can be deployed in legal argument on environmental matters.

In a 1997 Report by the UN Secretary-General on application and implementation of the Rio Declaration, an assessment is made of the legal nature of each Principle. In a general introduction to this commentary, the Secretary-General notes:

> The legal statutes of each of the principles varies considerably. Some are firmly established in international law, while others are only in the process of gaining acceptance. Some principles appear in global or regionally binding instruments, while others can only be identified in soft-law instruments. It is difficult in many cases to establish the parameters or the precise legal status of each principle. The manner in which each principle applies to a particular activity or incident would have to be considered in relation to the facts and circumstances of each case, taking account of various factors, including its sources and textual context, its language, the particular activity at issue, and the particular circumstances in which it occurs, including the actors and the geographical region.[183]

Recent history shows that a demand for more inventions and more technology has caused them to increase exponentially, and the concomitant increase in the rate of social change has exacerbated the differences between rich and poor nations and has caused demands for greater speed in dealing with them. These demands, while highlighting the problems, may tend to make their peaceful adjustment less likely.[184]

India, Bangladesh, Sri Lanka, Myanmar, Maldives and other possible littoral states while concerned have responsibilities to establish through all-round efforts and cooperation to promote and establish a legal regime for the Bay of Bengal environment.

References

1. U.N. Doc.A/CONF.48/14/Rev.1(1973.
2. Nicholas A. Robinson (ed): "Introduction: Ensuring Environmental Protection Globally", *Environmental Laws Treaties,* Vol. 1, Oceana Publications Inco. p. 3,
3. Convention on the Biological Diversity—Rio De Janeiro, 5 June 1992, Art 3: Principle.
4. Art 4: Jurisdictional Scope.
5. Art 22: Relationship with other International Conventions
6. For a study see H. Ringbon (ed.), *Competing Norms in the Law of Marine Environmental Protection—Focus on Ship Safety and Pollution Prevention* (London: Kluwer Law International, 1997).
7. Davor Vidas(ed), *Protecting the Polar Marine Environment Law and Policy for Pollution Prevention*, (2001), Cambridge University Press, p. 20.
8. Convention on the Territorial Sea and the Contiguous Zone, Art 4(4) (straight baselines) and Convention on the High Seas (search and rescue), Art. 12(2). The Conventions are available in UNTS, Vol. 516, p. 205ff and UNTS, Vol. 450, p. 82ff. See J. Crawford, "Universalism and Regionalism from the Perspective of the Work of the International Law Commission", in *International Law on the Eve of the Twenty First Century: Views from the International Law Commission* (New York: United Nations), 1997), p. 99.
9. See Fisheries case (United Kingdom v. Norway), ICJ Reports 1951, p. 116; Fisheries Jurisdiction case (United Kingdom v. Iceland; Federal Republic of Germany v. Iceland), ICJ reports 1974, pp. 3 and 175; North Sea Continental Shelf (Federal Republic of Germany v. Denmark, Federal Republic of Germany v. Netherlands), ICJ Reports 1969, p. 3.
10. F.C. Garcia-Amador, "Latin America and the Law of the Sea" in L.M. Alexandere (ed.), *The Law of the Sea: A New Geneva Conference, Proceedings of the 6th Annual Conference of the Law of the Sea Institute,* Kingston, Rhode island, 21-24 June 1971 (Kingston, RI: University of Rhode Island, Law of the Sea Institute, 1972); A. Szekely, *Latin America and the Development of the Law of the Sea*, 2 vols, (Dobbs Ferry, NY: Oceana, 1976); F. Orrego Vicuna (ed.), *The Exclusive Economic Zone: A Latin American Perspective* (Boulder, CO: Westview Press, 1984).
11. A.E. Boyle, "UNCLOS, the Marine Environment and the Settlement of Disputes", in Ringbom (ed.), *Competing Norms*, pp. 241-256.
12. See Preamble to the LOS Convention.
13. LOS Convention, Arts. 122-123.
14. Arts. 61-70 and 116-120.
15. Text reprinted in ILM, Vol. 36, 1997, p. 7ff (Protocol).

16. ILM, Vol. 11, 1972, pp. 1, 291 ff (Convention); and ILM, Vol.36, 1997, p. 546ff (Protocol).
17. ILM, Vol. 12, 1973, pp. 1, 319ff(Convention); and ILM, Vol. 17, 1978, pp. 546ff (Protocol).
18. *Report of the UN Conference on Environment and Development, Annex II,* Agenda 21, Chapter 17, para. 1, U N Doc.A/CONF.151/26/Rev.1, Vol. 1; see U. Beyerlin, "New Developments in the Protection of the Marine Environment: Potential Effects of the Rio Process", *Zeitschrift fur auslandisches offentliches Recht und Volkerrecht,*Vol. 55, 1995, p. 544; P.W. Birnie and A.E. Boyle, *International Law and Environment* (Oxford: Clarendon Press, 1992), pp. 251-299; and A. Yankov, "The Law of the Sea Convention and Agenda 21: Marine Environmental Implications", in A. E. Boyle and D. Freestone (eds.), *International Law and Sustainable Development: Past Achievements and Future Challenges* (Oxford: Clarendon Press, 1999), pp. 271-296.
19. *North Sea Continental Shelf*, p. 3. To this end, see Budislav Vukus, "United Nations Convention on the Law of the Sea and the polar marine environment", Davor Vidas (ed.), *Protecting the polar marine environment* (Cambridge University Press), 2000, pp. 45-46.
20. Alan Boyle, "Globalism and regionalism in the protection of the marine environment", in Davor Vidas (ed.). *Protecting the polar marine environment* (Cambridge University Press), 2000, p. 23.
21. LOS Convention, Arts. 210, 211.
22. See Protocol, 1996 to the London Convention, 1972.
23. See The Oslo Convention for the Prevention of Marine Pollution by Dumping from Ships and Aircraft (ILM, Vol. 11, 1972, p. 262ff); the Helsinki Convention on the Protection of the Marine Environment of the Baltic Area (ILM, Vol. 13, 1974, p. 546ff); the Barcelona Protocol for the Prevention of Pollution of the Mediterranean Sea by Dumping from Aircraft and Ships, 1976 (ILM, Vol. 15, 1976, p. 300ff); and the Noumea Protocol for the Prevention of Pollution by Dumping, 1986 (ILM, Vol. 26, 1987, p. 38ff).
24. LOS Convention, Art. 211(5).
25. Annex, regulations 9 and 10.
26. See generally *International Journal of Marine and Coastal Law,* Special Issue on Particularly Sensitive Sea Areas, Vol. 9, 1994.
27. LOS Convention, Art. 218, which provides for post state jurisdiction over pollution offences at sea.
28. Boyle, pp. 23-24.
29. UNEP(OCA)/LBA/IG.2/L.4; reprinted in *Yearbook of International Environmental Law*, Vol. 6, 1995, pp. 883-886. See further T. A. Menshah, "The International Legal Regime for the Protection and Preservation of the Marine Environment from Land-Based Sources of Pollution", in Boyle and

Freestone (eds.), *International Law and Sustainable Development,* pp. 297-324.

30. For further discussion see David Vanderzwaag, "Land-based marine pollution and the Arctic: polarities between principles and practice", in Davor Vidas (ed.), *Protecting the polar marine environment,* Law and Policy for Pollution Prevention (Cambridge University Press), 2000, pp. 175-198.
31. See L.M. Alexander, "Regional Arrangements in the Oceans", 71(1977) AJIL, p. 84;. L.M. Alexander, "New Trends in Marine Regionalism", 11(1994) *Ocean Yearbook* 1-8; A. Vallega, "The Regional Scale of Ocean Management and Marine Regional Building", 24(1994) *Ocean and Coastal Management* 17-38; B.A,. Boczeck, "Global and Regional Approaches to the Protection and Preservation of the Marine Environment", 16(1984) *Case Western Reserve Journal of International Law* 39.
32. See Davor Vidas, 'The polar marine environment in regional cooperation", in Davor Vidas (ed.), *Protecting the polar marine environment* (Cambridge University Press), 2000, pp. 78-101.
33. See A. Vallega, "The Regional Scale of Ocean Management and Marine Regional Building, *op cit.*"
34. For an analytical discussion see David Vanderzwaag, "Land-based marine pollution and the Arctic: polarities between principles and practice", in Davor Vidas (ed.), *Protecting the polar marine environment,* Law and Policy for Pollution Prevention (Cambridge University Press, 2000), p. 199.
35. J.M. Broadus, S. Demisch, K. Gjerda, P. Haas, Y. Karou, G. Peet, S. Repeto and A. Roginko, *Comparative Assessment of Regional International Programs to Control Land-Based Marine Pollution: The Baltic, North Sea, and Mediterranean* (Woods Hole, MA: Marine Policy Center, Woods Hole Oceanographic Institution, 1993), p. 11.
36. The recommendations are reprinted in W. E. Bruhenne and N. A. Robinson (eds.), *International Protection of the Marine Environment: Conservation in Sustainable Development,* Vol. 3, Booklet 17-03-96/1(Dobbs Ferry, NY: Oceana, 1997), pp. 1-27.
37. See *United Nations Handbook* (New Zealand Ministry of Foreign Affairs & Trade, 2003), pp. 227-231.
38. For general treatments of the international law of marine pollution, see D. Brubaker, *Marine Pollution and International Law: Principle and Practice* (London: Belhaven Press, 1993); D. B. Macgraw (ed.), *International Law and Pollution* (Philadelphia, PA: University of Pennsylvania Press, 1991); and G. J. Timagenis, *International Control of Marine Pollution* (Dobbs Ferry, NY: Ocean, 1980).
39. For a detailed discussion see Budislav Vukas, "United Nations Convention on the Law of the Sea and the polar marine environment", in Davor Vidas (ed.) *Protecting the Polar Marine Environment* (Cambridge University Press, 2000), pp 34-56.

40. Christopher C. Joyner, "Protection of the Antarctic Environment against marine pollution under the 1991 Protocol", in Davor Vidas (ed.) *Proteting the polar marine environment,* Law and Policy for Pollution Prevention (Cambridge University Press, 2000), pp. 105-106.

41. See Alastair Couper & Edgar Gold (eds.), *The Marine Environment and Sustainable Development: Law, Policy, and Science* (The Law of the Sea Institute, University of Hawaii, Honolulu, 1993) pp. 533-537.

42. See Reports of the Meetings, Docs.UNEP/SAS/LWG.1/7EAS/LWG.1/5, both of 26 February 1990.

43. See Alastair Couper, Edgar Gold (eds.), *The Marine Environment and Sustainable Development: Law, Policy, and Science* (The Law of the Sea Institute, University of Hawaii, Honolulu, 1993), p. 534, fn. 4.

44. See *Management and Conservation of Renewable Marine Resources in the South Asian Seas Region.* UNEP RSRS No. 62 (*Nairobi*: UNEP 1985); Environmental Problems of the South Asian Seas Region: An Overview, UNEP/RSRSNo.82(Nairobi: UNEP 1987); Sen Gupto *et al.*, State of the Marine Environment in the South Asian Seas Region, UNEP /RSRS No. 123 (Nairobi: UNEP 1990).

45. *Annual Report of the Executive Director 1990, para. 116 at 40-41 (Doc.UNEP/GC.16/3 (Nairobi: UNEP 1991),* Cf. Criticism of Edgardo D. Gomez, "Whither the East Asian Seas", 21 (1990) 6 Marine Pollution pp. 262-263.

46. E.g., in relation to Eastern Africa (Central Western Indian Ocean) region, where the 1st Intergovernmental Meeting of the 1985 Nairobi Action Plan was held only in the end of 1989.

47. P.H. Sand, *Lessons Learned in Global Environment Governance,1* (Washington, D.C.: World Resources Institute, June 1990).

48. P.H. Sand, *Marine Environmental Law in the United Nations Environment Program* (London/New York: Tycooly Publishing, 1988) at xv.

49. See E. Brown Weiss, "Our Rights and Obligations to Future Generations for the Environment, in "Agora: What Obligation Does Our Generation Owe to the Next? An Approach to Global Environmental Responsibility", 84(1990) AJIL 198, 211; and also by Brown Weiss, *In Fairness to Future Generations: International Law, Common Patrimony, and Intergenerational Equity,* Innovation in International Law Series, R. Falk, gen.ed., (Dobbs Ferry: Transnational Publishers, Inc. 1989). Cf. Resolution of the ACP-EEC Joint Assembly on Third World Poverty and the Environment of 28 February 1991, Doc.ACP-EEC 327/91/Final (African-Caribbean-Pacific [ACP].

50. These factors include: enhancing the coordinating and catalytic role of UNEP; better appreciation of complex difficulties encountered by the East and South Asian states; adequate geographical coverage by the RSP of the EAS and SAS regions; and some aspects of the substantive scope of the both programs. For a detailed discussion see Alastair Couper & Edgar Gold

(eds.), *The Marine Environment and Sustainable Development: Law, Policy, and Science* (The Law of the Sea Institute, University of Hawaii, Honolulu, 1993) pp. 5537-552.)

51. See the 1989 Economic Declaration from the Paris Summit of Canada, European Economic Community (EEC), France, Germany, Italy, Japan, United Kingdom, and the United States in 28(1989) ILM 1202; the 1990 UN Declaration on International Economic Cooperation, in Particular the Revitalization of Economic Growth of the Developing Countries (General Assembly's Resolution S-18/3, Annex).

52. See L.A. Kimball, "Regional Marine Resources Development: Growth by Necessity", 3(1982) *Ocean Yearbook* 157-197; and also by Kimball, "International Law and Institutions: The Oceans and Beyond", 20(1989) *Ocean Development and International Law* 147-165; B. Kwiatkowska, "The Role of Regional Organizations in Development Cooperation in Marine Affairs" in A.H.A. Soons (ed.), *Implementation of the Law of the Sea Convention through International Institutions* (The Law of the Sea Institute, University of Hawaii, Honolulu, 1990) pp. 29-49; and also by Kwiatkowska, "Institutional Marine Affairs Cooperation in Developing State Regions, Part 1: General Problems and Prospects", 14(1990) *Marine Policy* 385-398. For an account of difficulties mounted in development cooperation by industrialized states, see speech delivered at the Africa Conference held in the Netherlands in July 1990 by Mozambican Minister of Finance, Mr. Abdul Magid Osman, "Africa Beyond Crisis?—A Mozambican Viewpoint", ACP-EC 124(1990) *The Courier* 20-22.

53. For an analysis of the whole range of complicating factors of historical/ cultural, political, strategic, geographic, scientific /technological, administrative, diplomatic, legal, and temporal nature, see D. M. Johnston and M.J. Valencia, *Pacific Ocean Boundary Problems—Status and Solutions,* (Dordrecht: Martinus Nijhoff, 1991), pp. 20-33.

54. See analysis by Hasjim Djalal, "Managing Potential Conflits in the South China Sea", 10(1990)2 *International Challenge* 39-44.

55. Johnston and Valencia, *supra.,* n 82 at 2.

56. *Ibid.*

57. Barbara Kwiatkowska, "Environmental Prospects for the East and South Asian Seas" in Alastair Couper and Edgar Gold (eds.), *The Marine Environment and Sustainable Development: Law, Policy, and Science* (The Law of the Sea Institute, University of Hawaii, Honolulu, 1993), pp. 543-544.

58. For a detailed analysis of IOMAC, see remarks by its Secretary-General, Ambassador H.W. Jayewardene, 'Commentary', in A. H. A. Soons (ed.), *Implementation of the Law of the Sea Convention through International Institutions* (The Law of the Sea Institute, University of Hawaii, Honolulu, 1990), pp. 123-128; B. Kwiatkowska, "Institutional Marine Affairs Cooperation in Developing State Region, Part 1: General Problems and Prospects", 14 (1990) *Marine Policy* 385-398, "Part 2: The Indian Ocean

and IOMAC", 399-420; and also "1990 Agreement on the Organization for IOMAC", 6 (1991) International Journal of Estuarine and Coastal Law 133-144. India also prevented in the FAO International Conference for the adoption of a Draft Agreement for the Establishment of the Indian Ocean Tuna Commission held in Rome on 3-7 April 1989 from establishing this Commission.

59. P.H. Sand, *Marine Environment Law in the United Nations Environment Program* (London/ New York: Tycooly Publishing, 1988), p. xii.
60. Alastair Couper and Edgar Gold (eds.), *op.cit.*, pp. 544-547.
61. Note that at the 9th EEC-ASEAN Ministerial Meeting in June 1991, the ASEAN leaders declined the EEC's suggestion of ASEAN exerting pressure to change the military leadership of Myanmar (Burma), which is the world's largest opium producer. See "ASEAN Cool to EC Request on Burma", *Bangkok Post* of 1 June 1991, at 6. The ASEAN's dialogue partners, especially the EEC and the United States renewed this pressure with success at the 24th ASEAN Ministerial Meeting held in Kuala Lumpur in July 1991. The ASEAN agreed to send Mr. Raul Manglapus, the Philippine Foreign Secretary to Rangoon, Myanmar, reaffirming, however, its opposition to punitive measures advanced by the West. See M. Richardson, "West to Press ASEAN on Burma Rights", *International Herald Tribune* of 22 July 1991, at 5, and also by Richardson, "ASEAN Will Send and Envoy to Press Burma on Rights", *International Herald Tribune* of 24 July 1991, at 3.
62. See M. Savini, *Summary Information on the Role of International Fishery Bodies with Regard to the Conservation and Management of Living Resources of the High Seas,* FAO Fisheries Circular No. 835 (Rome: FAO July 1991).
63. See Alastair Couper and Edgar Gold (eds.), *op.cit.*, 551.
64. For references to all activities in this respect within the United Nations, see UN General Assembly resolution 45/212 on Protection of Global Climate for Present and Future of Mankind of 21 December 1990.
65. Montevideo Convention of Rights and Duties of States, Dec. 26, 1933, Inter-American. Art. 8, 40 Stat. 3097, 165 L.N.T.S. 19 (entered into force Dec. 26, 1934).
66. *The Schooner Exchange* v. *M'faddon,* 11 U.S. (Cranch) 116, 137 (1812).
67. Susan H. Bragdon, "National Sovereignty and Global Environmental Responsibility: Can the Tension Be Reconciled for the Conservation of Biological Diversity?", 33(1992) 2 *Harvard International Law Journal*, p. 381.
68. *Trial Smelter Case* (U. S. A. v. Canada) [1941], 3 R. I. A. A. 1905 (1949) (Special Arbitral Tribunal).
69. "The Tribunal shall apply the law and practice followed in dealing with cognate questions in the United States of America as well as international law and practice." *Ibid.* at 1908. Pursuant to Article 1 of the special

agreement (Convention for the Settlement of Difficulties Arising From Operation of Smelter at Trail, B.C.), Canada agreed to pay out $3,50,000.00 to the United States "in payment of all damage which occurred in the United States, prior to the first day of January, 1932, as a result of the operation of the Trail Smelter." *Ibid.* 1907.

70. Constance O'Keefe, Transboundary Pollution and the Strict Liability Issue: The Work of the International Law Commission on the Topic of International Liability for Injurious Consequences Arising Out of Acts Not Prohibited by International Law, 16(1984) *Denver Journal of International Law & Policy* 145, 174-5.
71. Trail Smelter Case, 3(1941) R. I. A. A. at 1963.
72. Corfu Channel (U.K. v. Alb.), 1949 I.C.J. at 22 (April 22).
73. *Ibid.*, at 10.
74. *Ibid.*, at 6.
75. *Ibid.*, at 23.
76. *Ibid.*, at 26.
77. See Ved P. Nanda, *Trends in International Environmental Law*, 20(1990) CAL. W, INT'L L.J. 187, 198-199. "International environmental law obligates states to regulate activities within their jurisdiction so that these activities do not cause harm to the environment beyond their jurisdiction." See Ved P. Nanda, *Global Warming and International Environmental Law—A Preliminary Inquiry*, 30(1989) HARV. INT'l L. J. 375. Also see Restatement (Third) of the Foreign Relations Law of the United States 601 (1987) (hereafter Third Restatement).
78. *Lake Lanoux Arbitration* (France v. Spain), 24 (1957) I.L.R. 101; see also O'Keefe, *op.cit.* at 176.
79. *Lake Lanoux Arbitration*, at 101.
80. Third Restatement, *op.cit.*
81. *Ibid.*
82. *Ibid.*
83. Alan E. Boyle, "State Responsibility and International Liability for Injurious Consequences of Acts Not Prohibited by International Law: A Necessary Distinction?," 39(1982) International and Comparative Law Quarterly 1, 3.
84. Coveyt T. Oliver & Ors., *The International Legal System: Cases and Materials* (New York: The Foundation Press, Inc., 1995), pp. 417-422.
85. See the 1954 International Convention for the Prevention of Pollution of the Sea by (OILPOL), 12 USTS 2989; TIAS 4900; the 1973 International Convention for the Prevention of Pollution from Ships (MARPOL), 12 (1973) ILM 1319 and 17(1979) ILM 546; the 1990 International Convention on Oil Pollution Readiness, Response and Cooperation, 30(1991) ILM 735; the 1969 Convention for Civil Liability for Oil Pollution Damage, 9(1970) ILM 45; 1976 Protocol, 16 (1977) ILM 617,

1984 Protocol Misc. No. 8 (1981) Cmnd. 9927 and 1992 Protocol, IMO Doc.LEG/CONF.9/15 (1992); the 1971 International Convention on the Establishment of a Fund for Compensation for Oil Pollution Damage. 11 (1972) ILM 284, 1976 Protocol, 16(1984) ILM 621, 1984 Protocol, 23 (1984) ILM 195 and 1992 Protocol, IMO Doc. LEG/CONF.9/16)1962); the 1976 London Convention on Civil Liability for Oil Pollution Damage Resulting From Exploration for and Exploitation of Seabed Mineral Resources, 16(1977) ILM 1450, and the 1972 Convention on the Prevention of Marine Pollution by Dumping of Wastes and Other Matter, 26 USTS 2403, TIAS 8165, 11(1972) ILM 1291. Intervention Against Maritime Casualties is provided for in the 1969 Convention Relating to Intervention on the High Seas in Cases of Oil Pollution Casualties, 26 UST 765, TIAS No. 8068, 9(1970) ILM 25 and the Protocol Relating to Intervention on the High Seas in Cases of Pollution by Substances Other Than Oil, TIAS 10561, 13 (1974) ILM 605.

86. 1974 Helsinki Convention on the Protection of the Marine Environment of the Black Sea Area, 13(1974) ILM 546; the 1976 Barcelona Convention for the Protection of the Mediterranean Sea Against Pollution and its Protocols of 1976 and 1980, 15 (1976) ILM 290, 300, 306, and 19(1980) ILM 869; the 1978 Kuwait Regional Convention for Cooperation on the Protection of the Marine Environment from Pollution and Protocol, 17(1978) ILM 511, 526; the 1981 Abidjan Convention for Cooperation in the Protection and Development of the Marine and Coastal Environment of the West and Central African Region and Protocol, 20(1981) ILM 746, 756; the 1983 Cartenga Convention for the Protection and Development of Marine Environment of the Wider Caribbean Region and its Protocols, TIAS 11085, 22(1983) ILM 227, 240 and the 1986 Noumea Convention for the Protection of the National Resources and Environment of the South Pacific Region and Protocols, 26(1987) ILM 38, 58. The agreement, the 1992 Paris Convention for the Protection of the Marine Environment of the North-East Atlantic, 32(1993) ILM 1072, seeks to coordinate protection of the North-East Atlantic. Until it comes into force the 1972 Oslo Convention for the Prevention of Marine Pollution by Dumping from Ships and Aircraft, 11(1972) ILM 262 and the 1974 Paris Convention for the Prevention of Marine Pollution from Land-Based Sources and Protocols [13(1974) ILM 352, 27(1988) ILM 525] remain in force. The 1992 Bucharest Convention on the Protection of the Black Sea Marine Environment Against Pollution from Land-Based Sources, on Cooperation in Combating Pollution of the Black Sea Environment by Oil and Other Harmful Substances in Emergency Situations and on the Protection of the Black Sea Marine Environment Against Pollution by Dumping, is not yet in force, 32(1993) ILM 1110, 1122, 1127 and 1129.

87. UN Doc.A/AC 138/S.C III/L.26, August 18, 1972, 733 and Draft Articles UN.Doc.A/AC 138/S.III/L.28, March 8, 1973, 762.

88. See LOS Convention, Art. 195.

89. Sharon A. Williams and A.L.C. De Mestral, *An Introduction to International Law* (Butterworths, Canada: 1987), pp. 280-281 reprinted in Covey T. Oliver & ors, Cases and Materials on *The International Legal System* (Westbury, New York, 1995), pp. 463-464.
90. William O. Douglas "Pollution: An International Needing International Solution", 7(1971) 1 *Texas International Law Journal*, p. 2.
91. See *Report of the U.N. Conference on the Marine Environment*, UN. Doc.A/CONF.48/14(1972), revised by U.N. Doc.A/CONF./48/14/ Rev.1(1972) (Declarations and Recommendations of the Conference).
92. *Ibid*, Art. 5.
93. Consent can be either implicit or explicit. Implicit consent may be implied by custom based on state practice evidencing a sense of legal obligation. Explicit consent can be found in the signing and ratification of treaties. The mandatory character of treaties is attributed to the characteristics of sovereignty because such agreements are based on consensus and no sovereign state is obliged to sign or ratify any treaty.
94. Some of the principles have already become part of customary international law by virtue of the fact that many of them form basis of international conventions such as the London Dumping Convention (1972), the Convention on International Trade in Endangered Species (1973), and the U.N. Convention on the Law of the Sea (1982).
95. G.A. Res. 2996, U.N. GAOR, 27th Sess., Supp. No. 30 (A/8730), at 42, U.N. Doc.A/8901(1972).
96. See *ibid*.
97. U.N. Charter Art. 13(1).
98. G.A. Res. 3232, U.N. GAOR, 29th Sess., Supp. No. 31, at 142, U.N. Doc.A/ 9631(1974).
99. G.A. Res. 523, U.N. GAOR, 6th Sess., Supp. No. 20, at 20, U.N. Doc.A/ 2119(1952); G. A. Res. 626, U. N. GAOR, 7th Sess., Supp. No. 20, at 18, U.N. Doc.A/2361 (1952); G.A. Res. 1314, U.N. GAOR, 13th Sees, Supp. No. 18, at 27, U.N. Doc.A/4090 (1958).
100. G.A, Res. 35/7, U.N. GAOR, 35th Sess., Supp. No. 48, at 15, U.N. Doc. A/ 35/48 (1980).
101. Susan H. Bragdon, "National Sovereignty and Global Environmental Responsibility: Can the Tension Be Reconciled for the Conservation of Biological Diversity?", 33(1992) 2 *Harvard International Law Journal*, pp. 383-387.
102. *Beijing Declaration on Environment and Development*, Xinhua, Gen. Overseas News Service, June 20, 1991, item no. 0620135 (Lixis Database, Nexis Library).
103. "Access to technologies" is meant to be broad, including access to information and training so that research relevant to the needs of developing countries can be pursued both by and within those countries. The physical transfer of technologies would also be included.

104. "Open access" would not mean access free of charge, but rather that access would not be regulated in such a way as to effectively deny it.

105. Considering genetic resources to be part of the common heritage of humankind has obvious implications for national sovereignty over those resources. Although raised in several environmental contexts, international law is still far from recognizing such a concept. Reactions among states to this concept have varied according to the context. For example, the United States and other industrialized nations rejected a common heritage regime as laid down by the Law of the Sea Convention for the deep seabed beyond the limits of national jurisdiction. The regime was generally supported by developing countries. Nonetheless, despite refusing to accept a common heritage regime in an area beyond national jurisdiction, many of the same industrialized nations proposed its introduction in the draft convention on biological diversity where the resources reside primarily within *other* states' jurisdictions.

106. It must be noted, however, that this interpretation would be a departure from the conventional approach to state liability which required a tangible injury translatable into provable monetary damages for responsibility to be found. The cause-effect link between the loss of species and global environmental harm is often indirect.

107. See The Brundtland Report "Towards Common Action: Proposals for Institutional and Legal Change", Our Common Future in World Commission on Environment and Development reprinted in Covely T. Oliver & ors, *The International Legal Systems*: *Cases and Materials* (Westbury, New York: The Foundation Press, Inc., 1995), p. 535.

108. *Ibid.*

109. One of the more surprising and significant achievements of the UN Conference on Environment and Development (UNCED), the Rio "Earth Summit" held in June 1992, was the agreement to create a new high-level organ within the UN secretariat specifically to coordinate further work on sustainable development. The headline achievements of the UNCED included the adoption of binding conventions on climate change and on bio-diversity. The conference also adopted the Rio Declaration (a statement of principles derivative of the Stockholm Declaration of 1972) and an extensive action programme of some 800 pages call *Agenda 21*. It is in this last document that the Sustainable Development is mooted. See Mark Imber, "Too many cooks/The Post Rio reform of the United Nations", 69(1993) *International Affairs 55*.

110. The notion "sustainable development" addresses views such as:

(a) Philosophical point of view—while one side of the philosophical part of sustainable development is spiritual—the earth and its preservation over man, a direct perversion of Genesis One, the other side is a direct inversion of the principles found in the Constitution of the United States and represented by the U.S. flag. Any philosophy which has principles found in the Constitution of the USSR as its basis is against personal freedom as all freedoms are given by the state and therefore can be altered, changed, amended, and abolished at any time—for any reason versus unalienable rights which cannot change and cannot be taken away and which come from God not the state.

(b) Environmental point of view—

Since the Rio "Earth Summit" in June, 1992, there has been a concerted effort by the United Nations and environmental groups to change the face of America. The outcome of Rio was Agenda 21 which is an agreed "programme of cooperative international work for the sustained and responsible development of the planet for the 21st century." "Biodiversity" is a phrase coined to describe the variety of the genes, species and ecosystems found on our planet. Al Gore wrote in his book, *Earth in the Balance*, "We must make the rescue of the environment the central principle for civilization...use every policy and program, every law and institution, every treaty and alliance, every tactic and strategy, every plan and course of action...to halt the destruction of the environment and to preserve and nature our ecological system." Although the Biodiversity Treaty did not pass in the Senate, the President, by Executive Order, established the President's Council on Sustainable Development to effect the Programme, pacts and treaties agreed to at the Rio Earth Summit.

Today, many of these ideas are being implemented around the country by a number of U.S. Agencies and environmental non-governmental organizations. If you ask farmers and ranchers across America, they will tell you their farms and property are endangered by these ideas. Should the Environmental Protection Agency come around and determine that there is an endangered species on your property, your property could be condemned so as to protect this species and "save the ecosystem." This action cuts to the heart of personal property rights. If we have no personal property rights, then we have no freedom. The potential loss of future property rights is seen in the Wetlands Project which wants to ultimately force people to live in "human islands" surrounded by buffer zones while 50% of the surface of America is returned to natural wildlife.

(c) Economic point of view—

Sustainable development is economic—who would have ever thought that there was a possibility that the air we breathe and the water we drink would be measured by a global body and that our use could then be measured according to how much we produce (or how we think), a Marxist/Leninist concept. Production and consumption are at the heart of sustainable development—if you don't produce, you don't consume. When we ask ourselves who cannot produce, the answer is babies and toddlers as well as the elderly. Do we wonder why there is an upward trend in abortion and euthanasia? A women who is not pregnant and who has a limited number of children can produce more for the state than the woman who has three children. In addition, welfare is not sustainable as those living off of it are not producing.

> Lastly, would it be inappropriate to mention the fact that there are many industries and individuals who will and have already benefited from sustainable development?

Quoted in Joan M. Veon, "Sustainable Development", visit at http://www.womensgroup/SUSD.html

111. Mukul Sanwal, "Sustainable Development, the Rio Declaration and Multilateral Cooperation", 4(1993) *Colorado Journal of International Law 48-49.*
112. *Rio Declaration*, Prin. 1.
113. *Ibid.* Prin. 2.
114. *Ibid.* Prin. 4.
115. *Ibid.* Prin. 3.
116. *Ibid.* Prin 11.
117. *Ibid.* Prin. 10.
118. *Ibid.* Prin 15.
119. *Ibid.* Prin. 16.
120. *Ibid.* Prin. 17.
121. *Ibid.* Prins. 18 & 19.
122. *Ibid.* Prin. 5.
123. *Ibid.* Prin. 9.
124. *Ibid.* Prin. 12.
125. *Ibid.* Prin. 14.
126. *Ibid.* Prin. 16.
127. *Ibid.* Prin. 8.
128. *Ibid.*
129. *Ibid.* Prin. 9.
130. *Ibid.*
131. *Ibid.* Prin. 12.
132. *Supra.*
133. *Supra.*
134. *Rio Declaration,* Prin. 7.
135. Prin. 21.
136. Mukul Sanwal, "Sustainable Development, the Rio Declaration and Multilateral Cooperation", 4(1993) 1 *Colorado Journal of International Environmental Law and Policy 49-52.*
137. Robert W. Hahn & *Kenneth R. Richards,* The Internationalization of Environmental Regulation, *30(1989) Harvard International Law Journal 421.*

138. Audra E. Dehan, "An International Environmental Court: Should There be One", 3(1992) *Touro Journal of Transnational Law 33.*

139. The Preamble of the Maastricht Treat states that parties are "[d]etermined to promote economic....progress....within the context of....environmental protection...." Treaty on European Union, *opened for signature* Feb 1, 1992, 31(1992) ILM 253.

140. Mukul Sanwal, *op.cit.,* 57-68.

141. H.L. Dickstein, "International Law and the Environment: Evolving Concepts", 26(1972) *The Year Book of World Affairs 1972,* 249.

142. Krishan Saigal, "Sustainable Management of Ecosystems", OCEAN Yearbook 13, 1998 (The University of Chicago Press) 56, 57.

143. World Commission on Environment and Development, *Our Common Future* (New York: Oxford University Press, 1987), p. 43.

144. Thomas E. Graedel & Paul J. Crutzen, *The Changing Atmosphere, 261 (1989) SCI. AM. 58,61-64 in Thomas J. Schoenbaum & Ronald H. Rosenberg,* Environmental Policy Law: Problems, Cases, and Readings (2nd. 1991) 1049 quoted in Nimby, "Not in Mexico's Backyard? A Case for Recognition of a Human Right to Healthy Environment in the American States", 23(1993) *Georgia Journal of International and Comparative Law 419, n. 33, 48.*

145. *Ibid.*

146. Mark Starik and Gordon P. Rands, "Weaving an Integrated Web: Multilevel and Multisystem Perspective of Ecologically Sustainable Organizations", 20(1995) 4 *Academy of Management Review 908-935.*

147. Krishan Saigal, *op.cit.* at 57-58.

148. Jentje Management 129-148.van Weide, "A System of View of Integrated Coastal Management", 21(1993) *Ocean and Coastal Management* 129-148.

149. Krishan Saigal, *op.cit.* at 74.

150. United Nations Environment Programme, *Ethics and Agenda* 21 (New York: United Nations Publications, 1994). A look at some other systems reveals a similar convergence. Zarathustra (3,000 B.C.), for example, has the following in his book *Zend Avesta*:

     Do not pollute earth, air, and water;

     Do not cut trees nor destroy green vegetation but transform waste lands And deserts into gardens;

     Refrain from killing birds and animals. Treat them with love and affection and make use of them to improve the lot of mankind. *Thus Spake Zarathustra*, compiled by B.S. Surti (Madras: Ramkrishna Mission, 1993). In the Indian scripture the Atharva Veda (contemporaneous with *Zend Avesta*) the following is stated:

     What of Thee I dig out,
     Let that quickly grow over,

Let me not hit thy vitals,
Or thy heart.

Atharva Veda, 12.35, quoted in M. S, Swaminathan, "Biodiversity and Peace on the Oceans", in *Pacem in Maribus XXII* ed. K. Saigal, R. Rajagopalan, and L.S. Ganesh (Madras: International Ocean Institute Operational Centre [India], 1995), p. 69.

151. The proceedings of the first symposium in 1984 are found in Variability and Management of Large Marine Ecosystems, K. Sherman and L. Alexander (eds.) (Boulder: Westview Press, 1986). LMEs are defined as areas of coastal and ocean space of a minimum of "... 2,00,000 square kilometres or some 60,000 square nautical miles" that are "...characterized by distinct bathymetry, hydrography, productivity, and tropically dependent populations." Sherman, one of the leading scholars on the subject, has divided the world's coastal and ocean areas into 49 LMEs in need of transboundary management. See Elisabeth Mann Borgese & ors (eds), *OCEAN* Yearbook 16 (The University of Chicago Press: 2002), 430.

152. See M. H. Belsky, "Management of Large Marine Ecosystems: Developing a New Rule of Customary International Law", 22(1985) 4 *San Diego Law Review* 733-763, 736.

153. Brundtland Report: World Commission on Environment and Development, *Our Common Future* (Oxford: Oxford University Press, 1987), pp. 44-45. This document is the final report of the WCED, an independent commission chaired by G. H. Brundtland, established by the United Nations General Assembly in 1983 by General Assembly Resolution 38/161.

154. *Ibid.*, p. 43.

155. E.M. Borgese and K. Saigal, "Managerial Implications of Sustainable Development in the Ocean", *OCEAN* Yearbook 12 (Chicago: University of Chicago Press, 1996) pp. 1-18 at p. 2.

156. During the 1980s, UNEP initiatives included: the formation of an Action Plan for the East Asian Seas and the strengthening of the Mediterranean Regional Programme by the passing of further protocols on the protection of the Mediterranean Sea against pollution from land-based sources and on specially protected areas and biological diversity, see Vander Zwaag and Johnston, "Towards the Management of the Gulf of Thailand: Charting the Course of Cooperation", in SEAPOL Integrated Studies of the Gulf of Thailand, vol. 1, ed. D.M. Johnston (Bangkok: SEAPOL, 1998), p. 61.

157. Premiers of New Brunchwick and Nova Scotia and Governors of Maine, Massachussetts, and New Hampshire, 1989 Agreement on the Conservation of the Marine Environment in the Gulf of Maine, reprinted in Gulf of Maine Council on the Marine Environment, *The Gulf of Maine Action Plan* 1991-2000 (New Castle, Maine: Gulf of Maine Council, 1991), Appendix.

158. See Vander Zwaag and Johnston, *op.cit.* 79.

159. K. von Molke, *The Vorsorgeprinzip in West German Environmental Policy*, Report prepared for the Royal Commission on Environmental Pollution

(United Kingdom) (London: HMSO, 1987), p. 5, writes that the principle, first appearing under the term "*Vorsorgeprinzip*" in German federal law in 1976, is stated as follows: Environmental policy is not fully accomplished by warding off imminent hazards and the elimination of danger which has occurred. Precautionary environmental policy requires furthermore that natural resources are protected and demands on them are made with care. Reprinted in: Vander Zwaag, *Canada and Marine Environmental Protection: Charting a Legal Course Towards Sustainable Development* (London: Kluwer Law International, 1995), p. 7.

160. See for example, paragraph 7 of the Bergen Ministerial Declaration on Sustainable Development in the ECE Region, 14 May 1990, where the meeting of 34 Ministers at Begen marked the first time that states declared the precautionary approach as a legal principle having general application. It read as follows: "In order to achieve sustainable development, policies must be based on the precautionary principle. Environmental measures must anticipate, prevent, and attack the causes of environmental degradation. Where there are threats of serious or irreversible damage, lack of full scientific certainty should not be used as a reason for postponing measures to prevent environmental degradation." Reproduced in D. Freestone and E. Hey (eds), *The Precautionary Principle and International Law: The Challenge of Implementation* (London: Kluwer Law International, 1996), p. 29.

161. Rio Declaration Prin. 15., the precautionary approach reads as follows: "In order to protect the environment, the precautionary approach shall be widely applied by States according to their capabilities. Where there are threats of serious or irreversible damage, lack of full scientific certainty shall not be used as a reason for postponing cost-effective measures to prevent environmental degradation."

162. *Ibid.*, Prin. 7.

163. *Ibid.*, Prin. 13.

164. *Ibid.*, Prin. 17.

165. *Ibid.*, Prins 10 and 22, respectively.

166. Agenda 21: *The Earth Summit: The United Nations Conference on Environment and Development* (UNED) (London: Graham & Trotman/ Martinus Nijhoff, 1993), pp. 123-508.

167. *Ibid.*, paras 17.1, 17.21, and 17.22(a).

168. *Ibid.*, para 17.5, which asks that states "... commit themselves to integrated management and sustainable development of coastal areas and the marine environment under their national jurisdiction" and paragraph 17.6, which encourages states to establish and strengthen coordination mechanism for integrated coastal zone management.

169. The Convention on Biological Diversity, 5 June 1992, UN.Doc.UNEP/ Bio.Div/N 7-INC.5/4, reprinted in 31(1992) ILM 818-841, entering into force on 29 December 1993.

170. The precautionary approach is found implicitly in the Preamble of the CBD, *ibid., where if there is: "...threat of significant reduction in loss of biological diversity, lack of full scientific certainty should not be used as a reason for postponing measures to avoid or minimize such a threat."*

171. The Jakarta Mandate on Marine and Coastal Biodiversity, adopted at the Second Meeting of the Conference of the Parties to the CBD (November 1995), UN.Doc.UNEP/CBD/COP/2/19 and UN Doc.UNEP/CBD/COP/2/5.

172. *Ibid*., see: Thematic issue-1 Integrated Marine and Coastal Area Management, and Thematic Issue-2 Marine and Coastal Protected Areas.

173. *Ibid.*

174. Richard K. Gardiner, *International Law* (London Pearson Longman; 2003) 429.

175. Sam Blay & ors (eds.), *Public International Law: An Australian Perspective* (Melbourne: Oxford University Press, 1997) 361.

176. *Legality of the Threat or Use of Nuclear Weapons*, Advisory Opinion, [1996] ICJ Rep 226, at 241-2, para. 29.

177. Concern about the degradation of the environment is credited to the "flower power" era of the 1960s, although, historically, the international community has responded to specific concerns on an *ad hoc* basis, reflected in the adoption of the 1902 Convention on the Protection of Birds Useful to Agriculture, the 1911 Convention for Preservation of the Fur Seal and the 1936 Convention for the Regulation of Whaling. 155 LNTS 351. Also see Steven Wheatley, *International Law* (London: Blackstone Press Ltd., 1996) 106.

178. K.B. Lali, "Economic Inequality and International Law", 149 (1974) 1 IJIL 11-12.

179. Michael Stopford, "Locating the Balance: The United Nations and the New World Disorder", 34(1994) *Virginia Journal of International Law* 687.

180. Carl August Fleischer, "An International Convention on Environment Cooperation Among Nations: Proposed Draft, Policies and Goals", 7(1971) 1 *Texas International Law Journal* 73.

181. See Bob Eckhardt, "How we got the dirtiest Stream in America Regulation of Local Hazards—The Houston Ship Channel", *ibid. 26.*

182. SAARC consists of Bangladesh, Bhutan, India, Maldives, Nepal, Pakistan, and Sri Lanka.

183. Report to the Commission on Sustainable Development of the Economic and Social Council, U.N. Doc.E/CN.17/1997/8 of 10 February 1997.

184. See Charles M. Hassett, "Weather Modification and Control: International Organizational Prospects", *ibid.* 104-105.

4

DEEP SEABED MINING AND MARINE ENVIRONMENT

4.1. Scope of the Study

The deep seabed mining regime has come to being in the United Nations Convention on the Law of the Sea, 1982.[1] Part XI of the Convention entitled as "The Area" deals with the regime of deep seabed and ocean floor. For the purposes of the Convention:

(1) 'Area' means the sea-bed and ocean floor and subsoil thereof, beyond the limits of national jurisdiction;

(2) 'Authority' means the International Sea-Bed Authority;

(3) "Activities in the Area" means all activities of exploration for, and exploitation of, the resources of the Area;

(4) "Pollution of the marine environment" means the introduction by man, directly or indirectly, of substances or energy into the marine environment, including estuaries, which results or is likely to result in such deleterious effects as harm to living resources and marine life, hazards to human health, hindrance to marine activities, including fishing and other legitimate uses of the sea, impairment of quality for use of sea water and reduction of amenities;

(5) (a) 'dumping' means:

(i) any deliberate disposal of wastes or other matter from vessels, aircraft, platforms or other man-made structures at sea;

(ii) any deliberate disposal of vessels, aircraft, platforms or other man-made structures at sea;

(b) 'dumping' does not include:

(i) the disposal of wastes or other incidental to, or derived from the normal operations of vessels, aircraft, platforms or other man-made structures at sea and their equipment, other than wastes or other matter transported by or to vessels, aircraft, platforms or other man-made structures at sea, operating for the purpose of disposal of such matter or derived from the treatment of such wastes or other matter on such vessels, aircraft, platforms or structures;

(ii) placement of matter for a purpose other than the mere disposal thereof, provided that such placement is not contrary to the aims of this Convention.[2]

"States Parties" means States which have consented to be bound by the LOS Convention and for which this Convention is in force.[3]

For the purposes of Part XI of the Convention:

(a) 'resources' means all solid, liquid or gaseous mineral resources *in situ* in the Area at or beneath the seabed, including polymetallic nodules;

(b) resources, when recovered from the Area, are referred to as 'minerals'.[4] The Area and its resources are the common heritage of mankind.[5]

In all matters, peace is warranted and in the case of marine environment any activity needs to be for peaceful purposes. In exercising their rights and performing their duties under the LOS Convention, States Parties shall refrain from any threat or use of force against the territorial integrity or political independence of any State, or any other manner inconsistent with the principles of international law embodied in the Charter of the United Nations.[6]

Marine environment gives rise to mean the marine areas within and beyond the limits of national jurisdiction.[7] The deep seabed mining area conventionally seems to consider the Area and above it, its water space as well. That is to say, the marine environment beyond national jurisdiction relates to the high seas and the common heritage regimes.[8] The LOS Convention's six high seas freedom have practically some limitations in the sense that the freedoms shall be exercised by all States with due regard for the interests of other states in their exercise of the freedom of the high seas, and also with due regard for the rights under this Convention with respect to activities in the Area.[9] The limitations seem to promote reciprocal approaches to peace and order. In effect, "the high seas shall be reserved for peaceful purposes."[10]

4.2. Marine Environment for Peaceful Purposes

The UN Convention on the Law of the Sea, 1982 has provided ocean space to be used for various concerns subject to peaceful purposes. The objective of environment and development is to take measures congenial to peace at every stage. The LOS Convention bestows sea regimes within and beyond national jurisdiction to be peacefully concerned.[11] Beyond national jurisdiction environment regime is to be concerned with the regime relating to the high seas and the Area. The high seas do not sustain claims to sovereignty. "No State may validly purport to subject any part of the high seas to its sovereignty."[12] This principle identically is also applicable in the case of the Area and its resources. Specifically, "No State shall claim or exercise sovereignty or sovereign rights over any part of the Area or its resources, nor shall any State or natural or juridical person appropriate any part thereof. No such claim or exercise of sovereignty or sovereign rights nor such appropriation shall be recognized."[13]

The general conduct of States in relation to the Area shall be in accordance with the provisions of Part XI of the LOS Convention, the principles embodied in the Charter of the United Nations and other rules of international law in the interests of maintaining peace and security and promoting international co-operation and mutual understanding.[14] The LOS Convention envisages marine scientific research to be carried out under its Part XIII. That means, marine scientific research in the Area shall be carried out exclusively for peaceful purposes and for the benefit for mankind as a whole, in accordance with Part XIII. The thing to note here is the fact that at every stage the measures to be taken are needed for peaceful purposes. The use of Area is reiterated for peaceful purposes and to this end the LOS Convention gives provision. The Area shall be open to use for peaceful purposes by all States, whether coastal or land-locked, without discrimination and without prejudice to the other provisions of Part XI.[15] It enables to emphasise that all states need to be committed to promoting peace and security in any situation as to the use of the Area.

States and competent international organizations shall, in accordance with the principle of respect for sovereignty and jurisdiction and on the basis of mutual benefit, promote international co-operation in marine scientific research for peaceful purposes. In this context, without prejudice to the rights and duties of States under the LOS Convention, a State, in the application of Part III, shall provide, as appropriate, other States with a reasonable opportunity to obtain from it, or with its co-operation, information necessary to prevent and control damage to the health and safety of persons and to the marine environment.[16]

As a matter of fact, global change is now being produced, more than any factor, by what hundreds of millions of individuals (and couples) are doing. Its pace and direction will only be changed by what hundreds of millions of individuals (and couples) do or stop doing. Since the new *genere* or problems depend on such wide participation, reaches into so many technical and professional fields, and touches so many economic interests and political sensitivities, it is not to be expected that any one system of governance would "work". The Global Commons will be governed pluralistically or not at all.[17] There is no alternative to peace and security for the states and organizations without whose cooperation it is not possible to activate in the case where common interests are involved. States and competent international organizations shall co-operate, through the conclusion of bilateral and multilateral agreements, to create favourable conditions for the conduct of marine scientific research in the marine environment and to integrate the efforts of scientists in studying the essence of phenomena and processes occurring in the marine environment and the interrelations between them.[18]

States, directly or through competent international organizations, shall cooperate in accordance with their capabilities to promote actively the development and transfer of marine science and technology on fair and reasonable terms and conditions. States shall promote the development of the marine scientific and technological capacity of States which may need and request technical assistance in this field, particularly developing States, including land-locked and geographically disadvantaged States, with regard to the exploration, exploitation, conservation of the marine environment, marine scientific research and other activities in the marine environment compatible with the LOS Convention, with a view to accelerating the social and economic development of the developing States. States shall endeavour to foster favourable economic and legal conditions for the transfer of marine technology for the benefit of all parties concerned on an equitable basis.[19]

In terms of international machinery for environmental assessment, it seems to be doing rather well these days. Worldwide scientific cooperation in this field is well established and functional; it includes formal bilateral and multilateral channels as well as informal transnational mechanisms for information sharing and "peer review." While global demand for environmental knowledge remains enormous, there are indeed many examples of successful assessment programs at hand—from the International Geosphere-Biosphere Programme of the International Council of Scientific Unions (ICSU) to the 1987 report of the World Commission on Environment and Development (Brundtland Commission).

When it comes to international environmental management or governance, the focus of current performance evaluations is on the structure established by and after the 1972 Stockholm Conference on the Human Environment, i.e., primarily the united Nations Environment Programme and global and regional institutions formed after UNEP. Yet the history of international environmental cooperation did not begin at Stockholm. Conventions for marine pollution control were already drafted twenty years earlier by the International Maritime Organization (IMO).

The constitutional mandate of the UN Food and Agriculture Organization (FAO) for the "conservation of natural resources" was formulated in 1945. Standards to protect workers against occupational hazards in the working environment were adopted by the International Labour Organization (ILO) as early as 1920s. Transboundary agreements for the protection of migratory birds and for the management of shared water resources date to well before World War I, as do international arrangements for the sharing of atmospheric data by nineteenth century precursors of the World Meteorological Organization. The first serious, if unsuccessful, attempt at global environmental management was probably Theodore Roosevelt's initiative in 1909 to convene at the Hague a world conference for natural resource conservation.[20]

Principle 21 of the Stockholm Declaration expressly refers to the United Nations Charter and to the principles of international law. The most important of these is the principle of good neighbourliness which is more properly expressed in its broader form as the rule of harmless use of territory, which means that cooperation between states must be developed for preventive purposes.

The reference to the United Nations Charter has the effect of strengthening this allegiance to the general principles and means that states, in their mutual relations, must abstain from the use of force or any other method, such as deliberative massive pollution of neighbouring territory, which would violate the sovereignty of the polluted country and constitute aggressive behaviour.

Confirmation of the existing law is also found in the actual wording of Principle 21, since to say that states "have the responsibility to ensure that activities within their jurisdiction or control do not cause damage to the environment of other states" is to reaffirm the obligation to take all reasonable steps, an obligation placed on them by the principles. The Earth Summit (Rio Declaration) subsumes Stockholm's Principle 2 in its Principle 21 in which attempts have been made to balance the right of states to be free from external interference (in exploitation of their resources) with that of state responsibility (i.e. not to cause damage beyond its territory).

The Earth Summit lays stress on providing cooperation to result in promoting environment. It means cooperation not only in environment issues but social matters as well. "All States and all people shall cooperate in the essential task of eradicating poverty as an indispensable requirement for sustainable development, in order to decrease the disparities in standards of living and better meet the needs of the majority of the people of the world."[21] Needs have been warranted for global partnership. "States shall cooperate in a spirit of global partnership to conserve, protect and restore the health and integrity of the Earth's ecosystem. In view of the different contributions to global environmental degradation, States have common but differentiated responsibilities. The developed countries acknowledge the responsibility that they bear in the international pursuit of sustainable development in view of the pressures their societies place on the global environment and of the technologies and financial resources they command."[22]

In strengthening cooperation transfer of technology and related necessities have been taken into account. "States should cooperate to strengthen endogenous capacity-building for sustainable development by improving scientific understanding through exchange of scientific and technological knowledge. And by enhancing the development, adaptation, diffusion and transfer of technologies, including new and innovative technologies."[23] Marine environment implementation is highly capital oriented. It is therefore, inevitable to make capital capabilities accessible to states. "States should cooperate to promote a supportive and open international economic system that would lead to economic growth and sustainable development in all countries, to better address the problems of environment degradation. Trade policy measures for environmental purposes should not constitute a means of arbitrary or unjustifiable discrimination or a disguised restriction on international trade. Unilateral actions to deal with environmental challenges outside the jurisdiction of the importing country should be avoided. Environmental measures addressing transboundary or global environmental problems, as far as possible, should be based on an international consensus."[24]

The Earth Summit pays heed to environmental damage to be compensated. "States shall develop national law regarding liability and compensation for the victims of pollution and other environmental damage. States shall also cooperate in an expeditious and more determined manner to develop further international law regarding liability and compensation for adverse effects of environmental damage caused by activities within their jurisdiction or control to areas beyond their jurisdiction."[25] Urges are made for cooperation to discourage or prevent environmental degradation. "States should effectively cooperate to discourage or prevent the relocation and transfer to other States of any activities and substances that cause severe environmental degradation or are found to be harmful to human health."[26] The ever-growing approaches have been taken into account stating that "States and people shall cooperate in good faith and in a spirit of partnership in the fulfilment of the principles embodied in this Declaration and in the further development of international law in the field of sustainable development."[27]

In order to foster a regime for marine environment emphasis is laid on states to provide cooperation. In doing so, there seems obligation is likely to be promoted. The extent of the obligation may be seen in the LOS Convention, which provides that "where a state becomes aware of cases in which the marine environment is in imminent danger of being damaged or has been damaged by pollution, it shall immediately notify other states likely to be affected by such damage.[28] Since threats in environment are trans-frontier problems that affect all states, states and organizations subregional, regional and global require to strengthen their efforts aimed at peaceful purposes for ensuring marine environment and development. The very doctrinal approach is seen in the Rio Declaration to be: "Peace, development and environmental protection are interdependent and indivisible."[29] All this results in saying that environmental regime is committed to peaceful purposes for realities.

4.3. High Seas Regime and Marine Environment

The high seas is that area of the sea that lies beyond the jurisdiction of coastal states. Under the LOS Convention, the high seas encompasses all parts of the sea that are not included in the internal waters, territorial sea, EEZ or archipelagic waters of a state.[30] In the early development of international law the juridical nature of the high seas was subject to much controversy, as was mentioned earlier in relation to the debate between Selden and Grotius over 'closed' or 'open' seas. By the nineteenth century the debate had been resolved in favour of the latter, and it is now a general principle of customary international law, codified in the Convention on the High Seas, 1958 and in the 1982 LOS Convention, that the high seas are open to all states and that no state may subject any part of the high seas to its sovereignty.[31]

The first corollary of this principle is that no state may interfere with the exercise by a foreign ship of the freedoms of the high seas. In the Convention on the High Seas 1958, these freedoms are listed as freedom of navigation, freedom of fishing, freedom to lay submarine cables and pipelines, and freedom of overflight. To these, the 1982 LOS Convention adds the freedom of scientific research and the freedom to construct artificial islands and installations.[32] These freedoms are subject to exceptions, both general and particular.

The high seas freedoms shall be exercised by all States with due regard for the interests of other States in their exercise of the freedom of the high seas, and also with due regard for the rights under this Convention with respect to activities in the Area.[33] Additionally, the freedom of fishing is subject to conservation measures for the living resources of the high seas, and the freedom to lay submarine cables and pipelines is subject to the right of a coastal state to regulate the laying of pipelines on its continental shelf.

Notwithstanding the wide freedoms given to all states in respect of the high seas, controversies do arise over conflicting uses of the area. In the 1970s, Australia and New Zealand protested against French nuclear testing in the Pacific Ocean, in the course of which France closed large areas of the high seas to foreign shipping. Australia and New Zealand argued, among other things, that interference with ships on the high seas, and with aircraft in the superjacent airspace, infringed their freedoms of navigation and overflight, thus raising the question of whether France had acted with due regard to the interests of other states. The resultant cases before the ICJ, the *Nuclear Test* cases, were never determined on their merits because the Court decided that the cases are moot, following France's announcement that it would cease atmospheric testing. None the less, the cases provide a good example of conflicts of interest that may arise from the exercise of high seas freedoms.

The second corollary of the principle that no state may subject any part of the high seas to its sovereignty is that states may exercise neither legislative nor enforcement jurisdiction over the foreign ships on the high seas. Alternatively stated, as a general rule ships are subject to the exclusive jurisdiction of the state whose flag they fly while on the high seas.[34] It is for this reason that principles of international law with respect to marine pollution, safety at sea, and so on, commonly operate by requiring states to adopt and enforce laws governing vessels flying their flag. To the general principle of exclusive flag state jurisdiction there are a number of defined exceptions by which states are permitted to interfere with foreign ships on the high seas. All states have legislative jurisdiction, enforcement jurisdiction, or both, for the purpose of suppressing piracy, slave trading, unauthorised broadcasting, illicit trafficking, and pollution arising from collisions on the high seas.[35]

Moreover, a coastal state has the right to use its warships or government ships in hot pursuit of a foreign ship that is believed to have violated the laws and regulations of the coastal state.[36] This right entitles the coastal state to arrest a foreign ship on the high seas, provided the foreign ship has been pursued uninterrupted from a maritime zone within the coastal state's jurisdiction.[37]

At present the regime of ocean space beyond national jurisdiction embodies in two dimensional approach. That means, the regime of the Area under the common heritage doctrine and the regime of the high seas under the freedom of the seas principle. The regime relating to the high seas is then aimed at water space and its living resources.

Besides the reduction in geographical scope, the foundations of the freedom of the high seas put forward by Grotius's "Mare Liberum" have now come to be subjected to the due regard principle in article 87(2) of the LOS Convention. Nothing more clearly demonstrates the change in emphasis in the relationship of flag states and coastal states with regard to state rights and responsibilities. Firstly, it limits the freedom of navigation through exercise of ordinary jurisdiction of the flag state. Secondly, with a view to prevent piracy, illegal immigration, drug trafficking, unauthorised broadcasting and pollution of the marine environment the LOS Convention through extraordinary jurisdiction of the coastal state imposes restriction on the freedom of navigation on the high seas. It provides for the right of hot pursuit and subsequent arrest on the high seas and also the right of visit to a coastal state. The traditional freedom of fishing on the high seas also has under article 87(1) a qualifying clause subject to conditions laid down in section 2, which is titled conservation and management of the Living Resources of the high seas. Again when viewed along with the 'due regard rule' in article 87(2) shows that the freedom of fishing is no longer an absolute and unrestricted freedom but there is an obligation for conservation and international co-operation.

Specifically speaking, due to the ever increasing demands and abuses of the seas the international community has been obliged to ensure the effective exercise of freedom by controlling and regulating it even more closely. The LOS Convention has provided for the change of emphasis from freedom of the high seas to control and regulation in the relationship of flag states and coastal states with regards to state rights and responsibilities on the high seas. Coastal States have been quick to exercise their rights by establishing their maritime zones for control and regulation. However, the effectiveness of control and regulation depends not only upon establishing jurisdiction in the coastal state legislation but actually exercising such jurisdiction in practice. Thus there is a need to recognise the associated responsibilities if the rationale of the LOS Convention changing the emphasis from freedom of the high seas to control and regulation is to be not only understood but also to be met. Similarly, there is a need to recognise that along with the freedom of the high seas there is a corresponding responsibility for those seeking to exercise that right.

The LOS Convention in its various provisions repeatedly mentions that states while adopting laws and implementing them must take into account "international standards and rules" and "applicable international standards and rules and recommended practices". But then, what are the international standards to which the LOS Convention refers? Do such standards exist? Strictly speaking, are there universally accepted standards prescribed by a multilateral treaty like the U.N. Charter?

Again, pollution of the high seas is a matter to which no convention, including the 1982 LOS Convention, has provided a permanent solution. A radical change of approach is called for. It is necessary to find a clear-cut solution for this problem. The present jurisdictions (namely, flag, coastal and port state jurisdiction) ought to give way to universal jurisdiction. Pollution of the seas should also become a subject of universal jurisdiction very much like piracy, narcotic drugs traffic, slave trade, etc. Consequently, the offending vessel could be sued in any court for damages and the "flag of convenience" theory or nationality of the owner would not stand in the way of full realisation of damages from the offending vessel.

The argument advanced here is that one who deprives others of the use of marine resources either by destroying them or rendering them unfit for human consumption should be declared an enemy to all mankind—*hostis humani generis*—and subject to penal jurisdiction of any state that captures him.[38]

It is interesting to note that in 1930, much before the first international convention to regulate pollution was adopted in 1954, the International Conference for the Unification of Penal Laws had included *pollution and deliberate poisoning of drinking water or food* among the crimes subject to universal jurisdiction.[39] No doubt at that time focus was on small scale such as urban drinking waters and food. But the changes in the expansion of human demands for food stuffs in the seas make the provisions and demands of 1930 correspondingly relevant to the modern problems of conservation of the ocean environment. Only recently, legal scholars who attended the First International Criminal Court Conference listed "criminal pollution endangering the health and safety of mankind" among the universal crimes recommended for the jurisdiction of the proposed International Criminal Court, where the offender is neither prosecuted by the state having custody of him nor extradited,[40] i.e., he should be surrendered to the International Criminal Court. One private agency concerned with tanker safety called for universal condemnation of polluters.[41]

Clearly, therefore, it is desirable to have universal substantive regulations and procedures ensuring the protection of marine environment generally, rather than simply legally protected interests of particular states and their nationals. That a polluter is an enemy of all peoples and states should acquiesce it in the high seas matters, thereby promoting a regime for marine environment worthily in the high seas.

4.4. Common Heritage for Deep Seabed Mining v. Human Heritage for Environment

We all have some notion of the Common Heritage of Mankind, the air we breathe, the natural energy of the earth, the natural resources of land and sea, our gene pool, which makes a single but diverse family out of the family of humans. The heritage includes many other attributes of nature which are or ought to be shared universally and equitably throughout the earth. Was it the great sixteenth/seventeenth century legal scholar Grotius who first defined the Common Heritage as it relates to the sea? In his words God himself says, "speaking through the voice of nature" in as much as it is not His will to have Nature supply every place with all the necessaries of life. He ordains that some nations excel in one art and others in another..." So by the decree of divine justice it was brought about that one people should supply the needs of another.

Those, therefore, who deny this law, destroy this most praiseworthy bond of human fellowship, remove the opportunities for doing mutual service, in a word do violence to Nature herself. For no hindrance causes to inflict the oceans navigable in every direction, with which God has encompassed all the earth, and the regular and the occasional winds which blow now from one quarter and now from another offer sufficient proof that Nature has given to all peoples a right of access to all other peoples.[42]

Nearly four hundred years later Ambassador Pardo of Malta redefined the oceanic common heritage, going beyond the freedom of the seas to include the resources of the ocean outside the areas of national jurisdiction. This concept was embodied in the now ratified Law of the Sea Treaty. Here the United Nations appointed themselves Trustee for the Common Heritage but limited that trusteeship to the seabed outside a 200 mile exclusive economic zone. The resources of this vast zone were reserved for the coastal states.[43]

Although the common heritage notion is not new, but there seems to be a feeling about the global vision, knowledge and intellectual integrity of Arvid Pardo, together with his lucid presentation of the proposals in 1967, that convinced the United Nations General Assembly to convene the Third United Nations Conference on the Law of the Sea. It is then significant to consider Arvid Pardo for his imagination and clear justification of the principle of the Common Heritage of

Mankind in his presentations to the General Assembly and subsequently during the initial considerations thereof. His elaboration of the principle was adopted as a basis for General Assembly Resolution 2749 (XXV) of 17 December 1970 containing the Declaration of Principles Governing the Sea-Bed and the Ocean Floor beyond the Limits of National Jurisdiction, and the Resolution 2750 (XXV) of the same date wherein the General Assembly decided to convene in 1973, the Third United Nations Conference of the Law of the Sea.

Human heritage seems to mean as attributes pertaining to or characterizing man or mankind who inherits or can inherit. Common heritage bears a concept to inherit the concerned resources. Human heritage is a pre-concept of common heritage. Human heritage gives rise to renewable and non-renewable resources to be in preservation for producing. Specifically speaking, where there will be no environment there will be no growth of resources whether living or non-living. From the viewpoint of the LOS Convention, the Area and its mineral resources—the common heritage are a part of human heritage. Human heritage results in environment, its approach is general than specific as in the case of common heritage.

In the case of human heritage, the need arises for protection and promotion of environment for habitats. Habitats can be defined as the place or type of site where an organism or population naturally occurs and may be classified in a number of ways. Very simple descriptions, such as mangrove/sea-grass/reef/sand, can be useful in some circumstances. However, for sampling marine biodiversity, it is important to realise that the species associated with these basic habitat types vary with factors such as: *depth, e.g.*, algae may dominate at shallow depths, with invertebrates dominating as light penetration decreases; *bottom* type, *e.g.*, granite reefs support different species than do limestone reefs, and muddy bottoms differ from sandy ones; *wave* exposure—influences the type of sea-grass and algae that dominate. Moreover, particular conditions (such as strong currents, upwellings or estuaries) may provide a habitat that may not be typical but nevertheless contributes significantly to the marine biodiversity. Like all natural systems, the marine environment is a sum total of many different parts.[44]

Human heritage is inter-linked with human habitation. Human beings are at the centre of concerns for sustainable development, including adequate shelter for all and sustainable human settlements, and they are entitled to a healthy and productive life in harmony with nature. Human health concerns related to climate change result from a complex set of interacting human and environmental factors. These concerns are particularly serious for the elderly and other vulnerable populations (the very young, the poor, and those whose health is already compromised). Air and water quality, seafood safety, and storm related risks are of great concern for the people particularly surrounding the marine areas.[45]

The risk of water-borne illness, such as gastrointestinal or respiratory diseases and skin, ear, or eye infections, can increase with warmer temperatures and extreme rainfall and runoff. Micro-oganisms associated with diseases in coastal waters, such as toxic algae, red-tide dinoflagellates, vibrio vulnificus (a pathogen contaminating shellfish), and others, can damage habitat and shellfish nurseries and be toxic to both marine species and humans.

As to human habitat steps had been taken globally under the auspices of the United Nations since 1976. More emphasis was reiterated to it in pursuance of the United Nations Conference on Environment and Development, 1992.[46] In order to promote a healthy environment that will continue to support adequate shelter for all and sustainable human settlements for current and future generations, stress is laid on:

(a) Promoting the conservation and sustainable use of urban and peri-urban biodiversity, including forests, local habitats and species biodiversity; the protection of biodiversity should be included within local sustainable development planning activities;

(b) Protecting existing forest resources and promote, where possible, afforestation around and within human settlements in order to fulfil basic needs relating to energy, construction, recreation and food security;

(c) Encouraging, where appropriate, the establishment of productive and recreational green belts around urban and rural agglomerations in order to protect their environment and contribute to the provision of food products;

(d) Reducing significantly the degradation of the marine environment emanating from land-based activities, including municipal, industrial and agricultural wastes and run-off, which have a pernicious impact on the productive areas of the marine environment and coastal areas;

(e) Ensuring that children have access to the natural world on a daily basis through free play outdoors, and establish education programmes to help children investigate their community environments, including natural ecosystems;

(f) Ensuring adequate opportunity for public participation by all interested parties at all levels of environmental decision-making.[47]

The deep seabed regime as embodied in Part XI is one of the innovative attainments of LOS Convention. Truly, not surprisingly, the law of the sea is complex and increasingly important. It is complex because it involves many competing and potentially conflicting state interests (coastal v. non-coastal, land-locked v. shelf-locked, maritime v. non-maritime, developed v. underdeveloped, etc.) and many competing and potentially conflicting uses (commercial and military navigation, coastal and deep sea fishing, hard and soft mineral mining, scientific and strategic exploration, etc). And it is increasingly important because, since the Truman Proclamation of September 28, 1945, 59 Stat. 884, which declared United States jurisdiction over the natural resources of the subsoil and the seabed of the continental shelf, it has been even more challenged by technologically advances and jurisdictional claims that threaten the ecologically wise and politically just management of those ocean bounties upon which a world urgently in need of alternative sources of energy, food, and wealth is manifestly dependent.

At the outset of a small but eloquent book concerning these matters, in anticipation of the Third United Nations Conference on the Law of the Sea (UNCLOS III), the late Wolfgang Friedmann put it this way: "Among the many challenges that face mankind in the remaining decades of the twentieth century two stand out as of crucial importance for the very survival of civilization. One is the ecological problem of man's ability to cope with an environment of his own creation, which now threatens to overwhelm him. The other is the political problem of choosing between a competitive race of nations for power and wealth—a race that can only lead to the ultimate confrontation of a few superpowers—and ordered co-operation, in which countries can combine their purposes, their ingenuity, their resources in an international order that envisages mankind as a whole. The ecological and political challenges are closely concerned. And of all the many areas in which a fateful choice must be made, there is none more important or urgent, both qualitatively and quantitatively, than the future status of the oceans. Towards the close of his book, after reviewing the positive as well as negative developments in ocean use and management, Professor Friedmann warned—ominously—that "the tragedy of mankind may prove to be the inability to adapt its modes of behaviour to the products of its intellect. Twentieth-century man threatens to be a new kind of dinosaur, an animal suffering from a brain ill-adjusted to its environment."[48]

Global sustainable development and poverty reduction requires healthier and more sustainably managed oceans and seas. The fisheries sector alone is the main source of protein for one billion people as well as a major provider of livelihoods: it provides some 5-10% of the world's food supply. There is growing pressure on the marine environment. The decline in marine biodiversity and the depletion of fish stocks are of increasing concern, as is the use of Flags of Convenience, especially for fishing vessels, as a means to avoid management conservation measures.[49]

The marine environment is vulnerable and sensitive to various issues. Climate and atmospheric changes are day to day matter to it. Rational use and development of coastal areas, all seas and marine resources, as well as conservation of the marine environment, requires the ability to determine the present state of these systems and to predict future conditions. The high degree of uncertainty in present information inhibits effective management and limits the ability to make predictions and assess environmental change. Systematic collection of data on marine environmental parameters will be needed to apply integrated management approaches and to predict effects of global climate change and of atmospheric phenomena, such as ozone depletion, on living marine resources and the marine environment. In order to determine the role of the oceans and all seas in driving global systems and to predict natural and human-induced changes in marine and coastal environments, the mechanisms to collect, synthesize and disseminate information from research and systematic observation activities need to be restructured and reinforced considerably.[50]

There are many uncertainties about climate change and particularly about sea level rise. Small increases in sea level have the potential of causing significant damage to small islands and low-lying coasts. Response strategies should be based on sound data. A long-term cooperative research commitment is needed to provide the data required for global climate models and to reduce uncertainty. Meanwhile, precautionary measures should be undertaken to diminish the risks and effects, particularly on small islands and on low-lying and coastal areas of the world.[51] In the case of the Bay of Bengal marine environment small island state like Maldives and low-lying coastal state as Bangladesh need to be seriously considered.

It should be noted that the aftermath of deep seabed mining is still unpredictable. Questions arise as to whether activities in the Area will affect resources otherwise such as the living resources and others too. In Agenda 21 paragraph 17 deals with protection of oceans, all kinds of seas, including enclosed and semi-enclosed seas, and coastal areas and the protection, rational use and development of their living resources, but it has not paid heed to the aftermath of activities in the Area. However, it is not possible until and unless data regarding deep sea bed mining is made available.

4.5. Protection of Marine Environment in the Area

The notion that elements of the environment were to be seen as resources to be safeguarded and managed for future generations, introduced by the Stockholm Declaration, 1972 led to the development by the International Union for the Conservation of Nature, sponsored by UNEP, of the World Conservation Strategy. The Strategy, which takes a global and ecosystem approach, called for the maintenance of essential ecological processes, the preservation of genetic diversity and the sustainable use of species and ecosystems. Much of the Strategy was incorporated into the World Charter for Nature 1982, which was adopted by the UN General Assembly by solemn proclamation, with only the USA dissenting, on 28 October 1982. The Charter, which "proclaims... principles of conservation by which all human conduct affecting nature is to be guided and judged", represents a synthesis of the Stockholm Declaration and the World Conservation Strategy. The Charter marks a firm departure from the notion of conservation for the purposes of consumptive uses. The environment and the living resources within it are to be protected and conserved for their own worth and for non-consumptive uses. Many of the principles espoused in the Charter have now been incorporated into binding treaties, such as the Biodiversity Convention 1992.

Also significant was the adoption of the UN Convention on the Law of the Sea, 1982 (LOS Convention). This imposes on states parties the obligation to protect all of the marine environment, including all the resources therein. This obligation extends both to areas outside and those within a state's jurisdiction. It also contains provisions relating to the protection of the marine environment from marine and land-based pollution.

The Earth Summit which met in Rio, 1992 took into account the Stockholm Declaration and the particular needs of developing countries. One of the outcomes of the Summit was the Rio Declaration, adopted by consensus by more than 175 states. It is a statement of principles or goals, some of which have already been incorporated into treaties and into domestic state practice and may, therefore, constitute customary norms. Its Preamble states that it reaffirms and seeks to build on the Stockholm Declaration "with the goal of establishing a new and equitable partnership through the creation of new levels of cooperation among states, key sectors of societies and people, working towards international agreements which respect the interests of all and protect the integrity of the global environmental nature of the Earth, our home...". In addition, the conference produced a non-binding Declaration on Forest Principles to guide states in their forestry practices and to lay the foundation for subsequent treaty provisions. It also adopted the equally non-binding, but very influential, Agenda 21. This a comprehensive 600-page action plan covering all aspects of the environment and development, which is intended as a guide for states in designing and pursuing their environmental and developmental policies and international relations into the twenty-first century. The conference also produced the Biodiversity Convention and the Framework Convention on Climate Change (the Climate Change Convention). Thus, in the outcome we can see how the continuing development of principles and the proliferation of resolutions and declarations is adding to the formation of customary rules and has led to negotiations for specific treaties focusing on the prevention of environmental harm and the conservation sustainable development of the environment and its resources.[52]

Marine environment is included in Chapter 17 of Agenda 21. The chapter on oceans is the longest and one of the most complex Chapter of Agenda 21. There are 137 paragraphs of this chapter. Neither is seen to deal specifically with environment as to the Area, its resources *in situ* and *on situ*. There is no mention of marine environment to result from activities in the Area. However, the LOS Convention is seen to deal with the matter to some extent. In the case of protection of the marine environment the Convention bestows upon the Authority to take measures. To this end it addresses:

> Necessary measures shall be taken in accordance with this Convention with respect to activities in the Area to ensure effective protection for the marine environment from harmful effects which may arise such activities. To this end the Authority[53] shall adopt appropriate rules, regulations and procedures for *inter alia*:
>
> (a) the prevention, reduction and control of pollution and other hazards to the marine environment, including the coastline, and of interference with the ecological balance of the marine environment, particular attention being paid to the need for protection from harmful effects of such activities as drilling, dredging, excavation, disposal of waste, construction and operation or maintenance of installations, pipelines and other devices related to such activities;
>
> (b) the protection and conservation of the natural resources of the Area and prevention of damage to the flora and fauna of the marine environment.[54]

It seems that the Authority is the machinery through which marine environment is to be ensured. The notion "natural resources" conventionally signifies as mineral (non-living) resources but the notion "flora and fauna" signifies plants and animal life. It thus results in taking into account botanical and biological species and as such, there are obligations to maintain and protect marine environment to ensure all these. That means, the LOS Convention here has embodied means in broader perspective in the sense that the Authority should not be only concerned with the matters of the mineral resources. The Authority has a role to safeguard and promote the ecosystem in the Area. In respect of protection and promotion of ecosystem measures are to be taken against harmful effects to cause or caused by activities in the Area.

Paragraph 1 of article 147 bestows: "Activities in the Area shall be carried out with reasonable regard for other activities in the marine environment" and paragraph 3 says: "Other activities in the marine environment shall be conducted with reasonable regard for activities in the Area" Accommodation of 'activities in the Area' and 'in the marine environment' has been emphasised, of course, reciprocally effective in respect of the 'Area' and the 'marine environment.' There is nothing to question as to any step to be taken in the seas, ocean floor and subsoil thereof within and beyond national jurisdiction for peaceful purposes. Protection of human life is reiterated in "With respect to activities in the Area, necessary measures shall be taken to ensure effective protection of human life. To this end the Authority shall adopt appropriate rules, regulations and procedures to supplement existing international law as embodied in relevant treaties."[55] With respect to activities in the Area if human life is endangered, there is a need to take measure for protection for whatever causes it occurs. There is then an opening to count environmental hazards if caused for activities in the Area for protection of human life.

The Authority is the organization through which States Parties shall, in accordance with Part XI of the LOS Convention, organize and control activities in the Area, particularly with a view to administering the resources of the Area. The powers and functions of the Authority shall be those expressly conferred upon it by this Convention. The Authority shall have such incidental powers, consistent with this Convention, as are implicit in and necessary for the exercise of those powers and functions with respect to activities in the Area.[56] Part XII as regards protection and preservation of the marine environment in its article 209 in connection with pollution from activities in the Area it is said:

1. International rules, regulations and procedures shall be established in accordance with Part XI to prevent, reduce and control pollution of the marine environment from activities in the Area. Such rules, regulations and procedures shall be re-examined from time to time as necessary.

2. Subject to the relevant provisions of this section, States shall adopt laws and regulations to prevent, reduce and control pollution of the marine environment from activities in the Area undertaken by vessels, installations, structures and other devices flying their flag or of their registry or operating under their authority, as the case may be. The requirements of such laws and regulations shall be no less effective than the international rules, regulations and procedures referred to in paragraph 1.

There is no mention about the Authority to exercise jurisdiction over the vessels of flag states or of their registry or operating under their authority in the sphere of marine environment if polluted from activities in the Area. That is to say, the states of those vessels have jurisdiction as a result, those states have authority over the vessels. Where there is Area, there is Authority this normative approach is absent here.

Anyway, the Legal and Technical Commission of the Council can exercise an authority about environment amounting to degradation to recommend to the Council. That is to say, the Commission shall:

"...(d) prepare assessments of the environmental implications of activities in the Area;

(e) make recommendations to the Council on the protection of the marine environment, taking into views of recognized experts in that field;

(f) formulate and submit to the Council the rules, regulations and procedures..., taking into account all relevant factors including assessments of the environmental implications of activities in the Area; ...

(h) make recommendations to the Council regarding the establishment of a monitoring programme to observe, measure, evaluate and analyse, by recognized scientific methods, on a basis, the risks or effects of pollution of the marine environment resulting from activities in the Area, ensure that existing regulations are adequate and are complied with and co-ordinate the implementation of the monitoring programme approved by the Council;...

(k) make recommendation to the Council to issue emergency orders, which may include orders for the suspension or adjustment of operations, to prevent serious harm to the marine environment arising out of activities in the Area. Such recommendations shall be taken up by the Council on a priority basis;

(l) make recommendation to the Council to disapprove areas for exploitation by contractors or the Enterprise in cases where substantial evidence indicates the risk of serious harm to the marine environment."[57]

The Council in addition to its powers and functions, shall: "...(o)(ii) adopt and apply provisionally, pending approval by the Assembly, the rules, regulations and procedures of the Authority, and any amendments thereto, taking into account the recommendations of the Legal and Technical Commission or other subordinate organ concerned....; (w) issue emergency orders, which may include orders for the suspension or adjustment of operations, to prevent serious harm to the marine environment arising out of activities in the Area; (x) disapprove areas for exploitation by contractors or the Enterprise in cases where substantial evidence indicates the risk of serious harm to the marine environment."[58]

It is remarkable that the Assembly of the Authority has no specific function about marine environment in connection with activities in the Area. As regards the powers and functions, the Assembly, though the sole organ of the Authority seems "...(f)(ii) to consider and approve the rules, regulations and procedures of the Authority, and any amendments thereto, provisionally adopted by the Council pursuant to article 162, paragraph 2(o)(ii)...."[59] This paragraph is a concern of the Legal and Technical Commission and the Council but the point to this end is that the Assembly has no function towards marine environment arising out of activities in the Area. That is to say, the marine environment matters in relation to activities in the Area are what should be effected by the Council.

Virtually, marine environment is a domain for progressive development that gives rise to development of international law. The approaches to common heritage of mankind, and human heritage for environment with respect to the Area will work in entirety if heed is paid to protection and preservation of marine environment.

4.6. Studies of Environmental Consequences of Deep Seabed Mining

The deep seabed covers an area twice the size of the land area of the earth. There are three main groups of deep-seabed minerals: polymetallic nodules, crusts, and sulfides. There is a need to concentrate a study on nodules, because it is with this category that the greatest progress has been made in exploration, evaluation of environmental consequences, development of technology, economic analysis, and the development of a legal and political framework.[60] Commercially interesting deposits of polymetallic nodules have been identified at depths of 4,500–5,500 metres in the Clarion Clipperton area of the central eastern Pacific Ocean, and in the Central Indian Basin of the Indian Ocean. To be regarded as commercial, the deposits should have an average content of nickel and copper of at least 2.25 per cent, and a nodule density of approx. 10 kilograms per square metre. The nodules contain some fifty metallic and non-metallic elements, of which nickel, cobalt, copper, manganese, molybdenum, and zinc are the most important metals. Nodule deposits represent major reserves of metals. Cautious analyses show, for instance, that there is twice as much cobalt in the Clarion Clipperton area alone as in total land-based reserves. It should be mentioned here that studies have been made on environmental consequences of deep seabed mining[61]:

(i) The USA and Germany have long been the leading nations in terms of studies of environmental consequences of deep seabed mining. The USA was the pioneer; in 1975 the US National Oceanic and

Atmospheric Administration initiated the Deep Ocean Mining Environmental Study. This five-year project was organized as a collaborative effort between the National Oceanic and Atmospheric Administration and four US registered industrial groups. The project consisted of two phases: the first, to characterize the region environmentally, and the second, to monitor the effects of industrial pilot-scale equipment tests therein. The specific objectives of the project were to develop: (1) environmental baselines (biological, geological, physical, and chemical) at the three sites chosen as representative of the range of environmental parameters likely to be met during mining; (2) predictive capabilities, to identify potential environmental effects of nodule recovery; and (3) an information base, to prepare environmental guidelines for government and industry.

(ii) As a part of the second phase, the National Oceanic and Atmospheric Administration monitored test mining operations conducted by the industrial groups in the Pacific Ocean in the late 1970s. For example, Ocean Mining Associates conducted on 10 November 1978 an integrated test of approximately twenty hours of continuous mining at 15,000 feet, during which time 400 tons of nodules were collected and lifted to the ship as various system concepts were examined.

(iii) Ocean Mining Associates employed a passive towed collector unit for the tests, while another industry group, Ocean Minerals Company, used an active self-propelled collector unit for its integrated tests. In 1981, the National Oceanic and Atmospheric Administration published the first comprehensive Deep Seabed Mining Environmental Impact Statement.

(iv) The Deep Ocean Mining Environmental Study concluded, *inter alia*, that there was a need to look more closely into the environmental impacts on the deep seabed—including the effects of the collector unit in and near the mining tracks, and the effects of the benthic (bottom) plume on benthic life, and its food supply, away from the mining activity. In line with these recommendations, the organization has over the past ten years concentrated its work on the deep seabed. The National Oceanic and Atmospheric Administration has designated Interim Preservational Reference Areas in the Clarion Clipperton Fracture Zone. These are stable reference areas which will be unaffected by nodule mining activities, but are similar to mining sites so that they can effectively serve as controls. The National Oceanic and Atmospheric Administration has worked actively to Commonwealth of Independent States, and France; an exchange arrangement for scientists with the German project has taken place. The collaborative project between the USA and the Commonwealth of Independent States is a large-scale Benthic Impact Experiment. Japan and the United States plan to carry out joint monitoring of the Japanese mining tests in 1996, where Japan focuses on the surface problems, while the US side concentrates on the deep seabed. The Japanese scientists plan to create a model illustrating what happens at the surface level and in the water column. The planned monitoring is a part of a comprehensive Japanese environmental impact study, initiated in 1990 and coordinated by the Metal Mining Agency of Japan.

(v) The German 'Disturbance and Recolonization Experiment' commenced in 1989 as the first long-term, large-scale disturbance recolonization project. The programme is financed by the German Ministry of Research and Technology and is co-ordinated by the University of Hamburg.

(vi) After obtaining pre-impact baseline environmental data, an area of 10.8 sq. km. in the eastern South Pacific was disturbed in February-March 1989 using a "plough harrow" device. An initial post-impact sampling series was carried out immediately after disturbance; the site was revisited again for renewed repeated visits to the site at two-year intervals to monitor the anticipated slow recolonization process until the area is inhabited by a new, stabilized community.

(vii) The Disturbance and Recolonization Experiment is one of several projects in the German Tiefsee-Umweltschutz-programme for research for the precautionary environmental protection of the deep sea. DM17 million has been invested in the programme from 1989 to 1993.

(viii) Currently Germany has the highest level of activity in deep-sea environmental research. Summarily, comprehensive work is currently being carried out to study the environmental consequences. This type of research is not new; it has been conducted in parallel with developments in technology. During the last four years considerable growth is seen in efforts in this area. Environmental consequences thus constitute a major area of research in deep seabed mining today. Moreover, research in this area is far more than mere office work, the greater part of it being practical scientific work carried out at sea. However, it should be emphasized that up to the present it has only been possible to study the effects of small-scale, short-term mining. Not until very recently have long-term, large-scale disturbance recolonization projects been started. The results from this research are already emerging, but many decades will pass before anything certain can be said about what actually happens on the deep seabed with regard to repopulation and recolonization. A large-scale project like the German one will, however, never be able to take the place of actual mining. There is broad agreement among scientists that only under long-term pilot mining operations will be possible to study the environmental consequences satisfactorily. Here, it should be pointed out that the Japanese test planned for 1996 cannot be seen as a long-term comprehensive pilot mining operation, though this is not to say it may not prove useful in an environmental context.

4.7. Main Environmental Problem Areas

There are three main environmental problem areas to be expected from exploitation of nodule deposits:

(i) The first relates to what happens on the seabed. As the collector unit gathers nodules, it will seriously destroy the top few centimetres of the seabed, causing major disturbance and disruption to the flora and fauna in the mining tracks. In addition, the propulsion system of the collector unit will stir up sediments; as a result, organisms in and around the tracks will be partially or entirely buried. In the mining tracks, for instance, a mortality rate of 95-100 per cent may be expected for organisms found there.

(ii) The second relates to the discharge of waste water from the *mining ship*. After the nodules have been gathered by the collector unit, they will be washed clean by water jets. The nodules will then be crushed and brought to the surface as slurry containing both crushed nodules and water. When the slurry reaches the surface, there will be a partial discharge of waste water containing particulate matter and trace metals. This discharge may interfere with light penetration and reduce photosynthesis in the surface layers. Furthermore, the waste water will be considerably colder than the surface water.

(iii) The third relates to onshore processing. This includes waste water, tailings, and slag. Here roughly the same problems will be encountered as in land-based mining operations. Two of the three chief problem areas involve the mining operation, the effects on the deep seabed and the effects in the water column. To understand this better, it will be useful to look more closely at just what goes on in the various zones of the water column. There are four biological zones.

Zone 1: the epipelagic zone:

This zone extends from the surface down to approximately 200 metres. An important part of this zone is the portion through which sufficient light penetrates to enable photosynthesis to take place. This layer—the euphotic zone—is defined as the depth interval from the surface down to the depth where light intensity is reduced to 1 per cent of the intensity immediately beneath the surface. The lower limit of the layer will necessarily vary both as regards the geographical co-ordinates and the time of year. Typical examples from the Pacific and the Atlantic have the 1 per cent limit at about 50 metres, although in tropical waters this limit lies at about 90 metres. The epipelagic zone is by far the most productive part of the water column, estimates indicating that 80 per cent of the total biomass in the oceans is found here. The biomass in this zone comprises phytoplankton and zooplankton, fish, and fish spawn. It is here that almost all the world's fishery resources are to be found.

Zone 2: the mesopelagic zone

The mesopelagic zone extends from about 200 metres to about 1,000 metres. In this intermediate zone we find layers featuring extreme values as regards important chemical and physical parameters. Here we find, for instance, minimum values for the content of oxygen in solution. In this layer certain species of pelagic fish-stocks and deep-sea shrimp are found, rendering the mesopelagic zone of some importance for commercial fishery.

Zone 3: the bathypelagic zone

As a lower intermediate zone, the bathypelagic zone extends from about 1,000 metres down to about 4,000 metres below the surface. The biomass in this zone is relatively sparse, due to minimal energy in the form of sunlight penetrating to such depths, and a scant supply of nutrients. For the few animals living in this area, conservation of energy is a cardinal principle.

Zone 4: the abyssopelagic zone

In the high seas, this zone extends from about 4,000 metres below the surface down to the seabed, and is characterized by a high degree of stability. Temperatures are low, ranging between 1 and 4 degrees Celsius, and very stable. Stability characterizes the abyssopelagic zone in other contexts as well: low rate of sedimentation, extremely low light penetration, and limited supply of nutrients. The low supply of elements necessary to living organisms means that the few biological resources existing here are to be found on the sea floor and in the upper few centimetres of the seabed sediments. Although many species are found down at the deep seabed, there are relatively few specimens of each species.

4.8. Environmental Uncertainty on the Deep Seabed

It is important to distinguish between problems that are manageable and possible to live with, and significant adverse changes that cause serious harm to the environment. A 'significant adverse environmental impact' may be defined as: important harmful changes in ecosystem diversity, the productivity of the biological communities with the environment; or the threat to human health through direct exposure to pollutants, or through consumption of exposed aquatic organisms; or important loss of aesthetic, recreational, scientific, or economic values.

The most significant environmental impacts will be those caused by the collector unit on the deep seabed. German scientists describe the effects on the deep seabed like this: Most of the nodules constituting a hard substrata for the settlement of organisms will be collected, a small number will be missed by the collector system, but these are likely to be buried from resedimentation of the plumes. The soft sediment around the nodules will be severely disturbed, compression of sediment will occur to several decimeters, and much of the fauna will be destroyed. Next to the collector system tracks sediment will be piled up. Small areas may remain undisturbed by these actions, but they will most certainly receive a cover of sediment from the plume. Sediment surface feeding fauna will die from food shortage if these manage to survive the direct mining impact. Some chance of survival remains only for stalked organisms penetrating high above the blanketing layer. Their food sources, drifting plankton or other particles, will pass by with the currents, after the plume has disappeared. In total the community will be tremendously altered and recolonization will be a very slow process. The reestablishment of a balanced community may finally take decades. It is yet too early to say how serious the environmental consequences on the deep seabed will be. US researchers have studied the effects of pilot mining operations conducted in the late 1970s, but these were limited and short-term test operations. As mentioned, comprehensive long-term studies started only three or four years ago, so limited empirical data is available. There is broad agreement on the need for more research...such as investigation of the direct bottom disturbance by the collector system and its indirect influence through resedimentation of the plume.

The second chief problem area is related to the discharge of waste water from the mining ship. The slurry loaded on board the mining ship at the riser outlet will have an approximately 10 to 20 per cent content of mineral material. To minimize the volume-to-weight ratio of the material to be temporarily stored on board the mining vessel, a de-watering process will be carried out to separate the seawater from the mineral material and dispose it off outside the ship. Discharge of the waste water from this process implies adding to the euphotic zone a significant volume of water with different physical and chemical characteristics. Such waste water comprises seabed water, sediments, fragments of nodules, and benthic biota from the seabed. Its temperature is lower than that of surface-layer water—normal seabed water being between 1 and 4 degrees Celsius. This will rise somewhat in the course of pumping and de-watering, and is calculated to be between 7 and 10 degrees Celsius at discharge. By contrast, in the test mining area where these calculations have been made, normal surface temperature is 26 degrees Celsius; thus, discharging waste water involves a considerable reduction in temperature the moment the water meets the surface.

Temperature is an important parameter for life in the euphotic zone. US investigations have concluded that discharge of waste water is unlikely to represent any serious problem. Particles have been found to sink more rapidly to the bottom than had been anticipated. It will be interesting to see if the Japanese study fully confirms these results. The Germans have recommended further research in this area as well.

The discharge depth for the waste water is a much-debated subject. Rather than discharge everything at surface level, several sources have recommended a depth of 200 metres or even 1,000 metres. By choosing the former, disturbance of the most productive part of the water column, the epipelagic zone, would be avoided. Those recommending a discharge depth of 1,000 metres or more justify this by the need to avoid disturbing the processes going on in the mesopelagic zone as well.

The third chief problem has to do with processing operations ashore. Various hydrometallurgical and pyrometallurgical processes have been developed for extracting the metal content from the nodules. In a hydrometallurgical process—a leaching process—chemical additives and electrowinning are used to refine the mineral material. In a pyrometallurgical process—a smelting process—the mineral material is melted to a crude alloy before the metal products are extracted by use of chemical additives. Environmental consequences will mainly be of two types. The first category is impacts caused during operation of the processing plant—primarily because of gas emissions from pyrometallurgical processes, the integrated power plant, and from the integrated sulphuric acid plant. Emissions of sulphur dioxide, nitrogendioxide, hydrogen sulphide, and carbon monoxide will have effects on air quality. The second category comprises the environmental impacts caused during pre-treating, handling, and disposal of waste material. Main impacts here are caused by onshore disposal of waste material—slag, tailings, process water, and cooling water—from the processing operations.

To summarize: the effects of onshore processing are in many ways similar to those caused by land-based production.

Mining deep seabed minerals thus represents no new source of environmental impacts, but rather an alternative source of supply of the same end-products. However, this does not apply to the effects on the seabed and the water column. Here deep seabed mining will create *new* types of environmental impact. Future exploitation of the nodules will represent the first large-scale activity ever attempted at such depths, and considerable uncertainty attends the environmental consequences. The greatest uncertainty concerns the deep seabed.[62]

Though the Indian Ocean is large and biologically diverse, corals here face enormous overall pressure from population increase and illegal fishing methods like dynamite blast fishing and cyanide fishing. Also, sediment runoff from agriculture has been a problem region-wide, smothering corals offshore. The United Nations Environment Programme estimated that 20 per cent of the region's coral reefs had already been destroyed—and that was in 1984.[63]

Deep Seabed Mining is being carried out in the Central Indian Basin of the Indian Ocean by India.[64] The Area granted by the Prep Com is near Diego Garcia Island.[65] Speculations are accountable to degradation of marine environment that cannot be said not inevitable in the Bay of Bengal. However, the Indian Ocean States are seen to be careful of maintaining it in all respects.[66] In the case of the environment the Bay of Bengal littoral states should consider themselves to be bound in duty and obligation to promote a viable regime for marine environment in the Bay of Bengal.

4.9. The Bay of Bengal: Environment Paradigm

Marine environment in the Bay of Bengal is a concern of the bay, its bed and subsoil within and beyond national jurisdiction. The Bay of Bengal environment concerns are highly related with its littoral states. In reality, natural and man-made activities in the bay have the very impact on environment for the littoral states. That means, the coastal states like Bangladesh, India, Maldives, Myanmar (Burma), Thailand, Sri Lanka have prime approaches to the marine environment in the Bay of Bengal. Due to the fact that sea matters are not limited only to certain areas, concerns of some other states specifically in the Bay of Bengal matters Malaysia and Indonesia may somehow be involved. The recent untold tsunami havoc geographically seems to be caused in Indonesia and other regions on 26 December 2004 but virtually has resulted in the whole world to be wholeheartedly committed to disaster management. Disaster Management has gained global importance in the wake of the killer tsunami that claimed more than 2,00,000 lives and caused untold miseries to thousands of people in several countries in one of the world's greatest disasters in recent history.[67] To this end, the marine environment has unquestionably been a domain to be considered for promotion and preservation, here the Bay of Bengal for environment.

The LOS Convention has provided provisions concerning prevention, reduction and control of marine environment. Stress is laid on the coastal states for their exercise of jurisdiction to prevent, reduce and control marine environment within national jurisdiction. Jurisdiction is given to the state of flags, and registry of concerned vessels. Jurisdiction in matters of environment resulting from activities in the Area lies with the Authority. To mention specifically, coastal states have been empowered to exercise jurisdiction in environment matters relating to the areas within national jurisdiction. "States have the obligation to protect and preserve the marine environment.[68] States have the sovereign right to exploit their resources pursuant to their environmental policies and in accordance with their duty to protect and preserve the marine environment."[69] It is remarkable that in marine environment matters states are under obligation but their sovereign rights are certainly reimbursed. Practically, states have 'obligation' and 'duty' to protect and preserve the marine environment. There is no specification about right in connection with the environment. In reality environment effects are not territorially limited. Consequently, it is not possible to innovate 'right' as possible in jurisprudence or international law. Environment, particularly marine environment, is an all concerned matter, as a result, all states have an obligation and duty towards its protection and preservation. The matter can be addressed by stating some extracts such as:

1. States shall take, individually or jointly as appropriate, all measures consistent with this Convention that are necessary to prevent, reduce and control pollution of the marine environment from any source, using for this purpose the best practicable means at their disposal and in accordance with their capabilities, and they shall endeavour to harmonize their policies in this connection.

2. States shall take all measures necessary to ensure that activities under their jurisdiction or control are so conducted as not cause damage by pollution to other States and their environment, and that pollution arising from incidents or activities under their jurisdiction or control does not spread beyond the areas where they exercise sovereign rights in accordance with this Convention.

3. The measures taken pursuant to this Part shall deal with all sources of pollution of the marine environment. These measures shall include, *inter alia,* those designed to minimize to the fullest possible extent:

(a) the release of toxic, harmful or noxious substances, especially those which are persistent, from land-based sources, from or through the atmosphere or by dumping;

(b) pollution from vessels, in particular measures for preventing accidents and dealing with emergencies, ensuring the safety of operations at sea, preventing intentional and unintentional discharges, and regulating the design, construction, equipment, operation and manning of vessels;

(c) pollution from installations and devices used in exploration or exploitation of the natural resources of the sea-bed and subsoil, in particular measures for preventing accidents and dealing with emergencies, ensuring the safety of operations at sea, and regulating the design, construction, equipment, operation and manning of such installations or devices;

(d) pollution from other installations and devices operating in the marine environment, in particular measures for preventing accidents and dealing with emergencies, ensuring the safety of operations at sea, and regulating the design, construction, equipment, operation and manning of such installations or devices.

4. In taking measures to prevent, reduce or control pollution of the marine environment, States shall refrain from unjustifiable interference with activities carried out by other States in the exercise of their rights and in pursuance of their duties in conformity with this Convention.

5. The measures taken in accordance with this Part shall include those necessary to protect and preserve rare or fragile ecosystems as well as the habitat of depleted, threatened or endangered species and forms of marine life.[70]

These provisions are actually with general approach to obligation and duty for states to prevent, reduce and control pollution of marine environment. Moreover, specification is seen about the sources of pollution of environment. All sources are of course man made. There are no elaborate approaches to sources caused by unnatural events. However, the notion like "in particular measures for preventing accidents and dealing with emergencies,..." covers the likely occurrence. As regards rights, jurisprudence makes a person vested with the so-called *right in rem,* e.g., right in general applicable to all. But in the marine environment states are not called to have right but are embodied with obligation and duty as if *in re*. That is to say, in the case of marine environment states are required to consider themselves to be under obligation and duty *in re* for its protection and preservation. As regards marine space like the territorial sea, exclusive economic zone and the continental shelf it is the coastal state which has jurisdiction to exercise for protection and preservation of marine environment. That means:

1. Coastal States shall adopt laws and regulations to prevent, reduce and control pollution of the marine

environment arising from or in connection with seabed activities subject to their jurisdiction and from artificial islands, installations and structures under their jurisdiction, pursuant to articles 60 and 80.

2. States shall take other measures as may be necessary to prevent, reduce and control such obligation.
3. Such laws, regulations and measures shall be no less effective than international rules, standards and recommended practices and procedures.
4. States shall endeavour to harmonize their policies in this connection at the appropriate regional level.
5. States, acting especially through competent international organizations or diplomatic conference, shall establish global and regional rules, standards and recommended practices and procedures to prevent, reduce and control pollution of the marine environment referred to in paragraph 1. Such rules, standards and recommended practices and procedures shall be re-examined from time to time as necessary.[71]

It should be mentioned here that states are empowered to adopt "laws and regulations" in compliance with "regional rules, standards and recommended practices" for protection, reduction and control of marine environment. Whether pollution of marine environment is caused by dumping[72], from vessels[73], from or through the atmosphere[74] states have jurisdiction equally to prevent, reduce and control marine environment. The notion like "recommended practices" carries no specification of its own. This then, gives rise to confusion about 'recommended practices.' However, the extract like "such rules, standards and recommended practices shall be re-examined from time to time as necessary" provides an opening to deal with confusion so arises. Thus, a practicable step can be taken for protection and preservation of marine environment.

As a practical consideration, the very recent tsunami disaster reminds the world to be as determined as possible to control natural calamities in the ocean space. Although it is beyond human control, but efforts must be made for control, thereby protecting and preserving marine environment. Earthquakes affect the seas in many ways; they generate submarine landslides, destructive tsunamis, and intense water-borne sound; they are associated with shoreline modifications that affect marine life, harbour installations, even political boundaries. The most important scientific information is that which earthquakes can provide on the tectonic processes that are responsible for the very existence of ocean basins and for other features of lesser scale but major importance, such as island arcs, deep-sea trenches, and ocean rifts.[75]

It is generally known that the Pacific region is more and more vulnerable to natural calamities like the tsunami, but the present tsunami disaster in the Indian Ocean region adjoining the Bay of Bengal reminds the states in the region to be committed to strengthen their measures for protection and preservation of marine environment. States—particularly the littoral states—bordering on the Bay of Bengal must consider themselves to be in obligation and duty bound for promotion, protection and preservation of its environment.

References

1. United Nations Convention on the Law of the Sea, 1982 (LOS Convention) has been ratified on 16 November 1994 and since then it is enforceable.
2. Art. 1(1) of the LOS Convention.
3. Art. 1 2.(1).
4. Art. 133.
5. Art. 136.
6. Art. 301.
7. Within national jurisdiction the exclusive economic zone (EEZ) and the continental shelf provide a wide extent of jurisdiction to the coastal state. As to peaceful purposes regarding marine scientific research in the exclusive economic zone and on the continental shelf in paragraph 3 of Art. 246 of the LOS Convention it is said: "Coastal States shall, in normal circumstances, grant their consent for marine scientific research projects by other States or competent international organizations in their exclusive economic zone or on the continental shelf to be carried out in accordance with this Convention for peaceful purposes and in order to increase scientific knowledge of the marine environment for the benefit of all mankind. To this end, coastal States shall establish rules and procedures ensuring that such consent will not be delayed or denied unreasonably."
8. Arts. 87, 136.

9. *Ibid.*
10. Art. 88.
11. The sea zones within national jurisdiction are such as: territorial sea, contiguous zone, exclusive economic zone (EEZ), and continental shelf. None of these zones can be said as infringing peace and tranquillity. It is to note that the regime of innocent passage is exclusively peace oriented. Passage is innocent so long as it is not prejudicial to the peace, good order or security of the coastal State. Such passage shall take place in conformity with the LOS Convention and with other rules of international law. Passage of a foreign ship shall be considered to be prejudicial to the peace, good order or security of the coastal State if in the territorial sea it engages in any of the following activities: (a) any threat or use of force against the sovereignty, territorial integrity or political independence of the coastal State, or in any other manner in violation of the principles of international law embodied in the Charter of the United Nations; (b) any exercise or practice with weapons of any kind; (c) any act aimed at collecting information to the prejudice of the defence or security of the coastal State; (d) any act of propaganda aimed at affecting the defence or security of the coastal State; (e) the launching landing or taking on board of any aircraft; (f) the launching landing or taking on board of any military device; (g) the loading or unloading of any commodity, currency or person contrary to the customs, fiscal, immigration or sanitary laws and regulations of the coastal State; (h) any act of wilful and serious pollution contrary to this Convention; (i) any fishing activities; (j) the carrying out of research or survey activities; (k) any act aimed at interfering with any systems of communication or any other facilities or installations of the coastal State; (l) any other activity not having a direct bearing on passage (Art. 19). The contiguous zone is entirely based on security for promotion of peace for the coastal State (Art. 33). In the EEZ, the coastal state has jurisdiction as provided for in the relevant provisions of this Convention with regard to the protection and preservation of the marine environment (Art. 56).

    The coastal State shall have exclusive jurisdiction over artificial islands, installations and structures in the EEZ , including jurisdiction with regard to customs, fiscal, health, safety and immigration laws and regulations (Art. 60). That means, in this zone the coastal State is entitled to exercise contiguous zone regime possibly in Art. 33.

    Article 60 applies *mutatis mutandis* to artificial islands, installations and structures on the continental shelf (Art. 80).
12. Art. 89.
13. Art. 137(1).
14. Art. 138.
15. Art. 141.
16. Art. 242.
17. Robert N. Wells, Jr. (ed), *Law, Values, and the Environment* (The Scarecrow Press, Inc., London, 1996) 28.

18. Art. 243 of LOS Convention.
19. Art. 266.
20. Jessica Tuchman Mathews (ed.), *Preserving the Global Environment* (W. W. Norton & Company, New York 1991) 238-239.
21. Prin 5 of Earth Summit.
22. Prin 7.
23. Prin 9.
24. Prin 12.
25. Prin 13.
26. Prin 14.
27. Prin 27.
28. Art. 198.
29. Prin 25.
30. Art. 86.
31. Arts. 87, 89.
32. Art. 87.
33. The high seas are open to all States, whether coastal or land-locked. Freedom of the high seas is exercised under the conditions laid down by LOS Convention and by other rules of international law. It comprises, *inter alia*, both for coastal and land-locked States: (a) freedom of navigation; (b) freedom of overflight; (c) freedom to lay submarine cables and pipelines, subject Part VI; (d) freedom to construct artificial islands and other installations permitted under international law, subject Part VI; (e) freedom of fishing, subject to the conditions laid down in section 2; (f) freedom of scientific research, subject to Parts VI and XIII. Art. 87 (1).
34. Art. 92.
35. Arts. 99 to 109, 221.
36. Art. 111.
37. Sam Blay & ors (eds.), *Public International Law: An Australian Perspective* (Oxford University Press, Oxford 1997) 337-338.
38. Some of the offences for which such universal jurisdiction has been claimed or proposed are: piracy, slave trade (slavery), crimes against humanity, genocide, terrorism, apartheid. The list of offences for which universal jurisdiction is considered desirable has been expanding and will almost certainly continue to expand. Okididi also has suggested the relevance of the principle to pollution of the seas. Okididi, *Regional Control of Ocean Pollution: Legal and Institutional Problems and Prospects* (Netherlands, 1978) 40, 126; Swan. International and National Approaches to Oil Pollution Responsibility", 50(1971) *Oregon Law Review* 506, 545.
39. U.N. Doc.A/Conf. 6/418, 1972, Art. 1.

40. Art. VI of the Draft Convention on International Crimes: Report of the First International Criminal Law Conference, Washington, 1971, 156 quoted in Okididi, *ibid.*, 136.
41. Okididi, *ibid.*, 128-136.
42. http://www.aloha.com/conven/chlos.html
43. *Ibid.*
44. http://www.environment.sa.gov.au/coasts/marine_paps.html
45. Incidences of disease, illness, or death are determined only in combination with human factors, such as the effectiveness of water and sewage treatment and the responsiveness of the public health system. Thus, climate-related health risks will place greater demands on public health resources.
46. The Second United Nations Conference on Human Settlements (Habitat II) took place in Istambul, Turkey, from 3—14 June 1996 the 20th anniversary of the first Habitat Conference in Vancouver in 1976. Habitat II received its impetus from the 1992 United Nations Conference on Environment and Development and General Assembly resolution A/RES/47/180. The purpose of the second United Nations Conference on Human Settlements (Habitat II) is to address two themes of equal global importance: "Adequate shelter for all" and "Sustainable human settlements development in an urbanizing world." Human beings are at the centre of concerns for sustainable development, including adequate shelter for all and sustainable human settlements, and they are entitled to a healthy and productive life in harmony with nature. http://www.iisd.ca/habitat/recent.html
47. Habitat II Texts para 139. http://www.iisd.ca/habitat/recent.html. It can be searched as Istambul Declaration on Human Settlements, 1996.
48. See Burns H. Weston, Richard A. Falk & Hilary Charlesworth, *International Law and World Order: A Problem-Oriented Coursebook* (West Group St. Paul, MINN, 1997) 1002-1003.
49. See Wolfgang E. Burhenne & Nicholas A. Robinson (eds.), *International Protection of the Environment: Conservation in Sustainable Development* (Oceana Publications, Inc., New York, 2003), Evian Summit 2003: G8 Summit 2003/ Sustainable Development 7.
50. Agenda 21, para 17.97.
51. Agenda 21, para 17.98.
52. Sam Blay & ors (eds.), *Public International Law: An Australian Perspective* (Oxford University Press, Oxford, 1997) 359-361.
53. The Authority has three principal organs, e.g., an Assembly, a Council and a Secretariat (Art. 158). It also has an organ, e.g., Enterprise through which the Authority shall carry out the functions referred to in Article 170, paragraph 1.
54. Art. 145.
55. Art. 146.

56. Art. 157.
57. Art. 165.
58. Art. 162.
59. Art. 159f(2).
60. Proposals to mine deposits and manganese nodules in the deep sea could lead to destruction of the sea floor and pollution of the local ecosystems. Oil and gas mining around the world has the potential to pollute the local environment through leaks and spills as well as by disrupting the local flora and fauna. Deepsea dumping of redundant installations has been proposed before, as in the case of the Brent Spar. This instance was resolved at that time, but dumping remains an issue that needs attention. http://www.bbc.co.uk/nature/blueplanet/alien/further_mine.shtml
61. The Oceans of the world are a tremendous resource for food and there needs to be much more concern for their protection...Not Tomorrow when we get around to it or when comes too late...but 'Now'.ihttp://www.sealand.tv/environmental.html
62. Jan Magne Markussen, "Deep Seabed Mining and the Environment: Consequences, Perceptions, and Regulations", *Green Globe Yearbook,* 1994, 31, 32, 33, 34.
63. http://www.motherjones.com/news/special_reports/coral_reef/indi...
64. In 1987, India was registered with the Preparatory Commission for the International Seabed Authority and for the International Tribunal for the Law of the Sea as the first pioneer state to carry activities in the Central Indian Basin of the Indian Ocean.
65. Just getting to Diego Garcia is a challenge in itself—the sandy ridge has no other land within 1,000 miles with India to the north, Madagascar to the west, Indonesia to the east and nothing but Antarctica way to the south. The only way in and out is through government ships or planes. Diego Garcia is part of the British Indian Ocean Territory (BIOT) formed in 1965 from territory belonging formerly to Mauritius and the Seychelles. The island is one of 52 in the Chagos Archipelago, which extends over an area of 10,000 square miles. The archipelago is located in the heart of the Indian Ocean, south of India and between Africa and Indonesia. The tropical island is a narrow coral atoll with a land area of about eleven square miles, nearly enclosing a lagoon. Its configuration is that of a 'V' drawn by a shaky hand. The island stretches 37 miles from tip to tip, with an opening to the north-northwest. Three small islands dot the mouth of the lagoon which is approximately 13 miles long and up to 6 miles wide. The lagoon is from sixty to one hundred feet deep with numerous coral heads in most areas. Shallow reefs surround the island on the ocean side, as well as in the lagoon. The island's mean height above sea level is 4 feet. Diego Garcia is the largest of many atolls that form the Chagos Archipelago. The horseshoe-shaped atoll is located seven degrees south of the equator in the North Central Region of the Indian Ocean. It is heavily vegetated, has a land area of 6,720 acres and is 37 miles long, tip- to-tip. The maximum elevation is 22

feet, with an average elevation of four feet above sea level. The enclosed lagoon is approximately seven miles wide and thirteen miles long. The three small islands at the mouth of the lagoon and the shape of the atoll give the impression of a footprint, hence the term "Footprint of Freedom". Annual rainfall averages 102 inches with the heaviest precipitation occurring during October to February. Humidity remains high throughout the year and temperatures are generally in the upper-80s Fahrenheit by day, falling to the mid-70s by night. The almost constant breezes keep conditions reasonably comfortable. The atoll has been used primarily for the harvesting of coconuts from which coconut oil and copra were processed. It has also been a coal station and guano mining was carried out for a brief period. Britain granted independence in the 1950s and 1960s to many of its former colonies in the Indian Ocean. The remaining islands were joined under the title of the British Indian Ocean Territories (BIOT), Diego Garcia being one of these islands. The British and United States Government agreements allowed the US access to part of the island to construct a communication station and subsequently a Naval Support Facility. The British do not charge the US any rent.

66. The Indian Ocean Consultative Business Network (IOCBN) in which the Indian Ocean Countries like: Australia, Bahrain, Bangladesh, India, Indonesia, Iran, Kenya, Kuwait, Madagascar, Malaysia, Maldives, Mauritius, Mozambique, Oman, Pakistan, Saudi Arabia, Seychelles, South Africa, Singapore, Sri Lanka, Thailand, the United Arab Emirates and Yemen are in work for overall activities about this Ocean. http://www.curtin.edu.au/curtin.centre/ioc/revjunex.htm
67. http://www.indiadaily.com/breaking_news/ The disaster has made the Bay of Bengal bordering countries like Maldives, India, Myanmar, Sri Lanka, Thailand and Indonesia the very targeted zone.
68. LOS Convention, Art. 192.
69. Art. 193.
70. Art. 194.
71. Art. 208.
72. Art. 210.
73. Art. 211.
74. Art. 212.
75. Arthure E. Maxwell, *The Sea* (John Wiley & Sons, New York 1970) 353.

5

SETTLEMENT OF ENVIRONMENTAL DISPUTES: THE BAY OF BENGAL PHASE

5.1. Forwarding Approach

Marine environment is not a concern limited to territorial boundary. Marine pollution is transboundary and global in character. At present protection and preservation of environment has been unquestioned. As per the principles laid down in the LOS convention: "States have the obligation to protect and preserve the marine environment."[1] The dominant story of transboundary environmental impact assessment in international law has the following elements:

(a) customary international law prohibits transboundary pollution;

(b) according to the classic version of this prohibition, contained in Principle 21 of the 1972 Stockholm Declaration, states must ensure that activities within their territory or under their control do not harm the environment beyond their territory;

(c) to ensure that activities within their jurisdiction will not cause transboundary harm, states must assess the potential transboundary effects of the activities; and

(d) to that end, states enter into international agreements requiring them to carry out transboundary environmental impact assessment for activities that might cause transboundary harm.[2]

Transboundary harms seems to be a logical requirement of Principle 21 of the 1972 Stockholm Declaration, which says:

> States have, in accordance with the Charter of the United Nations and the principles of international law, the sovereign right to exploit their own resources pursuant to their own environmental policies, and the responsibility to ensure that activities within their jurisdiction or control do not cause damage to the environment of other States or of areas beyond the limits of national jurisdiction.[3]

Treatises,[4] textbooks,[5] and scholars[6] state that Principle 21 is considered to be customary international law. Indeed, it has been called the cornerstone of international environmental law.[7] But despite the near unanimity on the importance of Principle 21 and the great amount of scholarly attention given to it, its meaning has remained indefinite. The problem does not consist in reconciling its two apparently contradictory clauses.[8] The prevailing view is that the responsibility must be read as a limitation on the right—in other words, that states have the right to exploit their own resources provided that they ensure that activities within their jurisdiction or control do not harm the environment beyond their territory. Otherwise, the second clause would be a nullity. And, unsurprisingly, negotiators of the language said at the time that they intended the second clause to limit the first.[9] The focus has therefore centred on the second clause, so much so that when scholars refer to Principle 21, they often refer only to the limiting language.

The more difficult issue has been to decide exactly what that language means. What are states required to do with respect to activities within their jurisdiction or control that cause or might cause) transboundary environmental damage? On its face, the language seems clear: each state must ensure that such activities do not harm the environment outside its territory. Therefore, states must take steps to avoid any such harm, including that committed by private actors, and if harm nevertheless occurs, states must be accountable under traditional notions of state responsibility for the damage. This reading meshes nicely with the language of Principle 21 but has a problem—an uncomfortable one, for a would-be principle of customary international law—that it does not seem to enjoy the necessary support in state practice. As Oscar Schachter has observed, "To say that a state has no right to injure the environment of another seems quixotic in the face of the great variety of transborder environmental harms that occur every day."[10]

Although some scholars have still argued that all transboundary environmental harm should be presumptively unlawful,[11] the idea that Principle 21 prohibits all transboundary harm has generally been rejected. Instead, most scholars adopt one or both of two limitations. First, they add the term *significant* or *substantial* before *damage*, so that the rule becomes that states should prevent all *significant* or *substantial* transboundary environmental harm from activities under their jurisdiction or control.[12] Second, they construe Principle 21 as reflecting an obligation of performance—*due diligence*—rather than an obligation of result.[13] Although the limitations may be combined in various ways, the majority probably includes both limitations. The result would be to read Principle 21 to require states to undertake due diligence to prevent significant (or substantial) transboundary environmental harm from activities within their jurisdiction or control.[14]

5.2. Environment—No One's Exclusive Matter

The world Ocean provides the greatest interface with the earth's atmosphere, digesting carbon dioxide, releasing oxygen, and affecting weather in a thousand known and unknown ways. On a grand scale the effect of pollutants upon the broad reaches of the seas is still subject to extensive investigation, but within the surface zones of water where light penetrates, particularly in the coastal regions or narrow seas, the action of pollutants can be easily observed.

The word 'ecology', the study of living systems in relation to their environment, was used by Ernest Haeckel in 1867. In the marine 'ecosystem', photosynthesis provides the basis for life. The interruption or destruction of photosynthesis by pollutants, therefore, is a serious matter. Without light, which generally cannot reach below ninety meter of the ocean's surface, microscopic plants (phytoplankton) cannot thrive and thereby furnish the food needed by microscopic animals (zooplankton) and higher orders of life. Creatures swimming, floating, or lying below the euphotic or light zone of the sea must depend upon the organic matter that falls from that zone. Moreover, in the coastal areas, where the ocean is shallow with abundant light, the mixture of nutrient fresh waters from the rivers running into the sea as well as the varieties of temperature and salinity make plant and animal life extraordinarily productive. In this near-shore or neritic zone, extending up to a depth of some 200 meters, the breeding grounds of most commercial fish and the habitat of crustaceans and molluscs can be found, all dependent upon a marine ecosystem easily damaged by some pollutants. It is also possible for some toxic metals and some chemicals to work their way through the food chain after primary ingestion by simple marine organisms to the level of fish eaten by man.

Disease and death of animal and plant life, with hazards to human health, are not the only effects of marine pollution. The seaside has always served as a recuperative environment for the body and spirit of mankind, with the vision and touch of foaming salt water calling forth poetic and artistic natures.[15]

Marine pollution is a global problem in several senses. It affects the health of the oceans in all parts of the world; it affects all countries, both developed and developing. Some marine pollution problems are local, but many have international implications. It is not only a global but complex problem with interlocking economic, technological, political and legal aspects. Wastes are disposed of in the ocean partly because the costs and risks of putting them elsewhere are greater. In many cases the blame for the damage cannot be assigned. Even where it can be assigned, liability may not be a deterrent. Outright prohibition may be necessary to prevent pollution but that may involve substantial deprivation to legitimate users. It may well be that new structures of authority are required but the effective exercise of authority would still be limited by the gaps and uncertainties of scientific knowledge and by the hard facts of economics and political interests.[16]

Knowledge—strict and demonstrable cause and effect data—about the number, kind, and effect of pollutants upon the world ocean is far from being exact. Indeed, the very definition of marine pollution may be open to challenge. In 1969, a group of scientists formulated the definition of marine pollution that, in one way or another, has been introduced into a number of declarations, national laws and treaties; namely: "the introduction by man into the marine environment (including the estuaries), directly or indirectly, of substances or energy, which bring about deleterious effects, such as damage to the biological resources, hazards to human health, lessening of the quality of the sea water for use, and a reduction of the possibilities offered for its enjoyment."

The emphasis of publicists concerned about marine pollution rests upon the activities of man, not nature. Indeed, the industry of man has changed the quality of water, injured aquatic life, posed dangers to human safety, and reduced the opportunities for aesthetic or recreational enjoyment of the seas. Nature itself, of course, is ruthless in violating environments suddenly and altering ecosystems over periods of time. Earthquakes, typhoons, and forests fires or infestations, swarming, and mass deaths due to temperature changes, extraordinary rains and dryness, or other shifts of the ecosystem all occur without the presence of man. Natural oil seeping from submerged fissures of the seabed, for example, have allowed untold millions of tons of oil to enter the world ocean without the piercing of drills. Yet the argument that man has deliberately polluted the seas, worsening his own environment, if not endangering the life system of the planet itself, cannot be avoided, and the plea that he can reasonably modify his domestic and economic activities to limit pollution must be heard.

Pollutants from the daily life of man reach the oceans in a variety of ways.

First, there is the runoff of human, agricultural, and industrial wastes into streams and rivers whose waters flow into estuaries and the world ocean. Torrents of water wash down the land into streams or pour through pipes into the rivers or seas all the powders, clippings, shavings, grimes, greases, oils, urine, scum, faeces, filth, fragments, spoils, acids, alkalis, dregs, and infinite other dirty residues of human civilization. In only a very small percentage of flushing systems of the planet is waste treated in any way before reaching the world ocean. Increasing populations, stimulated by economic development, have produced more and more wastes.[17]

A *second* way in which pollutants have entered the ocean is through the atmosphere. The political movement for protection of the environment was largely launched by groups of scientists deeply concerned about the fallout of transuranic elements upon the earth and seas. Between 1946 and 1963, a total of 429 tests of atomic weapons in the atmosphere were conducted by the United States, the Soviet Union (Federation of Russia), Great Britain and France, raising the anxieties of scientists that radioactive particles might be accumulating in the food chain, including marine plankton. Other toxic substances or chloronated hydrocarbons used in agriculture or industry as well as some gases can be transported by the atmosphere to the seas with dire effects. Petroleum hydrocarbons are also blown out to sea, perhaps as much as 6,000,000 tons in a year.[18]

A *third* way in which pollutants enter the world ocean is through the deliberate dumping of materials into the sea. Dredged sediments in rivers, bays and offshore channels which may contain toxic substances, have usually been dumped at sea. Sludge from treated sewage, garbage, industrial wastes, which may contain caustic acids, plating solutions, pharmaceuticals, metals, or non-degradable plastics have been dropped into the ocean, often not far from land and in shallow water.

A *fourth* way in which pollutants enter the world ocean has been the deliberate or accidental discharges from ships, chiefly oil. Ships at sea may leak engine oil and greases while tankers may wash their tanks clean of residues and oil and other contaminants, mix sea water into the tanks for ballast and later discharge it as oily water, and clear their bilges of the slops of the ship into the ocean. More dramatic, of course, are the collisions, strandings, and ruptures of tankers that quickly engorge the ocean with tons of oil that float like black seas toward the land, polluting a coastal zone rich in plant, animal, and human activity.[19]

Finally, a *fifth* source of marine pollution has been the exploitation of petroleum in the submerged continental shelf, where floating or submersible rigs have made possible the drilling of the seabed and forced the rise of gas and oil into pipes for loading into tankers or for transfer to land-connected pipelines.[20]

Furthermore, the deep seabed mining seems to be an added phase to cause pollution of marine environment. Activities in the Area are carried out under the auspices of the International Seabed Authority. The Authority is empowered to adopt appropriate rules, regulations and procedures for prevention, reduction and control of pollution and other hazards to the marine environment.[21] But question arises as to the machinery to provide remedy against marine pollution. As a practical consideration, the high seas and the Area's matters in respect of marine environment are undetermined in the sense that no machinery seems to take action against the entity causing pollution. Of course, it is now possible to talk about some remedial measure, for example in the case of an accident causing pollution in the high seas to be intervened. Article I(1) of the 1969 Intervention Convention on the high seas states:

> Parties to the present Convention may take measures on the high seas as may be necessary to prevent, mitigate or eliminate grave and imminent danger to their coastlines or related interests from pollution or threat of pollution of the sea by oil, following upon a marine casualty or acts related to such a casualty, which may reasonably be expected to result in major harmful consequences.[22]

Marine pollution matter accounts no limit as to sources, causes and the area of effects. Nature and man made actions may be somehow controlled, but practically, the same cannot be said about the marine environment. In reality, marine environment is a multi-issued matter in which conflicting issues are not unusual. Nevertheless, in spirit and letter, at least, the world is bound by its obligation and duty to preserve and protect the marine environment.

5.3. Settlement of Disputes Mechanisms

The Earth Summit is not an end in itself but the first step on a new pathway to our common future. A massive 600-page tome called Agenda 21 was adopted as a guideline for future national and international action in the "field of environment and development." Few international conferences can have been so comprehensively prepared as the United Nations Conference on Environment and Development. Much of the work of the Preparatory Committee and of UNCED's staff was devoted to the preparation of Agenda 21.[23]

Even after the Rio Conference, the precise legal status of Agenda 21 remains a matter of some speculation. It is clearly not a legally-binding text to which governments have subscribed in every detail. It does not have to be ratified in a post-Rio phase. Governments will not be hauled before the International Court of Justice in the Hague if they fail to deliver the goods. There is, nevertheless, a case to be made for considering that Agenda 21 is an example (possibly the most far-reaching and voluminous of its kind ever to be attempted) of "international soft law", a text which has moral if not legal force and which may subsequently serve to underpin both national actions and subsequent, possibly more stringent, international agreements in specific areas.[24] Agenda 21 consists of 40 topics in which ocean marine environment matters are embodied in chapter 17 dealing with protection of the oceans, all kinds of seas, including enclosed, semi-enclosed seas, and closed areas and the protection, rational use and development of their living resources.

Agenda 21 in its chapter 17 embodies 137 topics, but none is concerned specifically with settlement of disputes about marine environment matters arising whether within or beyond the limits of national jurisdiction. Of course, the agenda has paid heed to the Law of the Sea Convention with respect to management related activities. "States should ensure that marine living resources of the exclusive economic zone and other areas under national jurisdiction are conserved and managed in accordance with the provisions of the United Nations Convention on the Law of the Sea."[25] States, in accordance with the provisions of the United Nations Convention on the Law of the Sea on marine scientific research, commit themselves to improve the understanding of the marine environment and its role on global processes."[26] There are such references embodied in the LOS Convention in connection with the marine environment. But all these are only in matters for promotion of marine environment within national jurisdiction. Nothing is seen in Agenda 21 about the marine environment beyond the limits of national jurisdiction such as the high seas and the Area.

The diversity of interests, both national and international, and the probability of the conflict of these interests through the acts of the users of the sea, has rendered the sea a potential source of disputes. Being aware of this fact, the First United Nations Conference on the Law of the Sea in 1958 made an effort, though in vain, to adopt a compulsory disputes settlement system for State Parties to any of the four conventions resulting from that conference. The system was instead relegated into an Optional Protocol which was supplemented to the conventions.[27]

When in 1970, the General Assembly decided that UNCLOS III would convene in 1973, the need for the incorporation of a comprehensive compulsory system of disputes settlement in the treaty resulting from the Conference was acutely felt.[28]

The fact that the future convention would not only modify or update the existing rules of international law, but also create new rules entailing rights and duties in spheres of great economic interest for States, had lent even more importance to the creation of comprehensive procedures including binding judicial settlements in the Convention. Moreover, the establishment of a new international organization of the sort preached by the Group of 77 and in a field of direct economic and political importance to industrialized countries could breed even more conflicts, and made access to a compulsory disputes settlement method indispensable.[29]

Disputes settlement was not included in the mandate of any of the three Main Committees of the Conference. In the first substantive session of the UNCLOS III in Caracas, a group of delegations formed an Informal Working Group on Settlement of Law of the Sea Disputes. The initial basis of the deliberations of this group was a proposal submitted by the United States to the Sea-Bed Committee.[30] The result of the discussions at this forum, which was submitted to the Conference at the end of the session, highlighted the common points of view of the participating delegates concerning disputes settlement procedures. The gist of the expressed opinions was the need of a compulsory disputes settlement system for the uniform interpretation of the Convention, and the indispensability of the incorporation of this system, as an integral part, into the Convention.[31]

The Informal Working Group continued its work in 1975, and produced a document containing 17 articles to be submitted to the Conference. In this, document procedures for both non-compulsory disputes settlement were included. The I.C.J., the International Court of the Law of the Sea and an arbitral tribunal were named in this document as appropriate fora for the compulsory settlements. The fact that the parties to disputes could be States as well as international organizations and even individuals, made it necessary to establish a new international tribunal different from the I.C.J.[32]

At the end of 1975 Geneva Session of the Conference, on the basis of the above mentioned document, the President of the Conference produced an Informal Single Negotiating Text on Settlement of Disputes.[33]

At the same time, the question of the settlement of disputes relating to the sea-bed was dealt with at the First Committee of the Conference. The ISNT, prepared by the Chairman of the First Committee, contained provisions for the establishment of a tribunal as a principal organ of the

Authority[34] with the jurisdiction for the interpretation and application of the Convention and the contracts.[35]

In 1976, the general debate in the Conference on the question of disputes settlement was held on the basis of the text prepared by the President, and as a result of discussions a revised text on the disputes settlement procedures was produced which was incorporated into the RSNT. At this juncture, there was a general agreement that the States Parties to the Convention and their entities or nationals on the one hand, and the Authority on the other should have the right to bring any breach of the Convention or the contracts before a tribunal with binding powers.[36] Besides, expressed views were in favour of a general obligation to submit any disputes relating to the interpretation and application of the Convention to judicial settlement.

The question of disputes settlement was left open for discussion in the following sessions of the Conference, and except for the settlement of disputes relating to the activities in Area which was specifically discussed at the First Committee, the features of the general disputes settlement methods were touched upon by all delegates in different fora. In this respect, mention should be made particularly of the Group of Legal Experts on Disputes Settlement chaired by Harry Wuensche from the German Democratic Republic.[37]

With respect to the disputes concerning the sea-bed, the Group of 77 was in favour of compulsory disputes settlement providing a reasonable limitation was to be imposed on the competence of the International Tribunal for the Law of the Sea so that the implementation of such a system would not lead to the substitution of the discretion of the Authority by that of the Tribunal. To allay this fear, the ICNT included a proviso based on formulation prepared by Jens Evensen, which reads: "The Sea-Bed Disputes Chamber shall have no jurisdiction with regard to the exercise by the Assembly or by the Council or any of its organs of their discretionary powers under this Part of the present Convention; in no case shall its discretion will be applicable for that of the Authority."[38] At length, the

Treaty on the Law of the Sea established a special and novel system of dispute settlement. However, this development does not appear to have produced a magic solution to the traditional difficulties in this area. Nevertheless, by abandoning a doctrinaire approach, delegations managed to establish by consensus a body of rules characterized by the two fold concern for encouraging peaceful means of dispute settlement to resolve conflicts on the one hand and guaranteeing relative uniformity of interpretation and application of the Convention on the other.[39]

It is a matter of fact that serious attention was paid in UNCLOS III deliberations towards incorporation of settlement of disputes mechanisms. In international law it deserves credit to innovate an improved version towards settlement of disputes. As to dispute resolution, Part XV: Settlement of Disputes of the LOS Convention may be considered to stand where necessary. In its article 311, it is said:

> This Convention shall not alter the rights and obligations of States Parties which arise from other agreements compatible with this Convention and which do not affect the enjoyment by other States Parties of their rights or the performance of their obligations under this Convention.

The LOS Convention does not oppose the states that comply with other agreements which are compatible with this Convention. It is also possible to add that the LOS Convention provisions can be applicable in matters of other agreements if the Convention provisions are not contrary to those agreements. It is a matter of fact that there is an excellent scope to work on settlement of dispute matters in relation to the Earth Summit (Agenda 21) topics. Since environment, particularly the marine environment, is too much open ended, as such, no one can deal with it as a matter of its exclusive sovereign authority. Rights emerging from sovereignty aspect may more or less be absolute. Hence, this right if infringed, remedial approaches instantly arise. This may be materialised through settlement of dispute mechanisms as provided. There is then an opening for the LOS Convention mechanisms applicable to the settlement of disputes.

5.4. Facilitating Settlement of Disputes

Although the United Nations is a multifunctional organization, foremost among its functions is the maintenance of world peace. Both the League of Nations and the United Nations were created near the end of the greatest wars of the century primarily to act as instruments for eliminating armed conflict and for strengthening means for conflict control and resolution. In the long run, arms reduction and control and the development of world law might serve as a means for promoting peace, and on occasion, collective action against threats to or breaches of the peace might be required, but the keystone of the formula for avoiding international violence is to strengthen the commitment to and the machinery for peaceful settlement of disputes.

The primacy of peaceful settlement processes in both the League of Nations and the United Nations is evidenced by the emphasis upon these processes in the Covenant and in the Charter—an emphasis based on both placement and detail within the documents. The goals of promoting peace and security are mentioned first in these texts, and peaceful settlement of disputes is also first and fundamental among the means for goal attainment. Other goals, such as (1) developing friendly relations among nations, (2) harmonizing the actions of nations, (3) taking appropriate measures to strengthen universal peace, and (4) practicing tolerance and living together in peace (included in the United Nations Charter), reinforce the desire for avoiding war. The principles of the organizations emphasize the obligations of members states to refrain from the threat or use of force and to settle international disputes by peaceful means.

In an age of nuclear, biological, and chemical weapons, the attention to peaceful settlement procedures is a prudent approach to world order. The risks of mass annihilation, the insecurity of massive deterrence, the increase of interdependence among nations, the proliferation of increasingly destructive weapons, the psychological uncertainty of the behaviour of leaders under stress, and the threats of escalation, human error, and accident place the future of much of the human race in constant jeopardy. If survival is a foremost human value, then peaceful settlement of disputes is salient as an alternative to the risks of conflict and nuclear war. The other goals of the United Nations may be worth striving to attain for the enrichment of human welfare, but if rivalries and tensions are unrestrained and if peaceful settlement fails to prevent nuclear holocaust, all other human gains may be wiped out in a few moments. Such tragic prospects should provide sufficient incentive to use all means available to avoid international confrontations and to seek new and imaginative methods for reducing tensions. Any risks involved in taking such initiatives are probably less than those involved in a blind contest of wills among competing sovereign states. Peaceful settlement requires a spirit of cooperation and compromise among nation states, but any other course holds little promise for survival in an interdependent world of states with nuclear capability.[40]

The Charter provides a logical progression of steps to be followed by states involved in disputes. Each member promises to adhere to the Charter to settle all disputes by peaceful means and to refrain from the threat or use of force. If a dispute does arise, the parties should, before submission to a United Nations organ, "seek a solution by negotiation, inquiry, mediation, conciliation, arbitration, judicial settlement, resort to regional agencies or arrangements, or other peaceful means of their own choice."[41]

5.5. LOS Convention Settlement of Disputes Mechanisms

The Law of the Sea Convention calls for disputes between states parties concerning the application or interpretation of the Convention to be settled under the terms and conditions of relevant specific agreements or by another peaceful means agreed to by the parties involved. Compulsory provisions would come into play only for certain classes of disputes and only after other available approaches had failed to produce a resolution. The dispute settlement procedures established by the Convention are available only to states parties, and only states parties are subject to its compulsory and binding provisions.

5.5.a. Compulsory Conciliation

Third party as a commission or an international body while rendering assistance for settlement of disputes stands to be a conciliatory body. Furthermore, while a commission or an international body works as a third party in regard to a dispute for settlement, this mechanism is called conciliation. That is to say, conciliation is a mechanism that may enable disputes to be peacefully settled. Conciliation can be treated as a mechanism applicable to settle any dispute. There is no class category to deal with disputes by conciliation mechanism.

Certain disputes, such as a charge that a coastal state was refusing to share surplus fish from its EEZ, are subject to compulsory conciliation, and states enmeshed in other disputes may also opt for conciliation. Such disputes are handled by a five-member *conciliation commission* constituted under Annex V of the LOS Convention. The recommendations of a conciliation commission are not binding on either party; thus, even compulsory conciliation may fail to resolve a dispute.

5.5.b. Compulsory and Binding Arbitration

The Convention provides four venues for the compulsory settlement of disputes. With certain exceptions, when they become party to the Convention or at any time thereafter, states parties can declare which venues they intend to use for dispute settlement. The four venues are:

- The International Court of Justice.
- *The International Tribunal for the Law of the Sea* The Tribunal's Sea-Bed Disputes Chamber is the authorized venue for disputes relating to the Area (Part XI and its annexes).
- A five-member *arbitral tribunal* constituted in accordance with Annex VII of the LOS Convention. If the parties to a dispute (not involving seabed mining) cannot agree on any other venue, the dispute will be handled at this venue.
- A five-member *special arbitral tribunal* constituted in accordance with Annex VIII of the LOS Convention,

for disputes involving fisheries, protection and preservation of the marine environment, marine scientific research, and navigation including pollution from vessels and by dumping.

Although the procedures for setting up the two sorts of arbitral tribunals are a bit different, they are both designed to establish a level playing field in which neither disputant would have an innate advantage and cases would be decided solely.[42]

It should be noted that "Limitations and Exceptions to Applicability of Section 2"[43] are applicable to "Disputes concerning the interpretation or application of this Convention with regards to the exercise by a coastal State of its sovereign rights or jurisdiction provided for in this Convention...." Limitations and applicability of section 2 shall be subject to the procedures provided for in section 2 in cases such as:

(a) when it is alleged that a coastal State has acted in contravention of the provisions of this Convention in regard to the freedoms and rights of navigation, overflight or laying of submarine cables and pipelines, or in regard to other international lawful uses of the sea specified in Article 58;

(b) when it is alleged that a State in exercising the aforementioned freedoms, rights or uses has acted in contravention of this Convention or of laws or regulations adopted by the coastal State in conformity with this Convention and other rules of international law not incompatible with this Convention; or

(c) when it is alleged that a coastal State has acted in contravention of specified international rules and standards for the protection and preservation of the marine environment which are applicable to the coastal State and which have been established by this Convention or through a competent international organization or diplomatic conference in accordance with this Convention.

There seems some confusion to limitations and exceptions to compulsory procedures entailing binding decisions as enumerated in section 2 particularly in Article 287. In the case of protection and preservation of marine environment special arbitral tribunal has been empowered to deal with matters as such.

5.6. LOS Convention Dispute Settlement Machinery and Marine Environment

As time goes on, human activities in the globe are accelerating. In the seas, oceans and their bed, floor and subsoil activities are increasing. As a result, the spectrum of regime is also diverging. Science and technology have bestowed mankind with advantages and disadvantages. Environment is a matter concerning all. Nothing can exist without environment. The regime of the seas and oceans in the style of hydrospace is now in a certain spectrum. The part of the seas as territorial sea is in the stronghold of national jurisdiction lying in the sway of the coastal state. The exclusive economic zone and the continental shelf—the widest jurisdictional sea areas are in the jurisdiction of the coastal state. From a conceptual point of view, all concerns of hydrospace need to be regarded as marine environment. The LOS Convention provides a notion on "pollution of marine environment."[44] This defines the meaning of marine environment. Regulations on Prospecting and Exploration for Polymetallic Nodules in the Area (Mining Code), 13 July 2000 have defined the term marine environment as:

> "marine environment" includes the physical, chemical, geological and biological components, conditions and factors which interact and determine the productivity, state, condition and quality of the marine ecosystem, the waters of the seas and oceans and the airspace above those waters, as well as the seabed and ocean floor and subsoil thereof.[45]

A marine environment dispute is justified to arise if there is "serious harm to marine environment." The term "serious harm to marine environment" seems not specific but open-ended. There may be several variables to be taken into account. However, it is now possible to say:

> "serious harm to the marine environment" means any effect from activities in the Area on the marine environment which represents a significant adverse change in the marine environment determined according to the rules, regulations and procedures adopted by the Authority on the basis of internationally recognised standards and practices.[46]

The marine environment approaches relate to (a) coastal state, flag state, port state, state of registry, Authority and the concerned International Organizations. They may be in concern for redress against environmental harms. Within national jurisdiction coastal state, flag state/state of registry are to be in the phases of marine environment. In the case of the sea areas beyond national jurisdiction particularly the high seas, the matters seem to be with the flag state/state of registry or the port state. The Authority is bestowed with legal authority if environment is degraded in carrying activities of the Area. The International Organizations like UNEP and IMO play an important role to promote cooperation for protection and preservation of marine environment. Difficulties lie in specifying machinery exclusively destined for the settlement of marine environment disputes.

It is generally recognised that most effective measures for preventing deterioration of the human environment will depend primarily upon national and local regulations and enforcement. It is likely that sovereign states will subject themselves to supranational authority in ecological matters in sharp contrast to the lack of such authority in other areas. Nevertheless, the problems of global pollution, with the threat of eco-catastrophes from many existing sources and trends, present to human kind one more opportunity for cooperative action for the benefit, and possibly the survival, of the whole human race. National action without global planning will probably prove insufficient. A failure to meet potential ecological threats on a global front with foresight and imagination could prove disastrous. Should the scientific evidence suggest the necessity for drastic global measures to preserve a healthy environment, is a world of competing sovereign states capable of developing flexible responses in time to avert catastrophe?[47]

The LOS Convention's compulsory procedures entailing binding decisions as specified in Article 287 have limitations and exceptions to applicability.[48]

In reality, there are obligations to promote environment. Cooperation and understanding for its promotion by states and international organizations are preconditions to help establish a regime of marine environment. International agencies have given limited attention to problems of the human environment for many years, but the programs have been selective, low-scale, and often incidental to the main thrust of the efforts of these agencies. The pressure for a comprehensive and better-coordinated effort is of recent origin. A perusal of the activities of the specialized agencies affiliated with the United Nations reveals that the agencies giving the greatest attention to environmental problems are the World Meteorological Organization (WMO), which is concerned with air pollution and the climatic effect of pollutants; the World Health Organization (WHO), which is involved in a wide range of projects in environmental health; UNESCO, which has sponsored several studies and conferences of experts; the Food and Agriculture Organization Organisation (FAO), whose interests include pesticide accumulation and misuse of the environment; the International Atomic Energy Agency (IAEA), which is concerned with nuclear wastes; the International Maritime Organization (IMO), which has a special interest in oil pollution of the oceans; and the International Labour Organization (ILO), whose concerns include exposure to toxic substances in the working environment.[49]

Principle 21 of the Stockholm Declaration on the Human Environment...was reaffirmed in General Assembly resolutions: resolution 2995(XXVII) of 15 December 1972... and by Principle 2 of the Rio Declaration on Environment and Development.... The draft articles follow the well-established principle of *sic utere tuo ut alienum non laedas* (use your own property so as not to injure the property of another) in international law. As Lauterpacht stated, this maxim "is applicable to relations of States not less than those of individuals; ... it is one of those general principles of law ... which the Permanent Court is bound to apply by virtue of Article 38 of its Statute."[50]

Principle 15 of Rio Declaration seems an authoritative pronouncement of the "precautionary principle." According to this principle:

> In order to protect the environment, the precautionary approach shall be widely applied by States according to their capabilities. Where there are threats of serious or irreversible damage, lack of full scientific certainty shall not be used as a reason for postponing cost-effective measures to prevent environmental degradation.

Impacts on the environment can only be detected after they have taken place. The precautionary approach means that in case of doubt as to effects on the marine environment, preventive or remedial action is to be taken if scientific evidence makes it plausible that detrimental effects for the marine environment may result, i.e., a decision to err on the safe side. The precautionary approach is a way of handling and considering something whereas the precautionary principle takes up this approach and establishes it as a general principle adopted as a guide to action. The starting point of both is the lack of scientific certainty, or in other words the problem that perfect knowledge cannot be guaranteed before serious or even irreversible consequences become avoidable.[51]

There is an argument that this principle has been included in so many treaties, declarations and resolutions, with an absence of opposition, that it has achieved a general binding effect as customary law.[52] This raises the same difficulties as in many other instances of provisions that are included in treaties with unremitting regularity. Can the proposition be asserted as a customary rule? For a lawyer giving advice or preparing a case, the task is to find arguments. Even if there is no certainty as to whether there is a rule of custom, or what its precise content is, arguments can be deployed in good faith to justify action, or to persuade a tribunal what the law is and how it applies.

There is also a role for lawyers in assisting further development of the law, which is most likely to occur in the form of treaties. Even if there is a rule of custom, the practice of the community of nations is to prefer the rule to be entered into relevant treaties. Lawyers identify, refine and formulate the principles that are embodied in treaties. The precautionary principle has been invoked before the ICJ:

> New Zealand invoked the precautionary principle in support of its application to the International Court of Justice to review France's decision to recommence nuclear tests. Nuclear Tests Case (New Zealand v. France), request by New Zealand for an examination of the situation, 21 August 1995, at paras. 105-108. France replied that the legal status of the principle was "uncertain". ICJ, Verbatim Record (CR 95/20), 12 September 1995, p. 71.[53]

It is because of such uncertainty that so many treaties have been concluded in this area. While general international law includes established customary rules on state responsibility relevant to environmental law, the way forward is plainly through treaties.[54]

As marine environment is no one's exclusive concern, it is a technology oriented matter. Consequently, specialists need to contribute to it as experts. In its formulation the Law of the Sea Treaty, required an expert's role in concerned matters.

In theory, the participation of experts in the proceedings of a court of law does not raise any particular difficulties in national law. The judge's task is to take judicial decisions, while experts provide clarification on questions of fact. At most, the experts' contribution has the status of a qualified testimony explaining the relationship of causality between the various elements submitted to the court. Thus in non-traditional procedural law, experts are involved in adducing evidence. In general international dispute settlement the same principles apply.

However, the framework of the law of the sea is somewhat special, since the importance of technical and scientific issues and problems had been constantly highlighted during the negotiations. In fact, the role of technical and scientific experts was raised during discussion of the nature, role and function of special procedures. The so-called 'functional' approach proposed favouring settlement of disputes involving fisheries, pollution and scientific research by bodies made up of experts rather than professional jurists. The States of the Group of 77 were averse to such an exclusively technocratic approach which might ultimately establish a preserve legally separate from the Convention. Excluding any appeal, procedure against decisions handed down by the bodies established under special procedures was ruled out by technical bodies.

The initial version of the Single Negotiating Text had considered the question of recourse to technical experts in relation to precise questions, namely fisheries, pollution, navigation and scientific research. For this purpose, the court or tribunal selected could choose either to set up a committee of experts responsible for proposing solutions to the dispute or to invite experts to sit as technical assessors in the court or tribunal on an advisory basis. The opinion of the committee of experts was not binding on the parties to the dispute, which could discuss it before the designated judicial court or tribunal. However, this technically authoritative opinion was the document on the basis of which the court or tribunal considered the dispute. Discussions revealed that the negotiators were reluctant to adopt this proposal, which was construed as imposing an obligation on the court or tribunal to respect the experts' opinion, whereas the intention, on the basis of the declarations made, was to confine experts to an advisory capacity at the request of the court or tribunal. The first revision took up this general approach and amended the text to extend recourse to experts to technical and scientific problems instead of restricting it to the four areas mentioned above.

The second revision of the Single Negotiating Text made a number of extensive changes which were more or less incorporated into the final version. Recognition of the judicial power of the courts or tribunals established within the framework of special procedures meant that the problem of an experts' committee and the status of its opinions was considered to have been virtually resolved. On the other hand, the discretion of the court or tribunal to call experts as technical or scientific assessors in an advisory capacity but without the right to vote was strengthened. Thus, the final outline of the present Article 290 began to take place.[55] According to this article of the LOS Convention:

> In any dispute involving scientific or technical matters, a court or tribunal exercising jurisdiction under this section may, at the request of a party or *propriomotu*, select in consultation with the parties no fewer than two scientific or technical experts chosen preferably from the relevant list prepared in accordance with Annex VIII, Article 2, to sit with the court or tribunal but without the right to vote.

The LOS Convention has taken into account technical and scientific approaches to marine environment. There is no opening to consider marine environment as one's exclusive matter. This gives rise to marine environment disputes to be of concern to the victim and the actor whose activities have resulted in environment pollution. While harm to marine environment results from activities in the Area the concerned court has authority to consider provisional measures. That means:

> If a dispute has been duly submitted to a court or tribunal which considers that *prima facie* it has jurisdiction under this Part XI, section 5, the court or tribunal may prescribe any provisional measures which it considers appropriate under the circumstances to preserve the respective rights of the parties to the dispute or to prevent serious harm to the marine environment, pending the final decision.[56]

Provisional measures are prescribed to meet urgency of the situation. These measures are actually provisional in the sense that "Provisional measures may be modified or revoked as soon as the circumstances justifying them have changed or ceased to exist."[57] With regard to a dispute for causing serious harm to environment the party afflicted is entitled to provisional measures in the court or tribunal. "Provisional measures may be prescribed, modified or revoked under this article only at the request of a party to the dispute and after the parties have been given an opportunity to be heard."[58]

It should be noted that arbitration seems to be a means of applying legal principles to a controversy within limits previously agreed upon by the disputing parties. A panel of judges or arbitrators is created either by special agreement of the parties or by an existing arbitral treaty. In agreeing to submit the dispute to arbitration, the disputants also agree in advance to be bound by the decision. An arbitral agreement known as a *compromis* specifies the method of selecting the arbitral panel, the time and place of the hearing, and any limitations upon the facts to be considered or the principles of law or equity to be applied in arriving at a decision.[59] The LOS Convention has prescribed arbitration as a mechanism specified as Annex VII; Arbitration that includes 13 articles The Convention's Annex VIII is Special Arbitration whose jurisdiction is concerned with the matters in which technical and scientific expert's opinion is taken for the ends of decision. The two mechanisms are related with similar aspects but a difference on subject matters and arbitrators' qualifications. The special arbitration has limited scope of jurisdiction concerning only on four subjects as specified. To this end Article 1 of this annex says:

> Subject to Part XV, any party to a dispute concerning the interpretation or application of the articles of this Convention relating to (1) fisheries, (2) protection and preservation of the marine environment, (3) marine scientific research, or (4) navigation, including pollution from vessels and by dumping, may submit the dispute to the special arbitral procedure provided for in this Annex by written notification addressed to the other party or parties to the dispute. The notification shall be accompanied by a statement of the claim and the grounds which it is based.

Recourse to experts involves disputes relating to "scientific or technical matters." It is only for these cases that provision is made for the procedure for selecting no fewer than two experts from the relevant official list maintained by specialized international agencies: the Food and Agriculture Organization (FAO), the United Nations Environment Programme (UNEP), the Inter-Governmental Oceanographic Commission and the International Maritime Organization. Given the way in which the procedure for selecting experts is organized, it can be assumed that any other disputes only involve the interpretation or application of the Convention and that the experts nominated may only sit as assessors. However, the court or tribunal is in any case still free to decide on enquiries or expert assessments which it feels are necessary for the taking of evidence (Art. 27 of Ann. VI). Summarily, there is an opening for disputing parties to resolve disputes resulting in marine environment through the LOS Convention mechanisms one of which specifically designed as in Annex VIII: Special Arbitration.

5.7. Marine Environment Dispute: The Bay of Bengal Phase

Like some gigantic sickle fashioned by the Eternal Creator, with its handle formed by the base of the Indian subcontinent to the west, its cutting edge in the north-eastern part of the Indian Ocean and the tip of its blade nestling in the southern part of Thailand to the east, the Bay of Bengal is one of the world's most spectacular natural features. It occupies an area of 21,72,000 sq. kms. and its waters wash the shores of India, Sri Lanka, the Maldives, Bangladesh, Myanmar, Malaysia, Indonesia and Thailand. Its southern boundary may be said to be formed by an imaginary line connecting Dondra Head at the southern end of Sri Lanka to the northern tip of the Indonesian island of Sumatra. A number of great rivers, whose names and legends are inextricably intertwined with the region's myths and memories—Ganga, Brahmaputra, Irrawady, Godavari, Mahanadi, Krishna, and Cauvery—debouch into the Bay of Bengal, bringing with them vast quantities of silt during the monsoon season from July to September each year, and producing a warm, low-salinity, nutrient and oxygen-rich layer to a depth of 100 metres.

5.7.a. Separate and Diverse Ecosystem

The Bay of Bengal is one of the world's over 60 large marine ecosystems, with the fresh water from the major rivers impacting the salinity of the coastal and estuarine waters as well as coastal circulation patterns. This ecosystem is strongly affected by monsoons, storm surges and cyclones and in turn the Bay critically affects the climate of the countries bounding it. For instance, it is the warm moisture laden clouds over the Bay of Bengal that eventually precipitate as rainfall during the south-western monsoon season from July to September each year, upon which its surrounding littoral states are even today so critically dependent and it is again the north-easterly winds over the Bay of Bengal which bring the winter rains over much of south India.

The Bay has many critically important areas of biological diversity. These include the Sundarbans, which are one of the world's most extensive mangrove systems; the Palk Straits; the Gulf of Mannar; the Maldive Atolls; the MuKo Similan National Park and the Mu KSurin National Park in Thailand, and the Marine (Wandur) National Park in the Andaman and Nicobar Islands. Indeed, set in the midst of the Bay of Bengal as if it were a diadem in the forehead of the Bay, the Andaman and Nicobar Islands are a chain of some three hundred islands, big and small, stretching nearly seven hundred km. north to south.[60]

5.7.b. Present Day Socio-Economic Conditions

In many respects the consequences of relationship are still with us. Today the eight littoral nations that bound the Bay of Bengal are collectively home to over 1.5 billion people. Approximately 400 million of them live in the Bay's catchment area, including those residing in the large coastal cities such as Kolkata, Cuddalore, Kakinada, Machlipatnam, Chennai, Paradip and Vishakapatnam, to name those in India and Chittagong in Bangladesh.

Despite the region as a whole being rich in natural and mineral resources, the socio-economic condition of the vast majority of the people remains mired in poverty and subject to recurrent and devastating natural calamities. For instance, the sediment loading in the Ganga-Brahmaputra watershed caused by accelerated soil erosion in the Himalayas leads to large scale downstream flooding. More than four-fifth of Bangladesh consists of a delta plain positioned below the conveyance of the Ganga, Brahmaputra and Meghna Rivers. Each year, the inhabitants have to flee the flooded plains in large numbers. It is estimated that 7% of Bangladesh could be permanently flooded.

5.7.c. Fish and Fisheries

Industry and manufacturing in the Bay region are localized, and largely of the enclave type; agriculture, barring certain pockets, is at subsistence level and the economic activities centre mainly around tourism (especially in the Maldives), the mining of coral and sand for use as construction materials, and of course fishing, which is of major importance because it gives direct employment to over 2 million fishermen. Fishing is generally artisanal and involves many disadvantaged groups, such as poor villagers, women, migrant families etc. However, in the last three decades, the marine catch has increased more than four-folds with the steady intrusion of large scale mechanised fishing. India and Thailand account for the bulk of the fish catch, followed by Myanmar and Malaysia.

The main commercial species of fish are shrimp, tuna, yellow fin, big eye and skipjack. Of these species, shrimp (or prawn) is the major export earner. The coastal areas also support significant aquaculture production of shrimp and fish. Over-exploitation of marine resources, destructive fishing practices, habitat destruction, and pollution from land and sea-based sources are already posing serious threats to the continued survival of the region's marine bounty. A recent study of the trawl fisheries off India's south east coast found more than 40 per cent reduction in the catch, and nearly two-thirds decline in the catch rate. The ever present threats of oil spills from the heavy tanker traffic through the Bay of Bengal region and their impact on its marine life, as well as the concentration of shrimp aquaculture farms in certain coastal areas and their impact on the region's eco-system, are also cause for concern.

The growing competition and tension between artisanal and mechanised, large scale fishermen, the alarming increase in cyanide fishing to meet the needs of the lucrative live food fish markets of Hong Kong and Singapore, and the destruction of critical fish spawning and nurseries, such as mangroves and estuaries through pollution sedimentation and dams for flood control, are some of the other serious threats to the fishing industry, which is the mainstay of the economic life of the Bay of Bengal community.

5.7.d. Pollution Threats

Indeed a brown haze of pollution from the ocean's surface up to a height of one to three kms. blankets much of the Indian Ocean including the Bay of Bengal, according to a recent study conducted by an international team of oceanographers and scientists. These findings (reported in the June 2003 issue of WISTA: Ocean Wealth under the feature IN FOCUS-Pollution Haze Over The Indian Ocean) have a deep impact on the climate and marine life of the Bay region, and unless checked would degrade the environment irretrievably.

5.7.e. Oil and Natural Gas

It is oil today which fuels industry, and practically the entire oil tanker traffic from West Asia to China, Japan and the other countries of East Asia passes through the Bay region south of Sri Lanka before entering the Straits of Malacca via a passage below the Nicobar Islands. Furthermore, significant quantities of natural gas have been discovered offshore in Bangladesh, and recently the discovery of natural gas fields have been reported off the coast of Andhra Pradesh in India too. The risk of a major oil spill causing serious pollution and contamination of the fish stock is a matter of continuing concern. As regards the exploitation of natural gas as an energy source, it will replace other forms and to the extent those other forms are non-renewable, it will be for good. But whether it will have any lasting negative effect on the Bay environment, only time will tell.

5.7.f. Probing the Bay's Mysteries

Meanwhile, exciting developments are taking place to probe the Bay's mysteries, and utilise its wealth sustainably Here are a few by way of illustration and they are by no means exhaustive. India itself has organised experiments to utilise oceanic thermal energy by exploiting the difference between the surface temperatures and the deep sea temperatures in the Bay area to drive a turbine off Tuticorin. Satellite derived chlorophyll imageries are being used to present phytoplankton blooms in the Bay area during the north-east monsoons.

The monsoons govern the very pulse of life in our sub-continent. Therefore, observational experiments, under the Indian Climate Research Programme, called the Bay of Bengal Monsoon Experiment (BOBMEX), have been carried out extensively to measure the variables of the atmosphere, ocean and their interface to better understand the processes that govern the variability of organised convection over the Bay area.

The two Ocean Research Vessels, Sagar Kanya and Sagar Sampada, of the Department of Ocean Development, have been extensively deployed in the Bay area for systemic research and understanding of the oceanic environment, to determine the potential of various non-living and living sea resources in the Bay region and beyond.

Recently acquired data has served to dispel the impression that the Gulf of Mannar was bereft of rift configurations and now, with that Asian Development Bank assistance, the Sri Lankan Government is girding up its efforts towards exploration for petroleum resources, off-shore for the first time in almost twenty years.

Even the various commercial, ornamental, poisonous and venomous species of fish inhabiting the Andaman Seas, have not escaped attention. In recent years, taxonomic studies have led to as many as 1200 species of fish being identified. Of these, 147 species belonging to 33 families are known to be poisonous.

5.7.g. Towards a Bay of Bengal Community

The Bay can well act as a unifying force and be the focus of regional cooperation between the eight littoral nations that bound its rim. They face common problems in areas such as fisheries, oil spills, pollution control etc. To tackle these problems determinedly, regional agreements will have to be implemented in letter and spirit, and national legislation will have to be harmonised. Enforcement capacities will have to be strengthened, and sound management practices introduced. The multitude of international, regional and sub-regional institutions working in the Bay area, many of whose mandates overlap, will have to be rationalized and streamlined.

If even some of these measures are implemented sincerely, the nations bordering the Bay can look forward to a bright, common future as equal progressive members of a Bay of Bengal Community. Furthermore, in the case of marine environment disputes, duties and obligations must be hailed at every stage. There seems a serious feeling to do that on the part of each and every state concerned with the environment resulting in dispute for harm caused to it. The marine environment dispute as to the Bay of Bengal phase will then be effective for solution as duty and obligation for its littoral states. It is, submitted, the Bay of Bengal Community will encourage as if in duty and obligation bound to promote a legal regime of marine environment in the Bay of Bengal.

5.8. Overview

The Indian Ocean is a zone of tectonic activity. It is now known to all particularly from the recent earthquake and tsunami disaster.[61] The earthquake originated in the Indian Ocean just north of Simeulue island, off the western coast of northern Sumatra, Indonesia. The resulting tsunami devastated the shores of Indonesia, Sri Lanka, India, Thailand and other countries with waves of up to 15 m. (50 feet) high, even reaching the east coast of Africa, 4500 km. (2,800 miles) west of the epicentre.

The hypocentre of the main earthquake was at 3° 19' N, 95° 51.24 E (3.316°N, 95.854°E), some 160 km. (100 miles) west of Sumatra, at a depth of 30 km. (18.6 miles) below mean sea level (initially reported as 10 km.). This is at the extreme western end of the Ring of Fire, an earthquake belt that accounts for 81 per cent of the world's largest earthquakes. The earthquake itself (apart from the tsunami) was felt as far away as Bangladesh, India, Malaysia, Myanmar, Thailand, Singapore and the Maldives.

The earthquake was unusually large in geographical extent. An estimated 1200 km. (750 miles) of faultline slipped about 15 m. (45 ft) along the subduction zone where the India Plate dives under the Burma Plate. The slip did not happen instantaneously but took place in two phases over a period of several minutes. Seismographic data indicate that the first phase involved the formation of a rupture about 400 km. long and 100 km. wide, located 30 km. beneath the sea bed. The rupture proceeded at a speed of about 2 km/s, beginning off the coast of Aceh and proceeding north-westerly over about 100 seconds. A pause of about another 100 seconds took place before the rupture continued northwards towards the Andaman and Nicobar Islands.[62]

The India Plate is part of the great Indo-Australian Plate, which underlies the Indian Ocean and Bay of Bengal, and is drifting north-east at an average of 6 cm/year (2 inches/year). The India Plate meets the Burma Plate (which is considered a portion of the great Eurasian Plate) at the Sunda Trench. At this point the India Plate subducts the Burma Plate which includes the Nicobar Islands, the Andaman Islands and northern Sumatra. The India Plate slips deeper and deeper beneath the Burma Plate until the increasing temperature and pressure turns the subducting edge of the India Plate into magma which eventually pushes the magma above it out through the volcanoes. This process is interrupted by the locking of the plates for several centuries until the build up of stress causes their release resulting in a massive earthquake and tsunami. The volcanic activity that results as the Indo-Australian plate subducts the Eurasian plate has created the Sunda Arc.

Marine environment is tremendously concerned with natural activities. In no cases, marine environment can be considered to be at man's sway. Nature's role is a must but human endeavours are aimed so far to control the concerned nature activity. What happens at uncontrolled natural activities, human activities are prescribed to ameliorate its aftermath. Consequential steps for future control are provided, but human activities cannot be a guarantee to nature activities. In marine environment, this proposition cannot be ruled out. The recent earthquake and tsunami disasters have confirmed it. But human efforts must not end to promote a regime in the case of present deal, of marine environment viable and congenial for all concerned.

In common parlance, marine pollution involves the destruction of the quality of water by fouling, defiling and making it filthy by contamination. In scientific terms, pollution constitutes a distortion of the marine ecosystem. To understand, therefore, what marine pollution is, one must be in a position to appreciate the marine ecosystem.[63]

The marine ecosystem is composed of land, saline water and living things—each of which is dependent on the other two.[64] Living organisms interact in this ecosystem in an intricate way. In a two dimensional classification of water and bottom, the water mass is technically known as the pelagic zone and the land mass beneath it, the benthic zone. Fish and fauna, the planktonic and nektonic organisms from one ecological unit known as the 'community'. This community functions and survives on a very delicate balance. The marine ecosystem, therefore, is a complex interaction of community and environmental processes.

The history of life in the ocean depicts the evolution of the interaction between living creatures and the oceanic environment: the water, the air and the land. The ocean environment shapes the habits and forms of the creatures living therein. A series of delicately adjusted, interlocking relationship have developed because of one's responsiveness to the other. The life of all parts of the oceans is interlinked, from tiny plants to big marine mammals.[65]

The equilibrium of the food and energy in the oceans is often characterised as a food web—a complex network of paths of food energy transfer, the nutritional inter-relationship of marine organisms. Plants and animals that float or drift passively in the sea constitute the initial links in the complex marine food chain. Tiny plants, often of only microscopic dimension, trap some of the abundant energy of sunlight through photosynthesis. Starches and sugar resulting from this process are then available to the animals. Marine plants, like their terrestial counterparts, are the ultimate synthesisers of amino acids, the building blocks out of which proteins are formed or constructed. In general, these acids cannot be produced by the animals. Certain other fatty acids that occur abundantly in the fats of bony fishes are also produced by phytoplanktons. A continuous cyclic transfer of matter and energy from miscroscopic plants to larger animals typifies the complicated food web of the oceans. These exchanges are effected as grazing animals feed on the plants and are, in turn, preyed upon by larger predators. On the death of the ultimate predator, the energy rich material of their bodies is returned to the micro-organisms of the sea, to begin a new rotation of the food cycle.

A distortion of the above intricately balanced marine ecosystem occurs through pollution. Pollution upsets the ecological balance by poisoning the animals through plants with which they come into contact; dissolving oxygen in the sea water which is essential to the life of marine animals; and breaking the food chain.[66]

There is no alternative to marine environment for ecosystem to prevail and grow in it. Human activities need to be regulated for promotion of marine environment. The states bordering the seas need particular attention. In the case of the Bay of Bengal its bordering countries are in a positive phase for promotion of its environment. The Bay of Bengal bordering states like Bangladesh, Myanmar, India, Maldives, Sri Lanka even Thailand have to take many steps individually and regionally aiming at maintaining the environment in the Bay at any cost. The South Asian states are mainly littoral states in the Indian Ocean. The Indian Ocean provides these states foreign policy motivations, strategic importance and great potential for energy, non-living and living resources. The attitude of the South Asian states emerges out of their needs of the Indian Ocean.

Historically, the Indian Ocean was called the British Lake, dominated exclusively by the British. After the World War II, the area has been shared by many and thus attained significance.

The total area of the Indian Ocean is about 7 crore sq. kms. It stretches from the Cape Camorin in the north to the Antarctic continent in the west. The coastline of the Indian Ocean has 10 big, 20 middle and 300 small ports on it. The region is the most densely populated area in the world; now nearly 200 crore people live in this region. It has 47 states including 36 littoral and hinterland states. In the present international fora it has attained significance due to the super power rivalry in Indian Ocean.

The region is rich in natural resources. It has about 80.7% gold, 56% tin, 28.5% uranium, 98% diamond and 90% tea, and jute of the world. Thus, the resources of the Indian Ocean states are vital. The Indian Ocean is an important communicational link between the east and the west. It is a sea link between Europe, Far East, South-East Asia, Africa, the Middle East and Australia.[67] The Indian Ocean is a zone of peace and its 43-members of the Ad Hoc Committee are continuing their commitment for peace, security and stability in this area.[68] The internationalization of the issues of the Indian Ocean, has really been asserted of collective effort to reduce the super powers conflicts in Indian Ocean, though bilateral tensions are to be resolved in the littoral and hinterland states of the Indian Ocean.

The Indian Ocean provides these states great potential for energy, non-living and living resources. The energy resources, i.e., wind, tides, currents, waves, thermal gradients and salinity gradients are some of the resources towards which the South Asian states feel attracted. The natural resources of the Indian Ocean are easily available to the South Asian States. Their weak economies and ever increasing cost of production makes it impossible to use the Indian Ocean's resources. The Bay of Bengal bordering states are asymmetric in the phase of which India is in the high up position. In reality, the Asian States are practically Indo-centric.

Participation of South Asian States in the UNCLOS III deliberations was effective. Sri Lanka chaired the different sessions of the conference. Pakistan was the chairman of the group of 77. India, Nepal and Bangladesh contributed in their own way. South Asian States, indeed, had their own problems and therefore joined different geographical groups as well. India, Pakistan, Sri Lanka and Bangladesh belong to coastal states. Maldives among the archipelagic groups of states, Nepal and Bhutan in the group of land locked states.

Regional approach exclusively to the Bay of Bengal is at virgin stage compared to others steps taken about the related seas in the world. However, the ongoing development phase among the Bay of Bengal states is of particular significance. The ongoing SAARC role although confined to development sectors avoiding political issues, practically has an opening for promotion of marine environment. Bangladesh-India-Sri Lanka-Thailand Economic Co-operation (BIMST-EC) is a subregional grouping combining some geographically contiguous South Asian and ASEAN countries in the Bay of Bengal. It was formed by the member countries to exploit the synergies in their capabilities and resource endowments for their development.[69] The idea of BIMST-EC may have commenced in order to activate economic interaction around the Bay of Bengal community.[70]

At present regional grouping in regard to the Bay of Bengal concerns appears to be SAARC, BIMST-EC and the Bay of Bengal Community. Marine environment cannot be governed by geographical or political boundary in entirety. Neither ego nor deterrent approach whether individual or in group can be made effective to resolve environment dispute. Environment dispute is not to be only in the purview of the state affected. It is practically a matter of common concerns owing which environment matters need to be taken for protection, preservation and promotion at all levels.

The LOS Convention settlement of dispute mechanisms to all intents and purposes are cooperation oriented for peace. This is stressed in the preamble of the convention which states:

> Prompted by the desire, in a spirit of mutual understanding and co-operation, all issues relating to the law of the sea and aware of the historic significance of this convention as an important contribution to the maintenance of peace, justice and progress of all peoples of the world.

Conscious that the problem of ocean space are closely inter-related and need to be considered as a whole, explaining the principles, the preamble viewed:

> Recognizing the desirability of establishing through this convention, with due regard for sovereignty of all states, a legal order for the seas and oceans which will facilitate international communication, and will promote the peaceful uses of the seas and oceans, the equitable and efficient utilization of their resources, the conservation of their living resources, and the study, protection and preservation of marine environment.

Practically speaking, the LOS Convention contains important new rules for the protection and preservation of the marine environment from pollution. The world community's interest in the peaceful settlement of disputes and prevention of use of force in the settlement of disputes between States have been advanced by the mandatory system of dispute settlement in the Convention.[71] Although the Convention consists of a series of compromises, they form an integral whole. This is why the Convention does not provide for reservations. It is therefore not possible for States to pick what they like and disregard what they do not like. In international law, as in domestic law, rights and duties go hand in hand. It is therefore legally impermissible to claim rights under the Convention without being willing to assume the correlative duties.[72]

South Asian States are in common realm to protect and preserve marine environment in particular to the issues of the Bay of Bengal. As South Asian States are too asymmetric in their capabilities almost in all respects, they must not carry the view that they have an unequal involvement in protecting and preserving the environment in the Bay of Bengal. To this end it is indispensable to take into account principle of the Earth Summit:

> In order to protect the environment, the precautionary approach shall be widely applied by States according to their capabilities. Where there are threats of serious or

irreversible damage, lack of full scientific certainty shall not be used as a reason for postponing cost-effective measures to prevent environment degradation.[73]

In fact and figure, there are no capabilities for taking measures against environmental degradation for the states like Maldives and Bangladesh too on their own against degradation resulted in nature or man-made activities in the Bay of Bengal. The position of Myanmar, Thailand or even Sri Lanka cannot be ensured as commitment to enable to take convenient measures to overcome marine environment constraints. The solitary star in the case of the Bay of Bengal environment seems to be India whose capabilities are of course viable towards marine environment. As a matter of fact, India is advancing in appreciable spate in science and technology. In marine science and technology India's advancement is of recent origin. But its progress is gaining momentum.[74]

The other Bay of Bengal bordering states' infrastructure with respect to marine environment—marine affairs can be taken into account. In fact, to each and every Bay of Bengal littoral state there are incentives for access at national, sub-regional, regional and global level for promotion of the Bay's environment. Besides India, capabilities constraints are obvious for other states to be at an initial stage. However, with the passage of time, states are coming in contact through regional and sub-regional arrangements. Regional arrangement should be highlighted for application in the settlement of disputes. This mechanism can be effected for settling environmental disputes and as such, in the marine environment. Regional approaches should be implemented in the settlement of disputes arising out of the marine environment in the Bay of Bengal. The ongoing role of the Bay of Bengal bordering states gives rise to approaches to their cooperative role for promotion of marine environment in the Bay.

The lead to promote activities for preservation and protection of marine environment in the Bay of Bengal virtually seems to be taken by India. It does not mean that the then lesser capacitated other states have less to do. The Bay of Bengal marine environment dispute if one arises will have to be considered as a common issue to be overcome by the littoral states. Work needs to be done for promotion not only of national interests but also the pursuit of the common dream of the Earth Summit.

References

1. LOS Convention, Art. 192.
2. John H. Knox, "The Myth and Reality of Transboundary Environmental Impact Assessment", 96(2002) 1 AJIL 291.
3. UN Conference on the Human Environment, Stockholm Declaration, June 16, 1972, UNDoc.A/CONF.48/14, Prin 21, 11(1972) ILM 1416. The nations of the world reaffirmed Principle 21 in only slightly modified form as Principle 2 of the 1992 Rio Declaration. See UN Conference on Environment and Development, Rio Declaration on Environment and Development, June 14, 1992, UNDoc.A/CONF.151/5/Rev.1, Prin 2, 31(1992) ILM 874. The usual custom in continuing to refer is to the principle as Principle 21 rather than Principle 2. Internationally, Principle 21 is the most authoritative expression of the principle that states should prevent transboundary harm.
4. Alexander Kiss & Dinah Shelton, *International Environmental Law* (1991) 130; Philippe Sands, *Principles of International Environmental Law* (1995) 190.
5. David Hunter, James Salzman & Durwood Zaelke, *International Environmental Law and Policy* (1998) 321, 345; Edith Brown Weiss, Stephen C. McCaff, Daniel Barstow Magraw, Paul C. Szasz & Robert E. Lutz, *International Environmental Law and Policy* (1998) 317.
6. David Wirth, "Rio Declaration on Environment and Development: Two Steps Forward and One Back, Vice Vesa?", 29(1995) GA.L. REV. 599, 620; Rudiger Wolfrum, "Purposes and Principles of International Environmental Law", (1990) GER.Y.B. INT'L 308, 310.
7. Sands, *supra* at 186; Weiss, *supra* at 316.
8. See Jeffrey L. Dunoff, " Institutional Misffits: The GATT, the ICJ & Trade Environment Disputes", 15(1994) MICH. J.INT'L L. 1043, 1094 (highlighting contradiction between the sovereign right to exploit resources and responsibility not to allow transboundary harm).
9. Louis B. Sohn, "The Stockholm Declaration on the Human Environment", 14(1973) HARV.INT'L.L. 423, 492 (citing statement of Canadian delegation that the "principle reflects existing rules of international law, the first element in it stressing the rights of states, while the second element made it clear that those rights must be limited or balanced by the responsibility to ensure that the exercise of rights did not result in damage to others."
10. Oscar Schachter, "The Emergence of International Environmental Law", 44(1991) J INT'L AFF. 457, 463; see also Daniel Bodansky, "Customary

(and Not So Customary) International Environmental Law, 3(1995) IND.J.GLOBAL.LEGAL STUD. 110, 111 ("Although I am unaware of any systematic empirical study of this issue, transboundary pollution seems much more the rule than the exception in interstate relations. Pollutants continuously travel across most international borders through the air and by rivers and ocean currents,"); Schachter, *supra,* at 462 ("On its own terms, [Principle 21] has not become state practice: States generally do not 'ensure that the activities within their jurisdiction do not cause damage to the environments of others.').

11. Sanford E. Gaines, "Taking Responsibility for Transboundary Environmental Effects", 14 (1991) HASTINGS INT'L & COMP.L.REV. 781, 796.
12. For examples of *substantial,* see *Experts Group on Environmental Law of the World Commission on Environment and Development, Environmental Protection and Sustainable Development: Legal Principles and Recommendations* 75 (Art. 10) (1987); International Law Association, Rules of International Law Applicable to Transfrontier Pollution, Art. 3(1), in 60 ILA, *Conference Report* (1982). For examples of *significant,* see *Restatement (Third) of the Foreign Relations Law of the United States* S.601 (1987). See also Kamen Sachariew, "The Definition of Thresholds of Tolerance for Transboundary Environmental Injury Under International Law: Development and Present Status", 37(1990) NETH. INT'L L. REV. 193, 196 (concluding that since the Stockholm Conference, 'significant' is the most common term "used to describe the threshold of tolerable transboundary environmental harm or interference."
13. See Gunther Handle, "National Uses of Transboundary Air Resources: The International Entitlement Issue Reconsidered", 26(1986) Id. J.405.
14. John, H. Knox, "The Myth and Reality of Transboundary Environmental Impact Assessment", 96(2002) 1 AJIL 292-294.
15. Gerard J. Mangone, *Law for the World Ocean* (Stevens & Sons, London, 1981) 252-254.
16. R.A. Malviya, *Environmental Pollution and Ist Control under Intenational* Law (Chugh Publications, Allahabad, India: 1987) 80-81.
17. It is to mention that in a single day a country like the United States uses about 400 billion gallons of water for agriculture, industry, commerce, and public utilities as well as in households. It is also to note that in 1973 the estimates of petroleum hydrocarbons that entered the sea from coastal refineries and runoffs from the land was 2.7 million metric tons. *Ibid.,* 255-256.
18. *Ibid.,* 257.
19. The 1967 spill of 1,00,000 tons of oil into the sea, caused by the accidental grounding of the tanker *Torrey Canyon,* raised the legal question of the coastal states, power to intervene promptly to prevent major oil pollution damage to the shoreline by a vessel that was outside the territorial sea or on the high seas. This occurred at the time when the concept of Exclusive

Economic Zone was beginning to take shape at the United Nations. In the *Torrey Canyon* case, the British authorities bombed the vessel by setting fire to the oil cargo in order to reduce pollution damage. The IMO (the IMCO) was instrumental in the drafting of the 1969 International Convention Relating to Intervention on the High Seas in Case of Oil Pollution Casualties (The Intervention Convention), which was adopted by the international conference at Brussels and opened for signature from November 29, 1969, to December 31, 1970. The 1969 Intervention Convention entered into force on May 6, 1975. James C.F. Wang, *Handbook on Ocean Politics & Law* (Grenwood Press- New York: 1992) 309. Moreover, the *Argo Merchant*, and the *Amco Cadiz* that caused spilling their grimy guts upon the seas have captured world attention. Cries were seen raised everywhere for remedies to avoid such catastrophes and to fix liabilities upon the responsible parties, Gerard J. Mangone, *Law for the World Ocean* Tagore Law Lectures (Stevens & Sons, London, 1981) 258. The National Academy of Science in the United States made a rough estimate that 2.13 million metric tons of petroleum hydrocarbons entered the ocean in 1973 from tanker accidents, terminal operations, dry-docking, and tanker operations, about one-third of which came from tankers that flushed their tanks of residual oils. More oil probably entered the world ocean through human activities in 1979 than ever before. In 1978 about 2,60,000 tons of oil were spilled into the seas by tankers; in only the first six months of 1979 the figure had mounted to 2,20,000 tons. Moreover, in July 1979, the worst oil spill disaster in history occurred when two tankers collided in the Caribbean, spilling 3,00,000 tons of oil into the ocean. *Ibid.*, 258-259.

20. Such operations have not only been subject to incidental spills and leakages but have led to accidents, such as the Santa Barbara surge of 14,000 tons of oil into the sea in 1969, containing a strip of the California coast forty miles long, or the blowout in the Bay of Campeche off the Yucatan coast of Mexico in June 1979 that gushed about 3,000 tons of oil into the sea day after day. *Ibid.*, 259.

21. LOS Convention, Art. 145.

22. Text of the Convention can be found in *U.S. Treaties and Other International Agreements*, 26, 767-831.

23. Agenda 21 was, at least as far as sheer volume was concerned, a far more ambitious exercise. The draft which was presented to the delegates who arrived in Rio was almost 600 pages long. It was divided into four parts. Part I (107 pages) was entitled *Social and Economic Dimensions*; Part II (275 pages) was entitled *Conservation and Management of Resources for Development*. Part III (44 pages) deal with *Strengthening the Role of Major Groups*. Part IV (65 pages) concerned the *Means of Implementation*. Agenda 21 emerged from Rio unchanged as far as the overall structure was concerned though the four Parts were now renamed Sections. The full contents of Agenda 21 is available in Stanley P. Johnson, *The Earth*

Summit: The United Nations Conference on Environment and Development (UNCED) (Graham & Trotman/Martinus Nijhoff: 1993).

24. Agenda 21 was preceded by a Preamble which was submitted to the Rio Conference as a Chairman's draft. It called for a "new global partnership and "political commitment at the highest level" on development and environment cooperation. The reference to "political commitment at the highest level was bracketed, as was paragraph 4 on new and additional financial resources for developing countries to cover the incremental costs of implementing Agenda 21.
25. Agenda 21: 17.78.
26. Agenda 21:17.100.
27. *U.N.T.S*, Vol. 450, p. 169.
28. C.L Rozakis & Or (eds.), "The Settlement of Disputes Relating to Activities in the International Seabed Area", in *The New Law of the Sea* (North-Holland, Amsterdam, 1983), 303-344, 403. See also A.O. Adede, *Settlement of Disputes Arising Under the Law of the Sea Convention*, 69(1975) AJIL 798-818, 898.
29. Caflisch, *ibid.*
30. A.O. Adede, "Prolegomena to the Disputes Settlement Part of the Law of the Sea Convention", 10 (1977) *New York University Journal of International Law and Politics*, 253-393, 455.
31. *Ibid.*, 256.
32. *Ibid.*, 258.
33. U.N.Doc.A/CONF.62/WP.9.
34. U.N.Doc.A/CONF.62/WP.8, Article 24.
35. *Ibid.*, Art 32(1)(a) and (b).
36. See Said Mahmoudi, *The Law of the Deep Sea-Bed Mining* (Almqvist & Wiksell International, Stockholm) 287-289.
37. *Ibid.*, 239.
38. Art. 191 of the ICNT.
39. Rene-Jean Dupuy & Ors (eds.), *A Handbook on the New Law of the Sea* (Martinus Nijhoff Pubs., Dordrecht, 1991) 2, p. 1338.
40. A. Le Roy Bennet, *International Organizations: Principles and Issues* (Prentice Hall, Eaglewood Cliffs, New Jersey: 1991) 96-97.
41. Charter of the United Nations, Art. 33.
42. LOS Convention, Art. 287. See also http://www.cia.gov/nic/special_endgame.html
43. Section 2 relates to Compulsory Procedures Entailing Binding Decisions (Arts. 286-296).
44. Art. 1(4).

45. Regulation 1(c) available in E.D. Brown, *Seabed Energy and Minerals: The International Legal Regime* (Martinus Nijhoff: The Hague, 2001), Vol. 3, p. 257.
46. Regulation 1(f), *ibid.*
47. A. LeRoy Bennet, *International Organizations: Principles and Issues* (Prentice Hall, Eaglewood Cliffs, New Jersey, 1991) 318.
48. LOS Convention, Arts. 287, 297.
49. A. LeRoy Bennett, *op.cit.*, 312.
50. ILC Draft Articles on International Liability for Injurious Consequences arising out of Acts not Prohibited by International Law, ILC Report (1996) Annex 1, Report of Working Group, text to note 10.
51. A. LeRoy Bennett, 432. See also http://www.greenpeace.org/~intlaw/nuk-law.html
52. *Ibid.*, 433.
53. Report of UN Secretary General to Commission on Sustainable Development of the Economic and Social Council, UN Doc E/CN.17/1997/8 of 10 February 1997. Also see Richard K. Gardiner, *International Law* (Longman: London, 2003) 433.
54. *Ibid.*
55. Rene-Jean Dupuy & Daniel Vignes (eds.), *A Handbook on the New Law of the Sea* (Martinus Nijhoff Pubs., Dordrecht, 1991) 2, pp. 1390-1391.
56. LOS Convention, Art. 290, para 1.
57. *Ibid.*, para 2.
58. *Ibid.*, para 3.
59. A. LeRoy Bennet, *op.cit.*, 99.
60. Since times immemorial the Bay of Bengal has acted as the link between the Indian Sub-Continent and East Asia. By Buddha's time, mariners had crossed the Bay and made contact with Myanmar, Malaysia, and the Islands of Indonesia. In the Mauryan age, Tamralipti, in the Ganges basin became the main seaport from whence ships sailed to Sri Lanka, and later in the Christian era to South-East Asia and Indonesia. During this period too, maritime trade with the West developed, fuelled by the Roman Empire's demand for Eastern luxuries. With Rome's fall trade with the West declined, till it grew again gradually with the rising material standards of medieval Europe. Meanwhile before the Gupta era, contact had been made across the Bay between South India, and China, and as trade with the West declined, that with China increased in many of the same commodities that India exported to the West. In return items such as Chinese porcelain found a market in South India and Sri Lanka. With trade followed Indian political ideas, institutions, religion, art and language, which profoundly influenced the countries of South-East Asia. In the 10th century, the Chola ruler Rajendra Chola Deva the First, sent a fleet across the Bay of Bengal, probably to break the stranglehold that the Srivijayan

empire had over the South-East Asian trade routes. He occupied Pegu as well as the Andaman and Nicobar Islands. Colonies were planted in places as distant as Borneo and even today the population of Bali is predominantly Hindu. With Islam's spread, trade across the Bay declined, at least partly because of the adoption of mercantilist policies in the states bordering the Bay, but religious influences carried by Muslim savants and merchants strengthened, leading eventually to flourishing Muslim populations in Malaysia, Indonesia, and as far afield as China and the Philippines. The advent of the Europeans in Asian waters in search of spices, textiles, gold and other eastern luxuries, brought the Bay of Bengal squarely within a trading system which soon became globalised. The Portuguese were the first Europeans to exploit the spice trade but were later supplanted by others. Those who had come as traders eventually stayed on as conquerors. In time with the growth of productive forces, the Bay of Bengal acted as a vast conduit along the global sea lanes through which flowed the raw materials of East and South-East Asia to the manufacturing centres of Europe for being processed and value added, before being imported back into the countries from where the raw materials had initially been taken in a classic relationship of colony and metropolis. At the time India attained Independence in 1947, a single power, Britain was in actual physical control of the entire territory bordering the Bay of Bengal, with the possible exception of Thailand, and the Bay was effectively a British lake. http:www.witts.org/oceanwealth_06_dec03/specialfeture.htmtttop

61. The 2004 Indian Ocean earthquake was an undersea earthquake that occurred at 00:58:53 UTC (07:58:53 local time) on December 26, 2004. The earthquake generated a tsunami that was among the deadliest disasters in modern history. At a magnitude of 9.0, it was the largest earthquake since the 9.2 magnitude Good Friday Earthquake off Alaska in 1964, and tied for fourth largest since 1900. At least 2,26,000 people are known to have died as a result of the tsunami, and the count is not yet complete. The true final toll may never be known due to bodies having been swept out to sea, but current estimates use conservative methodologies. Relief agencies warn of the possibility of more deaths to come as a result of epidemics caused by poor sanitation, but the threat of starvation seems now to have been largely averted (http://news.bbc.co.uk/2/hi/asia-pacific/4157947.stm). The plight of the many affected people and countries prompted a widespread humanitarian response. The earthquake was initially reported as 6.8 on the Richter scale. The Pacific Tsunami Warning Center (PTWC) also estimated it at 8.5 shortly after the earthquake. On the moment magnitude scale, which is more accurate for quakes of this size (http://earthquake.usgs.gov/faq/meas.html), the earthquake's magnitude was first reported as 8.1 by the US Geological Survey. After further analysis, this was increased to 8.5, 8.9, and finally to 9.0 (http://earthquake.usgs.gov/recenteqsww/Quakes/usslav.htm). Since 1900 the only earthquakes recorded with a greater magnitude were the 1960 Great Chilean Earthquake (magnitude 9.5), the 1964 Good Friday Earthquake in Prince William Sound (9.2), and the March 9, 1957

earthquake (http://neic.usgs.gov/neis/eq_depot/usa/1957_03_09.html) in the Andreanof Islands (9.1). The only other recorded earthquake of magnitude 9.0 was in 1952 off the south-east coast of Kamchatka (http://neic.usgs.gov/neis/eq_depot/world/1952_11_04.html) (see Top 10 earthquakes (http://neic.usgs.gov/neis/eqlists/10maps_world.html)). Each of these megathrust earthquakes also spawned tsunamis (in the Pacific Ocean), but the death toll from these was significantly lower; a few thousand for the worst one, probably because of the lower population density along the coasts near affected areas and the much greater distances to more populated coasts.

62. http://www.guardian.co.uk/life/feature/story/0,13026,1383675,00.html.
63. Tarsem Lal Gill, "Marine Pollution and International Law", R. P. Anand (ed.), *Law of the Sea: Caracas and Beyond* (Radiant Publishers, New Delhi, 1978) 312.
64. Rahmatullah Khan, "Marine Pollution and International Legal Controls", 13(1973) *Indian Journal of International Law* 391.
65. Marine Scientific Affairs, Annual Report of the (US) President to the Congress on Marine Resources and Engineering Development (April 1970), quoted in Donat Pharand, "Oil Pollution Control in the Canadian Arctic", (1971) *Texas International Law Journal* 46.
66. Arsen Lal Gill, *op.cit.*, 313-314.
67. Arun Chaturvedi. *South Asian States and the Sea Laws* (Printwell Publishers, Jaipur, India, 1987) 70-71.
68. The contemporary roots of the zone are found in Nehru's idea of an "area of peace". (*Jawharlal Nehru's Speeches*, vol. 3, Calcutta: Publications Divisions, Government of India, 1958, p. 268). Conceptually, an area of peace would keep the newly independent states free from the conflicts of the great powers, Nehru's proposal was, in reality, a modification of Gandhi's idea of "village republic" living in peace with each other (A. Ramamurti, "Trusteeship in Agriculture", in J.D. Sethi (ed.) *Trusteeship: A Gandhian Alternative* (New Delhi: Gandhi Peace Foundation, 1986, p. 142). The non-aligned movement, which Nehru helped launch, converted "area of peace" into a political zone of peace. As early as 1964, Sri Lanka "raised the proposal in effect of declaring the Indian Ocean as a peace zone" at the Cairo Non-aligned Conference (P.V. Narasimha Rao, "Comments of Minister of External Affairs India", in *Seminar on Indian Ocean as a Zone of Peace* (New Delhi: India International Centre, 1981, p. 6). The call for an Indian Ocean zone of peace again surfaced at the 1970 Non-aligned Conference at Lusaka Hugo Palma, *Seguridad, Desarmeyy Cooperation International* (Lima: Ignacio Prada Pastor, 1992, pp. 64-66). Finally, in December 1971, the United Nations declared the Indian Ocean a zone of peace. The General Assembly also declared the South Atlantic Ocean a zone of peace in 1986. See Ramon Lopez-Reyes, "Zones of Peace: Towards Institutionalizing a Regime of Peace on the Seas", Elisabeth Mann Borgese & Ors (eds.), *OCEAN Yearbook,* 13 (The University of

Chicago Press, 1998) 386-387. The 43 members of the Ad Hoc Committee are Australia, Bangladesh, Bulgaria, Canada, China, Djibouti, Egypt, Ethiopia, Germany, Greece, India, Indonesia, Iran, Iraq, Italy, Japan, Kenya, Liberia, Madagascar, Malaysia, Maldives, Mauritius, Mozambique, Netherlands, Norway, Oman, Pakistan, Panama, Poland, Romania, Russian Federation, Seychelles, Singapore, Somalia, Sri Lanka, Sudan, Thailand, Uganda, United Arab Emirates, United Republic of Tanzania, Yemen, Zambia and Zimbabwe. Ad Hoc Committee observers are Nepal, South Africa and Sweden. http://www.un.org/news/press/docs/2003/gai03doc.htm

69. The first meeting of the Economic/Trade Ministers held in August 1998 in Bangkok imparted a new dynamism to the grouping which had been formed in 1997 with the decision to constitute an Inter-Governmental Group (IGG) to prepare a concept paper on possible approaches towards a preferential trading arrangement leading to a Free Trade Area. Subsequently, BIMSTEC decided to establish a Free Trade Area in the region with the objective of promoting harmonious development of economic relations among member countries through expansion of trade by providing fair conditions of competition for trade among them. BIMSTEC has identified six sectors for cooperation, viz., trade and investment, technology, transport and communication, energy, tourism and fisheries. The regular interactions at the levels of experts, senior officials, economy/trade ministers and foreign ministers have started. Fresh momentum has been imparted to the Grouping at the Ministerial Meetings held in Phuket in February 2004 with the proposed first Summit, expansion of the membership to cover Nepal and Bhutan, and signing of the Framework Agreement on BIMSTEC Free Trade Arrangement. Therefore, a foundation for the launching of the process of deeper economic integration in the framework of the Grouping has been laid. This brief presents some thoughts on the future directions of the Grouping. The combined size of BIMSTEC member economies is US$ 750 billion with 1.3 billion population. The members are at different levels of economic and industrial development and different natural resource endowments. Hence, the complementarities between them are substantial. The geographical contiguity could also facilitate the exploitation of potential of efficiency seeking restructuring of industry, provided conditions for such restructuring are created. Although the intra-regional trade turnover is small, it is increasing faster than the overall trade of member countries. Full potential of intra-regional trade remains untapped because of tariff and non-tariff barriers, poor communication and transport links, lack of information about the supply capabilities, among other barriers. Similarly, the intra-regional investment is negligible despite tremendous potential that exists for market seeking as well as efficiency seeking investments within the region. Regional economic integration may help in exploiting this hidden potential of intra-regional cooperation for mutual benefit. This policy brief is based on the Executive Summary of a Report prepared by RIS for the BIMSTEC Ministerial Meetings in consultation with the Institute for Policy Studies,

Colombo; Centre for Policy Dialogue, Dhaka; and International Institute for Trade and Development, Bangkok. *RIS Policy Briefs*, *RIS 20 Years* (1984-2004), No. 12, February 2004.

70. On 6 June 1997, a new sub-regional grouping BIST-EC (Bangladesh, India, Sri Lanka, Thailand) was formed at a meeting of the trade ministers of these countries in Bangkok. After Myanmar joined the organisation as a full member at a special ministerial meeting in December 1997, the name of the grouping was changed to BIMST-EC. http://www.nepalnews.com/contents/englishdaily/trn/2001/mar/m...

71. See Tommy T.B. Koh, President of the Third United Nations Conference on the Law of the Sea entitled as "A Constitution for the Oceans", in *The United Nations Convention on the Law of the Sea with Index and Final Act of the Third United Nations Conference on the Law of the Sea* (United Nations, New York, 1983) xxxiii.

72. *Ibid.*, xxxvi.

73. *Rio Declaration*, Principle 15.

74. The Government of India, committed to ocean research, established the National Institute of Oceanography (NIO) at Goa in 1966 and today it is India's premier oceanographic institute. In 1975, NIO acquired the first Indian oceanographic vessel, the *R.V. Gavashini*. The Department of Ocean Development (DOD) was established in 1981 as the nodal department for India's ocean development activities and ocean policy statement and addresses the following: Seabed mining; Extractive metallurgy specific to polymetallic nodules; Ocean energy: waves and thermal; Coastal and environmental engineering; Marine instrumentation; Front ranking research in polar sciences; Exploration of marine resources and their correlation with oceanographic parameters; Integrated coastal and marine management, coastal community development; Human resource development; Creation of centres of excellence to facilitate optimum utilization of ocean and its resources; and Observing, understanding and modeling ocean processes. For details see D.V. Subba Rao, "Marine Sciences of the Seas around India between 1974 and 2000 and Prospects for the New Millennium", Elisabeth Mann Borgese & Ors (eds.), *OCEAN* (The University of Chicago Press, Chicago, 2002), 16, 195-227.

6

CONCLUSION

Wherever the intensity of human activity has increased, the emergence of management arrangements has been a prerequisite for rational utilization of such areas and their resources. So, in the international field, whether it be outer space, the polar regions or the deep ocean regions, international cooperative arrangements have evolved to circumscribe the limits of individual action and provide for cooperative use and joint management. Also, in the area of ocean space—the oceans—it may be seen as inevitable that inter-governmental arrangements would eventually develop as a basis for rational management.

In such a context, the process of Indian Ocean Marine Affairs Cooperation (IOMAC) may be seen as a pioneering ocean management movement initiated by countries of the region, joined by extra-regional user states. For reasons of comprehensiveness and effectiveness, IOMAC was founded on the concept of integrating relevant management disciplines in mandated fields, as well as integrating relevant national, regional, and global institutional elements in the regional management framework.

In furtherance of the primary commitment for the realization of the promised benefits to governments from the new ocean regime, IOMAC has consistently emphasized training as an essential tool in advancing national capabilities in the requisite fields of marine affairs. This would be essential for bringing about a true integration of the ocean sector in national development strategies.

Inspired by recognition of the finite character of the adjacent ocean and its resources, African and Asian states united in the context of a characterization of the Indian Ocean as the "village pond" in the largely underdeveloped African-Asian region of the world. In IOMAC, the Indian Ocean was then seen as a unifying rather than a dividing medium as it had appeared before. In addition to promoting cooperation between Indian Ocean States and entities outside the region, including technologically-advanced States and international organizations, IOMAC since its inception, has opened new vistas on regional cooperation and facilitated the broadening of intra-regional contacts which promote closer cooperation between African and Asian countries on a regular basis. In the future, such contacts could provide the platform on which closer integration of the rim community could be forged.

Already, a number of far-reaching management measures for the ocean, such as its Declaration as a Sanctuary for, Whales for All Time, Banning of Large-scale Drift Nets, Declaration of a New Era of Indian Ocean Exploration, Initiation of Process Leading to the Establishment of an Indian Ocean Tuna Management framework, or establishment of a regional network of focal points for marine affairs, represent significant progress by IOMAC in bringing about collective ocean management in the region.[1]

As of now, there is no concrete and specific regional convention for the protection and preservation of the marine environment of the South Asian States. Marine pollution is transboundary and global in character. A regional agreement for the control and prevention of pollution could contribute considerably to the effective implementation of the related regional plans in South Asia.[2] From an oceanographer's perspective, the Bay of Bengal and the Arabian Sea constitute an ideal laboratory. The round of meteorological, hydrological and biological events governed by (a) influx of large freshwater from several major rivers, (b) intense north-east and south-west monsoon winds of which the latter breeds cyclones in the Bay of Bengal, is unique to these waters. Additionally, these waters support various tropical biotopes such as estuaries, mangroves, brackish water lakes, coral reefs, islands, and offshore waters with a great diversity of fauna and flora. The steadily growing population (~200 million) heavily utilizes the coastal zone for urban settlements, fishing, mariculture, marine transport, recreation, offshore oil and gas exploration, and dumping of wastes.[3] The seas as provider of sustenance for plants and animals need to be seriously looked at for protection and preservation of environment.

6.1. Marine Environment—not a Piecemeal Matter

The sea provides sustenance for a vast variety of plants and animals. The animal life of the sea—as indeed that of the land—is dependent ultimately upon plant life for its continued existence. The plants of the sea are, therefore, the primary food providers on which the whole structure of the marine animal life depends. On the basis of mode of existence, the teeming life of the seas is classified broadly into three-fold division of *plankton, benthos* and *nekton.* The word *plankton* is derived from the Greek word meaning wanderer. It was first used in 1889 by Professor Victor Hunsen, the leader of the German Plankton Expedition, to denote the numerous forms of life—both animal and plant which are not endowed with the ability to move (other than feebly) on their own accord. *Plankton* are not fixed to the seabed: they, therefore, drift helplessly and are completely at the mercy of wind and current. The second group of marine life is known as *benthos*—a word derived from the Greek word meaning deep. This group includes all forms of the life which remain fixed to the sea floor, or which burrow into, or creep along, the bed of the sea. Certain sea weeds, which are attached to the seabed, are sometimes included in this group, but more usually the term is applied to animal life only.

The third group of marine life is known as *nekton,* a word derived from the Greek word meaning swimming. Included in the *nekton* group are all those animals, including fishes, sea mammals and certain other forms of marine life which have the ability to swim powerfully, and which are therefore, able to counteract the effects of currents. Geologists, in their investigations into the manner in which marine sedimentary rocks are found, the manner in which marine sedimentary rocks are formed and based on environmental conditions. The marine environment is normally regarded as being composed of three major zones or provinces, referred to respectively the neritic, *bathyal,* and *abyssal zones*. Cutting across these three depth-typed zones of the seabed is a fourth province known as the *pelagic zone*. The *pelagic zone* provides the habitat for pelagic life. *Pelagic* organisms are those which are not fixed to the seabed. They include all nekton and many plankton. Pelagic animals which live at depths of more than about 100 fathoms are referred to as *bathypelagic fauna*. These are not normally to be found in the waters resting on the continental shelf—the outer limit of which coincides roughly with the 100 fathoms isobath.[4]

This approach poses that marine environment strata cannot be singled out in the sense that the sea, its waters, bed and subsoil including the concerned air space require to be treated entirely as an integrated whole. In all respects, human measures must be made to promote marine environment, thus ensuring the ecosystem which is the fundamental need for a regime of marine environment.

6.2. Bay of Bengal Environment Inevitable for Surrounding Littoral States

The large marine ecosystem (LME) is characterized by its tropical climate. It is situated in the monsoon belt and receives high rainfall. Bangladesh, India, Indonesia, Malaysia, Maldives, Myanmar, Sri Lanka, and Thailand are the countries bordering the LME. Intensive fishing is the primary force driving the LME, with climate as the secondary driving force. The Global Environment Facility (GEF) is supporting a fisheries project, now in the preparation stage, to address critical threats to the coastal and marine environment, and to promote ecosystem-based management of coastal and marine resources.

6.2.a. Productivity

The LME is affected by monsoons, storm surges, and cyclones but has no seasonal upwelling. However, in nearshore areas, the mixing of nutrient rich bottom waters and warm surface waters creates conditions similar to upwelling. The number and intensity of cyclones in the northern part of the Bay of Bengal are likely to increase due to global warming. Major rivers such as the Brahmaputra and Ganges discharge large quantities of fresh water into the Bay of Bengal. This input of freshwater and silt impacts the salinity of the coastal and estuarine waters as well as coastal circulation patterns. It influences and governs LME dynamics during the south-west monsoon. Wetlands, marshes, and mangroves play an important role in the overall productivity. Changing environmental conditions are influencing currents, productivity and coastal pollution. Lakes connected to the Bay of Bengal LME are changing. Some coastal areas serving as nursery grounds for commercially valuable species of prawns are polluted. Six areas of critical biological diversity are: the Sundarbans—one of the world's most extensive mangrove systems, Palk Bay, the Gulf of Mannar, the Marine (Wandur) National Park in the Andaman and Nicobar Islands, the Maldives Atolls, Mu Ko Dimilan National Park and Mu Ko Surin Park in Thailand.[5]

6.2.b. Fish and Fisheries Sustainability

The FAO 10-year trend shows a steady increase in catch from 1.4 million tons in 1990 to 2.2 million tons in the LME region in 1990. The average catch is 2 million tons. This tropical region has a relatively great marine biodiversity that is reflected in the catch composition. There is a high catch percentage for miscellaneous coastal fishes and pelagic fishes (tuna, yellowfin, big eye and skipjack). Herrings, sardines and anchovies represent more than 15% of the catch. The crustacean catch (shrimp is the major export earner) is just below 15% of the total catch. Catch trends are quite diverse and it is difficult to identify a pattern due to the fact that there is inadequate information on the status of the fisheries resources and their exploitation. Despite a steady rise in total landings since 1999, there are signs that the harvest levels may not be sustainable, especially with regard to tuna fishing in the Maldives, Malaysia, Thailand, Andaman coast and Sri Lanka. Ecological changes in the estuaries and coastal areas have not yet affected total production trends. The GEF-supported project is examining the issue of sustainable fisheries and food security.

Heavy fishing through open access and the unauthorised incursions of foreign fleets is a comparatively recent phenomenon. There is an increase of competition and conflicts between artisnal and large-scale fishermen. There is an alarming increase in cyanide fishing in this LME's coral reefs for the lucrative live food fish markets in Hong Kong and Singapore. Mangroves and estuaries—critical fish spawning and nursery areas—are also under stress or threatened by pollution, sedimentation, dams for flood (as in Bangladesh), and intensive coastal aquaculture. In most of the countries surrounding the Bay of Bengal, clear policies, appropriate strategies and measures for the sustainable management of the fishery resources are weak. There is a need to establish a systematic data collection system in order to prepare a regional strategy.[6]

6.2.c. Pollution and Ecosystem Health

The ecosystem's stress experiences are concerned with the size of the coastal populations bordering the LME. Issues of ecosystem health that are common throughout the region are: environmental stresses on the Bay of Bengal's water quality; the degradation of many of the coral, mangrove, wetland and sea grass bed habitats that support fisheries; and the use of fishing gear that may affect the long-term sustainability of the fisheries resource. The major rivers bring in large concentrations of pollutants from agricultural pesticides and industrial waste that damage fish spawning and nursery areas, cause fish kills and lead to possible changes in trophic structure. High levels of pesticides can be found along the coast, especially near cities and ports. A major part of Bangladesh consists of a delta plain positioned below the confluence of the Ganges, Brahmaputra and Meghna Rivers. Environmental refugees regularly flee the flooded plain, and many deaths occur with the floods. Sediment loading in the Ganges-Brahmaputra watershed caused by accelerated soil erosion in the Himalayas is considered to be one of the main factors contributing to downstream flooding. In some regions of the Bay of Bengal, a change in composition of plank species has been observed. There is heavy oil tanker traffic between Japan and the Middle East, with the main shipping route passing South of Sri Lanka before entering the Straits of Malacca via a passage below the Nicobar Islands. For this reason, oil spills are a major concern. In 1993, India approved a national oil spill contingency plan. There is inadequate information on pollution and sedimentation loads entering the Bay of Bengal, on coastal habitats and endangered species. This information is necessary in order to understand the functioning of the ecosystem and its reaction to stress over time.[7]

6.3. Sea Level Rise Impacts: Specification for Bangladesh and Maldives

There has been much recent discussion in the media concerning both the tragic events in the Indian Ocean and sea level rise associated with global warming. They are of course not directly linked, but there are important lessons to be learned from the tsunami for coping with long-term sea level rise, especially in low-lying regions in the Indian and Pacific Oceans.

One obvious difference between a tsunami and global sea level rise is the duration of the events. The Indian Ocean tsunami travelled from its source (an earthquake off Sumatra) to most of the regions it devastated in under three hours. The effect on those living on the shore was even more rapid—they had only minutes to react to the oncoming waves. In comparison, the effects of climate change are much slower—significant changes only happen over decades. However, probably the most important difference is that, while a tsunami dies down completely in a day or two, sea level rise will be with us for many centuries. Tsunamis may also be much higher than the sea level rise that we speculate to occur during the present century. While the Indian Ocean tsunami was only a metre or so in height as it travelled across the oceans,[8] there are reports of it being amplified to many metres by the time it reached the land. On the other hand, the Inter-Governmental Panel on Climate Change has estimated that the global sea level will rise by 0.1-0.9 of a metre by 2100, relative to the level in 1990.[9] Although even the higher of these estimates may sound small, the effect on communities living on low-lying coastal land would be devastating as 100 million people live within about one metre of the present sea level.[10]

It is instructive to look at two regions that have previously received considerable attention regarding the effects of future sea level rise: Bangladesh and the Maldives. The populous low-lying land of the deltaic regions of Bangladesh will suffer severely from sea level rise—it has been estimated that a 1.5 metre rise in sea level would affect 17 million people.[11] So why was the impact of the recent tsunami on this country so small? There are a number of reasons. Firstly, the wave that propagated northwards to Bangladesh appears to have been weaker,[12] possibly due to the shape of the original earthquake zone.[13] Secondly, much of the energy of the arriving tsunami was dissipated in the large expanse of relatively shallow water offshore,[14] and thirdly, prior to the tsunami some 2,000 multi-storied shelters had been installed to protect the population from cyclones and storm surges.[15] Of course, none of these factors will be any protection against the impending sea level rise due to global warming.

The Maldives, on the other hand, suffered substantial damage and loss of life (around 70 people perished and 1,000 were displaced).[16] The height of the tsunami[17] was about 1 metre while 80% of the Maldives are less than one metre above normal sea level[18] and the highest point is only 2.4 metres above sea level.[19] The resulting devastation gives us a much better appreciation of the probable effects of sea level rise on such low-lying coastal communities.

While we can learn a little about the likely effects of sea level rise from the tragic events there is another vitally important message that should not be overlooked—that these events offer a unique opportunity. The tsunami has cleared much of the infrastructure from regions threatened by future sea level rise. Rebuilding of this infrastructure will need to proceed speedily for the many displaced people to return to more normal lives. There is a danger that redevelopment will occur on the same sites, with any future tsunami risk being accommodated through a combination of a warning system and a network of disaster shelters. It is, however, of utmost importance that any rebuilding takes account of expected future sea level rise.

Sea-level rise has two effects on a shoreline. On a hard (e.g., rocky) shore, the water surface simply moves up the sloping beach. However, on sandy shorelines, the beach and dune system is actually eroded, causing additional shoreline retreat. In the first case, the position of the new shoreline may be estimated simply from the rise in sea level, while the second case is far more complicated and requires knowledge of the way in which the coastal morphology responds. A crude rule of thumb is that, for every centimetre of sea level rise, the shoreline retreats by one metre.[20] Once these processes are reasonably well understood, a sound strategy is that of managed retreat, whereby development is restricted within a certain distance of the present shoreline, determined by the expected shoreline movement during the life of the structure. These set-backs may be supplemented by density restrictions and 'rolling easements' that allow development to be pushed back as sea levels rise.[21] Already some developed and developing countries have adopted such policies including no-build zones and set-backs of 50 metres or more.

The tragic events, therefore, offer the opportunity for large coastal regions in and around the Indian Ocean to be redeveloped in a way that affords appropriate protection from sea level rise during the coming centuries.[22] A wide range of expertise is required for this, including sea level scientists, geomorphologists, risk analysts and coastal planners—some of whom could and should be provided by the region's richer neighbours.

The South Asian states have many interests in the Indian Ocean. It is vital to their economics, with the increasing role of technology. The scope of the Indian Ocean resources increases. The deep sea mining, effective use of continental shelf and the potentials of living sea resources further enhance the importance of Indian Ocean. The South Asian states are essentially littoral states to the Indian Ocean. India, Pakistan, Sri Lanka, Bangladesh and Maldives are littoral states, therefore having deep interests in the Indian Ocean. Nepal and Bhutan are land-locked states, their problems arise out of their needs to share the economic resources of the Indian Ocean.[23] In the case of the Bay of Bengal, it is inevitable for the littoral states to promote the marine environment favourable to its ecosystems.

6.4. From National Interests to International Cooperation

The environmental priorities entail, among other things, a greater focus on the sustainable use of natural resources and biological diversity instead of classical protection. The importance of a precautionary approach in the management and use of natural resources is emphasised. Poverty orientation, emphasis on the role of women in environmental and natural resource management as well as local participation are important elements for all-round environmental coordination. Urges exist from national interests to international cooperation in order to reiterate a regime of environment and as such, of marine environment in the Bay of Bengal.

6.4.a. International and Global Processes

Agenda 21 is the international action plan for sustainable development into the next century. It emphasises that poverty and environmental degradation represent the greatest challenges facing developing and industrial countries today. The action plan deals with the utilisation of natural resources and measures in key environmental and development sectors. The plan is based on the principle that in order to achieve environmental gains all measures must be compatible with social and economic development, and safeguard the right of co-determination and participation of the groups affected in processes which influence their situation. The plan represents a broad common platform for international development cooperation in the years ahead. It is assumed in Agenda 21 that most of the resources that are required to ensure sustainable development must be mobilised from domestic sources. An important result of the Rio process is also the principle of "common but different commitments", which implies some burden sharing internationally, including transfers of resources (e.g., aid) for a satisfactory follow-up of the action plan in developing countries. The UN Commission for Sustainable Development (CSD) has been given the mandate to follow up Agenda 21.[24]

6.4.b. Conservation and Sustainable Use of Biological Diversity

Biological diversity is the basis of life-sustaining ecological systems which regulate the climate, form soil and clean water and air. Biological diversity is a basic prerequisite for agricultural development as well as food and commodity-based industrial production. A large part of the world's biological diversity is found in developing countries and is exposed to substantial, irreversible destruction. This includes the destruction of ecosystems and species as well as genetic variation within each species.

6.4.c. Measures to reduce Pollution of Soil, Air and Water

Measures to combat pollution will vary in different areas, both based on local environmental conditions and each country's level of development and degree of industrialisation. The integration of issues is linked to pollution and health figures prominently (e.g., energy, agriculture, industry, health, water management, transport). Pollution problems must be tackled from several aspects, e.g., through the development/ strengthening of institutions, programmes to increase awareness, the involvement of the private sector, the transfer of know-how combined with technology transfer and investment projects, etc.

6.4.d. Commitments Towards Processes and Conventions

In the wake of the UNCED meeting the relationship between trade and environment was placed on the agenda in the GATT/WTO because of the desire to reduce the risk of disputes between states in the relationship between trade and the environment, negative environmental consequences of free trade or the use of environmental arguments as hidden barriers to trade.

During the UNCED meeting, a number of countries signed the Convention on Climate Change (1992) and the Convention on Biological Diversity (1992). Many developing countries are signatories to these conventions as well as a number of other international agreements which impose obligations with regard to a sound management of natural resources and the environment. Among these are: The Convention on Desertification (1994) which attaches importance to the development of national, sub-regional and regional action programmes to combat a deterioration in arid agricultural areas, particularly in Africa. The Montreal Protocol (1987) followed by the Vienna Convention seeks to protect the ozone layer. The Basle Convention (1989) deals with the monitoring and control of hazardous waste. The FAO's Code of Conduct for Responsible Fisheries (1995) and the UN agreement on Fishing in the High Seas (1995) establish important guidelines for assistance in the fisheries area.[25]

Chapter 37 of Agenda 21 poses national mechanisms and international cooperation for capacity-building. The ability of a country to follow sustainable development paths is determined to a large extent by the capacity of its people and institutions as well as by ecological and geographical conditions. Specifically, capacity-building encompasses the country's human, scientific, technological, organizational, institutional and resource capabilities. A fundamental goal of capacity-building is to enhance the ability to evaluate and address the crucial questions related to policy choices and modes of implementation among development options, based on an understanding of environmental potentials and limits and of needs as perceived by the people of the country concerned. As a result, the need to strengthen national capacities is shared by all countries.[26]

Building endogenous capacity to implement Agenda 21 will require the efforts of the countries themselves in partnership with relevant United Nations organizations, as well as with developed countries. The international community at the national, sub-regional and regional levels, municipalities, non-governmental organizations, universities and research centres, and business and other private institutions and organizations could also assist in these efforts. It is essential for individual countries to identify priorities and determine the means for building capacity and capability to implement Agenda 21, taking into account their environmental and economic needs.

Skills, knowledge and technical know-how at the individual and institutional levels are necessary for institution-building, policy analysis and development management, including the assessment of alternative courses of action with a view to enhancing access to and transfer of technology and promoting economic development. Technical cooperation, including that related to technology transfer and know-how, encompasses the whole range of activities to develop or strengthen individual and group capacities and capabilities. It should serve the purpose of long-term capacity-building and needs to be managed and coordinated by the countries themselves. Technical cooperation, including that related to technology transfer and know-how, is effective only when it is derived from that related to a country's own strategies and priorities on environment and development and when development agencies and Governments define improved and consistent policies and procedures to support this process.[27]

As a matter of fact, nations too are interdependent. National frontiers too are porous. Transnational realities in the sphere of technology and investment on the one hand, and poverty and misery on the other, too dangerous to permit egocentric isolation. Marine environment is not a territorial concern. Its very concern is transboundary, and as such, measures must be taken for and by all those concerned. As far as possible individual measures need to be taken, and in order to face degradation and pollution of environment, this can eventually be urged through cooperative measures at sub-regional, regional and global levels. There is then an opening for cooperative measures to be taken for promotion of marine environment. As time passes, cooperative approaches are advancing all over the globe. The Bay of Bengal bordering countries are also in the commitment to protect and preserve marine environment.

6.4.e. Legal and Institutional Framework

International law, as reflected in the provisions of the United Nations Convention on the Law of the Sea (LOS Convention) and elsewhere, sets forth rights and obligations of

States and provides the international basis to pursue the protection and sustainable development of the marine and coastal environment and its resources.

In accordance with general international law, while States have the sovereign right to exploit their resources pursuant to their environmental policies, the enjoyment of such right shall be in accordance with the duty to protection and preservation of the marine environment. This fundamental duty is to protect and preserve the marine environment from all sources of pollution. Of particular significance for the Global Programme of Action are the provisions contained in articles 207 and 213 of the LOS Convention.

Also of particular importance for the Programme of Action is the emphasis, in parts XII, XIII and XIV of the Convention, dealing respectively, with protection and preservation of the marine environment, marine scientific research and the development and transfer of marine technology, on the obligation of States to cooperate in the development of the marine scientific and technological capacity of developing States and to provide them with scientific and technological assistance.

The duty of States to preserve and protect the marine environment has been reflected and elaborated in numerous global conventions and regional instruments (e.g., the Convention on the Prevention of Marine Pollution by Dumping of Wastes and Other Matter; Basel Convention on the Control of Transboundary Movements of Hazardous Wastes and Their Disposal; Convention on the Biological Diversity; United Nations Framework Convention on Climate Change; Regional Seas Conventions, International Convention for the Prevention of Pollution from Ships (MARPOL73/78, etc.). Innovative new principles and approaches applicable to the prevention of the degradation of the marine environment from land-based activities have been included in a number of such agreements.

In 1982, the United Nations environment Programme (UNEP) took the initiative to develop advice to Governments on addressing impacts on the marine environment from land-based activities. This initiative resulted in the preparation of the Montreal Guidelines from Land-based Sources in 1985.

The duty to protect the marine environment from land-based activities was placed squarely in the context of sustainable development by the United Nations Conference on Environment and Development in 1992. Therein, States agreed, it is necessary:

(a) To apply preventive, precautionary, and anticipatory approaches so as to avoid degradation of the marine environment, as well as to reduce the risk of long-term or irreversible adverse effects upon it;

(b) To ensure prior assessment of activities that may have significant adverse effects upon the marine environment;

(c) To integrate protection of the marine environment into relevant general environmental, social and economic development policies;

(d) To develop economic incentives, where appropriate, to apply clean technologies and other means consistent with the internationalization of environmental costs, such as the "polluter pays" principle, so as to avoid degradation of the marine environment;

(e) To improve the living standards of coastal populations, particularly in developing countries, so as to contribute to reducing the degradation of the coastal and marine environment.

It is recognized that the role of international cooperation is to support and supplement national efforts. Implementation of strategies and activities under the programme areas relative to marine and coastal areas and seas requires effective institutional arrangements at national, sub-regional, regional and global levels, as appropriate. There are numerous national and international, including regional, institutions, both within and outside the United Nations system, with competence in marine issues, and there is a need to improve coordination and strengthen links among them. It is also important to ensure that an integrated and multi-sectoral approach to marine issues is pursued at all levels.[28]

6.5. Marine Environment: Odds and Ends

If a path to the better there be, it begins with a full look at the worst.[29] The marine environment matters are concerned with so many attributes seemingly complementary and contradictory. However, contradictions are not viable to the fact that marine environment is not squeezed in territorial boundaries. In reality, the marine environment is an all concerned matter. In order to promote it, it is necessary to take measures against odds and ends that result in pollution of the marine environment. It is here that we address causes of odds and ends to pollution of the marine environment.[30]

(a) *Oil Pollution*

When it comes to mixing oil and water, oceans suffer from far more than an occasional devastating spill. Only 5 per cent of oil pollution in the oceans is due to major tanker accidents.

(b) *Toxic Materials*

Metals and slowly degrading chemicals threaten inland and coastal waters. Industrial, agricultural, household cleaning, gardening, and automotive products regularly end up in coastal waters.

(c) *Dangerous Debris*

When odds and ends of life on land—particularly plastics—end up in the sea, they pose hazards to marine life. Animals drown or strangle from getting tangled in discarded or lost fishing gear, or suffer and even die from eating plastics and other garbage.

(d) *Deposits and Withdrawals*

Coastal mining booms could lead to ecological problems. Not only are the oceans used as dumping grounds, but they have recently become the source for materials that by their removal, could have serious consequences.

6.5.a. Ocean in Human Affairs

Humankind has had much longer experience in regulating the rights of nations to the world's oceans, especially for navigation and for fishing. These rights have evolved over hundreds of years, are now seen in the freedoms of the seas and EEZ (exclusive economic zone) regimes. Through the efforts of UNEP we have seen cooperative attempts to manage "regional seas" and to develop an international law of the sea through UNLOS Convention. Although the concept of ocean management is thus not unfamiliar to people and their national representatives, it is still at a very early stage of elaboration. Concerns have been limited to traditional rights to transportation and fishing—the latter focused on a few readily exploitable species. In this century concerns have broadened to include offshore mining, principally for petroleum, but with a growing interest in seabed mining for metallic minerals. The ocean has always been a handy 'sink' for sewage and other human wastes; recently this has extended to incinerator ash, nuclear-weapons testing, and nuclear-waste disposal. A handful of nations use the sea as a source of desalinized water.

This *ad hoc* approach to ocean management is now changing under the pressure of the environmental crisis, which means nothing less than system closure at the global scale. Although many of the above uses of the sea by human beings are expected to continue, the viewpoint now required is much broader. Probably, the fundamental role of the ocean in human affairs today is that of a climatic regulator, a global thermostat and a sink for excess carbon dioxide, for example. Right now we urgently need to know much more about the interaction between air and sea. We have limitations to our knowledge, but efforts to gather knowledge are possible. All the unknowns associated with global warming, sea-level rise, and the vulnerability of fish and phytoplankton to ultraviolet radiation can be analysed only with the help of much more knowledge of the evolution and resilience of the ocean. The second change in human attitudes relates to the more traditional concern regarding human access to ocean resources—only now we attach the adjective renewable to those resources. It has often been said that so far people have simply hunted in the oceans, whereas now we need to farm them.

6.5.b. Ocean in Bio-Geochemical Cycles

Although the ocean covers 70 per cent of the earth's surface we know far too little about it. Some scientists think that the ocean's great capacity to absorb carbon dioxide will save us from global warming; others see the chemistry of the deep ocean as the key that flips the climate back and forth between glacial cycles. In order to use the ocean wisely we need to know far more about its chemistry and its physics; most important, right now, we need to know about how it interacts with the atmosphere, particularly with regard to the exchange of carbon dioxide. We should also learn more about the ocean's capacity to absorb the solid wastes that we deposit directly into it—like petroleum, sewage, etc.

In a number of ways the ocean operates as an environmental pathway in a fashion analogous to the atmosphere. Surface ocean currents run parallel to the prevailing winds; gases are deposited on the surface; then they are mixed, ingested by biota, and cycled through various life forms. Some are then returned to the air and some are deposited on the ocean bed. However, beyond the generalities, the specific interactions are even more difficult to measure than they are in the atmosphere.

The ocean acts as a sink or repository for material from atmosphere and from the land. For example, the ocean is estimated to hold about 70 per cent of the carbon in the world, compared with only 1 per cent in the atmosphere, the balance being on land or in sedimentary rocks. What we do not know is how much more carbon the ocean can absorb. As we are pumping additional carbon into the atmosphere every time we burn fossil fuels and as we are reducing the biosphere's carbon-recycling capacity every time we reduce the forest cover, this unknown absorptive capacity of the oceans becomes a factor of crucial importance. This is true not only for the carbon cycle but also for all the other major bio-geochemical cycles, like nitrogen, oxygen, and sulphur.

6.5.c. Ocean as a Sink for Wastes

Most of the deposition from the air to the ocean is invisible. It is possible to see the results only as pollution on the beaches and in analyses of the pollutants that bio-accumulate in the food chain, especially in crustaceans. Not only may the chemical characteristics of the ocean be changed (analogous to the change in the presence of trace gases in the atmosphere), but these changes may lead to changes in the ability of the ocean to act as a global sink. Unfortunately we will not know when the ocean's absorptive capacity has been exhausted until after it has happened, by which time it will probably be irreversible. There is some direct knowledge of what happens out of sight of land just from rough calculations of wastes dumped by ships.[31] What follows is a brief review of the various forms of dumping that may have, or already have had, a significant effect on the ocean's continued ability to act as the globe's major buffering agent.

The substances that have been multiplied in quantity, or been invented, during the chemical age and that may have harmful side-effects may be assigned roughly to four groups: nutrients, toxic metals, hydrocarbons, and radioactive materials. All the chemicals used as fertilizers, herbicides, and pesticides in modern agricultural systems flow through various environmental pathways. Some evaporate; some remain a long time in the soil; but a great many flow through streams into the ocean within a matter of days or weeks. The latter pathway is important because most agricultural areas are associated with major river systems, like the Po, Rhine, Ganges, Mekong, and Mississippi . Nutrients encourage the growth of algae. In a sense they intensify the natural eutrophication process, whereby protected bodies of water, like bays and deltas, are gradually filled in by biomass, such as plant litter, sewage, and agricultural run-off, to the eventual exclusion of aquatic life forms.[32]

So far, the impact of chemical-based agriculture is most clearly seen in the industrialized economies of the North. However, higher agricultural productivity in the South is expected to come from increased use of chemical inputs; this is one of the cornerstones of the green revolution. If this process continues, then we should expect to see harmful algal blooms in the deltas of the Yangtze, Ganges, Nile, and Niger.[33]

The second group of substances—toxic metals and compounds—have caused concern for some time, especially since the Minamata case of mercury poisoning in Japan in 1953, when at least seventeen people died and many more were permanently disabled. The main substances to cause concern are lead, mercury, cadmium, aluminium, and polychlorinated biphenyls (PCBs). These materials enter the pathways as residuals from industrial and mining activities. Some are put directly into ocean by incinerating dangerous wastes at sea, which is a common practice around the shores of North America, Japan, and north-west Europe. These, the most advanced industrial countries, determined that this was a safer practice than burying such wastes on land, even though by incinerating at sea these potentially dangerous substances were injected directly into the food chain. No practice more clearly illustrates the "out of sight, out of mind" attitude than our view of the ocean as the ideal global garbage dump.[34]

Hydrocarbons are the ocean-polluting substances that have received the most persistent coverage in the media, probably because of the spectacular nature of spills from oil tankers that run aground. Here the public can see the sea birds drowned in oil and the angry fishermen, hotel owners, and coastal residents. The public can see the problem and the villain is only too visible; the media can haul in the guilty owners of the vessel and the negligent captain of the ship.

It is not surprising to learn that only 22 per cent of the hydrocarbons deposited in the ocean, from marine sources, come from tanker spills. Another 2.7 per cent come from oil platform accidents, while 16 per cent come from natural seepage from hydrocarbon-rich sediments open to the ocean. The remaining 59 per cent come from the routine flushing of oil-tanker holds. The practice is banned, but it continues without interference.[35]

Perhaps the ultimate example of the ocean as the dump of last resort is the ocean disposal of radioactive waste. Until 1983, European countries like Britain, Belgium, Switzerland, and the Netherlands dumped their radioactive waste near Cape Finisterre, in north-west Spain. It seemed suitable because the water was 4,000 metres deep, and at that time it lay within "international waters." The potential impact on the coasts and fisheries of Spain and Portugal was presumably considered to be unimportant. Today the United Kingdom Atomic Energy Authority is developing a disposal site, off the coast of Cumberland, for the radioactive waste from the notoriously unsafe Sellafield nuclear-power station.[36]

6.6. Management of the Seas: Overview

In establishing the prevailing principles of international law with regard to the preservation of the marine environment there exist a number of specific legal instruments pertaining either to (a) types of pollution, such as oil pollution or pollution of the seas by radioactive wastes, or to the dumping of other hazardous or harmful matter or (b) regional agreements dealing with special regions of the oceans.[37] The fundamental significance of the 1982 Law of the Sea Convention cannot be over-emphasized. Those who partook in this endeavour from the beginning can whole-heartedly endorse the assessment made in the Preamble of the Convention that the work was inspired "by the desire to settle in a spirit of mutual understanding and co-operation, all issues relating to the law of the sea" and thus to contribute:

> to the strengthening of peace, security, co-operation and friendly relations among all nations in conformity with the principles of justice and equal rights and...promote the economic and social advancement of all peoples of the world....

with a view to conforming to the "Purposes and Principles of the United Nations as set forth in the Charter."

Equally significant is the emphasis in the Preamble on the concept of "the area of the seabed and the ocean floor as well as its resources" as the "common heritage of mankind." Part XI of the Convention elaborates and gives meaning to this "common heritage" concept in general and is a pioneering accomplishment. As a species mankind seems to possess certain characteristics and privileges. But by the same token, we must recognize our special obligations vis-a-vis the other living species of fauna and flora and vis-a-vis our globe and probably also the universe in general.

Significant in this context are the efforts of the Law of the Sea Convention to meet and neutralize the enormous ecological challenges to which the marine areas are increasingly exposed through a technological revolution running rampant. As a consequence, one of the most essential parts of the convention is Part XII thereof, introducing a number of the most modern and most comprehensive marine anti-pollution provisions of the modern law of nations with its natural emphasis on the marine environment.

The specific measures there laid down to prevent, reduce and control marine pollution were, as stated by the Chairman of the Third Committee Alexander Yankov:

> Viewed as part of a greater co-operative effort to check the alarming trend towards rapid and serious degradation of the marine environment. It was obvious that a viable international regime for the protection and preservation of the marine environment would require a comprehensive approach to the codification and progressive development of international law, namely one that established general rules that might serve as a basis for the further more specific regional or global agreements.[38]

As emphasized by Dr. Yankov, the increasing global dimensions of the protection and preservation of the marine environment were fully understood by main personalities in the Law of the Sea Conference. Thus, Part XII of the 1982 Convention on the Protection and Preservation of the Marine Environment is a reflection of the global dimension of marine pollution and of the realization that effective international actions are of paramount importance, indeed an absolute necessity.

It was accepted in the Conference that the rules elaborated for the protection of the marine environment would have to cover the major sources of pollution whether such pollution emanated:

(i) from land-based pollution;

(ii) from pollution through or from the atmosphere;

(iii) from navigation or accidents at sea like the Torrey Canyon accident of 1967 or the Amco Cadiz accident in March 1978;

(iv) from sea-bed exploration or exploitation including pollution caused by ordinary use or by accidents;

(v) from construction or operation or artificial islands, installations and structures;

(vi) from marine scientific research;

(vii) from dumping of disposal of wastes or other harmful matter at sea;

(viii) from environmental modification and similar techniques or technologies including international or accidental introduction of new or alien species in a part of the marine environment. Such techniques may "upset the normal functioning of the ecological system and cause adverse effects to the marine environment;"[39]

(ix) Finally pollution emanating from radioactive spills or wastes intentionally or accidentally released into the marine environment.

The increasing dilemma of marine pollution has been described by Professor Loius B. Sohn as follows:

> In the 1920s, the first statutes were enacted against oil pollution, but there was little international co-operation on the subject prior to the Second World War. Thereafter, however, wastes dumped from ever-growing coastal cities, pollution from cars, airplanes and ships, release into oceanflowing rivers of pesticides and other hazardous waste, and oil spills from wells on the continental shelf have made it clear that some international co-operation and regulation were necessary. The first step in this direction was the international convention for the Prevention of Pollution of the Sea by Oil, adopted in London in 1954.[40]

The preservation and conservation of the living resources in Antarctica as one of the agreed objectives of the Antarctic

Treaty, 1959[41] have been emphasised at different places. The Brussels Meeting (1964) was notable for its adoption of the Agreed Measures for the Conservation of the Arctic Fauna and Flora. Article VIII of which provided for the zoning of "Specially Protected Areas". A number of such areas have since then been designated, at the Tokyo Consultative Meeting (1970) one important recommendation that was adopted related to man's impact on the Antarctic environment, which provided for research in the matter and for interim measures to reduce harmful environmental interference. The Consultative Meeting at Oslo (1975), was a milestone in this continuing process of consultation. As a result enquiries have been in motion as to the ecological effects involved in the Antarctic mineral exploitation. Another recommendation adopted at Oslo provided for the continuing protection of the Antarctic environment, with a prohibition of disposal of nuclear wastes there, and for scientific and technical cooperation between the Parties.[42] The Antarctic Treaty Consultative Meeting in 1991 agreed to a regime that prohibited mining in Antarctica and that substantially enhanced existing environmental protection provisions.[43]

The problems relating to the protection and distribution of the stationary and migrating living resources of the oceans have been a concern of coastal States over the centuries. But the economic and political importance thereof increased with the development of modern fishing techniques developed from the latter part of the 19th century.

The problems pertaining to the pollution of the marine environment are of a more recent date and have arisen especially in connection with the increased risks of severe oil pollution from the growing fleet of oil tankers in the world. An additional, more recent source is the danger of pollution stemming from the exploration and exploitation of the mineral resources (especially petroleum resources) of the sea-bed and the ocean floor.[44]

By now, there exist a great number of conventions and agreements regulating specific aspects pertaining to the prevention or abatement of marine pollution. A number of these specific instruments are of a special character. That is they relate to special types of pollutants and/or sources of pollution. A number of such conventions for the prevention of and liability for oil pollution have been concluded. Mention must be made of the two Brussels Conventions of 29 November 1969; the first relating to Intervention on the High Seas in Cases of Oil Pollution and the second relating to Civil Liability for Oil Pollution Damage. An additional protocol thereto was the London Protocol of 19 November 1976. Strict provisions have also been concluded for the pollution of the seas by radioactive matter. Thus the Convention on the Liability of Operators of Nuclear Ships concluded in Brussels on 25 May 1972 defines a nuclear ship as a ship "equipped with a nuclear power plant"(Art. I). Article II provides, *inter alia*, that:

> An operator of a nuclear ship shall be *absolutely liable* for any nuclear damage upon proof that such damage has been caused by a nuclear incident involving the nuclear fuel of or radioactive products or waste produced by such ship.

Attention may also be drawn to the Treaty banning Nuclear Weapon Tests in the Atmosphere, in Outer Space or under Water of 5 August 1963 (entered into force on 10 December 1963).

The preamble of this pioneering treaty contains interesting observations on the armaments race as well as on the ecological repercussions of the nuclear arms race. The preamble proclaims as the principal aim of this treaty "The speediest possible achievement of an agreement on general and complete disarmament under strict international control." Furthermore, it expresses as its purpose:

> To achieve the discontinuance of all test explosions of nuclear weapons for all times, determined to continue negotiations to this end and desiring *to put an end to the contamination of man's environment by radioactive substances.*

Consequently, the Contracting Parties undertake in Article I:

> To prohibit, to prevent and not to carry out any nuclear weapon test explosions or any other nuclear explosion at any place under its jurisdiction and control." Whether the parties have lived up to the letter and spirit of this commitment is doubtful. Even more regrettable is the assumption that certain countries, including France, South Africa, Pakistan, India and China, may have exploded nuclear test bombs in such a manner as to cause nuclear contamination of the marine environment.[45]

Mention may also be made of a subsequent international law instrument dealing with the threat of nuclear contamination of the marine environment, namely the Treaty on the Prohibition of the Emplacement of Nuclear Weapons of Mass Destruction of the Seabed and Ocean Floor and in the Subsoil thereof concluded on 11 February 1971. The Preamble of this Convention emphasizes the "common interest of mankind" in peaceful developments and peaceful exploration and exploitation of the sea-bed and ocean floor. The Convention further states that the prevention of a nuclear arms race on the sea-bed and ocean floor serves the best interests of mankind as it contributes to reducing international tension and strengthening friendly relations between States. Consequently, Article I of this Convention contains prohibition against implanting or emplacing on the sea-bed and the ocean floor or in the subsoil thereof outside the 12, outside the 12 mile limit of the territorial sea "any nuclear weapons or other weapons of mass destruction."

The special concerns with regard to the prevention of pollution of the seas from radioactive matter came to the fore at the first Geneva Conference on the Law of the Sea in 1958. Although the four 1958 Conventions on the Law of the Sea did not devote so much time or space to marine pollution as the Third Law of the Sea Conference and the United Nations Law of the Sea Convention of 1982 have done, certain important principles were laid down in the 1958 Convention especially in the Convention on the High Seas.

Article 24 of the High Seas Convention provides that each State party to the convention has the obligation to:

> Draw up regulations to prevent pollution of the seas by the discharge of oil from ships or pipelines or resulting from the exploitation and exploration of the sea-bed and its subsoil.

Thus the concern relating to oil pollution and a strict obligation to prevent such pollution were expressed in this Convention.

Article 25 of the 1958 Convention was even more adamant with regard to radioactive material and radioactive waste. Firstly, this Article prescribes that "every State shall take measures to prevent pollution of the seas from the dumping of radioactive waste." Furthermore, states have the obligation to take account of "the standards and regulations" in this respect. Article 25 further provides that "all States shall cooperate" with such international organizations: "for the prevention of pollution of the seas or airspace above, resulting from *any activities with radioactive materials or other harmful agents.*"[46] Evensen views that these provisions must be considered as expressing basic general principles of existing international law with regard to the marine environment.[47] The purpose of the High Seas Convention of 1958 was—as stated in the Preamble—"to codify the rules of international law relating to the high seas." The preamble further emphasizes that the provisions of the High Seas Convention are "generally declaratory of established principles of international law", Evensen equally shares this view. Thus, Articles 24 and 25 of the 1958 High Seas Convention give expression to prevailing principles of international law for the prevention of pollution and the protection of the marine environment.

Additional expressions of these legal principles are found in the Convention on the Dumping of Wastes at Sea in London on 19 December 1973. The London Convention constitutes a valiant effort to prevent and control the dumping of wastes at sea. In its preamble the Convention ascertains two basic facts as to the marine environment and its management.

First it contains a belated recognition of the fact:

> That the marine environment and the living organisms which it supports are of vital importance to humanity. And people have an interest in assuring that it is so managed that its quality and resources are not impaired.
>
> And secondly:
>
> That the capacity of the sea to assimilate waste and render them harmless and its ability to regenerate natural resources is not unlimited...

The Dumping Convention of 1973 formulates the general legal principle on management and protection of the marine environment as follows in Article I:

> Contracting Parties shall individually or collectively promote the effective control of all sources of pollution of the marine environment, and pledge themselves especially to take all practicable steps to prevent the pollution of the sea by the dumping of waste or other matter that is liable to create hazard to human health, to harm living resources and marine life, to damage amenities or to interfere with other legitimate uses of the sea.

Actually this interesting formulation of the general legal principle for the protection of the marine environment has obviously been influenced by Principle 7 of the Declaration on the Human Environment at the United Nations Conference on the Human Environment held at Stockholm from June 5 to 16, 1972. This principle, expressing a fundamental rule of the modern law of nations, restates the following universal obligation:

> States shall take all possible steps to prevent pollution of the seas by substances that are liable to create hazards to human health, to harm living resources and marine life, to damage amenities or to interfere with other legitimate uses of the sea.

The technological revolution of the last couple of decades has exposed another dimension of mankind's global environment to abuse and serious danger. It refers to Outer

Space. The two main legal instruments for the management and protection of Outer Space are:

(i) Treaty on the Principles Governing the Activities of States in the Exploration and Use of Outer Space, including the Moon and Other Celestial Bodies of 27 January 1967.

(ii) Agreement Governing the Activities on the Moon and Other Celestial Bodies of 5 December 1979.

The 1967 Moon Treaty provides that outer space including the Moon "shall be the province of all mankind", and the Moon Agreement of 1979 likewise provides that the Moon and its natural resources are "the common heritage of mankind." The terminology differs somewhat in these two instruments, but they complement each other. With regard to questions pertaining to the protection and preservation of these mind-boggling regions, these treaties contain provisions prohibiting contamination of these areas of the common heritage of mankind. The 1967 Treaty provides as its point of departure in Article VI that:

> States Parties to the Treaty shall bear international responsibility for national activities in outer space including the Moon and other celestial bodies whether such activities are carried on by governmental agencies or by non-governmental entities...

Article IX of the Treaty contains prohibitions against harmful contamination. It provides that States Parties to the Convention shall conduct exploration of Outer Space:

> So as to avoid harmful contamination and also adverse changes in the environment of the Earth resulting from the introduction of extra-territorial matter and ... shall adopt appropriate measures for this purpose.[48]

The United Nations Conference on Environment and Development (Rio Declaration, 3—14 June 1992) reaffirms the Declaration of the United Nations Conference on Human Environment, adopted at Stockholm on 16 June 1972. Basically the Rio Declaration seeks to build itself on the Stockholm Declaration. In the Preamble, the Rio Declaration addresses to devote to "Working towards international agreements which respect the interests of all and protect the integrity of the global environmental and developmental system." It stresses on "Recognizing the integral and interdependent nature of the Earth, our home." The Stockholm Declaration's 26 principles have been in text and spirit together with some inclusion and exclusion incorporated in 27 principles of the Rio Declaration. The additional texts seem to concern more or less with development spectrum. The soft law impact of the Stockholm Declaration cannot be said to be strengthened through the Rio mechanism to take measures against pollution of environment. Agenda 21 basically is based on Principle 21 of the Stockholm Declaration embodied in Principle 2 of the Rio Declaration. It addresses:

> States have, in accordance with the Charter of the United Nations and the principles of international law, the sovereign right to exploit their own resources pursuant to their own environmental and developmental policies, and the responsibility to ensure that activities within their jurisdiction or control do not cause damage to the environment of other States or of areas beyond the limits of national jurisdiction.

The extract is the substitute of Principle 21 of the Stockholm Declaration with only addition of word "and developmental" along with the word 'environmental' of this Principle. Thus it emerges as Principle 2 in the Rio Declaration.

Few international conferences can have been so comprehensively prepared as the United Nations Conference on Environment and Development. Much of the work of the Preparatory Committee and UNCED's staff was devoted to the preparation of Agenda 21. In his speech to the first meeting of the UNCED Preparatory Committee in the Secretary-General, Maurice Strong, indicated that:

> Agenda 21 would go well beyond the kind of "Action Plans" which have traditionally emerged from UN conferences. It should provide the basic framework and instrumentality which will guide the world community on

> an ongoing basis in its decisions on the goals, targets, priorities, allocation of responsibilities and resources in respect of the many environment and development issues which will determine the future of our planet. It should therefore incorporate provisions for monitoring of progress and periodic review and revision.
>
> Agenda 21 would be one of the most important products of the Conference. In providing a coherent and manageable framework for dealing with the vast array of subject matter confronting the Conference, it would constitute an instrumentality through which the world community and its many institutions and mechanisms can continue to deal effectively on an ongoing basis with this complex and inter-acting system of issues.[49]

The regime of marine environment is a reality of concerned states obligations. The LOS Convention in its article 192 says that: "States have obligation to protect and preserve the marine environment." In the MOX Plant Case, 2001, the International Tribunal for the Law of the Sea unanimously prescribed, pending a decision by the Annex VII arbitral tribunal, the following measures under article 290, paragraph 5, of the Convention[50]:

> Ireland and the United Kingdom shall cooperate and shall, for this purpose, enter into consultations forthwith in order to:
>
> (a) exchange further information with regard to possible consequences for the Irish Sea arising out of the commissioning of the MOX plant;
>
> (b) monitor risks or the effects of the operation of the MOX plant for the Irish Sea;
>
> (c) devise, as appropriate, measures to prevent pollution of the marine environment which might result from the operation of the MOX plant.

How to conceptualize obligation as to protect and preserve marine environment may be treated as a matter of additive views. Judge Wolfrum in his separate opinion gives a clarification saying:

> In general it has to be taken into consideration, though, that the provisions of the Convention on the Law of the Sea formulate obligations rather than rights. Is it possible to argue that obligations of States Parties under a multilateral treaty create, as a corollary, rights for each single other State Party. This is correct in bilateral relations. It would, however, be a simplification to say so in multilateral relations, such as the ones established by the Convention on the Law of the Sea. Some guidance may be drawn in this respect from the most recent draft of the International Law Commission on state responsibility. This draft distinguishes between obligations vis-a-vis another State in bilateral relations and obligations towards States Parties and obligations towards States Parties of a multilateral agreement. However, one may assume that Ireland at least has a legally protected interest that the United Kingdom lives up to its obligations to co-operate in the protection of the marine environment of the Irish Sea.

The impact of obligation should cover protection and preservation of the marine environment with which states are directly concerned. That is to say, the prime concerned states with the environmental matters are those who are bilaterally related. As a practical consideration, states seem to be sub-regionally or regionally grouped together owing to their identical or some common approaches in certain matters. These are largely in practice on geographical factors and to some extent on some other parameters more or less of political and economic nature. It then justifies, if states particularly of sub-regional or regional groups are identically in obligation for protection and preservation of the marine environment.

There is yet to regard state's obligation towards protection and preservation of the marine environment as having a position of customary international law, but the ongoing trends of states gives rise to consider it to be in the realm of such law. The preamble of Earth Charter (The Hague, June 29, 2000) states:

> We stand at a critical moment in Earth's history, a time when humanity must choose its future. As the world

> becomes increasingly interdependent and fragile, the future at once holds great peril and great promise. To move forward we must recognize that in the midst of a magnificent diversity of cultures and life forms we are one human family and one Earth community with a common destiny. We must join together to bring forth a sustainable global society founded on respect for nature, universal human rights, economic justice, and a culture of peace. Towards this end, it is imperative that we, the peoples of Earth, declare our responsibility to one another, to the greater community of life, and to future generations...[51]

At a time when major changes in how we think and live are urgently needed, the Earth Charter challenges us to examine our values and to choose a better way. It calls on us to search for common ground in the midst of out diversity and to embrace a new ethical vision that is shared by growing numbers of people in many nations and cultures throughout the world. The Earth Charter devotes to a declaration of fundamental principles for building a just, sustainable, and peaceful global society in 21st century. It seeks to inspire in all peoples a new sense of global interdependence and shared responsibility for the well-being of the human family and the larger living world. It is an expression of hope and a call to help create a global partnership at a critical juncture in history. The Earth Charter's inclusive ethical vision recognizes that environmental protection, human rights, equitable human development, and peace are interdependent and indivisible. The Charter provides a new framework for thinking about and addressing these issues. The result is a fresh, broad conception of what constitutes a sustainable community and sustainable development.[52]

Mention can also be made as to conservation and management of straddling fish stocks and highly migratory fish stocks that relates to protection and preservation of ecological systems. Agreement for the Implementation of the Provisions of the United Nations Convention on the Law of the Sea of 10 December 1982 Relating to the Conservation and Management of Straddling Fish Stocks and Highly Migratory Fish Stocks commits to be "Conscious of the need to avoid adverse impacts on the marine environment, preserve biodiversity, maintain the integrity of marine ecosystems and minimize the risk of long-term or irreversible effects of fishing operations..."[53]

There may arise a need for some cursory examination of legal instruments pertaining to the protection and preservation of marine environment, attention may be drawn to a number of regional conventions for the protection and preservation of special ocean stretches or marine areas.[54]

It is now possible to come to the conclusion that there is an urge for protection and preservation of the marine environment at all levels globally, regionally, sub-regionally and at individual national level. The Bay of Bengal which is a domain of nature catastrophe draws attention particularly of its bordering states which committed to protect and preserve environment for maintaining of ecosystems in entirety, otherwise, to a sustainable extent. Although, in environment and development phases, the Bay of Bengal Community appears not at pace with the other regions nevertheless, it seems to be making progress in taking steps for promotion of the Bay's environment.

6.7. Towards the Bay of Bengal Environment

It is a fact that as time passes, changes take place. There is no alternative but to accept changes. Ultimately, it is inevitable to concede to the saying "We must become change, we wish to see."[55] Since 1964, the United Nations Conference on Trade and Development (UNCTAD) the world nations saw two camps of the economically rich, scientifically and technologically developed states as "developed states" and the economically backward states as "developing states". The role of developing states in international forum was to uphold interests and to do that despite differences among themselves. Their stand was to assert their common interests collectively. There was enthusiasm among the developing states to activate their stand strongly. The demarcation of world states was also for the developing states as 'Third World states', and the developed states as the 'First World states'. The rarely noted "Second World states" were the socialist and communist block states. The distinctive phases of world states were seen as 'Western' and 'Eastern' states—the former signifies the developed states and the latter—developing states.

The distinction between rich and poor countries was symbolized by a line drawn across the globe between the 'North' and the 'South' by the Brandt Commission in 1980. The 'North' consisted of North America, Europe, the Soviet Union (now Russian Federation), Japan, Australia, and New Zealand. All the rest belong to the 'South'. The Commission's concern was focused on inequalities in economic development, but the general distinction serves quite well for the increasingly divisive impacts of the global environmental crisis. Indeed the Brandt Commission mentioned the linkages between environment and development.[56]

Environmental issues that already affect international relations include global warming, regional acidification, depletion of ozone in the upper atmosphere, marine pollution, nuclear safety, and the disposal of toxic wastes. These are issues that have come to public attention quite recently, and most governments remain ambivalent about how much should be done to control them. There is much scope for disagreement especially when the actions of one country affect the quality of life, even the livelihood, of its neighbours. Clean technology costs money to develop, to install, and to maintain. The benefits are difficult to quantify, there are limits to the extent to which an individual country can clean up its own environment and enjoy the benefits of its own investments and regulations without the active cooperation of its neighbours.

The great achievement of the World Commission on Environment and Development, or Brundtland Commission, authors of *Our Common Future* (1987), was to make explicit the linkages between global environmental deterioration, poverty, and rapid population growth. It described how both industrialization and over-population contribute to the degradation of environmental support systems. Thus, any solution to the current global crisis should also be linked through these issues—industrial activities must be cleaned up, poverty eradicated, and the size of the global population stabilized.[57]

Environmental development measures are conveniently effective if taken bilaterally. In the case of sub-regional and regional states the effects may also be significant. The Bay of Bengal bordering states belong to the group of developing states. The position of India is rather somehow different in the sense that it has made its nation building approaches successful compared to scientific and technological development of the neighbouring as well as the regional states. Although India seems to belong to the group of developing states, its development enables to regard it as a developed country of the developing states. In reality, no other Bay of Bengal bordering states can be compared with India as to the economic, scientific and technological advances.

The Bay of Bengal bordering states are endowed with some regional forum like SAARC, and BIMSTEC. The SAARC countries like Bangladesh, Bhutan, India, Pakistan, Maldives, Nepal, and Sri Lanka are developing countries with varying position. Bangladesh, Bhutan, Maldives, and Nepal belong to the category of least developed countries. Moreover, Bhutan and Nepal are land-locked and Maldives and Sri Lanka are island states. Pakistan is developing whereas the position of India is unbeatable with regard to economic, scientific and technological considerations. There are certain objectives of SAARC but these are seen not to include specification about environment. It can be noted that the SAARC aims at: "promoting peace, stability, amity and progress in the region through strict adherence to the principles of the United Nations Charter and Non-Alignment, particularly respect for the principles of sovereign equality, territorial integrity, national independence, non-use of force and non-interference in the internal affairs of other States and peaceful settlement of all disputes."[58] However, as time passed, the programme under SAARC Charter appears to include environment matter in the theme of reorganization.

Under the new SAARC Integrated Programme of Action (SIPA), the number of Technical Committees has been reduced from eleven to seven mainly through the amalgamation of the different sectors covered by the various Technical Committees and eliminating overlapping, duplication and waste. The prime objective of the reorganisation has been to enhance clarity in terms of the goals and targets of the activities undertaken, as well as to improve its quality and efficacy.

The seven Technical Committees under SIPA now cover:

1. Agriculture and Rural Development;
2. Communications and Transport;
3. Social Development;
4. Environment, Meteorology and Forestry;
5. Science and Technology;
6. Human Resources Development; and
7. Energy.

An in-built mechanism for automatic review of activities under SIPA has been provided for. The review will be undertaken every three years by an independent multi-disciplinary Expert Group that would be constituted by the Secretary-General in consultation with Member States. The SAARC programme on "Environment, Meteorology and Forestry" is in formative stage and as such, it is not significant presently to the environmental aspects especially of marine environment concerns. But in reality SAARC's pace as time passes, goes on to be in constraint.

Bangladesh-India-Myanmar-Sri Lanka-Thailand Economic Co-operation (BIMSTEC) is a sub-regional grouping combining some geographically contiguous South Asian and ASEAN countries in the Bay of Bengal. It was formed by the member countries to exploit the synergies in their capabilities and resource endowments for their development. The first meeting of the Economic/Trade Ministers held in August 1998 in Bangkok imparted a new dynamism to the grouping which had been formed in 1997 with the decision to constitute an Inter-Governmental Group (IGG) to prepare a concept paper on possible approaches towards a preferential trading arrangement leading to a Free Trade Area. Subsequently,

BIMSTEC decided to establish a Free Trade Area in the region with the objective of promoting harmonious development of economy among member countries through expansion of trade by providing fair conditions of competition for trade among them. BIMSTEC has identified six sectors for cooperation, viz. Trade and investment, technology, transport and communication, energy, tourism and fisheries. The regular interactions at the levels of experts, senior officials, economy/ trade ministers and foreign ministers have started.

Fresh momentum has been imparted to the Grouping at the Ministerial Meetings held in Phuket in February 2004 with the proposed first Summit, expansion of the membership to cover Nepal and Bhutan, and signing of the Framework Agreement on BIMSTEC Free Trade Arrangement. Therefore, a foundation for the launching of the process of deeper economic integration in the framework of the Grouping has been laid. The BIMSTEC has recently included Nepal and Bhutan as members.[59]

It has been argued that the grouping has a rich potential for regional economic integration owing to complementarity of economies and resources. While establishment of a free trade area is described as a good beginning, it is felt the grouping should set a goal to form a Bay of Bengal Economic Community by 2020. It notes that Bangladesh and Myanmar have large natural gas reserves while Nepal and Bhutan have hydropower resources. With net energy importers like India and Sri Lanka available to utilise surplus gas and hydro power, it is felt the BIMSTEC can ultimately form a Bay of Bengal Energy community. It may be recalled that the European Union began as a Coal and Steel community and only later metamorphosed into a comprehensive economic grouping.[60] It is argued that the Bay of Bengal Community so considered would facilitate speedier trade liberalisation and increased regional capital flows and offer prospects of widening the network for outward oriented growth in this part of Asia. This forum appears to emerge as the natural bridge between South Asia and South-East Asia and to play a very important role given the inability of SAARC to widen economic links within the subcontinent. The BIMSTEC then is obvious for the liberalised Indian market to meaningful opportunities to the ASEAN countries. Strategically, a closer linkage with the Indian Subcontinent would go a long way in ensuring the prospects of peace and stability in the region.

As a matter of fact, BIMSTEC is now at a formative stage, and its role is in question to what extent it will concern with environment issues generally, and marine environment specifically. Taking into consideration its aims and objectives, it is obvious that BIMSTEC will mainly commit to promoting economic activities and to do that a regime of free trade in the assumed geographic region may be reiterated. Anyway, it is possible to see some urges of cooperation among the Bay of Bengal bordering countries and in so doing, they will come together with matters, they feel should dealt with. Although the notion like the "Bay of Bengal" is seen to continue with the BIMSTEC, but there is no mention of the Bay as regards its environment.

The Bay of Bengal needs to be considered for promotion of ecosystems and environment as a whole. Pollution of the Bay requires to be prevented, reduced and controlled. There is a need to make out causes and sources of pollution of the Bay. Nature and man-made activities result in sorrows for coastal populations and pollution of the Bay. The Bay of Bengal shallows in such a way that any major storm pushes a massive storm-surge of floodwaters over the low-lying, heavily populated, adjacent areas of Bangladesh and India. Every year or so, a tropical cyclone comes into the Bay at just the right angle to push a surge over these areas, killing thousands of human beings.

Sea level rise has become a crucial matter foı Bangladesh and Maldives. Sea level rise causes are to be taken into consideration for the states so affected. One of the most important consequences of an increase in mean global temperatures will be a possible rise in the sea level around the planet. The reasons for this rise in sea level include:

The expansion of the ocean's volume when water temperatures increase. Although small, such thermal expansion can translate to a considerable rise in mean sea levels.

Mountain glacier melt will also contribute a sizeable amount of water to the oceans, which will also contribute to sea level rise. It should be noted that such mountain glaciers melt will not only contribute to sea level rise once the water reaches the sea, but will also contribute to increased flooding in flood plains.

Melting water from the land is expected to be the third component. In addition to the rise in sea level due to increased temperatures, as described above, the land surface of the planet is also undergoing changes in elevation due to a number of factors, including tectonic changes, sedimentation etc. As a part of the Indian Ocean, the Bay of Bengal is a domain of tectonic activity and as such the Bay of Bengal bordering states need to consider them to be active in entirety.[61]

With the passage of time, the Bay of Bengal countries are advancing towards organisational forum. Agreement on the Institutionalisation of the Bay of Bengal Programme as an Inter-Governmental Organisation gives rise to acceleration of such move. The Inter-Governmental Organisation for the Bay of Bengal is committed to the promotion of coastal fisheries and regional cooperation and to that end the contracting parties have agreed to[62]

take into account paramount importance of coastal fisheries as an essential sector of development in the Bay of Bengal region;

recognise that coastal fisheries plays a vital role in economy of the Bay of Bengal countries;

recognise the establishment and maintenance of an Inter-Governmental Organisation in the region can make a significant contribution to the development of coastal fisheries;

consider that the success of such an Inter-Governmental Organisation will depend largely on close regional co-operation;

consider that co-operation in this field can best be achieved through the establishment of an Inter-Governmental Organisation carrying out its activities in collaboration with other governments as well as organisations and institutions that may be able to provide financial and technical support.

The Bay of Bengal region is being considered to be vulnerable in consideration of its living and non-living resources. The Bay of Bengal Inter-Governmental Organisation is devoted to coastal fisheries and in order to activate the programme there is a need to give attention towards protection and preservation of ecosystems. Truly, new approaches to marine and coastal area management and development, at the national, subregional, regional and global levels are required, approaches that are integrated in content and are precautionary and anticipatory in ambit, as reflected in the following programme areas[63]:

(a) Integrated management and sustainable development of coastal areas, including exclusive economic zones;
(b) Marine environment protection;
(c) Sustainable use and conservation of marine living resources of the high seas;
(d) Sustainable use and conservation of marine living resources under national jurisdiction
(e) Addressing critical uncertainties for the management of the marine environment and climate change;
(f) Strengthening international, including regional, cooperation and coordination;
(g) Sustainable development of small islands.

In order to intensify marine environment concerns, clarification is almost readded to the relevant infrastructure of the Bay of Bengal. Marine environment of the Bay of Bengal is directly or indirectly becoming polluted due to addition of so many polluting agents. To protect water pollution and control of mine drainage, large scale drilling and production of natural gas from the offshore gasfields, and exploration of beach sand placer deposits from the offshore islands must follow standard regulations both from mine safety and environmental protection point of view.

The coastal environment is contaminated by oil tanker traffic, harbour operations and effluents discharged from petroleum processing. Sewage disposal by the rivers into the Bay of Bengal contains higher concentration of Biochemical Oxygen Demand (BOD). Moreover, the coastal environment has also been affected by industrial effluents, agricultural residues, some other human activities like deforestation and irrational expansion of coastal shrimp farming, etc. resulting in ecological degradation. Overfishing and dumping of discarded fishes in these areas are becoming a threat to the resourcefulness of the fishing grounds. Only proper management of the existing grounds and finding of new fishing grounds can ensure the continuous harvest of fisheries

The occurrence of marine species—both plants and animals—has largely been controlled by the physico-chemical properties of ocean water. Water discharges from the surrounding river catchments carry huge influx of sediments full of nutrients to the Bay, particularly along the near shore region. This has turned the Bay into a fertile marine fishing ground of the region. The near-shore up-welling zone not only has a high yield of nutrients, but also is a high primary production area for the phytoplankton and related zooplankton zones.

The hydrological conditions of the Bay of Bengal is favourable for a variety of shrimps and fishes. Although fishes remain scattered in the Bay in some places they get concentrated and constitute important fishing grounds.

The surface salinity at the mouths of some large rivers like the Ganges, Brahmaputra, Irrawady, Krishna, Godavari, Cauvery and Mahanadi varies widely from one day to another, especially in summer. Salinity of water also changes vertically. The influence of the fresh water is experienced up to depths of 200-300 m. From the surface, the salinity gradually increases downward and at about 200-300 m. it reaches 35% and at about 500 m. the salinity is more than 35.10%, but at

1,000 m. it decreases slightly and attains 34.95%. With further increase of depth salinity decreases and at 4,500 m. it is close to 34.7%.

6.8. The End Phase

The Large Marine Ecosystem (LME) is situated in the monsoon belt and receives high rainfall. Bangladesh, India, Indonesia, Malaysia, Maldives, Myanmar, Sri Lanka, and Thailand are the countries bordering the LME. Intensive fishing is the primary force driving the LME, with climate as the secondary driving force. The Global Environmental Facility (GEF) is supporting a fisheries project, now in the preparation stage, to address critical threats to the coastal and marine environment, and to promote ecosystem-based management of coastal and marine resources.

Knowledge has no end in itself. This deal on the Bay of Bengal environment is first of its kind, as a result, there is a scope to applaud the move that relates to the concerns of the Bay. Although the regional agreements like SAARC, BIMSTEC do not appear to include specific provisions on protection and preservation of the Bay of Bengal environment, the Bay's bounties of living and non-living resources and hydro-electric utilities compel the bordering states to protect, preserve and promote its environment. Confrontations at bilateral, and sub-regional levels may not be unabated, but the marine environment realm needs to be enriched through cooperation aimed at an obligation upon each and every member of the Bay of Bengal community. If it is taken up actively, the Bay of Bengal Environment might enrich at pace with the other marine regions environment.

At present while a state is environmentally affected by work done by the neighbouring state, the affected state has a lot of scope to bring it to others' notice citing specifically the UN Law of the Sea Convention, the Earth Summit and possibly other global and related regional and subregional agreements. Whatever allegations and counter-allegations might come to public, the environment concerned states must be committed to settle the conflict peacefully devoting themselves to the commitment of protecting, preserving and promoting the Bay of Bengal environment. This commitment will encourage the Bay of Bengal community through equigeneration system in which all members large, small and tiny can share to enrich and strengthen the Bay of Bengal environment. Future generations should look back at an epoch of peace, harmony and cooperation in order to find appropriate means for the preservation and protection of the marine environment. Given the inextricably interconnected nature of the environment, cooperative solutions are the strategy of choice now and in the future. To end, the legal regime of marine environment in the Bay of Bengal cannot help emphasising on huge funds to be met by organisations particularly the international organizations without which "environment and development" objectivity cannot come to fruition.

References

1. The following 38 entities have so far been associated with IOMAC activities: Asian-African Legal Consultative Committee (AALCC), Commonwealth Secretariat, Division of Global and Interregional Projects, Economic and Social Commission for Asia and the Pacific (ESCAP), Economic Commission for Africa (ECA), Food and Agriculture Organization of the United Nations (FAO), Gulf Cooperation Council (GCC), Intergovernmental Oceanographic Commission (IOC), International Bank for Reconstruction and Development (IBRD), International Centre for Ocean Development (ICOD), International Hydrographic Bureau (IHB), International Maritime Organization (IMO), International Ocean Institute (IOI), International Telecommunications Union (ITU), International Union for Conservation of Nature and Natural Resources (IUCN), International Whaling Commission (IWC), Issue-based Indian Ocean Network (IBION), Law of the Sea Institute (LSI), Netherlands Institute for the Law of the Sea (NILOS), Office of the Special Representative Organization of African Unity (OAU), Project Jonah (Australia), Regional Bureau for Africa, Regional Bureau for Asia and the Pacific, UN Ad hoc Committee of the Indian Ocean Peace Zone, UN Department of Political and Security Council Affairs, United Nations Development Programme (UNDP), UN Division for Outer Space Affairs, United Nations Educational, Scientific and Cultural Organization (UNESCO), United Nations Environment Programme (UNEP), United Nations Fund for Population Activities (UNFPA), United Nations Industrial Development Organization (UNIDO), UN International Economic and Social Affairs Department, UN Legal Counsel, UN Division of Ocean Affairs and the Law of the Sea, UN Revolving Fund for Natural Resources Exploration, United Nations University, World Meteorological Organization (WMO) http://www.unu.edu/unupress/unupbooks/uu15oe/uu15oe0n.htm

2. Marine studies over the Indian Ocean began actually by India. The Indian Ocean, the only ocean named after a country, is unique because unlike other oceans it is bounded in the north by the Asian continent. The Indian Seas cover 3 million kilometers squared, larger than its land area. India, a peninsular country with major rivers, divides the north Indian Ocean into two basins, the Bay of Bengal on the east and the larger Arabian Sea on the west, bounded approximately between 0°N to 24°N and 60°E to 100°E. Their total shelf area of about 0.84 million kilometers squared, approximates that of the Gulf of Mexico plus the Caribbean Seas, excluding Antilles. The Indian coastline is 7,515 km. The Bay of Bengal and the Arabian Sea contribute 59 per cent and 41 per cent, respectively, to the 2.02 million kilometers squared Indian Exclusive Economic Zone. D.V. Subba Rao, "Marine Sciences of the Seas around India between 1874 and 2000 and Prospects for the New Millenium" in Elisabeth Mann Borgese & Ors (eds.), 16(2002) OCEAN (The University of the Chicago Press, Chicago) 195.
3. The pursuit of marine science during the British colonial rule (pre-1947) was limited only to a few individuals and was purely descriptive. In contrast, independent India has acquired certain capabilities in marine science comparable with other similar nations. *Ibid.* 197.
4. Charles H. Cotter, *The Physical Geography of the Oceans* (Hollis & Carter, London, 1965) 142-143.
5. http://www.nefsc.noaa.gov/lme/text/lme34.htm
6. http://na.nefsc.noaa.gov/lme/text/lme34.htm
7. *Ibid.*
8. http://www.pmel.noaa.gov/tsunami/tidegauge200441226.html(Maldives); http://www.noaanews.noaa.gov/stories2004/s2358.htm (Cocos Islands)
9. http://www.grida.no/climate/ipcc_tar/wg1
10. http://www.marine.csiro.au/LeafletsFolder/45slevel/45.html
11. http://www.grida.no/climate/vital/33.htm
12. http://www.ppk.itb.ac.id/aceh/simulasi_tsunami_aceh.htm
13. http://earthobservatory.nasa.gov/NaturalHazards/shownh.php3?img_id =12646
14. http://independent-bangladesh.com/news/jan/01/01012005mt.htm#A5
15. http://en.wikipedia.org/wiki/2004_Indian_Ocean_Earthquake
16. http://www.pmel.noaa.gov/tsunami/tidegauge200441226.html
17. http://www.environment.gov.mv/climate.htm
18. http://www.gesource.ac.uk/worldguide/htm/950_map.html
19. http://www.physicstoday.org/pt/vol-57/iss-2/p24.html
20. http://www.grida.no/climate/ipcc_tar/wg2/301.htm#663
21. *Ibid.*
22. http://www.tai.au

23. Arun Chaturvedi, *South Asian States and Sea Laws* (Printwell Publishers, Jaipur, India, 1987) 113.
24. http://odin.dep.no/ud/engelsk/publ/handlingsplaner/032005-990965/index-dok000-b-n-a.html
25. A Panel on Forestry has been appointed to examine all issues related to the protection and sustainable use of forests. The results of the Food Security Summit: Global Plan of Action (1996) figure prominently in relation to the development of sustainable production systems. In the social sphere it is necessary to take into account: the Conference on Population in Cairo (1994), the Social Summit in Copenhagen (1995) and the Conference on Women in Beijing (1995). The World Heritage Convention is formally not a part of the Rio umbrella, but it will be important to take this into account along with the Habitat II-City Summit and the Global Plan of Action for plant genetic resources in 1996. Several of the global conventions also cover development aspects, which make it imperative to secure optimal accord between commitments in the conventions and the guidelines in development assistance policy. http://odin.dep.no/ud/engelsk/publ/handlingsplaner/032005-990965/index-dok000-b-n-a.html
26. Chapter 37.1 of Agenda 21.
27. Chapter 37.2 of Agenda 21.
28. Chapter 17.117 of Agenda 21.
29. Thomas Hardy.
30. http://seawifs.gsfc.nasa.gov/OCEAN_PLANET/HTML/peril_pollution...
31. This is estimated as an annual input of 6.4 million tons of general shipboard litter, plus 1,36,000 tons of plastics, nets, lines, and buoys and 22,000 tons of plastic containers from fishing boats. See Rodney R. White, *North, South, and the Environmental Crisis* (University of Toronto Press, Toronto, 1993) 85.
32. The northern Adriatic has become particularly susceptible to "red tides" caused by algal blooms, mainly in response to excessive inputs of phosphorus in detergents. In 1988, an algal bloom in the Venice lagoon led to "an invasion of insects and the release of hydrogen sulphide with extremely disagreeable consequences for the population and the tourists". Grenomn, Michael, and Michael Batisse (eds.), *Futures for the Mediterranean Basin: The Blue Plan* (Oxford University Press, Oxford, 1989) 254.
33. White, *supra* 85.
34. *Ibid.* 86.
35. *Ibid.* 86.
36. *Ibid.*
37. A study has already been made on it. *Supra*...
38. Dr. J. Evensen, "Management of the Seas: Legal Issues with Special Emphasis on Pollution" in Will D. Verwey (ed.), *Nature Management and*

Sustainable Development (T.M.C. Asser Instituut, The Hague, 1989) 506-507.

39. *Ibid.*

40. *Ibid.* 507.

41. 409 UNTS, 71; UKTS 97(1971), Cmnd. 1535; 54(1960) AJIL (Supplement) 476-483. The treaty entered into force in 1961. The following 27 states are parties to it: Argentina, Australia, Belgium, Brazil, Bulgaria, Chile, Czechoslovakia, Denmark, France, GDR, Italy, Japan, Netherlands, New Zealand, Norway, Papua New Guinea, Peru, Poland, Romania, South Africa, UK, USA, USSR, and Uruguay.

42. R.A. Malviya, *Environmental Pollution and Its Control Under International Law* (Chugh Publications, Allahabad, India, 1987) 253.

43. Sam Blay & Ors (ed.), *Public International Law: An Australian Perspective* (Oxford University Press, Oxford, 1997) 399-401.

44. A pollution accident in Santa Barbara, California of 1969 (the Santa Barbara oilspills) was a reminder of the pollution hazards involved in such oil-drilling activities. What happened was as follows:

    On January 28, 1969, one of the wells owned by the Union Oil Company suffered a blow-out resulting in the Oil Disaster of 1969. For the next eleven days, the well lost reddish-brown crude oil in the Pacific Ocean at the rate of 1,000 gallons per hour. A claim was based, *inter alia,* on the principle of absolute (strict liability) for ultra hazardous activities. The oil company concerned, the Union Oil Company, settled the claim out of court. The court verdict entailed responsibility for marine pollution. See *ibid.* 507.

45. *Ibid.* 508.

46. *Ibid.* 508-509.

47. *Ibid.* 509.

48. *Ibid.* 515.

49. Quoted in Stanley P. Johnson, *The Earth Summit: The United Nations Conference on Environment and Development (UNCED)* (Martinus Nijhoff, London, 1993) 125.

50. International Tribunal for the Law Of the Sea (ITLOS): The MOX Plant Case (Ireland v. United Kingdom), December 3, 2001, cited in 41(2002) ILM 405. Shortly stating, Ireland alleged against the United Kingdom that the MOX plant operation will cause environmental pollution in the Irish Sea. The dispute was adjudicated in the International Tribunal for the Law of Sea on December 3, 2001. See furthermore the text appearing at the ITLOS website (visited March 19, 2002). Http://www.itlos.org.

51. In 1987, the United Nations World Commission on Environment and Development issued a call for creation of a new charter that would set forth fundamental principles for sustainable development. The drafting of an Earth Charter was part of the unfinished business of the 1992 Rio Earth

Summit. In 1994, Maurice Strong, the secretary general of the Earth Summit and chairman of the Earth Council, and Mikhail Gorbachev, president of Green Cross International, launched a new Earth Charter initiative with support from the Dutch government. An Earth Charter Commission was formed in 1997 to oversee the project and an Earth Charter Secretariat was established at the Earth Council in Costa Rica. Early in 1997, the Earth Charter Commission formed an international drafting committee. The drafting committee helped to conduct the international consultation process, and the evolution and development of the document reflects the progress of the worldwide dialogue on the Earth Charter. Beginning with the Benchmark Draft issued by the Commission following the Rio+5 Forum in Rio de Janeiro, drafts of the Earth Charter were circulated internationally as part of the consultation process. Meeting at the UNESCO Headquarters in Paris in March 2000, the Commission approved a final version of the Earth Charter.

Website: http://www.earthcharter.org.

52. Together with the Earth Charter consultation process, the most important influences shaping the ideas and values in the Earth Charter are contemporary science, international law, the teachings of indigenous peoples, the wisdom of the world's great religions and philosophical traditions, the declarations and reports of the seven UN summit conferences held during the 1990s, the global ethics movement, numerous non-governmental declarations and people's treaties issued over the past thirty years, and best practices for building sustainable communities. A new phase in the initiative began with the official launching of the Earth Charter at the Peace Palace in the Hague in June 29, 2000. The mission of the Initiative is to establish a sound ethical foundation for the emerging global society and to help build a sustainable world based on respect for nature, universal human rights, economic justice, and a culture of peace.

53. UNDoc. A/CONF.164/37 of 8 September 1995. Jean-Pierre Levy & Gunnar G. Schram, *United Nations Conference on Straddling Fish Stocks and Highly Migratory Fish Stocks* (Martinus Nijhoff, The Hague, 1996) 763.

54. Among such instruments are the well-known Barcelona Convention of 16 February 1976 with two protocols for the Protection of the Mediterranean Sea Against Pollution. Other agreements pertaining to the Protection and Preservation of the Mediterranean are the Athens Protocol of 17 May 1980 (pollution from land-based sources); the Geneva Protocol of 3 April 1982 (Mediterranean Specially Protected Areas) and the Monaco Agreement of 10 May 1976 (Protection of the Waters of the Mediterranean Shores) Among other relevant material sources can be drawn to: The Kuwait Convention of 24 April 1978 on the Persian Gulf; The Abidjan Convention of 23 March 1981 for Central and West-Africa; The Jeddah Convention of 14 February 1982 on the Red Sea and the Persian Gulf; The Cartagena Convention of 24 March 1983 on the Wider Caribbean Region; and the Noumea Convention of 1986 for the South Pacific Region.

55. M.K. Gandhi.
56. Brandt Commission (Independent Commission on International Development Issues), 1980: *North—South: A Programme for Survival,* Pan Books, 113-116.
57. Rodney R. White, *North, South, and the Environmental Crisis* (University of Toronto Press, Toronto, 1993) 3-4.
58. The South Asian Association for Regional Cooperation (SAARC) comprises the seven countries of South Asia, i.e., Bangladesh, Bhutan, India, the Maldives, Nepal, Pakistan and Sri Lanka. It is an Association based on the consciousness that in an increasingly interdependent world, the objectives of peace, freedom, social justice and economic prosperity are best achieved in the South Asian region by fostering mutual understanding, good neighbourly relations and meaningful cooperation among the Member States which are bound by ties of history and culture. The Charter of SAARC provides for the following: The highest authority of the Association rests with the Heads of State or Government, who meet annually at Summit level. To date, twelve meetings of the Heads of State or Government have been held respectively in Dhaka (1985), Bangalore (1986), Kathmandu (1987), Islamabad (1988), Malé (1990), Colombo (1991), Dhaka (1993), New Delhi (1995), Malé (1997), Colombo (1998), Kathmandu (2002), and Islamabad (2004).
59. *The Hindu*, February 22, 2004.
60. *Ibid.*
61. There is a positive need for protection and preservation of the Bay of Bengal environment and to that end geographically, economically and environmentally vulnerable states like Bangladesh and Maldives draw particular attention. It is to mention that, Bangladesh, one of the most densely populated countries in the world with over 755 people per square km has a per capita income only about US$235. Over 40% of the population live in poverty. With its high population density, low level of development, and low lying deltaic mass, Bangladesh has already been facing a number of natural and man-made problems. Natural hazards like cyclones, floods, droughts and socio-economic problems such as poverty, low literacy, poor health delivery systems, high unemployment are some of them. In the future Bangladesh may also have to face adverse impact of development across its border which among other things, are expected to have reduced availability of water during the dry season and has to deal with impacts of climate change and sea level rise. To better prepare the country for dealing with these impacts pragmatic planning is needed; it should be based on authentic data and analyses from scientific studies. http://www.sdnpbd.org/sdi/international_day/wed/2004/banglades...
62. The BOBP-IGO Agreement was formally signed by the Governments of Bangladesh, India and Sri Lanka at Chennai on 26 April, 2003 and by the Government of Maldives at Chennai on 21 May 2003 (BOBP-IGO Agreement. For details see Annex A.

63. See "Introduction" of Agenda 21, Chapter 17. Quoted in Stanley P. Johnson, *The Earth Summit: United Nations Conference on Environment and Development* (UNCED) (Graham & Trotman/Martinus Nijhoff, London, 1993) 308.

ANNEXURES

ANNEXURE A: AGREEMENT ON THE INSTITUTIONALISATION OF THE BAY OF BENGAL

PROGRAMME AS AN INTER-GOVERNMENTAL ORGANISATION

The Contracting Parties,

Conscious of the paramount importance of coastal fisheries as an essential sector of development in the Bay of Bengal region;

Recognising that coastal fisheries plays a vital role in economy of the Bay of Bengal countries;

Recognising that the establishment and maintenance of an Inter-Governmental Organisation in the region can make a significant contribution to the development of coastal fisheries;

Considering that the success of such an Inter-Governmental Organisation will depend largely on close regional co-operation;

Considering that co-operation in this field can best be achieved through the establishment of an Inter-Governmental Organisation carrying out its activities in collaboration with other governments as well as organisations and institutions that may be able to provide financial and technical support;

Have agreed as follows:

Article 1

ESTABLISHMENT

The Contracting Parties hereby establish the Bay of Bengal Inter-Governmental Organisation on coastal fisheries with the objectives and functions set out hereinafter.

Article 2

DEFINITIONS

For the purpose of this Agreement:

"Organisation" means the Inter-Governmental Organisation for the Bay of Bengal Programme on coastal fisheries (BOBP-IGO).

"Agreement" means this agreement for the establishment of the BOBP-IGO.

"Member" means a government, which is a contracting party to this Agreement.

"Council" means the Governing Council of the BOBP-IGO.

"Director" means the Director of the BOBP-IGO.

"Contracting Parties" mean the members who are signatories of the Agreement for the establishment of the BOBP-IGO as well as others who may desire to join the BOBP-IGO in future.

"Donor Government" means a government, other than a Member Government, which makes a substantial contribution to the activities of the Organisation and has concluded an agreement pursuant to Article 15 of this Agreement.

Article 3

OBJECTIVES

The objectives of the Organisation shall be to enhance co-operation among member countries, other countries and organisations in the region and provide technical and management advisory services for sustainable coastal fisheries development and management in the Bay of Bengal region.

Article 4

FUNCTIONS

In order to facilitate the achievement of the foregoing objectives, the Organisation shall:

(a) *implement* programmes and activities which are of immediate requirement for the sustainable development and management of coastal fisheries;

(b) *consolidate* the establishment of an expanded network to share the responsibility of fisheries management, training and information exchange essential to coastal fisheries development in the region;

(c) *assist* the Members in increasing the livelihood opportunities and improving the quality of life of the small-scale fishers in the region;

(d) *increase* awareness and knowledge of the needs, benefits and practices of coastal fisheries management;

(e) *assist* the Members in harmonisation of policy and legal framework necessary for sustainable development and management of coastal fisheries resources of the region;

(f) *train* and upgrade core personnel needed for coastal fisheries planning, research, training, extension and development;

(g) *establish* a regional information system to provide appropriate information;

(h) *assist* the Members in strengthening their national capabilities in development and management of coastal fisheries;

(i) *transfer* to the Members appropriate technologies and techniques for development of small-scale fisheries;

(j) *promote* regional self-reliance in small-scale fisheries development through Technical Co-operation among Developing Countries (TCDC) and facilitate the exchange of national experts, technical know-how and information within the framework of TCDC;

(k) *develop* programmes for the promotion of women's participation in coastal fisheries development at all levels;

(l) *assist* the Members in feasibility studies and project formulation; and

(m) *undertake* such other activities related to the objectives of the Organisation as may be approved by the Governing Council.

Article 5

SEAT

1. The office of the Organisation shall be determined by the Governing Council, subject to the consent of the Members concerned.

2. The Host Government shall provide free of charge or at a nominal rent, such accommodation and facilities as are necessary for the efficient conduct of work at the seat of the Organisation.

3. If necessary, the Governing Council may establish subsidiary offices, subject to the consent of the Members concerned.

Article 6

MEMBERSHIP

1. The Members of the Organisation shall be the Contracting Parties to this Agreement.

2. The original Members of the Organisation shall be the Governments in the Bay of Bengal region invited to the meeting of Plenipotentiaries at which this Agreement was adopted, which have ratified the Agreement or have acceded thereto. A list of invited Governments is given in Annex to this Agreement.

3. The Governing Council of the Organisation may, by a majority of not less than two-thirds of the Members, authorise any Government not referred to in paragraph 2 above, which has submitted an application for membership, to accede to this Agreement as in force at the time of accession, in accordance with Article 16, paragraph 3.

Article 7

RIGHTS AND OBLIGATIONS OF MEMBERS

1. Members shall, in accordance with this Agreement, have the right:

(a) to attend the meetings of the Governing Council and other appropriate meetings that may be called by the Organisation;

(b) to obtain on request, free of charge within reasonable limits, information available within the Organisation, on matters of their concern, including guidelines for obtaining technical assistance, and collaboration in the study of their problems; and

(c) to receive free of charge publications and other information that may be distributed by the Organisation.

2. Members shall, in accordance with this Agreement, have the following obligations:

(a) to settle their financial obligations towards the Organisation;

(b) to collaborate in determining the technical activities of the Organisation;

(c) to provide, promptly, information reasonably requested by the Organisation, to the extent that this is not contrary to any laws or regulations of the Member;

(d) to undertake assignments that may be mutually agreed between individual Members or groups of Members and the Organisation;

(e) to accord to the Organisation and its Members, in so far as it may be possible under the constitutional procedures of the respective Members, facilities which are deemed essential for the successful functioning of the Organisation; and

(f) to collaborate, in general, in the fulfilment of the objectives and functions of the Organisation.

Article 8

THE GOVERNING COUNCIL

1. The Organisation shall have a Governing Council on which each Member shall be represented. The Governing Council shall be the supreme body of the Organisation.

2. The Governing Council shall hold an annual session at such time and place as it shall determine.

3. Special sessions of the Governing Council may be convened by the Director at the request of not less than two-thirds of the Members.

4. The Governing Council may, in its Rules of Procedure, establish a procedure whereby the Chairman of the Governing Council may obtain a vote of the Members on a specific question without convening a meeting of the Council.

5. The Governing Council shall elect a Chairman and a Vice-Chairman.

6. Each Member shall have one vote. Unless otherwise provided in this Agreement, decisions of the Governing Council shall be taken by a majority of the votes cast. A majority of the Members shall constitute a quorum.

7. The Food and Agriculture Organization of the United Nations (FAO) shall be invited to be represented at meetings of the Governing Council in an advisory capacity. Donor Governments may be represented at meetings of the Governing Council in accordance with an agreement concluded with the Organisation under Article 15 of this Agreement.

Article 9

FUNCTIONS OF THE GOVERNING COUNCIL

1. The functions of the Governing Council shall be:

(a) to determine the policy of the Organisation and to approve by a majority of not less than two-thirds of the Members its programme of work and its budget, giving due consideration to the conclusions and recommendations of the Technical Advisory Committee referred to in Article 11;

(b) to assess, by a majority of not less than two-thirds of the Members, the contribution of Members as provided in Article 13;

(c) to establish special funds to enable the acceptance of additional resources for the development of programmes and projects;

(d) to lay down general standards and guidelines for the management of the Organisation;

(e) to evaluate the progress of work/activities of the Organisation including the auditing of accounts, in accordance with policies and procedures established for the purpose by the Governing Council, and to give guidance to the Director on the implementation of its decision;

(f) to formulate and adopt the Financial Regulations and the Administrative Regulations, and to appoint auditors;

(g) to appoint the Director of the Organisation and to determine his conditions of service;

(h) to adopt rules governing the settlement of disputes, referred to in Article 19;

(i) to approve formal arrangements with governments, as well as other organisations or institutions, including any headquarters agreement concluded between the Organisation and the Host Government;

(j) to adopt the Staff Regulations which determine the general terms and conditions of employment of the staff;

(k) to approve agreements for co-operation to be concluded pursuant to Article 15; and

(l) to perform all other functions that have been entrusted to it by this Agreement or that are ancillary to the accomplishment of the approved activities of the Organisation.

(m) The Governing Council shall adopt its own Rules of Procedure.

Article 10

OBSERVERS

Non-member Governments, organisations and institutions that are able to make a significant contribution to the activities of the Organisation may, in accordance with the Rules of

Procedure adopted under Article 8, paragraph 2, be invited to be represented at sessions of the Governing Council as observers.

Article 11

TECHNICAL ADVISORY COMMITTEE

1. The Governing Council shall establish a Technical Advisory Committee composed of one representative designated by each Member of the Organisation.

2. The representatives designated on the Technical Advisory Committee shall be persons with special competence and expertise in the field of coastal fisheries.

3. The Technical Advisory Committee shall meet at least once a year and at any time at the request of the Governing Council.

4. At its annual meeting, the Committee shall designate one of the Committee members as Chairman who shall convene the next annual meeting of the Technical Advisory Committee.

5. The Technical Advisory Committee shall advise the Governing Council on all technical aspects of the activities of the Organisation.

6. At each session, the Technical Advisory Committee shall adopt a report, which shall be submitted to the Governing Council within seven days of such adoption.

7. FAO shall be invited to be represented at Meetings of the Technical Advisory Committee. Where appropriate, representatives of Donor Governments and of other organisations or institutions shall also be invited to be represented at such sessions.

Article 12

DIRECTOR AND STAFF

1. The Organisation shall have a Director appointed by the Governing Council. The Organisation shall also have staff members and consultants as per clause 5 of this Article.

2. The Director shall be the legal representative of the Organisation. He shall direct the work of the Organisation

under the guidance of the Governing Council in accordance with its policies and decisions.

3. The Director shall submit to the Governing Council at each regular session:

(a) a report on the work of the Organisation, as well as the audited accounts; and

(b) a draft programme of work and a draft budget for the following year.

4. The Director shall:

(a) prepare and organise the sessions of the Governing Council and all other meetings of the Organisation and shall provide the secretarial services thereof;

(b) ensure coordination among Members of the Organisation;

(c) organise conference symposia, regional training programmes and other meetings in accordance with the approved programme of work;

(d) initiate proposals for joint action programmes with regional and other international bodies;

(e) be responsible for the management of the Organisation;

(f) ensure the publication of research findings, training manuals, information printouts and other materials as required;

(g) take action on other matters consistent with the objectives of the Organisation; and

(h) perform any other function as may be specified by the Governing Council.

5. Staff members and consultants shall be appointed by the Director in accordance with the policy, general standards and guidelines laid down by the Governing Council and in accordance with the Staff Regulations. The Director shall promulgate Staff Rules, as required, to implement the foregoing.

Article 13

FINANCES

1. The financial resources of the Organisation shall be:

(a) the contributions of the Members to the budget of the Organisation;

(b) the revenue earned from the provision of services against payment;

(c) donations and voluntary contributions, provided that acceptance of such donations and voluntary contributions is compatible with the objectives of the Organisation; and

(d) such other resources as are approved by the Governing Council and compatible with the objectives of the Organisation.

2. Members undertake to pay annual contributions in freely convertible currencies to the regular budget of the Organisation.

3. A Member which is in arrears in the payment of its financial contributions to the Organisation shall have no vote in the Governing Council if the amount of its arrears equals or exceeds the amount of the contributions due from it for the two preceding calendar years.

The Governing Council may, nevertheless, permit such a Member to vote if it is satisfied that the failure to pay was due to conditions beyond the control of the Member.

4. Unless otherwise agreed by the consensus of the Members of the Organisation, each Member's financial liability to the Governing Council and to other Members for the acts of omission and commission of the Governing Council shall be limited to the extent of its obligation to make contributions to the budget of the Organisation.

Article 14

LEGAL STATUS, PRIVILEGES AND IMMUNITIES

1. The Organisation shall have juridical personality and such legal capacity as may be necessary for the fulfilment

of the Organisation's objectives and for the exercise of its functions.

2. The Organisation shall be accorded the privileges and immunities necessary to perform its functions provided for in this Agreement. In addition, the representatives of Members and the Director and staff of the Organisation shall be accorded the privileges and immunities necessary for the independent exercise of their functions with the Organisation as generally accorded to international organisations in each country.

3. Each Member shall accord the status, privileges and immunities referred to above by applying, *mutatis mutandis*, to the Organisation, the representatives of Members, and to the Director and staff of the Organisation the privileges and immunities provided for in the Convention on the Privileges and Immunities of the Specialised Agencies adopted by the General Assembly of the United Nations on 21 November 1947.

4. Privileges and immunities are accorded to the representatives of Members and to the Director and staff of the Organisation, not for the personal benefit of the individuals themselves, but in order to safeguard the independent exercise of their functions in connection with the Organisation. Consequently, a Member not only has the right but is under a duty to waive the immunity of its representatives in any case where, in the opinion of the Member, the immunity would impede the course of justice, and where it can be waived without prejudice to the purpose for which the immunity is accorded. If the Member does not waive the immunity of the representative, the Member shall make the strongest efforts to achieve an equitable solution of the matter. Similarly, the Director not only has the right but is under a duty to waive the immunity of a staff member where, in the opinion of the Director, the immunity would impede the course of justice, and where it can be waived without prejudice to the purpose for which the immunity is accorded. If the Director does not waive the immunity of the staff member, he shall make the strongest efforts to achieve an equitable solution of the matter.

The immunity of the Director may only be waived by the Governing Council.

5. The Organisation shall conclude a headquarters agreement with the Host Government, and may conclude agreements with other states in which offices of the Organisation may be located, specifying the privileges and immunities and facilities to be enjoyed by the Organisation to enable it to fulfil its objectives and to perform its functions.

Article 15

CO-OPERATION WITH DONOR GOVERNMENTS AND OTHER ORGANISATIONS AND INSTITUTIONS

1. The Contracting Parties agree that there should be a close working relationship between the Organisation and the Food and Agriculture Organization of the United Nations (FAO). To this end, the Organisation may enter into negotiations with FAO with a view to concluding an agreement. Such agreement may provide, *inter alia*, that the Director-General of FAO may appoint a Representative who shall be entitled to participate in all meetings of the Organisation in an advisory capacity, without the right to vote.

2. The Contracting Parties agree that there should be co-operation between the Organisation and Donor Governments whose contribution would further the activities of the Organisation. To this end, the Organisation may enter into agreements with such Donor Governments wherein provision may be made for their participation in certain activities of the Organisation.

3. The Contracting Parties agree that there should be co-operation between the Organisation and other international organisations and institutions, especially those active in the fisheries sector, which might contribute to the work and further the objectives of the Organisation. The Organisation may enter into agreements with such organisations and institutions. Such agreements may include, if appropriate, provisions for participation by such organisations and institutions in activities of the Organisation.

Article 16

SIGNATURE, RATIFICATION, ACCESSION, ENTRY INTO FORCE AND ADMISSION

1. This Agreement shall be open for signature by the Governments of the Bay of Bengal countries listed in the Annex hereto, until 30 April 2003 and thereafter at the Headquarters of the Food and Agriculture Organization of the United Nations (FAO) in Rome. Governments which have signed the Agreement may establish their consent to be bound thereto by depositing an instrument of ratification. Governments referred to in the Annex, which have not signed the Agreement, may establish their consent to be bound by depositing an instrument of accession.

2. Instruments of ratification or accession shall be lodged with the Depositary.

3. Subject to Article 6, paragraph 3 of this Agreement, and at any time after the entry into force thereof, any Government not referred to in paragraph 1 above wishing to become a member of the Organisation shall notify the Director in writing of its intention to do so. The Director shall inform Members of the receipt of that application. The Governing Council shall then decide on the application in accordance with Article 6 and if a favourable decision is taken, invite the Government concerned to accede to this Agreement. The Government shall lodge its instrument of accession, whereby it consents to be bound by the provisions of this Agreement as from the date of its admission, with the Director-General of FAO within ninety days of the date of the invitation by the Governing Council.

4. This Agreement shall enter into force, with respect to all governments, which have ratified it or acceded thereto, on the date when instruments of ratification or accession have been deposited by at least four Governments listed in the Annex.

Article 17

AMENDMENT

1. The Governing Council may amend this Agreement by a

three-quarters majority of the Members as of the date on which the amendment is adopted. Amendments shall take effect, with respect to all Contracting Parties, on the thirtieth day after their adoption by the Governing Council, except for any Contracting Party which gives notice of withdrawal within thirty days of receipt of notification of the adoption of such amendments, subject to the condition that any obligation incurred by the Member *vis-à-vis* the Organisation shall remain valid and enforceable. Amendments adopted shall be notified to the Depositary forthwith.

2. Proposals for the amendment of this Agreement may be made by a Member in a communication to the Director, who shall promptly notify the proposal to all Members.

3. No proposal for amendment shall be considered by the Governing Council unless it was received by the Director at least one hundred and twenty days before the opening day of the session at which it is to be considered, and circulated by the Director to the Members not later than ninety days before the opening day of that session.

Article 18

WITHDRAWAL AND DISSOLUTION

1. At any time after the expiration of three years from the date when it became a party to this Agreement, any Member may give notice of its withdrawal from the Organisation to the Depositary. Such withdrawal shall take effect twelve months after the notice thereof was received by the Depositary or at any later date specified in the notice, provided, however, that any obligation incurred by the Member *vis-à-vis* the Organisation shall remain valid and enforceable.

2. The Organisation shall cease to exist at any time decided by the Governing Council by a three-quarters majority of the Members. The disposal of any real property belonging to the Organisation shall be subject to the prior approval of the Governing Council. Any assets remaining after the land, buildings and fixtures have been disposed of, after the balance of any donated funds that have not been used has been

returned to the respective donors, and after all obligations have been met, shall be distributed among the Governments, which were Members of the Organisation at the time of the dissolution, in proportion to the contributions that they made, in accordance with Article 13, paragraph 2, for the year preceding the year of the dissolution.

3. Subject to the provisions of paragraph 2, the Organisation shall also cease to exist if the number of Members falls to three, unless the remaining Members unanimously decide to continue its existence.

Article 19

INTERPRETATION AND SETTLEMENT OF DISPUTES

1. Any dispute concerning the interpretation or application of this Agreement, which cannot be settled by negotiation, conciliation or similar means may be referred by any party to the dispute to the Governing Council for its recommendation. Failing settlement of the dispute, the matter shall be submitted to an arbitral tribunal consisting of three arbitrators. The parties to the dispute shall appoint one arbitrator each; the two arbitrators so appointed shall designate by mutual consent the third arbitrator, who shall be the President of the tribunal. If one of the Parties does not appoint an arbitrator within two months of the appointment of the first arbitrator, or if the President of the arbitral tribunal has not been designated within two months of the appointment of the second arbitrator, the Chairman of the Governing Council shall designate the arbitrator or the President, as the case may be, within a further two-month period.

2. The proceedings of the arbitral tribunal shall be carried out in accordance with the rules of the United Nations Commission on International Trade Law (UNCITRAL).

3. A Member, which fails to abide by an arbitral award rendered in accordance with paragraph 1 of this Article, may be suspended from the exercise of the rights and privileges of membership by a two-thirds majority of the Members.

Article 20

DEPOSITARY

1. The Director-General of FAO shall be the Depositary of this Agreement.

ANNEXURE B: BIMSTEC

What is BIMST-EC ?

The idea of this regional co-operation was first mooted by Bangladesh, India, Sri Lanka and Thailand at a meeting in Bangkok in June 1997. The aim, purpose and principles are contained in Bangkok Declaration of 6th June 1997 on the Establishment of the Bangladesh-India-Sri Lanka-Thailand Economic Co-operation (BIST-EC).

At the special Ministerial meeting convened in Bangkok on 22 December 1997, the Union of Myanmar was admitted to the group where it was decided to rename it as BIMST-EC (Bangladesh-India-Myanmar-Sri Lanka-Thailand-Economic Co-operation). This is known as Declaration of 22 December 1997.

At the Ministerial meeting in February 2004, Bhutan and Nepal were welcomed as new members.

The inter-regional grouping will serve as a bridge between the five SAARC countries and two ASEAN countries. BIMST-EC will have a greater potential to increase the trade among member countries by taking advantage of their geographical location in the region of the Bay of Bengal and the Eastern coast of the Indian Ocean. Discussions have already been held with regard to building a Trans Asia Highway linking the five countries and also setting up a BIMST-EC Airline connecting the capitals and important cities of the member countries.

At the first meeting of BIMST-EC Economic/Trade Ministers meeting termed as the Retreat held in Bangkok on 7 August 1998, it was decided that BIMST-EC would initially begin co-operation efforts in six areas. It was agreed that each country would play the lead role in planning and implementing programs in each of the areas. The sectors and lead countries at the inception were:

Trade & Investment—Bangladesh
Technology—India
Transportation & Communication—Thailand
Energy—Myanmar
Tourism—Sri Lanka
Fisheries—Sri Lanka

As the lead country status for each country was for a period of approximately 3 years, the lead countries have changed. Since 2002 the lead countries are:

Trade & Investment—Bangladesh
Technology—Sri Lanka
Transportation and Communication—India
Energy—Myanmar
Tourism—India
Fisheries—Thailand

Since some of the sectors are very broad, for greater efficiency in achieving the aims and objectives of BIMST-EC, the six sectors have been further divided into sub-sectors with each sub-sector having a chair country responsible for co-ordinating activities of that sub-sector, reporting to the lead country.

In March 1998, at a meeting organised by UN ESCAP in Bangkok the businessmen from the five BIMST-EC countries formed an expert group known as BIMST-EC Business Forum. The aims of this group are to enhance private sector co-operation among member countries in the BIMST-EC region, in the identified sectors and sub-sectors.

Recognizing the fact that sub-regional co-operation can progress only under the aegis of inter-governmental co-operation and co-ordination, and also recognizing the private sector as the engine of growth, for the purposes of enhancing interaction between government bodies and the private sector representatives of the five BIMST-EC countries, the BIMST-EC Economic Forum was conceptualized at a meeting in Dhaka in 1999. The BIMST-EC Economic Forum is a representative group of both the public and private sectors. Their role is to discuss matters pertaining to achieving the objectives of BIMST-EC and make recommendations to be taken up at the ministerial meetings each year.

First BIMSTEC Summit held in Bangkok, July 31, 2004

The First BIMSTEC Summit was held in Bangkok on July 31, 2004. To begin with, the leaders of Seven Asian countries agreed upon the rearranging the acronym BIMSTEC in view of the increasing membership and areas of cooperation, Thereby, the association will now be known as the "Bay of Bengal Initiative for Multi-Sectoral Technical and Economic Cooperation", or BIMSTEC for short.

The leaders adopted a Summit Declaration in which they urged further progress in ongoing areas of cooperation, including timely completion of the FTA negotiations, development of transportation infrastructure, interconnection of energy grids, enhancement of tourism and business travel, and people-to-people exchanges.

In this Retreat, they also paid special attention to poverty reduction and counter-terrorism.

They underscored the importance of empowerment, including through education and self-employment, rural development, access to credit, and making poor people bankable. Recognising the need to improve health-care and the involvement of the private sector, the leaders agreed that these experiences will be taken up at the Ministerial Meeting on Poverty Eradication to be hosted by Bangladesh.

The Meeting welcomed India's proposal to host a BIMSTEC Working Group meeting on Terrorism, which would involve senior officials with decision-making power. The Working Group would coordinate work in such areas as intelligence and capacity building.

Emphasising on the importance of protecting biodiversity and traditional knowledge, in particular traditional medicine. The leaders to set up a network of national centres of excellence to discuss ways to promote traditional medicine and generic drugs, so that the poor would have access to affordable treatment. The Meeting welcomed Thailand's offer to serve as lead country on this area of cooperation.

Bhutan's offer to host a Ministerial Meeting on culture was also welcomed. The Leaders also discussed practical ways to promote BIMSTEC as a single tourism destination. In this connection, India offered to host a Roundtable and Workshop of tourism ministers and industry representatives, so that they can work out concrete ideas to highlight the BIMSTEC area's historical and cultural attractions.

India also proposed to host a Ministerial Conference on Energy Cooperation in 2005, which was also welcomed by the other leaders at the summit. Thailand offered to extend a credit line on account trade for BIMSTEC members to buy agricultural products from Thailand. The size of the credit line would depend on each country's need.

The Leaders of the seven BIMSTEC concluded by agreeing to task their Foreign Ministers with the responsibility of coordinating overall BIMSTEC cooperation. The next BIMSTEC summit will be held in India in the year 2006.

(Source: Ministry of External Affairs, Thailand, Press Release)

ANNEXURE C: STOCKHOLM DECLARATION

The United Nations Conference on the Human Environment, having met at Stockholm from 5 to 16 June 1972, having considered the need for a common outlook and for common principles to inspire and guide the peoples of the world in the preservation and enhancement of the human environment,

Proclaims that:

1. Man is both creature and moulder of his environment, which gives him physical sustenance and affords him the opportunity for intellectual, moral, social and spiritual growth. In the long and tortuous evolution of the human race on this planet a stage has been reached when, through the rapid acceleration of science and technology, man has acquired the power to transform his environment in countless ways and on an unprecedented scale. Both aspects of man's environment, the natural and the man-made, are essential to his well-being

and to the enjoyment of basic human rights the right to life itself.

2. The protection and improvement of the human environment is a major issue which affects the well-being of peoples and economic development throughout the world; it is the urgent desire of the peoples of the whole world and the duty of all Governments.

3. Man has constantly to sum up experience and go on discovering, inventing, creating and advancing. In our time, man's capability to transform his surroundings, if used wisely, can bring to all peoples the benefits of development and the opportunity to enhance the quality of life. Wrongly or heedlessly applied, the same power can do incalculable harm to human beings and the human environment. We see around us growing evidence of man-made harm in many regions of the earth: dangerous levels of pollution in water, air, earth and living beings; major and undesirable disturbances to the ecological balance of the biosphere; destruction and depletion of irreplaceable resources; and gross deficiencies, harmful to the physical, mental and social health of man, in the man-made environment, particularly in the living and working environment.

4. In the developing countries most of the environmental problems are caused by under-development. Millions continue to live far below the minimum levels required for a decent human existence, deprived of adequate food and clothing, shelter and education, health and sanitation. Therefore, the developing countries must direct their efforts to development, bearing in mind their priorities and the need to safeguard and improve the environment. For the same purpose, the industrialized countries should make efforts to reduce the gap themselves and the developing countries. In the industrialized countries, environmental problems are generally related to industrialization and technological development.

5. The natural growth of population continuously presents problems for the preservation of the environment, and adequate policies and measures should be adopted, as appropriate, to

face these problems. Of all things in the world, people are the most precious. It is the people that propel social progress, create social wealth, develop science and technology and, through their hard work, continuously transform the human environment. Along with social progress and the advance of production, science and technology, the capability of man to improve the environment increases with each passing day.

6. A point has been reached in history when we must shape our actions throughout the world with a more prudent care for their environmental consequences. Through ignorance or indifference we can do massive and irreversible harm to the earthly environment on which our life and well-being depend. Conversely, through fuller knowledge and wiser action, we can achieve for ourselves and our posterity a better life in an environment more in keeping with human needs and hopes. There are broad vistas for the enhancement of environmental quality and the creation of a good life. What is needed is an enthusiastic but calm state of mind and intense but orderly work. For the purpose of attaining freedom in the world of nature, man must use knowledge to build, in collaboration with nature, a better environment. To defend and improve the human environment for present and future generations has become an imperative goal for mankind—a goal to be pursued together with, and in harmony with, the established and fundamental goals of peace and of worldwide economic and social development.

7. To achieve this environmental goal will demand the acceptance of responsibility by citizens and communities and by enterprises and institutions at every level, all sharing equitably in common efforts. Individuals in all walks of life as well as organizations in many fields, by their values and the sum of their actions, will shape the world environment of the future.

Local and national governments will bear the greatest burden for large-scale environmental policy and action within their jurisdictions. International cooperation is also needed in order to raise resources to support the developing countries in carrying out their responsibilities in this field. A growing class of environmental problems, because they are regional or global in extent or because they affect the common international realm, will require extensive cooperation among nations and action by international organizations in the common interest.

The Conference calls upon Governments and peoples to exert common efforts for the preservation and improvement of the human environment, for the benefit of all the people and for their posterity.

PRINCIPLES

States the common conviction that:

Principle 1

Man has the fundamental right to freedom, equality and adequate conditions of life, in an environment of a quality that permits a life of dignity and well-being, and he bears a solemn responsibility to protect and improve the environment for present and future generations. In this respect, policies promoting or perpetuating apartheid, racial segregation, discrimination, colonial and other forms of oppression and foreign domination stand condemned and must be eliminated.

Principle 2

The natural resources of the earth, including the air, water, land, flora and fauna and especially representative samples of natural ecosystems, must be safeguarded for the benefit of present and future generations through careful planning or management, as appropriate.

Principle 3

The capacity of the earth to produce vital renewable resources must be maintained and, wherever practicable, restored or improved.

Principle 4

Man has a special responsibility to safeguard and wisely manage the heritage of wildlife and its habitat, which are now gravely imperilled by a combination of adverse factors. Nature conservation, including wild-life, must therefore receive importance in planning for economic development.

Principle 5

The non-renewable resources of the earth must be employed in such a way as to guard against the danger of their future exhaustion and to ensure that benefits from such employment are shared by all mankind.

Principle 6

The discharge of toxic substances or of other substances and the release of heat, in such quantities or concentrations as to exceed the capacity of the environment to render them harmless, must be halted in order to ensure that serious or irreversible damage is not inflicted upon ecosystems. The just struggle of the peoples of ill countries against pollution should be supported.

Principle 7

States shall take all possible steps to prevent pollution of the seas by substances that are liable to create hazards to human health, to harm living resources and marine life, to damage amenities or to interfere with other legitimate uses of the sea.

Principle 8

Economic and social development is essential for ensuring a favourable living and working environment for man and for creating conditions on earth that are necessary for the improvement of the quality of life.

Principle 9

Environmental deficiencies generated by the conditions of under-development and natural disasters pose grave problems and can best be remedied by accelerated development through the transfer of substantial quantities of financial and technological assistance as a supplement to the domestic effort of the developing countries and such timely assistance as may be required.

Principle 10

For the developing countries, stability of prices and adequate earnings for primary commodities and raw materials are essential to environmental management, since economic factors as well as ecological processes must be taken into account.

Principle 11

The environmental policies of all States should enhance and not adversely affect the present or future development potential of developing countries, nor should they hamper the attainment of better living conditions for all, and appropriate steps should be taken by States and international organizations with a view to reaching agreement on meeting the possible national and international economic consequences resulting from the application of environmental measures.

Principle 12

Resources should be made available to preserve and improve the environment, taking into account the circumstances and particular requirements of developing countries and any costs which may emanate from their incorporating environmental safeguards into their development planning and the need for making available to them, upon their request, additional international technical and financial assistance for this purpose.

Principle 13

In order to achieve a more rational management of resources and thus to improve the environment, States should adopt an integrated and coordinated approach to their development planning so as to ensure that development is compatible with the need to protect and improve environment for the benefit of their population.

Principle 14

Rational planning constitutes an essential tool for reconciling any conflict between the needs of development and the need to protect and improve the environment.

Principle 15

Planning must be applied to human settlements and urbanization with a view to avoiding adverse effects on the environment and obtaining maximum social, economic and environmental benefits for all. In this respect projects which are designed for colonialist and racist domination must be abandoned.

Principle 16

Demographic policies which are without prejudice to basic human rights and which are deemed appropriate by Governments concerned should be applied in those regions where the rate of population growth or excessive population concentrations are likely to have adverse effects on the environment of the human environment and impede development.

Principle 17

Appropriate national institutions must be entrusted with the task of planning, managing or controlling the 9 environmental resources of States with a view to enhancing environmental quality.

Principle 18

Science and technology, as part of their contribution to economic and social development, must be applied to the identification, avoidance and control of environmental risks and the solution of environmental problems and for the common good of mankind.

Principle 19

Education in environmental matters, for the younger generation as well as adults, giving due consideration to the underprivileged, is essential in order to broaden the basis for an enlightened opinion and responsible conduct by individuals, enterprises and communities in protecting and improving the environment in its full human dimension. It is also essential that mass media of communications avoid contributing to the deterioration of the environment, but, on the contrary, disseminates information of an educational nature on the need to project and improve the environment in order to enable man to develop in every respect.

Principle 20

Scientific research and development in the context of environmental problems, both national and multinational, must be promoted in all countries, especially the developing countries. In this connection, the free flow of up-to-date scientific information and transfer of experience must be supported and assisted, to facilitate the solution of environmental problems; environmental technologies should be made available to developing countries on terms which would encourage their wide dissemination without constituting an economic burden on the developing countries.

Principle 21

States have, in accordance with the Charter of the United Nations and the principles of international law, the sovereign right to exploit their own resources pursuant to their own environmental policies, and the responsibility to ensure that activities within their jurisdiction or control do not cause damage to the environment of other States or of areas beyond the limits of national jurisdiction.

Principle 22

States shall cooperate to develop further the international law regarding liability and compensation for the victims of pollution and other environmental damage caused by activities within the jurisdiction or control of such States to areas beyond their jurisdiction.

Principle 23

Without prejudice to such criteria as may be agreed upon by the international community, or to standards which will have to be determined nationally, it will be essential in all cases to consider the systems of values prevailing in each country, and the extent of the applicability of standards which are valid for the most advanced countries but which may be inappropriate and of unwarranted social cost for the developing countries.

Principle 24

International matters concerning the protection and improvement of the environment should be handled in a cooperative spirit by all countries, big and small, on an equal footing.

Cooperation through multilateral or bilateral arrangements or other appropriate means is essential to effectively control, prevent, reduce and eliminate adverse environmental effects resulting from activities conducted in all spheres, in such a way that due account is taken of the sovereignty and interests of all States.

Principle 25

States shall ensure that international organizations play a coordinated, efficient and dynamic role for the protection and improvement of the environment.

Principle 26

Man and his environment must be spared the effects of nuclear weapons and all other means of mass destruction. States must strive to reach prompt agreement, in the relevant international organs, on the elimination and complete destruction of such weapons.

ANNEXURE D: RIO DECLARATION

REPORT OF THE UNITED NATIONS CONFERENCE ON ENVIRONMENT AND DEVELOPMENT

(Rio de Janeiro, 3-14 June 1992)

RIO DECLARATION ON ENVIRONMENT AND DEVELOPMENT

The United Nations Conference on Environment and Development,

Having met at Rio de Janeiro from 3 to 14 June 1992,

Reaffirming the Declaration of the United Nations Conference on the Human Environment, adopted at Stockholm on 16 June 1972, and seeking to build upon it,

With the goal of establishing a new and equitable global partnership through the creation of new levels of cooperation among States, key sectors of societies and people,

Working towards international agreements which respect the interests of all and protect the integrity of the global environmental and developmental system,

Recognizing the integral and interdependent nature of the Earth, our home,

Proclaims that:

Principle 1

Human beings are at the centre of concerns for sustainable development. They are entitled to a healthy and productive life in harmony with nature.

Principle 2

States have, in accordance with the Charter of the United Nations and the principles of international law, the sovereign right to exploit their own resources pursuant to their own environmental and developmental policies, and the responsibility to ensure that activities within their jurisdiction or control do not cause damage to the environment of other States or of areas beyond the limits of national jurisdiction.

Principle 3

The right to development must be fulfilled so as to equitably meet developmental and environmental needs of present and future generations.

Principle 4

In order to achieve sustainable development, environmental protection shall constitute an integral part of the development process and cannot be considered in isolation from it.

Principle 5

All States and all people shall cooperate in the essential task of eradicating poverty as an indispensable requirement for sustainable development, in order to decrease the disparities in standards of living and better meet the needs of the majority of the people of the world.

Principle 6

The special situation and needs of developing countries, particularly the least developed and those most environmentally vulnerable, shall be given special priority. International actions in the field of environment and development should also address the interests and needs of all countries.

Principle 7

States shall cooperate in a spirit of global partnership to conserve, protect and restore the health and integrity of the Earth's ecosystem. In view of the different contributions to global environmental degradation, States have common but differentiated responsibilities. The developed countries acknowledge the responsibility that they bear in the international pursuit of sustainable development in view of the pressures their societies place on the global environment and of the technologies and financial resources they command.

Principle 8

To achieve sustainable development and a higher quality of life for all people, States should reduce and eliminate unsustainable patterns of production and consumption and promote appropriate demographic policies.

Principle 9

States should cooperate to strengthen endogenous capacity-building for sustainable development by improving scientific understanding through exchanges of scientific and technological knowledge, and by enhancing the development, adaptation, diffusion and transfer of technologies, including new and innovative technologies.

Principle 10

Environmental issues are best handled with the participation of all concerned citizens, at the relevant level. At the national level, each individual shall have appropriate access to information concerning the environment that is held by public authorities, including information on hazardous materials and activities in their communities, and the opportunity to participate in decision-making processes. States shall facilitate and encourage public awareness and participation by making information widely available. Effective access to judicial and administrative proceedings, including redress and remedy, shall be provided.

Principle 11

States shall enact effective environmental legislation.

Environmental standards, management objectives and priorities should reflect the environmental and developmental context to which they apply. Standards applied by some countries may be inappropriate and of unwarranted economic and social cost to other countries, in particular developing countries.

Principle 12

States should cooperate to promote a supportive and open international economic system that would lead to economic growth and sustainable development in all countries, to better address the problems of environmental degradation. Trade policy measures for environmental purposes should not constitute a means of arbitrary or unjustifiable discrimination or a disguised restriction on international trade. Unilateral actions to deal with environmental challenges outside the jurisdiction of the importing country should be avoided. Environmental measures addressing transboundary or global environmental problems should, as far as possible, be based on an international consensus.

Principle 13

States shall develop national law regarding liability and compensation for the victims of pollution and other environmental damage. States shall also cooperate in an expeditious and more determined manner to develop further international law regarding liability and compensation for adverse effects of environmental damage caused by activities within their jurisdiction or control to areas beyond their jurisdiction.

Principle 14

States should effectively cooperate to discourage or prevent the relocation and transfer to other States of any activities and substances that cause severe environmental degradation or are found to be harmful to human health.

Principle 15

In order to protect the environment, the precautionary approach shall be widely applied by States according to their capabilities. Where there are threats of serious or irreversible damage, lack of full scientific certainty shall not be used as a reason for postponing cost-effective measures to prevent environmental degradation.

Principle 16

National authorities should endeavour to promote the internalization of environmental costs and the use of economic instruments, taking into account the approach that the polluter should, in principle, bear the cost of pollution, with due regard to the public interest and without distorting international trade and investment.

Principle 17

Environmental impact assessment, as a national instrument, shall be undertaken for proposed activities that are likely to have a significant adverse impact on the environment and are subject to a decision of a competent national authority.

Principle 18

States shall immediately notify other States of any natural disasters or other emergencies that are likely to produce sudden harmful effects on the environment of those States. Every effort shall be made by the international community to help States so afflicted.

Principle 19

States shall provide prior and timely notification and relevant information to potentially affected States on activities that may have a significant adverse transboundary environmental effect and shall consult with those States at an early stage and in good faith.

Principle 20

Women have a vital role in environmental management and development. Their full participation is therefore essential to achieve sustainable development.

Principle 21

The creativity, ideals and courage of the youth of the world should be mobilized to forge a global partnership in order to achieve sustainable development and ensure a better future for all.

Principle 22

Indigenous people and their communities and other local communities have a vital role in environmental management and development because of their knowledge and traditional practices. States should recognize and duly support their identity, culture and interests and enable their effective participation in the achievement of sustainable development.

Principle 23

The environment and natural resources of people under oppression, domination and occupation shall be protected.

Principle 24

Warfare is inherently destructive of sustainable development. States shall therefore respect international law providing protection for the environment in times of armed conflict and cooperate in its further development, as necessary.

Principle 25

Peace, development and environmental protection are interdependent and indivisible.

Principle 26

States shall resolve all their environmental disputes peacefully and by appropriate means in accordance with the Charter of the United Nations.

Principle 27

States and people shall cooperate in good faith and in a spirit of partnership in the fulfilment of the principles embodied in this Declaration and in the further development of international law in the field of sustainable development.

ANNEXURE E: SOUTH ASIA MAP FOR THE BAY OF BENGAL

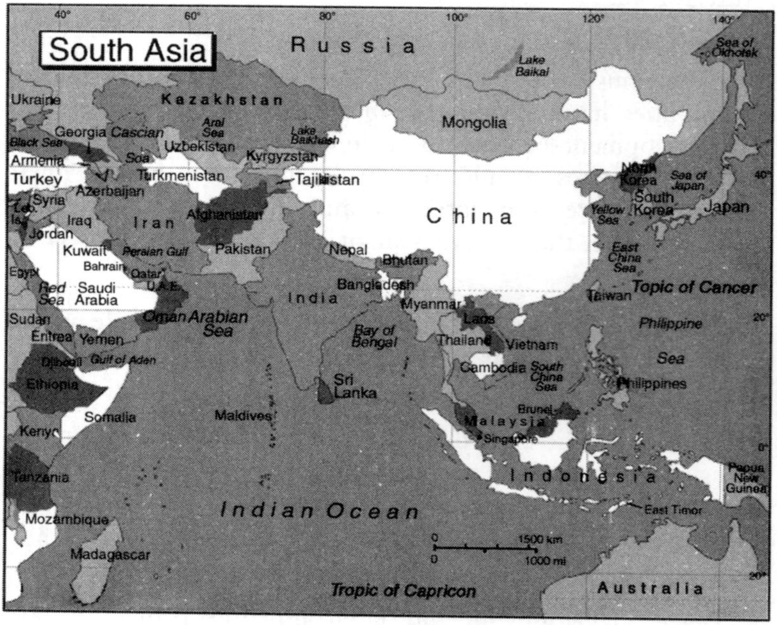

BIBLIOGRAPHY

I. BOOKS AND JOURNALS

Adede, A.O., "Settlement of Disputes Arising Under the Law of the Sea Convention", 69(1975) *AJIL*.

——., "Prolegomena to the Disputes Settlement Part of the Law of the Sea Convention", 10(1977) *New York University Journal of International Law and Politics*.

Alexander, L.M., "Regional Arrangements in the Oceans", 71(1977) *AJIL*.

——., "New Trends in Marine Regionalism", 11(1994) *Ocean Yearbook*.

Anand, R.P., *Law of the Sea Caracas and Beyond*, 1978.

Barcena, A., "Some Reflections on a New Approach to Ocean and Coastal Management", *The Marine Environment and Sustainable Development: Law, Policy, and Science*, 1993.

Belsky, M.H., "Management of Large Marine Ecosystems: Developing A New Rule of Customary International Law", 22(1985) 4 *San Diego Law Review*.

Bennet, A.L., *International Organizations*, 1991.

Beyerlin, U., "New Developments in Protection of the Marine Environment: Potential Effects of the Rio Process", 55(1995) Zettschrift fur auslandisches offentliches Recht und Volkerrecht.

Birnie, P.W. & Boyle, A.E., *International Law and Environment*, 1992.

Blay & others (eds), *Public International Law: An Australian Perspective*, 1997.

Boczeck, B.A., "Global and Regional Approaches to the Protection and Preservation of the Marine Environment",

16(1984) *Case Western Reserve Journal of International Law*.

Boyle, A.E., "State Responsibility and International Liability for Injurious Consequences of Acts Not Prohibited by International Law: A Necessary Distinction." 39(1982) ICLQ.

——., "UNCLOS, the Marine Environment and Settlement of Disputes", in Ringborm (ed) *Competing Norms*, 2000.

Borgese & Saigal, "Managerial Implications of Sustainable Development in the Ocean", *Ocean Yearbook* 12(1996).

Bragdon, S.H., "National Sovereignty and Global Environmental Responsibility: Can the Tension Be Reconciled for the Conservation of Biological Diversity", 33(1992) 2 *Harvard International Law Journal*.

Broadus, J.M. & others, *Comparative Assessment of Regional International Programs to Control Land-Based Marine Pollution: The Baltic, North Sea, and Mediterranean*, 1993.

Brown, E.D., *The Legal Regime of Hydrospace*, 1972.

——., *Seabed Energy and Minerals: The International Legal Regime*, 2001.

Brubaker, D., *Marine Pollution and International Law: Principle and Practice*, 1993.

Burenne & Robinson (eds), *International Protection of the Marine Environment: Conservation in Sustainable Development*, Vol. 3, 1997.

Chaturvedi, A., *South Asian States and the Sea Laws*, 1987.

Cotter, C.H., *The Physical Geography of the Ocean*, 1965.

Couper, A. & Gold, E. (eds), *The Marine Environment and Sustainable Development: Law, Policy and Science*, 1993.

Crawford, J., "Universalism and Regionalism from the Perspective of the Work of the International Law Commission", in *International Law on the Eve of the Twenty First Century: Views from the International Law Commission*, 1997.

Deshpande, V.S., "Indian Ocean as a Peace of Zone—Evolving the Legal Process", 14(1974) *IJIL*.

Dickstein, H.L., "Evolving Concepts International Law and the Environment", 26(1972) *The Yearbook of World Affairs*, 1972.

Dickstein, H.L., "*International Law and Environment*: *Evolving Concepts*", 26(1972).

Djalal, H., "Managing Potential Conflicts in the South China Sea", 10(1992) International Challenge.

Dunoff, J.L., "Institutional Misfits: The GATT. The ICJ & Trade Environment Disputes", 15(1994) *Michigan Journal of International*.

Dupuy & others (eds), *A Handbook on the Law of the Sea*, 1991.

Eckhardt, B., "How we got the dirtiest Stream in America Regulation of Local Hazards—The Houston Ship Channel", 7(1971) *Texas Journal of International Law*.

Evense, J., "Management of the Seas: Legal Issues with Special Emphasis on Pollution in Verwey" (ed), *Nature Management and Sustainable Development*, 1989.

Fleischer, C.A., "An International Convention on Environment Cooperation Among Nations: Proposed Draft, Policies and Goals", 7(1971) *Texas International Law Journal*.

Freestone & Hey (eds), *The Precautionary Principle and International Law*: *The Challenge of Implementation*, 1996.

Gaines, S.F., "The Emergence of International Environmental Law", 44(1991) *Hastings International Law & Comparative Law Review*.

Gar-Amador, F.C., "Latin America and the Law of the Sea" in L.M. Alexander (ed), The Law of the Sea: A New Geneva Conference, Proceedings of the 6th Annual Conference of the Law of the Sea Institute, 1972.

Gardiner, R.K., *International Law*, 2003.

Gill, T.L., "Marine Pollution and International Law", in Anand (ed), Law of the Sea Caracas and Beyond, 1978.

Gomez, E.D., "Whither the East Asian Seas", 21(1990) *Marine Pollution.*

Hahn & Richadrs, "The Internationalization of Environmental Regulation", 30(1989) *Harvard International Law Journal.*

Handle, G., "National Uses of Transboundary Air Resources: The International Entitlement Issue Reconsidered", 26(1986) *NAT'L RES. J.*

Hunter D. & others, *International Environmental Law and Policy*, 1998.

Johnson, S.P., *The Earth Summit: The United Nations Conference on Environment and Development (UNCED)*, 1993.

Johnston & Valencia, *Pacific Ocean Boundary Problems: Status and Solutions*, 1991.

Joyner, C.C., "Protection of the Antarctic Environment against marine pollution under the 1991 Protocol" in Vidas (ed), *Protecting the Polar Marine Environment Law and Policy for Pollution Prevention,* 2000.

Khan, R., "Marine Pollution and International Legal Controls", 13(1973) *IJIL.*

Kimball, L.A., "Regional Marine Resources Development: Growth by Necessity", 39(1982) *Ocean Yearbook.*

——., "*International Law and Institutions: The Oceans and Beyond*", 20(1989) *Ocean Development and International Law.*

Kiss & Shelton, *International Environmental Law*, 1991.

Knox, J.H., "The Myth and Reality of Transboundary Environmental Impact", 96(2002) *AJIL.*

Kwiatkowska, B., "The Role of Regional Organizations in Development Cooperation in Marine."

——., "Institutional Marine Affairs Cooperation in Developing State Regions, Part I: General Problems and Prospects" 14(1990) *Marine Policy.*

——., "Environmental Prospects for the East and South Asian Seas" in Cooper & others (eds), *The Marine Environment and Sustainable Development: Law, Policy, and Science*, 1993.

Lali, K.B., "Economic Inequality and International Law", 14(1974) *IJIL*.

Levy, J.P. & others, *United Nations Conference on Straddling Fish Stocks and Highly Migratory Fish Stocks*, 1996.

Mahmoudi, S., *The Law of the Deep Sea-Bed Mining*, 1987.

Malviya, R.A., *Environmental Pollution and Its Control under International Law*, 1987.

Mangone, G.J., *Law for the World Ocean*, 1981.

Markussen, J.M., "Deep Seabed Mining and the Environment: Consequences, Perceptions, and Regulations", *Green Globe Yearbook*, 1994.

Mathews, J.T., (ed), *Preserving the Global Environment*, 1991.

Maxwell, A.E., *The Sea*, 1970.

Menshah, T.A., "The International Legal Regime for the Protection and Preservation of the Marine Environment from Land-Based Sources of Pollution" in Boyle & Freeston (eds), *International Law and Sustainable Development*.

Molke, K., *The Vorsorgeprinzip in West German Environmental Policy*, 1987.

Nanda, V.P., "Trends in International Environmental Law", 20 Cal. W.Int'L.J.

——., "Global Warming and International Environmental Law—A Preliminary Inquiry", 30(1989) *Harvard International Law Journal*.

Nimby, "Not in Mexico's Back Yard? A Case for Recognition of a Human Right to Healthy Environment in the American States", 23(1993) *Georgia Journal of International and Comparative Law*.

Okididi, *Regional Control of Ocean Pollution: Legal and Institutional Problems and Prospects*, 1978.

Oliver, C.T. & others, *The International Legal System: Cases and Materials*, 1995.

Osman, M.A., *Africa Beyond Crisis: A Mozambican Viewpoint*, ACP-EC 124 (1990) *The Courier*.

Pharand, D., "Oil Pollution Control in the Canadian Arctic", 1971, *Texas International Law Journal*.

Palmer, G., "New Ways to make International Environmental Law", 86(1992) AJIL.

Rao, S., "Marine Sciences of the Seas around India between 1974 and 2000 and Prospects for the New Millenium" in Borgese & others (eds), 16 (2002) *Ocean*.

Richardson, M., "West to Press ASEAN on Burma Rights", *International Herald Tribune of 22 July 1991*.

——., "ASEAN Will Send an Envoy to Press Burma on Rights," *International Herald Tribune of 24 July 1991*.

Ringbon, H. (ed), *Competing Norm in the Law of Marine Environmental Protection—Focus on Ship Safety and Pollution Prevention*, 1997.

Robinson, N.A. (ed), "Introduction: Ensuring Environmental, Protection Globally", 1(1994) Environmental Law Treaties.

Rozakis & others, "The Settlement of Disputes Relating to Activities in the International Seabed Area" in *The New Law of the Sea*, 1983.

Saigal, K., "*Sustainable Management of Ecosystems*", 13(1998) *Ocean Yearbook*.

Sand, P., *Lessons Learned in Global Environment Governance*, 1990.

Sand, P.H., *Marine Environment Law in the United Nations Environment Program*, 1988.

Sands, P., *Principles of International Environmental Law*, 1995.

Sanfor, E.G., "Taking Responsibility for Transboundary Environmental Effects, 14(1991) *Hastings International and Comparative Law Review*.

Sanwal, M., "Sustainable Development, the Rio Declaration and Multilateral Cooperation", 4(1993) 1 *Colorado Journal of International and Environmental Law and Policy.*

Savini, M., *Summary Information on the Role of International Fishery Bodies with Regard to the Conservation and Management of Living Resources of the High Seas*, 1991.

Schachter, O., "The Emergence of International Environmental Law", 44(1991) J INT'L AFF.

Sohn, L.B., "The Stockholm Declaration on the Human Environment", 14(1973) Harvard. INTL'.L.

Starik & Rands, "Weaving an Integrated Web: Multilevel and Multisystem Perspective of Ecologically Sustainable Organizations", 20(1995) 4 *Academy of Management Review.*

Stopford, M., "Locating the Balance: The United Nations and the New World Disorder", 34(1994) *Virginia Journal of International Law.*

Swan, "International and National Approaches to Oil Pollution Responsibility", *Oregon Law Review* 506, 545.

Szekely, *Latin America and the Development of the Law of the Sea*, 2 vols, 1976.

T.B. Koh, T., "A Constitution for the Oceans" in the *United Nations Convention on the Law of the Sea with Index and Final Act of the Third United Nations Conference on the Law of the Sea*, 1983.

Timagenis, G.J., *International Control of Marine Pollution*, 1980.

Vallega, A., "The Regional Scale of Ocean Management and Marine Regional Building", 24(1994) 11(1994) *Ocean and Coastal Management.*

Vanderzwaag, D., "Land-based marine pollution and the Arctic: polarities between principles and practice" in Davor Vidas (ed), *Protecting the Polar Marine Environment Law and Policy for Pollution Prevention*, 2000.

Vicuna (ed), *The Exclusive Economic Zone: A Latin America Perspective*, 1984.

Vida, D. (ed), *Protecting the Polar Marine Environment Law and Policy for Pollution*, 2001.

Vidas (ed), *Protecting the Polar Environment*, 2000.

Vidas, D., "The Polar Marine Environment in Regional Cooperation", in Davor Vidas (ed), Protecting the polar Marine Environment, 2000.

Vukus, "United Nations Convention on the Law of the Sea and Polar Marine Environment" in Wells, (ed), Law, Values, and the Environment, 1996.

Weiss, E.B., *In Fairness to Future Generations International Law, Common Patrimony, and Intergenerational Equity, Innovation in International Law Series*, 1989.

—— "Our Rights and Obligations to Future Generations for the Environment in Agora: What Obligation Does Our Generation Owe to the Next? An Approach to Global Environmental Responsibility", 84(1990) *AJIL* in Soons (ed), *Implementation of the Law of the Sea Convention through International Institutions*, 1990.

Williams & Mestral, *An Introduction to International Law*, 1987.

White, R.R., *North, South and the Environmental Crisis*, 1993.

Yankov, A., "The Law of the Sea Convention and Agenda 21: Marine Environmental Implications" in A.E. Boyle and D. Freeston (eds), *International Law and Sustainable Development: Past Achievements and Future Challenges*, 1999.

Zwaag, D. and Johnston, D.M., "Towards the Management of the Gulf of Thailand: Charting the Course of Cooperation", 1(1998) SEAPOL Integrated Studies of the Gulf of Thailand.

Zwaag, V., *Canada and Marine Environmental Protection: Charting a Legal Course Towards Sustainable Development*, 1995.

Weide, J., "A System of View of Integrated Coastal Management", 21(1993) Ocean and Coastal Management.

Weston, Falk & others, *International Law and World Order: A Problem-Oriented Coursebook*, 1997.

Weiss, McCaff & others, *International Environmental Law and Policy*, 1998.

Wirth, D., "Rio Declaration on Environment and Development: Two Steps Forward and One Back, Vice Versa?", 29(1995) GA.L.REV.

Wolfrum, R., "Purposes and Principles of International Environmental Law," 1990 GER.Y.B.INT'L.

White, R.R., *North, South and the Environmental Crisis*, 1993.

Zwaag, V., *Canada and Marine Environmental Protection: Charting a Legal Course Towards Sustainable Development*, 1995.

II. INTERNATIONAL INSTRUMENTS AND DECLARATIONS

A. Treaties, Ageements, Convention and Declaration

Abidjan Convention for Cooperation in the Protection and Development of the Marine and Coastal Environment of the West and Central African Region and Protocol, 1981, 20(1981) ILM 746, 756.

AGENDA 21

Agreement Relating to the Implementation of Part XI of the United Nations Convention on the Law of the Sea of 10 December 1982 (1994), 33 (1994) ILM 1309.

Antarctic Treaty, 1959, 402 UNTS 71.

Barcelona Convention for the Protection of the Mediterranean Sea Against Pollution, 1976 and its Protocols of 1976 and 1980, 15 (1976) ILM, 290, 300, 306 and 19(1980) ILM 869.

Beijing Declaration on Environment and Development, 1991, Xinhua, Gen. Overseas News Service, 20 June 1991, item no. 0620135 (Lexis Database, Nexis Library).

Bucharest Convention on the Protection of the Black Sea Marine Environment Against Pollution from Land-Based Sources, on Cooperation in Combating Pollution of the Black Sea Environment by Oil and Other Harmful Substances in Emergency Situations and on the Protection of the Black Sea Marine Environment Against Pollution By Dumping, 1992, 32(1993) ILM 1110, 1122, 1127 and 1129.

Cartenga Convention for the Protection and Development of Marine Environment of the Wider Caribbean Region and Its Protocols, 1983, 22(1983) ILM 227, 240 Protocol, 1974, [13(1974) ILM 352, 27(1988) ILM 525].

Charter of the South Asian Association for Regional Cooperation (SAARC).

Charter of the United Nations.

Convention for Civil Liability for Oil Pollution Damage, 1969, 9(1970) ILM 45.

Convention on the Territorial Sea and the Contiguous Zone, 1958, 516 UNTS 205.

Convention on the Continental Shelf, 1958, 499 UNTS 285.

Convention on Fishing and Conservation of the Living Resources of the High Seas, 1958, 59 UNTS 285.

Convention on Biological Diversity, 1992, 31(1992) ILM 822.

Convention on the Prevention of Marine Pollution by Dumping of Wastes and Other Matter, 1972, 26 USTS 2403.

Convention Relating to Intervention on the High Seas in Cases of Oil Pollution Casualties, 1969, 9(1970) ILM 25.

Convention on the High Seas, 1958, UN.Doc.A/CONF.13/ L.53 and Corr. 1.

Convention for the Regulation of Whaling, 1931, 155 LNTS 351.

Convention on the Protection of Birds Useful to Agriculture, 1902.

Convention for Preservation of the Fur Seal, 1911.

Economic Declaration from the Paris Summit, 1989. 28(1989) 1202.

Economic and Social Council, UN.Doc.E/CN.17/1997/8 of 10 February 1997.

Helsinki Convention on the Protection for the Prevention of the Marine Environment of the Baltic Area, 1974, 13(1974) ILM 546.

International Convention for the Prevention of Pollution of the Sea by (OILPOL), 1954, 12 USTS 2989.

International Convention for the Prevention of Pollution from Ships (MARPOL), 1973, 12 (1973) ILM1319.

International Convention on Oil Pollution Readiness, Response and Cooperation, 1990, 30(1991) ILM 735.

International Convention for Establishment of a Fund for Compensation for Oil Pollution Damage, 1971, 11(1972) ILM 284; Protocol, 1976, 16(1984) ILM 621; Protocol, 23(1984) ILM 195, and Protocol, 1992, IMO Doc. LEG/CONF.9/16(1962).

Inter-Governmental Organisation for the Bay of Bengal Programme on Coastal Fisheries (BOBP-IGO).

Kuwait Regional Convention for Cooperation on the Protection of the Marine Environment from Pollution and Protocol, 1978, 17(1978) ILM 511, 526.

London Convention on Civil Liability for Oil Pollution Damage Resulting from Exploration and Exploitation of Seabed Mineral Resources, 1976, 16(1977) ILM 1450.

Montevideo Convention of Rights and Duties of States, 1933, 165 LNTS 19.

Noumea Convention for the Protection of the National Resources and Environment of the South Pacific Region and Protocols, 1986, 26(1987) ILM 38, 58.

Noumea Protocol for the Prevention of Pollution by Dumping, 1986, 26(1987) ILM 38.

Oslo Convention for the Prevention of Marine Pollution by Dumping from Ships and Aircraft, 1972, 11(972) ILM 1261.

Paris Convention for the Protection of the Marine Environment of the North-East Atlantic, 1992, 32(1993) ILM 1072.

Paris Convention for the Prevention of Marine Pollution from Land-Based Sources and Protocol, 1974, 13(1974) ILM 352, 27(1988) ILM 525.

Preparatory Committee of UNCED, Protection of the Oceans and All Kinds of Seas, Including Enclosed and Semi-Enclosed Seas, and of Coastal Areas and the Protection, Rational Use and Development of their Living Resources: Report of the Secretary-General of the Conference, 30 January 1991; reprinted in 7(1991) *International Organizations and the Law of the Sea Documentary Yearbook* 149.

Preparatory Commission for the International Seabed Authority and for the International Tribunal for the Law of the Sea, United Nations Convention on the Law of the Sea, 1982, 21(1982) ILM.

Protocol Relating to Intervention on the High Seas in Cases of Pollution by Substances Other Than Oil, 13 (1974) ILM 605.

Paris Convention for the Prevention of Marine Pollution from Land-Based Sources and Rio Declaration on Environment and Development, 1992, 31(1992) ILM 874.

Stockholm Declaration of the United Nations Conference on the Human Environment, 1972, 11(1972) ILM 1416.

Paris Convention for the Protection of the Marine Environment of the North-East Atlantic, 1992, 32(1993) ILM 1072.

Paris Convention for the Protection of the Marine Environment of the North-East Atlantic, 1992, 32(1993) ILM 1072.

Report of UN Secretary General to Commission on Sustainable Development of the United Nations Conference on

Straddling Fish Stocks and Highly Migratory Fish Stocks & Agreement for the Implementation of the Provisions of the United Nations Convention on the Law of the Sea of 10 December 1982 Relating to the Conservation and Management of Straddling Fish Stocks and Highly Migratory Fish Stocks, 1995, 34(1995) ILM 1542.

The Bay of Bengal Initiative for Multi-Sectoral Technical and Economic Cooperation (BIMST-EC).

United Nations Conference on Human Settlements (Habitat, I & II), 1976 & 1996, UN.Doc.A/RES/47/180, http://www.iisd.ca/habitat/recent.html

United Nations Framework Convention on Climate Change, 1992, 31(1992) ILM.

UN Declaration on International Economic Cooperation, in Particular the Revitalization of Economic Growth of the Developing Countries, 1990 (General Assembly's Resolution S-18/3, Annex).

United Nations Conference on Human Settlements (Habitat, I & II), 1976 & 1996, UN.Doc.A/RES/47/180, http://www.iisd.ca/habitat/recent.html

B. U.N. Resolutions and Documents

UNEP: 2994(XXVII)—UN Conference on the Human Environment.

2995 (XXVII)—Cooperation between States in the Field of the Environment.

2996 (XXVII)—International Responsibility of States in Regard to the Environment.

2997 (XXVII)—Institutional and Financial Arrangements for International Environmental Cooperation.

3001 (XXVII)—Measures for Protecting and Enhancing the Environment.

3002 (XXVII)—Development and Environment.

U.N.Doc.A/AC.138 S. III/L.26, 18 August 1972.

U.N.Doc.A/CONF.48/14(1972).

Report of the U.N. Conference on the Marine Environment, U N. Doc.A/CONF.48/14(1972), revised by U.N. Doc.A/ CONF./48/14/Rev.1(1972) (Declarations and Recommendations of the Conference) U.N.Doc.A/AC.138 S. III/L.26, 18 August 1972.

Draft Articles U.N.Doc.A/Ac138/8.III/L.28, 8 March 1973.

G.A. Res. 2996, U. N. GAOR, 27th Sess., Supp. No. 30 (A/ 8730), at 42, U. N. Doc.A/8901(1972).

G.A. Res. 3232, U. N . GAOR, 29th Sess., Supp. No. 31, at 142, U.N. Doc.A/9631(1974).

G.A. Res. 523, U. N. GAOR, 6th Sess., Supp. No. 20, at 20.

U.N. Doc.A/2119(1952); G. A. Res. 626, U. N. GAOR, 7th Sess., Supp. No. 20, at 18.

U.N. Doc.A/2361 (1952); G. A. Res. 1314, U. N. GAOR, 13th Sees, Supp. No. 18, at 27.

U.N. Doc.A/4090 (1958).

G.A, Res. 35/7, U. N. GAOR, 35th Sess., Supp. No. 48, at 15.

U.N. Doc. A/35/48 (1980).

U.N.Doc.E/CN.17/1997/8 of 10 February 1997.

U.N.Doc.A/CONF.62/WP.9.

U.N.Doc.A/CONF.62/WP.8.

U.N.Doc.A/CONF.164/37 of 8 September 1995.

U.N.Doc.A/35/48(1980).

Docs.UNEP/SAS/LWG.1/7EAS/LWG.1/5 both of 26 February 1990.

UNEP/RSRS No. 62(Nairobi:UNEP 1985).

Doc.UNEP/GC.16/3(Nairobi: UNEP/1991).

INDEX